D1635434

Citizenship:
Feminist Perspectives

Second Edition

Ruth Lister

Consultant Editor: Jo Campling

First edition 1997

Second edition published 2003 by
PALGRAVE MACMILLAN

Palgrave Macmillan in the UK is an imprint of Macmillan Publishers Limited,
registered in England, company number 785998, of Houndmills, Basingstoke,
Hampshire RG21 6XS.

Palgrave Macmillan in the US is a division of St Martin's Press LLC,
175 Fifth Avenue, New York, NY 10010.

Palgrave Macmillan is the global academic imprint of the above companies
and has companies and representatives throughout the world.

Palgrave® and Macmillan® are registered trademarks in the United States,
the United Kingdom, Europe and other countries.

ISBN 978-0-333-94819-4 hardback
ISBN 978-0-333-94820-0 paperback

This book is printed on paper suitable for recycling and made from fully
managed and sustained forest sources. Logging, pulping and manufacturing
processes are expected to conform to the environmental regulations of the
country of origin.

A catalogue record for this book is available from the British Library.

A catalog record for this book is available from the Library of Congress.

Printed and bound in Great Britain by
CPI Antony Rowe, Chippenham and Eastbourne

Contents

Preface to the First Edition

My approach to the question of citizenship reflects, in part, my own background in campaigning politics. The first sixteen years of my working life were spent with the Child Poverty Action Group, a leading UK charity that works for the eradication of child and family poverty. In a book I subsequently wrote to mark CPAG's 25th anniversary, I noted that 'looking back we find that citizenship was one of the ideals that inspired the Group's early development. Although it did not emerge again as an explicit theme until the mid-1980s, much of CPAG's work can be understood as a contribution to the wider struggle to extend full and genuine citizenship rights to those excluded by poverty' (1990a, p. 1). During some of that period I was also involved in the Women's Liberation Campaign for Financial and Legal Independence, which focused mainly on the treatment of women in the social security and tax systems, 'in rebellion against women's partial citizenship' (Rowbotham, 1989, p. 148). It was through that campaign that I came to identify myself as a feminist, an identity that for me still holds good even though we are supposed to be living in 'post-feminist' times.

At about the time that I moved into higher education, in 1987, the language of citizenship re-emerged on the political and academic agenda. Having been invited to give the 1989 Eleanor Rathbone Memorial Lecture, I was struck by how Eleanor Rathbone in *The Disinherited Family* (republished 1986), together with some of her contemporaries, drew on the language of citizenship to make the case for the endowment of motherhood between the wars. Their arguments were still relevant to more recent campaigns in defence of child benefit, the 'granddaughter' of the demand for the endowment of motherhood, and for women's financial independence. Furthermore, their gendered understanding of the concept of citizenship stood in contrast to the gender-ignorant, and therefore gender-biased, way in which it was being used by politicians in the late 1980s.

This led me to start asking a number of questions about women's role as citizens; about the limitations placed upon our rights as citizens and the constraints placed upon our ability to fulfil some of the obligations of citizenship. Those questions brought me eventually to this book. On the way I have developed my own understanding around these questions in three main ways. First, I have been able to pursue at a more theoretical level issues that previously I had approached primarily from the stance of an activist. From the new vantage point that this gives me, I blush slightly at the theoretical naivety of some of my writing then. Nevertheless, I would argue that our theoretical understanding of citizenship needs to be grounded in an appreciation of its practical and policy implications.

Second, at both a theoretical and political level, I have become more aware of the limitations of a gender analysis that suppresses the differences within the gender categories. This, in turn, has meant a greater consciousness of the, relatively privileged, standpoint from which I write: that of a Western, White, middle-class, heterosexual, non-disabled, childless, woman. (White and Black are capitalised to denote they are used as political categories.) In developing this feminist account of citizenship, I have tried on the one hand not to write as if from some universal woman's standpoint and on the other not to appropriate the voice of 'other' groups of women. In negotiating this difficult path, I have benefited from the work of other feminist authors, such as Kathleen B. Jones (1993); Anna Yeatman (1993); and Sue Wilkinson and Celia Kitzinger (1996). Similarly, in writing a piece of work that combines theory and policy, I have used examples from a range of countries to illuminate both similarities and differences, but am conscious of the dangers of superficial over-generalisation. It is for my readers to assess whether I have avoided such pitfalls.

Finally, my own perception of some of the practical manifestations of citizenship has shifted. In particular, I have become more conscious of the ways in which even, indeed in particular, some of the most disadvantaged women act as citizens and are not simply passive in their exclusion from the full panoply of citizenship rights. I have been helped here through my work with Peter Beresford of the Open Services Project looking at how people in poverty can exercise a voice in anti-poverty campaigns and through my membership of the independent Opsahl Commission into the future of Northern Ireland. The evidence given to the Commission by women's groups from working-class areas of Belfast provided an inspiring example of how women's active citizenship can flourish against all the odds.

The many people, including members of various research networks and contributors to conferences, whose ideas have helped me directly or indirectly on the long path from when the book was first conceived are too numerous to mention individually but a collective thank you is in order. There are nevertheless a number of people and organisations to whom individual thanks are due. First is my editor, Jo Campling, for her patience and her continued faith in the project despite my repeated failure to deliver. Second, I was lucky to have two committed research assistants at different stages of the project: Valerie Bryson and Parul Desai, whose contribution was invaluable. Valerie Bryson was funded by the Joseph Rowntree Foundation; and a Nuffield Foundation Social Science Research Fellowship enabled me to concentrate on writing the book for a whole academic year. I am most grateful to both Trusts. My heartfelt thanks go to Valerie Bryson again, along with Jane Lewis and Jim Kincaid who read the draft manuscript, and to Fiona Williams and Desmond King, who each read a couple of chapters. Anne Showstack Sassoon, who reviewed the manuscript for Macmillan, provided help beyond the call of duty. In each case, their comments have helped enormously in improving on the first draft; remaining weaknesses are of course my own responsibility. I am grateful to Vivian Dhaliwal for help with tidying up the bibliography and to Brian Negus for assistance in technical emergencies. Finally, I thank my closest friends, in particular J., for your loving support and tolerance, especially during those months when my anxiety levels were highest and my obsession with 'the book' was at its most tiresome.

RUTH LISTER

Preface to the Second Edition

It is difficult to believe that more than five years have passed since I wrote the preface to the first edition. During this time there has been an exponential increase in the citizenship literature and one of the purposes of this second, substantially revised and expanded, edition is to incorporate key developments in that and related literatures. The vibrant debates around citizenship in the past few years have meant that my own thinking has evolved further. In reflecting on the first edition, I have very much valued the stimulating exchanges with fellow members of the European Network for Theory and Research on Women, Welfare States and Citizenship, co-ordinated by Trudie Knijn. Among other things, these exchanges have helped me see more clearly the extent to which my understanding of citizenship is coloured by the British context within which I write. The growing deployment of a discourse of citizenship in the southern hemisphere has likewise served to influence my thinking.

There have also been important political and policy developments since I wrote the first edition, especially in the UK with the advent of New Labour. These have been of considerable significance for the politics and practice of citizenship. Important too has been the increased prominence of demands for the inclusion of people in poverty in decision-making that affects their lives. My understanding of this citizenship issue has been deepened through my membership of the Commission on Poverty, Participation and Power, half of whose members had direct experience of poverty. At the same time, the whole issue of global citizenship has become much more salient in the face of global protest movements and increased political discussion about the 'architecture' of global governance. Another aim of the second edition is to reflect these political developments.

As with the first edition, thanks are due to a large number of people whose intellectual contributions and personal support have been of great importance to me. The constructive engagement of reviewers of the book and referees of articles based on it has helped me to see some of the weaknesses in the original, which I hope this second edition addresses. Jan Flaherty provided invaluable research assistance. Jet Bussemaker, Ute Gerhard, Arnlaug Leira, Birte Siim and Jodie Raphael answered various queries about their countries. Jane Lewis and Jim Kincaid once again kindly gave up their time to read draft chapters. I am also grateful to Jo Campling and to Catherine Gray and Jo Digby at Palgrave for their continued help. And thanks, once again, to my closest friends and in particular to J. for still being there for me.

RUTH LISTER

List of Abbreviations

ANC	African National Congress
CI	Citizen's Income
CPAG	Child Poverty Action Group
DEG	Department of Employment Group
DSS	Department of Social Security
EAPN	European Anti-Poverty Network
EC	European Commission
EFTA	European Free Trade Area
EU	European Union
EWL	European Women's Lobby
HMSO	Her Majesty's Stationery Office
ILO	International Labour Organisation
IMF	International Monetary Fund
IPU	Inter-Parliamentary Union
NGO	Non-governmental organisation
OECD	Organisation for Economic Co-operation and Development
TUC	Trades Union Congress
UN	United Nations
UNDP	United Nations Development Programme
UNHCR	United Nations High Commissioner for Refugees
UNHCHR	United Nations Office for the High Commission for Human Rights
UNIFEM	United Nations Development Fund for Women
USAID	US Agency for International Development
WTO	World Trade Organisation

To my mother and the memory of my father;
and also in memory of Hilary Arnott, 1944–94,
a passionate opponent of exclusion and injustice

Introduction: Why Citizenship?

Why citizenship and, more specifically, why women's citizenship? I was asked this question at a conference by a feminist academic who clearly regarded current feminist preoccupation with what she perceived as an irretrievably White male, and therefore not very helpful, concept as a waste of time. To be asked such a provocative question is salutary; it is a useful reminder that not everyone shares one's own fascination with a subject. It is, therefore, perhaps appropriate to introduce this book by explaining why I believe the topic is an important one. In doing so, I hope to convey some of the intellectual and political excitement that I have experienced in exploring the question of women's citizenship and to persuade the sceptical that, despite the problems with the concept, it is one with which feminists can usefully engage.

At the same time, there are no doubt still some citizenship theorists who need to be reminded, or even convinced, that this ostensibly gender-neutral concept is, in fact, deeply gendered. The existence of a considerable body of academic and political writing about citizenship that ignores the gender perspective points to the first, more negative, reason for current feminist preoccupation: what we might call 'the Everest argument,' i.e. that it is there.[1] Not only is it there but, like Everest, both historically and today it dominates the terrain of Western political thought. Contemporary theorists have described the notion of citizenship as: 'a key aspect of Western political thinking since the formation of classical Greek political culture' (Turner, 1993, p. vii) and 'one of the central organising features of Western political discourse' (Hindess, 1993, p. 19).

Its re-emergence in recent years as a dominant concept has been attributed to a number of developments internationally (see also Bussemaker and Voet, 1998). Three broad interrelated trends affecting nation states have, in particular, served to revitalise debates about citizenship, while at the same time problematising it as a status and concept attached to the nation state (Scobey, 2001). The first concerns the reshaping of national boundaries (for example in Germany and the countries that comprised the former Yugoslavia); growing pressures in some nation-states for regional autonomy;

1

and the implications for all nation-states of the forces of globalisation. Second are the implications for citizenship rights and obligations of the growing movement across national borders of migrants and asylum-seekers, the increasingly multi-ethnic nature of many societies and the claims of indigenous peoples. Third, the notion of European citizenship has taken on greater prominence in the face of pressures towards increased integration and an expanding European Union and the desire to foster a stronger European identity among the peoples of Europe. The language of citizenship permeates many key documents of the European Commission.[2]

Issues of democracy have also been important. In societies as diverse as the United States and Sweden, there have been concerns about the demise of active political citizenship in representative democracies marked by increased bureaucratisation and technological advance. As these concerns have tended to focus in particular on young people's disengagement from formal political processes, there has been a growing preoccupation in some countries, such as the UK, with the role of citizenship education.[3] The UK New Labour government's desire to promote active citizenship, especially among young people, is mirrored in the more radical Charter 88 'Unlocking Democracy' campaign for a Citizens' Constitution that would provide a framework for a 'social, economic, political and cultural environment of citizenship' (Charter 88, 2000, p. 7). At the same time, the peoples of the new democracies of Central and Eastern Europe and South Africa have been able to exercise their rights as citizens for the first time. The impact of these revolutions has reverberated far beyond their own frontiers, contributing to the re-evaluation of civil and political citizenship rights in other societies. Although a concept originating in Western philosophy and associated with the northern hemisphere, it is no longer confined to the latter, and the discourse of citizenship, interpreted, and sometimes transformed, according to local context, has a growing salience for political movements in other parts of the world.[4] In Latin America, in particular, it has become increasingly prominent in political and cultural democratic struggles that have, in part, represented attempts to 'resignify the very meaning of received notions of citizenship'; and feminists have played a central role in these.[5]

Finally, there is the challenge to the values of social citizenship embedded in welfare states in the face of economic crises and political backlash. In response, the philosophy of citizenship has provided a means of reconciling the collectivist tradition of the left with notions of individual rights and responsibilities, in recognition that the alternative to the political credo of the new right cannot discard the individual to which the latter directed its appeal.[6] The particular prominence of debates about citizenship in the UK in the late twentieth century reflected its position as 'chief European testing ground for New Right theory' the influence of which then spread (Marquand, 1991, p. 329). The erosion of existing citizenship rights and processes of marketisation of welfare have provoked a renewed interest in citizenship in a wide range of other countries also.[7] At a global level, the

Guiding Principles for Social Developmental Welfare Policies adopted by the United Nations (UN) include as 'the central objective of social welfare policy … the enhancement of human well-being by raising the level of living, ensuring social justice and widening opportunities for people to develop their highest capacities as healthy, educated, participating and contributing citizens' (European Centre, 1993). In the UN–European region, the promotion of citizenship and social rights has been identified as a priority in applying the UN Guiding Principles.

A contested and contextualised concept

The academic literature on citizenship is flourishing, drawing in scholars from a wide range of countries and disciplines. Indeed, 1997 marked the launch of a new journal of *Citizenship Studies*, which emphasises the concept's strategic significance. One of the recurring themes of the literature is that citizenship is 'an essentially contested concept'.[8] It is contested at every level from its very meaning to its political application, with implications for the kind of society to which we aspire. Herein lies one of the reasons for the intellectual and political controversy that such an ancient concept is still able to generate.

Citizenship is also 'a contextualised concept' (Siim, 2000, p. 1). 'Vocabularies of citizenship' and their meanings vary according to social, political and cultural context and reflect different historical legacies. Citizenship is expressed in 'spaces and places'.[9] These perspectives are mirrored at the level of the individual in the idea of 'lived citizenship', that is 'the meaning that citizenship actually has in people's lives and the ways in which people's social and cultural backgrounds and material circumstances affect their lives as citizens' (Hall and Williamson, 1999, p. 2). Citizenship struggles are thus also shaped by cultural, political and historical context. The idea of 'nation-specific citizenship "complexes" or "regimes"' denotes these different contexts. A citizenship regime, Jenson and Phillips suggest, 'encodes within it a paradigmatic representation' of citizenship identity: of the 'national' and 'model' as well as the 'second-class' and non-citizen.[10]

The notion of citizenship identity derives from the most basic meaning of citizenship: membership of a community (itself a contested concept). It describes the relationship between individuals and the state and between individual citizens within that community. Increasingly, each element of this equation – membership, identity and relationships – is being interrogated. Likewise, longstanding questions as to whether that membership is defined primarily by the rights or the obligations that it entails, and the nature of such rights and obligations, have become increasingly salient. Looking at it from the perspective of the two great historical traditions of citizenship, is it in essence a status to which rights attach or a practice involving civic virtue and participation in the *polis* (Oldfield, 1990)? In addition to these old debates, new questions are being raised about the appropriateness of a concept that in modern times is tied to the nation-state, in the face of the erosion of national autonomy and the threat of ecological disaster. At the same time, new formulations are emerging such as cultural, sexual, intimate and ecological citizenship (see also Turner, 2001).

The combination of its salience and contested nature underlines the importance of a sustained feminist analysis of the meaning, limitations and potential of the notion of citizenship. Behind the cloak of gender-neutrality, which embraces the idea, there lurks in much of the literature a definitely male citizen and it is his interests and concerns that have traditionally dictated the agenda. The reappropriation of strategic concepts such as citizenship is central to the development of feminist political and social theory. A feminist project to (re)appropriate citizenship does not, however, imply an uncritical acceptance of its value as a concept. For a start, one of the fundamental questions addressed is whether an ideal, originally predicated on the very exclusion of women, can be reformulated so as satisfactorily to include (and not simply append) them. Moreover, in doing so, can it give full recognition to the different multiple and shifting identities that women simultaneously hold?

It also has to be recognised that citizenship, as an idea and practice, can have negative as well as positive connotations. Some commentators have pointed to its 'disciplinary possibilities' (Squires, 1998, p. 274; Carver, 1998). Aihwa Ong describes these as 'a cultural process of "subjectification"' to 'power relations that produce consent through schemes of surveillance, discipline, control, and administration' (1996, p. 737, cited in Joseph, 1999). Coercive 'workfare' type policies, often justified in the language of citizenship responsibility, might stand as one example (Harris, 1999; Fitzpatrick, 2001). Another might be the Dutch 'citizen's contract', which requires immigrants and refugees to participate in a citizenship course in the Dutch language and culture, and is geared towards labour market participation, as a condition of receipt of social assistance (Bussemaker, 1998).[11]

An example of the ambiguous relationship to citizenship of the victims of restrictive citizenship, immigration and asylum laws is afforded by a letter to the *Guardian* from 'Eleven Muslim Women'. They wrote of their sense of anger, as a group of British citizens either born in or brought to Britain as small children, yet denied the right to be joined by their husbands because of the 'primary purpose' rule.[12] Their letter ended: 'At present we must choose between our husband and our country. The pressures on us are forcing us out of our country of citizenship and into exile.' Yet it also illustrates the way in which those denied a basic right, such as to live as a united family, can use the notion of citizenship to make their case. It began by quoting the then Home Secretary who had spoken of 'a country where all citizens, whatever their origins, have a sense of belonging to Britain'. Their letter was a plea to be allowed to 'belong' as full and equal citizens.

Their letter illustrates the janus-faced nature of citizenship; it operates simultaneously as a mechanism of both inclusion and exclusion and also as a language of both discipline and resistance (Stychin, 2001). While not denying the ways in which legal definitions of citizenship and citizenship practices can exclude (often Black) outsiders and act more generally as a disciplinary force, as an ideal it can also provide a potent weapon in the hands of disadvantaged and oppressed groups of insiders. As such it has, in my experience, a resonance for many people. This is despite the fact that few speak the language of citizenship in their everyday lives. T. H. Marshall's classic exposition of modern citizenship incorporated the idea of 'an image of an ideal citizenship against which achievements can be measured and towards which aspirations can be directed' (Marshall, 1950, p. 29; Parker, 1998). In this way, it can provide both an inspiration and a yardstick against which progress can be measured. A critical question then becomes that of who defines the yardstick and in whose image.

Struggle and agency

Although Marshall's 'image of an ideal citizenship' lends itself to a dynamic approach, one of the criticisms of his work has been that it placed insufficient 'emphasis on the notion of social struggles as the central motor of the drive for citizenship'.[13] Much of the political history of the last century has been characterised by battles to extend, defend or give substance to political, civil and social rights of citizenship and, more recently, to forge new claims to, for instance, reproductive and cultural rights. Women have played a central role in these struggles, not just for the vote but also for social and other citizenship rights, often explicitly using the ideal of citizenship as their lode star. Women have also played a key role in the citizenship struggles of Black peoples in societies such as the United States and more recently South Africa. In the latter case, they have worked long and hard to ensure that Black women are full and equal citizens in the new South Africa. A massive exercise in participatory democracy was undertaken to involve women throughout South Africa in the drawing up of a Women's Charter for Effective Equality. In some ways, the process was seen to be as important as the outcome. And this outcome was itself significant: the Bill of Rights adopted by the ANC in 1993 makes provision for equal protection under the law, equal rights in the family and in all areas of public life. The constitution of the new South Africa emphasises the equal citizenship of women and men and people of all races. Not surprisingly, the gap between aspirations and reality is enormous. Nevertheless, the explicit constitutional recognition of women's claims to equal citizenship is of immense significance and women's formal political representation is better than in many longer established democracies (Kadalie, 1995; Kemp *et al.*, 1995). Indeed, it has been suggested that this is 'the closest any democracy has come to incorporating gender into the definition of citizenship' (Seidman, 1999, p. 303; McEwan, 2000).

Other social movements, in which women are active, are also employing the language of citizenship. In particular, the disabled people's movement in the UK, following the example of that in the US, has presented itself as a movement for full citizenship rights: 'To be disabled in Great Britain is to be denied the fundamental rights of citizenship to such an extent that most disabled people are denied their basic human rights ... It is possible to remove all the barriers to citizenship that disabled people face.'[14] The lesbian and gay movement has also begun to deploy the language of citizenship. For example, in the UK, Stonewall launched its manifesto for the new century under the rubric of 'equal as citizens'; its Citizenship 21 project aims to explore the meaning of equal citizenship in the context of a wider understanding of diversity. Increasingly, also, the discourse shapes the theorisation of lesbian and gay politics.[15]

A focus on citizenship as a process and not just an outcome, in which the struggle to gain new rights and to give substance to existing ones is seen as being as important as the substance of those rights, combines elements of the two historical traditions of citizenship: the participatory republican and liberal–social rights traditions. From this perspective, citizens appear on the stage of both theory and practice not simply as the passive holders of rights but as actively engaging with political and welfare institutions, both as individuals and in groups. In this way the idea of human agency becomes central to our understanding of citizenship and, I will argue in Chapter 1, provides the synthesising thread between the two historical traditions.

A feminist citizenship project thus encourages an approach to theory and practice that gives due accord to women's agency rather than simply seeing us as victims of discriminatory and oppressive male-dominated political, economic and social institutions. In the Australian context, a shift of interest in feminist debate from the nature of the state to the nature of citizenship has been interpreted as a switch in focus from the structural constraints on women's emancipation to that of women's political agency (Curthoys, 1993). In contrast, I shall argue that, following the work of social theorists such as Anthony Giddens, the study of citizenship has to involve both agency and structural constraints and the interplay between the two. This interplay is, in turn, mediated by cultural meanings and understandings (Pugh and Thompson, 1999), which are themselves gendered (Pfau-Effinger, 1998, 2001). Such an approach helps move us on from a preoccupation with 'victim feminism', while not exaggerating, as does Naomi Wolf (1993), the extent to which we have achieved power as a sex. It allows for recognition of the importance of psychology and identity without placing undue faith in Wolf's vision of 'a new psychology of female power' to transform gender power relations. In other words, I would argue that a feminist citizenship project offers some of the optimism of writers such as Wolf by recognising women's agency and achievements as citizens, both individually and collectively, without losing sight of the deep-seated inequalities that still undermine many of their citizenship rights and particularly those of 'minority group' women.[16]

Many of those inequalities are the subject-matter of social policy analysis and it is this analysis, together with that of relevant public policies, that constitutes one of social policy's main contributions to citizenship theory, be it from the perspective of membership, rights, obligations or political participation. Where social policy has until relatively recently been weak, as Fiona Williams has argued, is in its understanding of human agency.[17] One area where this is beginning to be addressed is in the study of citizenship, often in collaboration with other disciplines. An example is the work of Birte Siim, a political scientist who uses social policy to study women as social and political actors. For her, agency represents both a 'key to women's active citizenship' and an analytical tool for connecting different citizenship arenas and forms of participation (Siim, 2000, p. 4).

Within social policy itself, studies of young people have used the framework of citizenship to understand how the transition to adulthood is shaped by both the impact of structural constraints and young people's own agency and choices (Jones and Wallace, 1992; Coles, 1995). Similarly, Fred Twine has placed the relationship between structure and agency at the centre of his analysis of citizenship and social rights. Inspired by C. Wright Mills' *The Sociological Imagination* (1959), a recurrent theme in his exposition of social citizenship is, echoing Marx, that 'people make themselves, but not in circumstances of their own choosing' (1994, p. 7). Comparative welfare state analysis is, likewise, placing greater emphasis on the importance of agency (Misra and Akins, 1998; Korpi, 2000).

The notion of human agency, linked to that of autonomy, also figures prominently in Doyal and Gough's theorisation of human need (1991). In a summary of their work, Ian Gough highlights the link with citizenship: since need satisfaction is a prerequisite for the fulfilment of citizenship duties, 'social rights of citizenship follow from an unambiguous concept of human need' (1992, p. 8). One element of basic human needs, he argues, is that of 'autonomy of agency – *the capacity to make informed choices about what should be done and how to go about doing it*' (p. 9, emphasis in original). Crucial to personal autonomy is the opportunity to participate in the social roles of production, reproduction, cultural transmission and political authority. Beyond that lies 'critical autonomy – the ability to situate, criticise and, if necessary, challenge the rules and practices' of one's society (p. 10), in other words the ability to act as a critical citizen. Citizenship is also pivotal to the definition and interpretation of needs and to the struggle for their realisation and conversion into rights. Doyal and Gough identify civil and political rights, together with effective political participation and democracy, as essential to critical autonomy and the optimisation of needs satisfaction.

The book: outline and disciplinary approach

As will have become clear, the question of citizenship can be approached from a number of disciplinary paths. It has been described as 'a strategically important concept intellectually' and as providing 'a platform for interdisciplinary research on the problems of social membership in advanced societies'.[18] My own stance, based initially in social policy, attempts to interweave the insights it affords with an analysis derived also from political, social and feminist theory, as well as the literature on migration and the nation-state.

A number of theorists have also emphasised the way in which citizenship straddles the theoretical and the empirical on the one hand and the normative on the other. This combination of theory and praxis informs my approach here. However, although overall I am attempting to provide a synthesis of theoretical and more practical policy perspectives on citizenship, the book's structure is based on a division between the two. Part I provides the book's theoretical framework by working through the theoretical issues and dilemmas involved in developing feminist perspectives on citizenship. The earlier chapters, while written from a feminist standpoint, are not exclusively concerned with women's citizenship, whereas the later ones are grounded more centrally in feminist theory and women's concerns. Part II takes as its starting point the theorisation of the public–private divide before moving on to its practical and policy implications. The theoretical framework developed in Part I is then used to illuminate some of the policy dilemmas faced in the promotion of women's political and social citizenship. The Conclusion brings the two together again to summarise the theoretical themes and sketch out a broad political and policy agenda.

Chapter 1 poses the question: what is citizenship? Following a brief discussion of citizenship as membership, it considers different interpretations of citizenship rights and obligations and the implications of the liberal–social rights and republican participatory traditions. These, it is then argued, should be seen as complementary rather than competing approaches. A rounded and fruitful conceptualisation of citizenship, with the potential to enhance women's political agency as well as their structural position, has to embrace both individual rights (and, in particular, social rights) and political and other forms of participation as well as to analyse the relationship between the two. In this way citizenship emerges as a dynamic process in which the two dimensions of status and practice interact with each other, linked through human agency.

Chapter 1 also discusses the communitarian conception of citizenship and its emphasis on obligations and responsibilities, aspects of which some identify as a more coercive side of citizenship. This is one example of how the concept of citizenship is not unproblematic. Chapters 2 and 3 explore those problems that in the main represent the exclusionary side of citizenship's coin, looking in turn at those excluded from without and within the boundaries of the nation-state. Chapter 2 considers various aspects of the limitations of a concept associated in modern times with the nation-state at a time when the latter is becoming less pivotal economically and politically. Yet simultaneously nation-states exercise, often with increasing aggressiveness, the power to exclude 'outsiders' through the drawing and policing of the boundaries of citizenship and residence in an age when migration and asylum-seeking are increasingly commonplace. These considerations, the chapter argues, do not invalidate citizenship's use as a progressive political and analytical tool. Instead, what is needed is a multi-layered conceptualisation that embraces the notion of global citizenship and the complementary use of international human rights law.

Chapter 3 deals with the fundamental tension between the ideals of equality and universality embodied in the very idea of the citizen on the one hand and the 'postmodern' emphasis on difference and diversity on the other. Given that the original notion of the citizen was of its essence male, is the female citizen no more than oxymoron? Is it possible to expose the false universalism of the disembodied citizen while retaining the concept as an inspiring ideal? Is it valid to talk of women's citizenship when it is now understood that it is not possible to treat woman as an undifferentiated category? The conception of citizenship developed here attempts to answer such questions in relationship to citizenship both as a status and a practice by combining the strengths of both universalism and difference through the notion of a 'differentiated universalism'.

The question of difference re-emerges in Chapter 4 in the discussion of the equality *vs.* difference debate, one example of where the project of engendering and re-gendering citizenship engages with key debates in feminism and, for me, has helped to crystallise them. Indeed, one of my central questions is a reformulation of that controversy: is the goal an ostensibly gender-neutral conception of citizenship which enables women to participate as equals with men in the public sphere ('equality') or an explicitly gender-differentiated conception which recognises and values women's responsibilities in the private sphere ('difference')? The attempt to answer that question has drawn me into other important philosophical questions for feminism such as whether theory and practice should be governed by 'an ethic of care' (associated with 'difference') or 'an ethic of justice' (associated with 'equality') and whether the traditional goal of female independence should be discarded in recognition of the reality and importance of human interdependence.

Approaching each of these various questions from the standpoint of women's citizenship, it became clear that they were distorted by the binary logic underpinning them. Thus, to force a choice between a gender-neutral and a gender-differentiated conception of citizenship, based on *either* an ethic of justice and ideal of independence *or* of care and interdependence, simply leads women up a political and theoretical cul-de-sac. A more promising vision is that of a woman-friendly, 'gender-inclusive' citizenship that combines elements of the gender-neutral and gender-differentiated approaches, while at the same time remaining sensitive to the differences that exist between women. This is best advanced, I will argue, through the subversion, transcendence or critical synthesis of the original dichotomies.

A further dichotomy which has been challenged by feminist theory is that of the public–private divide which is pivotal to women's long-standing exclusion from full citizenship in both theory and practice. While few feminists would now argue for the complete dissolution of the two categories, women's citizenship cannot be understood or achieved so long as they are treated as rigidly separated in hierarchical opposition to each other. Chapter 5 elaborates the theoretical and practical implications. It emphasises the varying ways in which the private and the public impact on each other, with particular reference to first, women's physical and economic autonomy and secondly, the sexual division of labour and women's labour market position.

Chapters 6 and 7 then develop the analysis in relation to women's political and social citizenship. In Chapter 6, women's typical under-representation in political elites and the key formal channels of politics is contrasted with the major contribution that they often make to more informal forms of politics such as community groups. It is argued that participation in informal politics should be recognised as a legitimate form of political citizenship. Moreover, the disparity between women's involvement in formal and informal politics constitutes a challenge to the former by the latter. The case is argued for a more permeable model of formal politics, more open both to individual women and to the influence of the informal kinds of politics in which many women will probably still prefer to participate.

The issue of social rights is then taken up in Chapter 7 which poses the question 'who is a social citizen?'. Behind this question lies the traditional and widespread privileging of citizen-the wage-earner over citizen-the carer in the allocation of social citizenship rights. Are women (and different groups of women) better served through a challenge to the nature of social citizenship rights, so that earning is no longer privileged over caring, or through improving women's access to the labour market, so that they can compete on equal terms with men and thereby gain the same employment-linked social rights? This specific formulation of the equality *vs.* difference dilemma, still unresolved, can be traced back to feminist writings in the early years of the century. It is argued here that the way through it lies in a dual focus on men's caring obligations on the one hand and on the state's responsibility to help support those caring for children, or for older or disabled people, on the other.

The relationship between women in their diversity and the (welfare) state is examined more widely, drawing on notions of gendered and racialised welfare regimes and of a non-monolithic state. In its role as regulator of a range of citizenship rights, including immigration, cultural, reproductive and sexual as well as social rights, the state can both support and undercut the citizenship of different groups of women. At the same time, welfare states have provided an important arena in which women have developed their roles as active citizens – both through their contribution to struggles for welfare provisions and to their evolution and through their position within, and as negotiators with, welfare institutions. It can thus be seen that the social and political dimensions of citizenship are interlinked, which takes us back to the argument in Chapter 1.

Part I

A Theoretical Framework

1
What is Citizenship?

The question 'what is citizenship?' is not an easy one to answer in any definitive way. This is partly because it incorporates a number of different elements, reflecting competing political traditions, and partly because of both its contextualised and contested nature. It therefore runs the danger of meaning what people choose it to mean, and the question then is 'which is to be master', as Humpty Dumpty told Alice when she queried whether 'you can make words mean different things', (Carroll, 1947). The answers to both these questions are of considerable significance, for 'the way we define citizenship is intimately linked to the kind of society and political community we want' (Mouffe, 1992a, p. 25). It would be easy enough to proffer a bland definition, but to do so risks suppressing citizenship's contested nature. Instead, this chapter attempts to answer the question 'what is citizenship?' in two ways. First, it reviews the main elements that constitute the language of citizenship and that, in different combinations, provide the ingredients of the various definitions attempted in the literature – academic and political. Second, it discusses the main ways in which the concept is contested, leaving until later chapters the challenge from those who most certainly have not been 'master' when it comes to the articulation and practice of citizenship.

At heart, what is at issue in the mainstream debates is the balance between rights and obligations and the nature of each. The rights approach derives from the liberal political tradition, born in the seventeenth century, in which civil and political rights are the means by which the limited state guarantees the freedom and formal equality of the individual who is sovereign. Whether or not the state should also play a broader role in guaranteeing social rights was one of the key citizenship debates of the twentieth century. Citizenship as obligation has its roots in the more ancient civic republican tradition of classical Greece in which political participation as civic duty and the expression of the citizen's full potential as a political being represent the essence of citizenship, as articulated by Aristotle in particular.[1] Citizenship obligation can, though, also be construed more widely and today it is work obligations that dominate the increasingly prominent 'duties discourse' (Roche, 1992).

13

This discourse reflects a third, more recent, communitarian strand, which has strong affinities with the civic republican tradition, sharing some of its assumptions and concerns (in particular its rejection of individualistic rights-based citizenship), but which is nevertheless distinct from it.[2]

Having explored their contemporary articulation, I make the case for a synthesis of the rights and participatory traditions, using the notion of human agency as the common thread, and with particular reference to the importance of such a synthesis for women. However, these traditions have to be recast if they are to support rather than exclude women and, in particular, women who are also members of 'minority groups' such as disabled and, in White-dominated societies, Black women.

An essentially contested concept

The difficulty of arriving at an exhaustive and comprehensive definition of citizenship, commented on even by Aristotle, is a common refrain running through the literature, reflecting complex political, moral and ethical issues concerning the individual's relationship to the state and the wider society. Rather than attempt such a definition of this 'slippery concept', many fall back on that provided by T. H. Marshall, the British sociologist who, more than anyone else, shaped postwar thinking about citizenship, and not only in Britain:[3] 'Citizenship is a *status* bestowed on those who are full members of a community. All who possess the status are equal with respect to the rights and duties with which the status is endowed' (1950, pp. 28–9, my emphasis). The key elements here are membership of a community (itself an increasingly contested concept), the rights and obligations that flow from that membership, and equality.

Issues around membership are, according to Hall and Held, 'where the *politics* of citizenship begins' (1989, p. 17, emphasis in original). Marshall himself placed considerable emphasis on membership but, as the quotation suggests, he did so largely from the perspective of the status that derives from it. Rights (and especially social rights), in his formulation, are pivotal not only as an element of membership but also as an integrative force, which fosters 'a direct sense of community membership based on loyalty to a civilisation which is a common possession' (1950, pp. 40–1). A common culture or 'civilisation' was taken for granted, as was the associated matter of the identity of citizens (Turner, 1997). In contrast, questions of culture and identity are much more central and contested in the contemporary theorisation and politics of citizenship, in both their more conservative and radical manifestations.

At the level of the national community, culture and identity are seen as pivotal to processes of 'nation-building', in which national and citizenship identity all too easily become conflated.[4] The association with national identity and culture features prominently in communitarian approaches to citizenship (Delanty, 1997a, 2000; Cohen, 1999). In these, identity and culture are treated as relatively static and homogeneous and are not interrogated as they are in more radical formulations. Such interrogations contest the conflation of national and citizenship identity, locating the latter in local, sub-national and supra-national as well as national spaces; relate citizenship identity to the cultural politics of differentiated identities; and conceptualise it as dynamic, forged in part through struggles around membership and rights.[5]

An understanding of citizenship in terms of membership and identity underlines that what is involved is not simply a set of legal rules governing the relationship between individuals and the state but also a set of social relationships between individuals and the state and between individual citizens.[6] These relationships are negotiated and, therefore, fluid (Stasiulis and Bakan, 1997). Their nature and how they are understood reflects national context and culture. An emphasis on the bonds between individual citizens, for example, is a particular feature of the Scandinavian literature, reflecting the feelings of solidarity engendered by a long history of social democracy (Hernes, 1987). This literature also accentuates the participatory dimension of membership in a community, exemplified in Olof Petersson's formulation of citizenship as the right to have 'equal possibilities to participate in the governing of society' (1989, p. 16, cited in Siim, 1991). The notion of participation can be found in both Marshallian and more republican/communitarian approaches to citizenship. In the former there is a preoccupation with the formal political, legal and social rights that underpin that participation and the social and economic conditions under which those rights are exercised. In the latter, the focus shifts to the attitudes and actions that constitute the identity of a citizen. It places emphasis on 'civic virtues', that is the qualities necessary for good and responsible citizenship and on the culture of citizenship needed to nourish them.[7] Adrian Oldfield (1990) conceptualises the two different approaches as citizenship as a *status vs.* citizenship as a *practice*. The one prioritises the rights of the *individual* citizen; the other the interests of the *wider society* (Heater, 1990).

Among those who subscribe to the first approach are both classical liberals, who would confine citizenship to the formal (negative) civil and political rights necessary to protect individual freedom, and those in the tradition of Marshall, who would include also social rights as necessary to the promotion of a more positive notion of freedom. Proponents of the second approach include both contemporary apostles of civic republicanism, for whom the true citizen is actively involved in political and civic affairs, and those communitarians who propound the gospel of active responsibility to the wider community. For some this responsibility is articulated specifically as the obligations of citizens (or at least certain citizens) to undertake paid work and/or engage in voluntary service.[8] Increasingly significant too is an ecological interpretation of the needs of the wider community and the duties that they entail. The respective strength of the two approaches differs between societies, reflecting both contemporary conditions and debates and also the differential historical influence of the two citizenship traditions (as well as, more recently, of communitarianism). I shall argue that a rounded conception of citizenship needs to draw on a modernised and progressive interpretation of both traditions, having first looked more closely at how they are articulated in contemporary debate under the three headings of rights, general obligation and obligation in the more specific political sense.

Citizenship as rights

Most modern accounts of citizenship take as their starting point Marshall's celebrated exposition of its three elements: civil, political and social rights:

> The civil element is composed of the rights necessary for individual freedom – liberty of the person, freedom of speech, thought and faith, the right to own property and to conclude valid contracts, and the right to justice. The last is of a different order from the others, because it is the right to defend and assert all one's rights on terms of equality with others and by due process of law. ... By the political element I mean the right to participate in the exercise of political power, as a member of a body invested with political authority or as an elector of the members of such a body. ... By the social element I mean the whole range from the right to a modicum of economic welfare and security to the right to share to the full in the social heritage and to live the life of a civilised being according to the standards prevailing in the society (Marshall, 1950, pp. 10–11).

This tripartite formulation incorporates both classical and social–liberal notions of citizenship rights in what became the principal paradigm of the postwar period in the UK and many other countries, the US excluded.[9] It also, in its exposition of 'civil rights', conflates what Keith Faulks (1998, 2000) terms 'market rights' (such as 'the right to own property') and civil liberties (such as 'freedom of speech'). The renaissance of classical liberalism in the form of the new right, which accords primacy to market rights over all other forms of citizenship rights, has reopened the debate about the nature of rights and the validity of their extension beyond the civil and political spheres. Underlying this debate are opposed views about the nature of freedom and of the role of government in the protection or promotion of that freedom. The new right defines freedom in negative terms as the absence of coercion and interference so that the role of government is limited to the protection of the freedom of individual citizens. The promotion by government of a more positive notion of freedom as the ability to participate in society as full citizens is regarded as illegitimate. Moreover, it is argued that citizenship cannot embrace social rights because, implying a claim on resources, they are categorically different from civil and political rights.

In an important critique, Raymond Plant has countered this thesis in two main ways. First, he denies that social rights are categorically different from civil and political rights, for the protection of the latter also implies a claim on resources. Second, he suggests that if you ask what negative freedom is for, the obvious answer is to protect individual autonomy, that is to enable individual citizens to pursue their own ends. If this is the case, he argues, it cannot be separated from the ability to pursue those ends. Thus, the distinction between freedom and ability, which is critical to the neo-liberal conception of citizenship, breaks down.[10] The notion of autonomy, of the ability to determine the conditions of one's life and to pursue one's life projects, recurs in contemporary theorisations of social citizenship rights. Carol Gould, for instance, makes the case for a conception of positive freedom as 'self-development, requiring not only the absence of external constraint but also the availability of social and material conditions necessary for the achievement of purposes or plans'.[11]

The other main justification for recognising social rights as a legitimate expression of citizenship is that they help to promote the effective exercise of civil and political rights by groups who are disadvantaged in terms of power and resources. Without social rights, gross inequalities would undermine the equality of political and civil status inherent in the idea of citizenship. This is encapsulated in the increasingly influential notion of the 'indivisibility' of civil, political and social rights.[12] Social citizenship rights also promote the 'de-commodification of labour' by decoupling the living standards of individual citizens from their 'market value' so that they are not totally dependent on selling their labour power in the market.[13] This, of course, is one reason why neo-liberals, for whom the market rules supreme, resist their development. Market forces are thus tempered by recognition of an obligation on society to ensure that its members are able to meet their basic needs.

Again the notion of autonomy is key, linking the theorisation of social citizenship rights with that of human need. Personal autonomy, together with physical survival, constitutes the precondition for action in any culture and, as such, argue Doyal and Gough, represents one of the 'most basic human needs – those which must be satisfied to some degree before actors can effectively participate in their form of life to achieve any other valued goals' (1991, p. 54). As observed in the Introduction, their theory of human needs claims to provide a justification not only for civil and political rights but also for social rights of citizenship as critical to the promotion of autonomy. The role accorded social rights is in recognition that autonomy cannot be understood in purely individualistic terms but that it has a social dimension also.

The work of Doyal and Gough exemplifies a growing willingness on the left to engage in a rights discourse, which has also been used by many democratic political movements and civil society activists as a mobilising flag.[14]

This contrasts with the traditional Marxist approach, which has dismissed the idea of citizenship rights as an individualistic bourgeois charade designed to obscure fundamental economic and social class divisions behind a veneer of equality. Doyal and Gough themselves reject such arguments as 'counter-productive and dangerous', for they ignore the ways in which rights can contribute to the protection of human needs, thereby (although they do not finish the argument) helping to address economic and social inequalities. Others, such as Norman Ginsburg (1994b), observe that it is difficult to envisage a future welfare strategy that does not incorporate rights, even if those on the left remain divided as to their role.

Feminists too differ in their view of the role of rights. For liberal feminists, they are central to any reform programme. Others have underlined the importance of social rights in weakening the hold of patriarchal power and in strengthening women's position as political citizens. Feminists in a wide range of countries have also appealed to a more recent international rights discourse to fight gender inequalities and demand full citizenship status (Huq, 2000). In contrast, post-structuralists reject the very notion of unchanging, universal rights and radical feminists and some care theorists tend to dismiss rights as merely the expression of male values and power. Among feminists writing in a socialist tradition there is a concern about their individualistic nature and about the dangers of abstracting them from their historical and political context. The importance of context is also stressed by those who point to the gap that can exist between formal rights and 'really existing citizenship', which depends on the ability to access and exercise rights (Molyneux, 2000, p. 122). A number of contemporary feminist scholars caution against placing too much faith in rights but also counsel against outright rejection, in acknowledgement of the law's force as an agent of emancipation as well as oppression.[15]

Feminist scepticism about citizenship rights overlaps with that of some on the radical left who have highlighted 'the failure of citizenship rights vested in liberal democratic institutions to meet the needs of women and racialised groups and the socially and economically marginalised' (Taylor, 1989, p. 29). In part, this reflects citizenship's more general exclusionary tensions, but it also suggests a need to distinguish between different kinds of rights and the possibility of their 'radical extension' to embrace new categories, demanded by social movements (Doyal and Gough, 1991). Examples include various rights associated with recognition and identity politics, such as cultural and reproductive rights. The latter can be seen both as an extension of the civil–political–social rights triad and as inseparable from it.[16] Effectively ignored in most of the mainstream literature on citizenship, reproductive rights are, David Held argues, 'the very basis of the possibility of effective participation of women in both civil society and the polity'. He identifies seven clusters of rights corresponding to key sites of power: health, social, cultural, civil, economic, pacific and political rights. These bundles of

rights are, Held contends, key to the entrenchment of the principle of autonomy and to facilitating free and equal political participation.[17]

In similar vein, Gould argues that 'the right of participation in decision-
making in social, economic, cultural and political life' should be included in
the nexus of basic rights (1988, p. 212; see also Jones and Gaventa, 2002).
Thomas Janoski, another advocate of 'participation rights', suggests that
their recognition 'counters criticisms that the welfare state creates a dependent society' and 'pushes citizenship rights into the center of more recent
welfare state controversies and democratic struggles' (1998, pp. 42 and 50).
This position is echoed in attempts on the left to develop a more dynamic
form of social citizenship rights than those traditionally associated with the
postwar welfare state. These initiatives stem from dissatisfaction with the
'passive' nature of the latter in the face of welfare bureaucracy, resulting in
the 'depoliticisation' of social citizenship, and, more recently, also concerns
about the marketisation of welfare. The result has been explorations of the
potential for user involvement and greater democratic accountability of
welfare institutions, both statutory and voluntary.[18] Here a rights-based conception of welfare citizenship as status is being dynamised and complemented by an emphasis on citizenship as practice.

Citizenship as general obligation

It is not, though, this interpretation of citizenship as practice that is most
prominent at the turn of the twenty-first century. Instead, an increasingly
influential 'duties discourse' is, in various guises, supplanting the dominant
postwar social rights paradigm. Most importantly, in the US, the UK,
Australia and a number of continental European countries both the new
right (in particular neo-conservatives) and communitarians have deliberately
challenged the 'rights discourse' so as to shift the fulcrum of the dominant
citizenship paradigm (see *Critical Social Policy*, 1998). Most of the key texts
contributing to this shift originated in the US, notably Lawrence Mead's
Beyond Entitlement: The Social Obligations of Citizenship (1986) and Michael
Novak *et al.*'s *The New Consensus on Family and Welfare* (1987). Both
emphasise citizenship obligations over rights and both appeal to the common
good in identifying as the prime obligation engagement in paid work by
welfare recipients to support their families.

Work obligations

Paid work, as important to individual well-being, figured prominently in nineteenth and early twentieth century thinking about citizenship (Parker, 1998).
The question of work *obligations* was not ignored by Marshall who considered

'the duty to work' to be 'of paramount importance' in a modern economy. However, a voice from a different era, he suggested that 'the essential duty is not to have a job and hold it, since that is relatively simple in conditions of full employment, but to put one's heart into one's job and work hard' (1950, pp. 78–80). His perspective was thus very different from that of those writing in the late twentieth and early twenty-first centuries, when conditions of full employment can no longer be taken for granted and when welfare budgets have been under strain from the cost of supporting those without jobs. Moreover, neo-conservatives such as Mead and Novak, unlike Marshall, argue that social citizenship rights should be contingent on the duty to engage in paid work which, they maintain, represents 'as much a badge of citizenship as rights' (Mead, 1986, p. 229). The enforcement of this duty can be analysed both according to its intensiveness (namely the kind of work tests and sanctions applied) and its extensiveness (for instance, how it treats lone parents) (Kremer, 1994). The latter, in particular, has gender implications that raise questions about the status of care as a citizenship responsibility to which I return in Chapter 7.

An intensification of the obligation to work, reflecting the influence of new-right thinking, characterises policy developments in western nations, especially, though not exclusively, in the Anglo-Saxon world where they have led to 'work-welfare' programmes including most radically, in the US, work-fare.[19] In the UK, the widely accepted, longstanding principle that unemployed claimants should be available for work and should be expected to accept a reasonable offer of work or training was subject to increasingly punitive interpretation and application under the Conservatives, culminating in the replacement of unemployment benefit by a jobseeker's allowance, designed to 'make clear to unemployed people the link between their receipt of benefit and the obligations that places upon them' through a mandatory 'job-seeker's agreement' (DEG/DSS, 1994, p. 10). New Labour has continued this policy, intensifying both the rhetoric of responsibility, demanded in return for new opportunities, and the sanctions for those who do not comply. Although its New Deal schemes provide more support and assistance than existed previously, the obligations placed on the claimant are not matched by, what some would argue is, a reciprocal duty to ensure jobs are available (Rosanvallon, 2000; Hills, 2001).

This exemplifies the unequal terms under which the contract between state and individual is being renegotiated, as part of 'a new politics of welfare contractualism', particularly prominent in the US and the UK.[20] Under this contract, the state provides welfare benefits in return for which it can require individual citizens to fulfil certain obligations, most notably the obligation to seek and/or undertake paid work. Stuart White conducts a closely-argued defence of welfare contractualism on grounds of distributive justice and reciprocity: 'as a way of ensuring that those who willingly share in the social product satisfy a corresponding obligation to make a productive contribution back to the community in return and do not "free-ride" on the productive efforts of (and so exploit) their fellow citizens' (2000, p. 508). However, for this to represent 'fair reciprocity' requires the satisfaction of certain other considerations of justice. These he sets out as: a fair reward (from wages and/or tax-benefit policy) for those who meet the work requirement; decent work opportunities and choices; equitable treatment of non-market forms of 'productive contribution', in particular unpaid care; and the extension of the requirement of 'productive contribution' to the wealthy who do not need to work. To these we might add an adequate social infrastructure of welfare services, together with flexible employment practices, to support those who are expected to combine paid work and care responsibilities of any kind (White and Gardner, 2000). White also posits an 'equal opportunity' test, in which equal opportunity is defined in terms of the prevention or correction of 'inequalities in income attributable to differences in natural ability and [of] inequalities in capability due to handicaps that people suffer through no fault of their own' (p. 521). The imposition of work obligations under the reciprocity principle should, he suggests, be conditional on the satisfaction of 'a sufficiently high threshold of equal opportunity' (which is left vague).

White suggests that centre-left versions of welfare contractualism to some extent recognise these conditions, but only imperfectly. The imperfections are particularly conspicuous in the US workfare context, and least so in Scandinavia. In the UK, while the rewards attached to low-paid work have been improved, job opportunities in some parts of the country remain very poor indeed; there is only limited acknowledgement of non-market forms of 'productive contribution'; the low income and capital taxes imposed on the wealthy constitute a minimalist alternative obligation; and, in the context of wide class, gender and 'race' inequalities, the equal opportunity test is failed. Nor is there yet an adequate social infrastructure, although New Labour has begun the task of creating this. In this, inegalitarian, context, more coercive Anglo-American forms of work-welfare policies have been rejected by critics such as Bill Jordan as representing 'forced labour' rather than, what he dismisses as the 'new orthodoxy' of, the principle of reciprocity (1998, pp. 58, 61; Jayasuriya, 2001). White himself acknowledges the danger that in such conditions 'the burdens of reciprocity then fall with inequitable heaviness on the shoulders of the least well-off' (White and Gardner, 2000, p. 99).

The broader relationship between obligations and rights

The issue of the work obligations attached to social security entitlement is but one, politically charged, aspect of the wider question of the relationship between rights and obligations or responsibilities.[21] Few would dispute that responsibilities and obligations as well as rights enter into the citizenship equation. The question is: what is the appropriate balance and relationship between the two and how does that balance reflect gender and other power relations?

The balance and relationship between citizen rights and duties, although not central to Marshall's path-breaking essay, was not, as is sometimes believed, ignored by it. Marshall referred to the duties of citizenship in a number of places. For instance, he claimed that 'social rights imply an absolute right to a certain standard of civilisation which is conditional only on the discharge of the general duties of citizenship' and that 'if citizenship is invoked in the defence of rights, the corresponding duties of citizenship cannot be ignored'; these duties require that the citizen's acts 'should be inspired by a lively sense of responsibility towards the welfare of the community'. Towards the end of the essay, he raised explicitly the question of the 'changing balance between rights and duties'. He contrasted the precision of citizen rights with the vagueness of citizen duties other than a limited number of compulsory ones, namely payment of taxes and national insurance contributions, education and military service (and presumably jury service). The other, vaguer, duties, he suggested, 'are included in the general obligation to live the life of a good citizen, giving such service as one can to promote the welfare of the community' under which he included 'the duty to work'. However, he was sceptical as to the force of the appeal to a 'national community' in which any obligation 'appears remote and unreal' (1950, pp. 43, 70, 78).

While Marshall did not resolve the question of the balance between rights and duties, his exposition of the question did help to elucidate two key aspects of it. First, is the distinction between 'compulsory' and 'vague' duties and related to that is the nature of the relationship between these duties and rights, in particular social rights. Today, some like Ralf Dahrendorf (1988) (whose position was endorsed by the British Speaker's Commission on Citizenship) claim that the rights and duties of citizenship are separate from each other. This position, grounded in liberalism, is echoed by Jordan who argues that 'the first principle of liberalism – strong unconditional rights, weak and conditional duties – is clearly breached if rights are hedged about with restrictive obligations' (1998, p. 82).

Others see a closer and more reciprocal, or even conditional, relationship between rights and duties, which can work both ways. Thus, from one side, there is the argument that duties imply a right to the means to fulfil them; from the other is the increasingly vociferous claim, associated with communitarianism, that responsibilities are morally and logically prior to rights.[22] In the US, communitarianism's most politically influential advocate, Amitai Etzioni, has called for 'a moratorium on the minting of most, if not all, new rights', together with the re-establishment of a link between rights and responsibilities and recognition that the latter do not necessarily entail the former. His goal is correction of 'the current imbalance between rights and responsibilities' (1993, p. 4). In the UK, David Selbourne has similarly deplored 'a politics of dutiless right' characteristic of the 'civic deserts' of the modern nation with its attenuated civic bond (1994, p. 31).

Such thinking has had a considerable influence on the 'third way', as expounded by New Labour and by Giddens, its 'intellectual guru'. Indeed the latter has gone so far as to propose '*no rights without responsibilities*' as 'a prime motto for the new politics' (1998, p. 65, emphasis in the original). Interestingly, Etzioni has criticised this formulation as 'a grave moral error'. His argument is that 'while rights and responsibilities are complementary and necessitate one another', basic rights should not be denied to those who do not live up their responsibilities, just as they are not exempted from their responsibilities, if their rights are not fully honoured (2000, pp. 29–30). This would appear to acknowledge the danger that rights can be fundamentally compromised, if they become subservient to specific obligations and to come closer to a notion of a reciprocal rather than conditional relationship.

A helpful formulation of the principle of reciprocity, at a broader level than that articulated by White, has been proposed by Geraint Parry. Echoing Marshall, he posits a 'mutual society' based on the principle of 'from each according to his or her ability; to each according to his or her need for the conditions of agency' (1991, p. 186). In other words whatever is necessary to enable him or her to fulfil the potential of citizenship as a practice.

Active citizenship – conservative and radical

As I shall argue at the end of this chapter, the notion of agency helps knit together the different citizenship traditions. It can also be found implicitly in the idea of 'active citizenship', which has been promoted in the British context from a variety of standpoints, and in formulations of citizenship responsibility grounded in social movements such as feminism and environmentalism. Conservative ministers deployed 'active citizenship' as an exhortation to discharge the responsibilities of neighbourliness, voluntary action and charity (an example of Marshall's vaguer citizenship duty to promote the welfare of the community). It was largely discredited because of the context of the rundown of public sector services, benefit cutbacks and privatisation programme in which it was advanced.[23] Nevertheless, in both the UK and the US ideas for citizens' or community service have since been put forward.

Going further, the argument that community service should equate with paid work as a means of discharging the general obligations of citizenship has been gaining ground and has been partially acknowledged by some governments.[24] A parallel argument relates to care which, insofar as it is undertaken in the private sphere of the home, tends to be discounted as an expression of active citizenship responsibility. This has prompted feminist criticism of the contemporary preoccupation with paid work obligations and a more fundamental critique of dominant constructions of obligation, rooted in individualistic and legalistic notions of contract. The argument has been put, instead, for less formal understandings of responsibility, derived from the 'self-in-relationship' with others and from an ethic of care (see Chapter 4). This is a central issue in many feminist critiques of citizenship theory and practice, as we shall see.[25]

The case for acknowledging less formal expressions of citizenship responsibility has also been made in relation to mutual aid and self-help activities (Munn-Giddings, 1998; Barnes, 1999). These provide an example of more radical and collectivist conceptions of active citizenship, as embodied in Ray Pahl's alternative definition: 'local people working together to improve their own quality of life and to provide conditions for others to enjoy the fruits of a more affluent society' (1990, p. 8; see also Williams and Windebank, 1997). This is a form of active citizenship that disadvantaged people, often women, do for themselves, for instance through community groups, rather than a paternalistic top-down relationship; one that creates them as subjects rather than objects.

Another example is the development by the green movement of ideas of ecological citizenship duties, which stretch beyond the geographical and temporal boundaries of the individual citizen's community.[26] Fred Steward sums up green politics, which is becoming an increasingly important strand of political activism, as expressing 'aspirations of citizenship through its globalisation of the sense of community' as well as successfully fostering 'a culture of local, community activism and personal responsibility' (1991, pp. 65, 75). Ecological citizenship has been put forward as an additional element of citizenship, which both complements and acts as a corrective to the original civil–political–social triad and which broadens the idea of participation to include citizens' relationship to nature. Ecological citizenship can also be viewed from a rights perspective, for example the right to healthy foods and an unpolluted environment, which in turn implies obligations on corporate bodies and government as well as on individual citizens towards each other.[27] Both the rights and responsibilities of ecological citizenship are, Bryan Turner (2001) argues, critical to our ontological security.

There are some, though, such as David Marquand (1991) who, while placing active citizenship in the civic republican tradition, dismisses it as a 'deformed' variant thereof that does not engage with the essence of civic republicanism, which is the duty to take part in government. While Marquand is right to highlight the depoliticised nature of the Conservatives' active citizen, his position runs the danger of promulgating a narrow interpretation of active political citizenship that is not well suited to modern societies.

Citizenship as political obligation

The values to which modern civic republicanism appeals would be easily recognisable to the ancient Athenians: civic duty, the submission of individual interest to that of the common good, the elevation of the public sphere in which the citizen is constituted as political actor. In more modern times, this tradition was rekindled in the American revolution and the early history of the US. Today it is in the US where civic republicanism is once again being most vociferously promoted as an expression of disenchantment with the increased fragmentation of society and with the apathy and parochial self-interest seen as typical of modern American democracy (Phillips, 1993; Mouffe, 1993a). The renaissance of civic republicanism (together with the emergence of communitarianism) represents a reaction against the individualism of the liberal citizenship paradigm that has dominated contemporary political life. This, it is argued, represents an impoverished version of citizenship in which individual citizens are reduced to atomised, passive bearers of rights whose freedom consists in being able to pursue their individual interests. The reclaiming of active, collective politics as of the essence of citizenship is central to contemporary civic republicanism, the articulation of which has been heavily influenced by the work of Hannah Arendt.[28] For civic republicans, political activity is not a means to an end but an end in itself, associated with the pursuit of the 'public' or 'common good', which stands outside and separate from the interests of individual citizens. Nevertheless, political activity is also regarded as contributing to the self-development of the individual citizen: it is only through political engagement that the Self fulfils its full potential (Marquand, 1991).

Civic republicanism's appeal is not confined to any one point in the political spectrum, for elements of its creed resonate for many supporters of radical democracy as well as for communitarians. It has also been appropriated, suitably modified, by some feminist writers, most notably Mary Dietz. She advocates 'a vision of citizenship' that is 'expressly political and, more exactly, participatory and democratic' in which politics involves 'the collective and participatory engagement of citizens in the determination of the affairs of their community' and in which we conceive of ourselves as ' "speakers of words and doers of deeds" mutually participating in the public realm'. It is only, she argues, when active political participation is valued as an expression of citizenship in contrast to the 'politically barren' construction of the 'citizen as bearer of rights' alone, that feminists will 'be able to claim a truly liberatory politics of their own' (1987, pp. 13–15; 1985, 1991).

Other feminists have been attracted by civic republicanism's portrayal of citizenship as active political participation and involvement in decision-making and by the potential of collective deliberation in the public sphere for the articulation of the interests of women and 'minority groups' and for the debating and confronting of differences (see Young, 1989, 1990a; Phillips, 1991, 1993; Voet, 1998). Nevertheless, they have also been critical of some of its other key tenets. These criticisms centre on three main areas: its narrow conception of the 'political' and 'the citizen' built on a, generally, rigid separation of public and private spheres; its appeal to notions of universalism, impartiality and the common good; and the demanding nature of the obligations it entails, which has particular implications for women. It is through an examination of these criticisms, which come from outside the alternative conventional liberal paradigm, that the distinction between civic republicanism and other approaches to active political citizenship associated with participatory and radical democracy emerges (Phillips, 1991).

Broad vs. narrow conceptions of the 'political' and the 'citizen'

Which activities are deemed worthy of the labels of 'political' and 'citizenship' are two closely intertwined questions that are central to any feminist reinterpretation of civic republicanism. The classical civic republican model dictated that all citizens should be directly involved in governance of the community. A creature of the Athenian city state, the model does not translate easily into modern, large, complex societies. Nevertheless, the modern civic republicanism ideal is of citizenship as active ongoing engagement in the formal political process. It is in the relatively narrow definition of the 'political' and of the 'citizen' which is implied that one of the problems with civic republicanism lies. The significance of the definition of 'the political' for political theory and practice has been underlined by numerous feminist scholars who have exposed the extent to which conventional definitions have been steeped in male experience.[29] More generally, Parry *et al.* warn that 'any definition of 'political participation' is inevitably tendentious and contestable', given that the drawing of the line between the political and the non-political is itself a political act (1992, p. 20).

Proponents of participatory democracy broaden the sphere of 'the political' beyond that pertaining to the general government of a society to embrace other institutions in which, it is argued, individuals should have the opportunity to participate in decision-making. In extending the locus of 'the political' and of democratic relations, advocates of participatory democracy are challenging the sharp distinction between 'public' and 'private', which characterises civic republicanism, while sharing the latter's emphasis on active participation (Phillips, 1991; 1993). Although their main focus has been workplace democracy, some have broadened the case for democratic participation. Gould, for instance, argues that democracy is necessary not only in the conventional political and the economic spheres but also 'in the organisation and relations of social and cultural life' under whose rubric she includes not only welfare institutions and voluntary associations but also 'the family and other child-raising and living arrangements' (1988, p. 255; see also Pateman, 1989 and Janoski, 1998).

This broader conception of participatory democracy lays down an even more direct challenge to the conventional separation of the 'private' from the 'public' and 'political' by broadening appreciably the scope of the latter and by emphasising the interrelationship between the two, reflecting the tenor of much feminist writing on the subject. Carole Pateman thus rejects the idea of a political sphere as 'a reified abstraction' separated from the rest of social life; instead it exists 'whenever citizens gather together to make political decisions' (1989, p. 110). The definition offered by Held endorses such a conceptualisation of politics as 'unrelated to any specific "site" or set of institutions':

> In my view, politics is about power; that is about the *capacity* of social agents, agencies and institutions to maintain or transform their environment, social or physical ... Accordingly, politics is a phenomenon found in and between all groups, institutions (formal and informal) and societies, cutting across public and private life. It is expressed in all the activities of cooperation, negotiation and struggle over the use and distribution of resources. It is involved in all the relations, institutions and structures which are implicated in the activities of production and reproduction in the life of societies.[30]

This definition of politics incorporates what Patricia S. Mann terms 'micropolitics': 'embedded in the daily lives of individuals' (1997, p. 235). This, in turn, would embrace the process of negotiation with welfare state institutions, by individuals as well as groups, the main responsibility for which tends to fall to women (which does not necessarily mean that the women themselves define their actions as 'political' [Naples, 1998a and b]). Feminist theorists such as Barbara Nelson (1984) and Kathleen Jones (1990) have highlighted this aspect of contemporary citizenship politics; Parry *et al.* explicitly incorporate it into their definition of 'the political' as 'action directed at governmental authorities' (1992, p. 19). Although the latter concede that such action can be typified as that of the consumer pursuing her individual interests, they argue that the sum of individual complaints about a particular issue, such as council house repairs, can translate into a local political issue. Similarly, one could point to how the contestation of a particular decision by an individual social security claimant can result in an interpretation of, or even change in, the law which has implications for the wider body of claimants. Another example might be the attempts by some disabled people to challenge the attitudes of professionals who subscribe to the 'medical' or 'personal tragedy' models of disability and to insert their own definitions and interpretations of their needs and how they should be met.[31] However, not all engagement with welfare institutions has either direct or indirect wider political consequences, so that while I would include engagement with welfare institutions within the sphere of political citizenship, I recognise that it constitutes one of its fuzzier borders.

'Action directed at governmental authorities' can also take place outside formal political and institutional channels through the medium of, for instance, demonstrations, pickets and agitprop. Such alternative political action marked the protest politics of the late 1960s and re-emerged in

Britain in the mid-1990s particularly in relation to animal rights, green and public order issues. Most notably, it is now associated with anti-globalisation protests, in which a loose coalition of social movements come together in different countries, usually in connection with international summit meetings. Such action is not necessarily directed towards 'governmental authorities'; often the target is the activities of private companies, in particular multi-nationals, or there may be no specific target such as in the earlier Reclaim the Night marches in which women simply attempted to claim public space. Holloway Sparks has suggested the notion of 'dissident citizenship' to conceptualise

> the practices of marginalized citizens who publicly contest prevailing arrangements of power by means of oppositional democratic practices that augment or replace institutionalized channels of democratic opposition when those channels are inadequate or unavailable (1997, p. 75).

It is in the interests of the powerful to label such actions as disruptive (Young, 2000). Although they can cross the boundaries of what is deemed lawful, in certain circumstances acts of civil disobedience can constitute citizenship practice when executed in the name of a greater good. Examples might include the unlawful destruction of genetically modified crops (described by the executive director of Greenpeace UK as 'active citizenship') and the British women who were acquitted of criminal damage to missile programmes on the grounds that such programmes posed a threat to international law. Derek Heater suggests that, in such situations 'justice of cause, sincerity of belief and altruism of motive are valid indices of good citizenship'.[32]

It is through various forms of community-based and social movement politics that many women are most likely to become politically active. Not all civic republicans dismiss out of hand such broader notions of politics. Sheldon Wolin, for instance, is supportive of grassroots movements but nevertheless considers action of this kind to be 'politically incomplete' because of the very localism that is also its strength. Nevertheless, he accepts that not all such action is 'parochial', for increasingly it is directed at concerns, such as nuclear power, affecting a wider population (1992, p. 252). This distinction between the 'parochial' and the 'comprehensive' is also an important one in teasing out different approaches to what counts as citizenship. Any suggestion that the stage for the exercise of genuine political citizenship has to be national rather than local flies in the face of the realities of contemporary politics. As Parry *et al.* observe, most citizen participation is at the local level; indeed they suggest that it is the move beyond the local that almost marks out the professional politician from the ordinary citizen (although some citizens have now leap-frogged over the national to the global level). Global protests notwithstanding, the more remote the locus of politics, the less likely it is that people will become involved. Women, in particular, have tended to practice politics on the local stage, which is not to argue that their under-representation in the national political arena is a matter of indifference. Similarly, much green activism, the expression of active ecological citizenship, is rooted in particular localities, even if some of its focus is global.

Oldfield, in his exploration of the meaning of civic republicanism in the modern world, drawing on some of the classical civic republican texts, accepts that, in large states, the main site for citizen participation will be the locality (see also Lowndes, 1995). Since decisions made at local or neighbourhood level, as well as at the national and international, affect citizens, the practice of citizenship has to be able to encompass all of these levels. Indeed, he appears to be arguing that, in modern plural and heterogeneous societies, citizenship can be practised in a diversity of public arenas. For Oldfield, the importance of citizenship lies in part in its creation of a sense of community. He concludes his treatise on civic republicanism with the observation that 'to a large extent [citizens] will choose where to be active and, when and where they are active, they will create a sense of community. Community is found, therefore, not in formal organisation, but wherever there are individuals who take the practice of citizenship seriously' (1990, p. 174). In his, otherwise demanding, characterisation of modern citizenship, Oldfield thus appears to end up by endorsing an approach that could embrace at least some of the activities I have been discussing.

If an active participatory notion of citizenship, which embodies some of the spirit of civic republicanism, is to offer an attractive and realistic model to women and other groups traditionally marginalised in the political process, it has, I would argue, to embody a broad notion of 'the political', which incorporates a range of activities in the public sphere. Otherwise, the members of these groups face definitional hurdles to entry into the ranks of the citizenry which effectively rule many of them out. This is not the same as saying that the political sphere has no boundaries. Even Pateman, who has contributed powerfully to the feminist critique of the public–private divide, distinguishes political life from the 'private aspects of social life' but sees the two as being 'dialectically interrelated' rather than 'dualistically counterposed' (1989, p. 110). This points to a distinction between my broad conception of citizenship politics, which is nevertheless still located in the 'public' sphere, and what feminists have rightly identified as the personal politics which can also take place in the 'private' or 'intimate' sphere. This distinction helps in the next step of clarifying what is meant by political citizenship; in other words not all politics necessarily counts as citizenship, for the latter, in its political sense, implies active political participation, albeit broadly defined.

An example provided by Anne Phillips (1993) helps to illustrate the point, although the point I am making is rather different from that made by her. Phillips draws a distinction between campaigning in public for men to do their fair share of housework and simply sorting out the division of labour in one's own home; in the case of the former, we are acting as citizens, in the case of the latter, which is nevertheless significant for citizenship, we are not. It is thereby accepted that the terrain of political citizenship is the public sphere while underlining how it cannot be divorced from what happens in the private, which shapes its contours and which can be the proper object of citizenship struggles. This seems to me a helpful way of drawing a line between political action which merits the label citizenship and that which does not, while not losing sight of the relationship between the two, provided it is recognised that the line between the public and private spheres is not immutable. Indeed, actions in both public and private spheres can interact to enhance the capacity to act as a citizen. Thus, involvement in collective action can strengthen the ability to resist oppressive practices such as domestic violence in the private sphere; conversely such resistance can lead to and inform more public collective citizen action.[33]

However, Phillips goes further and argues that, in 'the new language of citizenship' as opposed to 'the older language of democratising everyday life', only action in the public arena (conventionally defined) can be accorded the label 'political', for 'politics is a particular kind of activity, and not to be dissolved into everything else' (p. 86). By treating 'the political' and citizenship as if they were interchangeable, Phillips is here unnecessarily narrowing the meaning of the former so that it can no longer encompass, as does for instance Held's definition and that of many feminists, the power relations that pervade the private domestic as well as the public sphere.

Impartiality and the common good

In locating citizenship, in its active political sense, in the public sphere, albeit a public sphere that is interlocked with the private, I, like Phillips, have accepted one of the tenets of civic republicanism. However, my delineation of the public sphere is broader; it pertains not just to the arenas of formal politics, set apart from everyday life and involving only a very small minority, but encompasses also what Jean Leca calls the 'reservoirs of citizenship': the myriad of voluntary associations of civil society, most particularly the kinds of campaigning and community groups in which women are most likely to be active.[34] Here I part company with civic republicanism, which does not include all forms of public political participation under the rubric of citizenship. Political participation designed to further individual or group interests is deemed outside the pale of citizenship which, as noted already, for civic republicans has to be directed towards the pursuit of the 'common good'.

In a sympathetic but critical assessment of civic republicanism, Michael Waltzer observes how those involved in 'the associational networks of civil society, in unions, parties, movements, interest groups, and so on' can contribute indirectly to the decision-making of the state; yet, they 'stand outside the republic of citizens as it is commonly conceived. They are only intermittently virtuous; they are too caught up in particularity' (1992, p. 99). Although Waltzer himself champions engagement in the associations of civil society, he appears to accept civic republicanism's withholding of the badge of citizenship from such activities. One reason is that their very ordinariness and inclusiveness does not make for the 'heroism' of classical citizenship. This is typical of the way in which the citizen has traditionally embodied a male image whose virtues are 'uniformly masculine' (van Gunsteren, 1994) and a non-disabled male at that.[35] The other reason, which figures more prominently in the contemporary literature, is the partial and particular nature of this kind of political participation. Citizens are supposed to come together to achieve common ends with those different from themselves and in so doing to transcend their specific interests and concerns and identify with the wider collectivity rather than with any particular group.

Iris Young (1989, pp. 255, 257, 1990a) and Anne Phillips (1991, 1993), who share this belief in the importance of coming together to debate and confront differences, have nevertheless developed a powerful feminist critique of this aspect of civic republicanism, as conventionally articulated, which stems from the latter's roots in a notion of the common good. Its essence lies in the observation that the ideals of impartiality and transcendence of individual and group differences impose 'a homogeneity that suppresses group differences in the public' and which in 'a society where some groups are privileged while others are oppressed ... serves only to reinforce that privilege'. To refuse to apply the label of citizenship to the involvement of community activists, the struggles of poor women, or Black or disabled women for justice, is to reinforce the very exclusion against which these groups are fighting, in the name of a 'common good' which has subordinated their interests to those of more powerful groups.

However, this position raises a question mark over the status of sectional interest group politics, as Phillips acknowledges. She poses the question as to where sectional interest ('bad') ends and group identity ('good') begins in feminist and socialist politics. 'What exactly', she asks, is 'the dividing line between pressing one's own selfish and sectional interest and organising around your needs as a disadvantaged or oppressed group?' (1993, pp. 81–2). It is a question that is difficult to answer in the abstract, for the answer probably depends in part on the way in which the politics are conducted and on whether one is a member of disadvantaged or privileged groups.[36] Interestingly, women community activists in low income North American neighbourhoods, interviewed by Nancy Naples, made a distinction between their own *collective* struggles for civil rights and economic equality and 'self-interested actions' rooted in 'the individual, self-promoting class basis of traditional electoral and interest group politics' (1998a, p. 180).

Young (1990a) suggests that the problem lies not in interest group politics as such but in their disconnection from an appeal to justice and in the

inequalities that permit some interests to dominate while others are effectively silenced. Moreover any rigid distinction between a particular and an
impartial perspective can be difficult to maintain in practice. As Young
(1989) notes, our perceptions of public issues are inevitably coloured by our
situated experience. Furthermore, the involvement of individuals in a particular political activity might be motivated initially by self-interest but the
outcome could nevertheless be to the benefit of the wider community and
that wider outcome might become more important to the individual as a
result of her involvement. Thus, for example, a mother of teenage children
might join a campaign for decent facilities for young people on her estate out
of concern for her own children; but that campaign could benefit the whole
community if it reduced vandalism and crime, and her involvement in it may
well have broadened her own concerns. Such a process is not uncommon
among women who get involved in local campaigns (see, for instance,
Krauss, 1998; Naples, 1998a; McCoy, 2000).

Local activism of this kind is important for citizenship from the perspective
both of its impact on the wider community and on the individuals involved.
Its contribution to the strengthening of 'social capital', promoted by Robert
Putnam (1993) and others, as a prerequisite for effective public policy and as
an expression of healthy citizenship, can all too easily be overlooked in formulations that ignore social capital's gendered dynamics and that foreground
more male-dominated activities (Lowndes, 2000). Parry *et al.* (1992) are
among those who note how collective action can boost self-confidence, as
individuals (and this has been particularly true of women) come to see themselves as political actors and effective citizens. For many women, involvement
in community organisations or social movements can be more personally
fruitful than engagement in formal politics, which is often more alienating
than empowering.[37] Thus, from the perspective of the self-development of
the individual citizen, the significance of which is emphasised by a number of
civic republicans, it makes sense to adopt a more inclusive notion of what
counts as citizenship. [38]

However, just as the lines are difficult to draw between action derived
from impartial and self-interested perspectives, so, also, troubling questions
can arise from certain kinds of community action. I have in mind an episode
widely reported and debated in the British media in summer 2000. Residents
(mainly women and children) of a disadvantaged housing estate carried out a
series of, often violent, attacks on and demonstrations against anyone
believed to be a paedophile. At one level, such action exemplifies what I have
been talking about: marginalised and powerless women emerged as effective
actors on behalf of their children and 'the community'. Katrina Kessel, one
of the leaders, said subsequently 'how else is anyone going to listen to a
common person like me? ... At least we were being listened to, and we got
something done', and she maintained that 'looking out for our kids has
helped bring people together' (*Observer*, 4 February 2001; and *Guardian*

6 February 2001). Yet such action was taken with total disregard for the civil rights of those believed to be paedophiles, some of whom were forced to flee. When lines have to be drawn, I would argue that the denial of the citizenship of unpopular groups stands outside the bounds of genuine citizenship action, even though it may resemble that action and perform many of the same functions for the individual and (part of) the wider community.

Notwithstanding such difficult instances, I am making the case for a conceptualisation of 'the political' and of citizenship no longer rooted in the experiences of men and divorced from those of women. When the perspectives of women and of 'minority groups' are written into the equation, the outcome is a broader, more inclusive, portrayal of what participatory political citizenship can mean in a large-scale complex society. This less rigid conceptualisation, which includes the struggles of members of oppressed groups and the everyday politics of community organisations, invokes the spirit of a gendered political theory that 'redefines and enlarges the scope of politics, the practice of citizenship and authority, and the language of political action' (Jones and Jónasdóttir, 1988, p. 9).

The demands of civic republicanism: an obligation or a right?

Frazer and Lacey have likewise called for a broader conception of the political, requiring a variety of public forums 'which allow for genuine involvement in self-government without being unrealistically time-consuming and without entailing that we must all live our lives primarily as citizens'. Their proviso, echoed by others sceptical about any call to full-time citizen duty in the modern world, underlines the final difficulty with civic republicanism in its pure form, namely its demanding nature.[39] Just how demanding is brought home by Oldfield:

> Civic republicanism is a hard school of thought. There is no cosy warmth in life in such a community. *Citizens are called to stern and important tasks which have to do with the very sustaining of their identity.* There may be, indeed there ought to be, a sense of belonging, but that sense of belonging may not be associated with inner peace and, even if it is, it is not the kind of peace that permits a relaxed and private leisure, still less a disdain for civic concerns (1990, p. 5, emphasis added).

The fulfilment of such exacting requirements, he warns, depends on motivation and will; on 'habits of the heart' a phrase inherited from de Tocqueville and popularised by Bellah *et al.* (1985). Citizenship is elevated to *the* defining identity, overriding all others (Mouffe, 1992; Conover *et al*, 1991).The more demanding the conception of citizenship, the more likely it is that those willing and able to meet its stringent tests will represent a minority. Given the sexual division of labour and of time, this minority is likely to be predominately male, as was the ideal citizen of classical republicanism who was largely freed from the necessity to labour and to meet his bodily requirements, facilitated by the ranks of non-citizens – women and slaves (Hartsock, 1985; Held, 1987). The dependence of the classical republican model on an exclusive minority of citizens, largely unencumbered by the demands of everyday living, is one reason why it cannot simply be transplanted into twentieth-century democracies and why it cannot be accepted uncritically by feminists.

Oldfield himself concedes that the civic republican tradition tends to assume that citizens have the time and other resources necessary to fulfil their obligations as citizens. It certainly takes no account of the gendered distribution of these resources. The notion of political participation, however defined, as an obligation of citizenship, together with the idealisation of collective political activity, therefore runs the danger of casting out from the body of citizens all those unable or unwilling to match up to its demanding requirements and of creating another source of guilt for already overburdened women. As Held argues with regard to his model of democratic autonomy, which places at its centre the ability of every citizen to participate in public life, this principle does not have to be translated into a necessity. What is important is that the conditions are created that enable all citizens to participate – to act as citizens – if they so wish; this then increases the likelihood that they will do so, thereby further developing their capacities as participating citizens in a virtuous circle of citizenship participation (Held, 1987, 1989; Gould, 1988).

Where this discussion of citizenship as political obligation has led to is a recasting of participatory political citizenship, broadly defined, as a right and an opportunity. This right can be justified with reference to its importance to the expression of human agency and to individual self-development through social cooperation, which is how Gould (1988) characterises human freedom. In the next, final, section of this chapter, I will suggest that the notion of human agency, rooted in its social context, provides the conceptual tool for a synthesis of the rights and participatory traditions of citizenship in a way that is particularly helpful from the perspective of women.

A critical synthesis

The way in which political participation can be conceptualised as a right as well as an obligation underlines its importance to both the broad liberal and republican traditions of citizenship. Together with civil rights, basic political rights form the core of the liberal tradition, guaranteeing the 'negative' freedom of individuals in the name of their autonomy. Perhaps too often taken for granted in the West, despite the relative recency of the struggles of women and Black peoples for their full extension, the claiming of such rights by the peoples of Eastern Europe and South Africa have helped to remind us of their importance to citizenship at the end of the twentieth century. In particular, the joy and seriousness with which the Black peoples of the new South Africa seized their newly achieved right to vote in 1994 underlined the importance of that basic component of political citizenship. Within the UK, concerns about 'disenchantment with and disengagement from traditional political structures' and the general weakness of democratic citizenship has prompted calls for a Citizens' Constitution, which would encourage 'a culture of citizenship and rights' (Charter 88, 2000, p. 23).

Developments such as these, as noted earlier, have contributed to a rather less suspicious attitude on the left and among some feminists towards a rights-based approach which had previously been rejected as individualistic and legalistic. (Non-market) civil and political rights are more likely now to be seen as a necessary precondition of full and equal citizenship. They are not, however, a sufficient condition, for they need to be backed up by social rights. Social rights play a pivotal role both as an antidote to the individualism of the classical liberal rights formulation and as the means of giving substance to such rights through the promotion of the 'positive' freedom of individuals as well as the protection of their 'negative' freedom. They also serve to weaken the hold of private patriarchal power and of family obligation (Yeatman, 1994; Finch,1989).

The case for understanding rights as constituting a mutually supportive web of the formal (civil and political) and the substantive (social and economic) has been made with reference to their status as a prerequisite for the realisation of human agency. Gould, for instance, proposes that 'human rights are grounded in the nature of human beings', one of the fundamental characteristics of which is 'free agency'. It is from these human rights, that the triad of citizenship rights derives.[40] Similarly, within citizenship theory itself, 'the typical justification [of social rights] is agency' (Marquand, 1991, p. 338): social rights (at least in theory) enable citizens to exercise their political and civil rights on equal terms and create the conditions for full social and political participation. In this way, they further the values of not only liberal rights but also classical republican citizenship (Oliver and Heater, 1994, pp. 5, 96), a point acknowledged by Oldfield from a civic republican standpoint:

> For activity of any kind, including that involved in the practice of citizenship, people need certain resources. Some of these have to do with what liberal individualism identifies as civil, political and legal rights. Others have to do with economic and social resources. Without health, education and a reasonable living income, for instance, individuals do not have the capacity to be effective agents in the world, and the possibilities of a practice of citizenship are thus foreclosed in advance (1990, p. 27).

Oldfield admits, though, that civic republicanism 'does not have much to say about providing individuals with the resources they require to become effective agents in the world – that is, to become citizens' (p. 156). (The same can be said for classical liberalism with regard to its preoccupation with formal as opposed to substantive rights.) Thus, a civic republican (and also communitarian) conception of citizenship needs to be underpinned by citizenship rights. Conversely, a traditional rights-based account of citizenship is also not sufficient. It needs to be developed in conjunction with some of the insights afforded by civic republicanism and communitarianism, but shorn of their more exclusionary tendencies. In particular, its exposition of rights has to be located not in a notion of atomised individuals but in the context of the wider society (without necessarily buying in to the republican/communitarian idea of 'the community'). At the same time, the active nature of republican citizenship points towards a more dynamic conceptualisation than that commonly associated with a liberal or social rights approach and reminds us that rights need to be defended and extended through political action. Thus, citizenship rights are not static but are always open to reinterpretation and renegotiation.

A similar point is used by Chantal Mouffe to argue that traditional rights and civic republican traditions are not incompatible, despite the claims of some of their respective proponents. While recognising the limitations of each, she argues that we need to build on their respective strengths in order to go beyond them in 'a new conception of citizenship adequate for a project of radical and plural democracy'.[41] Anna Yeatman goes further in her exposition of a politics of difference, which she distinguishes from both liberal and republican rights discourse. She conceptualises rights as 'dialectical and relational': 'they are dialogical rights, predicated fundamentally on a right to give voice and be listened to within the dialogical processes of decision-making' (1994, p. 90; see also Dean, 1996, pp. 93–6). Here a rights approach is defined in terms of process and political participation. This is also reflected in the notion of 'rights-claims', which remain an important mobilising tool for social movements in both the North and South. Social movements in Latin America, for instance, have developed radical understandings of citizenship around the idea of 'a right to have rights', which includes 'the invention and creation of *new* rights, which emerge from specific struggles and their concrete practices'.[42]

Thus, while the rights and participatory approaches to citizenship remain conceptually different, they do not necessarily have to conflict; indeed, they can be seen as being mutually supportive, even if tensions between them remain.[43] Parry (1991) suggests that Marshall's own articulation of modern citizenship, with its emphasis on full membership of a community as well as on rights, represented an early attempt to synthesise rights theories with a more communitarian approach. Moreover, Marshall maintained that the bonds of citizenship are stimulated by 'the struggle to win' rights as well as 'their enjoyment when won' (1950, p. 41). Certainly, the interplay between the rights and participatory strands of citizenship has been an important thread running through the development of welfare states. In the UK, it has been argued that an emphasis on passive entitlements at the expense of active participation in the building of welfare institutions contributed to a bureaucratised, alienating welfare system that, in the very process of offering social rights, denied those in poverty and other users the dignity and status of full citizens.[44] The interaction between social and political citizenship has also been key in the development of women's position as citizens in the twentieth century.[45] The nature of the social rights that have emerged has, in part, been a reflection of the extent to which women have been involved in their construction. Conversely, the extent of women's political involvement has, in part, been a reflection of the nature of the social and reproductive rights they have achieved and their mobilisation has been, in part, a function of their relationship with the welfare state. In the welfare state today, the two aspects of citizenship coalesce in the process of negotiation with welfare state institutions.

This perspective on citizenship is exemplified by the work of Scandinavian feminist scholars. Helga Hernes, for example, writes:

> The welfare state literature, to the extent that it deals with individual citizens, deals with those aspects of citizenship that are related to social policy entitlements. Democratic theories and empirical studies of democratic politics emphasise the participatory aspects of citizenship. Any adequate account of contemporary citizenship … must include all these dimensions if the interplay between material rights, multi-level participation, and political identities is to be grasped (1987, p. 138).

This helps to underline the importance of a synthetic approach, if citizenship is to provide a useful tool for feminist analysis. A rounded and fruitful theorisation of citizenship, which can be of potential value to women, has to embrace both individual rights (and, in particular, social and reproductive rights) and political participation and has also to analyse the relationship between the two (see also Sarvasy and Siim, 1994; Siim, 2000). The related issues of the construction of citizenship obligation or responsibility and of membership itself are picked up again in later chapters.

Human agency

By adopting a synthetic approach, which embraces elements of the two main historical citizenship traditions, citizenship emerges as a dynamic concept in which process and outcome stand in a dialectical relationship to each other. Moreover, this relationship is itself a fluid process as the content of citizenship rights is not fixed but remains the object of political struggles. At the core of this conceptualisation, as suggested already, lies the idea of human agency. Citizenship as participation represents an expression of human agency in the political arena, broadly defined; citizenship as rights enables people to act as agents.

The idea of human agency is typically used to characterise individuals as autonomous, purposive and creative actors, capable of choice.[46] The actions and choices of these actors constitute a process of self-development, 'of concretely becoming the person one chooses to be through carrying out those actions that express one's purposes and needs' (Gould, 1988, p. 47). Patricia Hill Collins similarly uses the image of 'a journey toward self-definition' through which 'Black women's power as human subjects' and their ability to exercise some control over their lives are validated (1991, pp. 106–7). In developing her self, the individual is also acting upon, and thereby potentially changing, the world, a world that at the same time structures the choices available. As Yeatman observes, 'it is because humans are attributed the freedom to make themselves and the world they live in that citizenship becomes necessary' (1994, p. 58).

The conception of human agency which informs my approach to citizenship is one that not only locates it in a dialectic relationship with social structures, but that also conceives of it as embedded in social and cultural relations (see also Mann, 1997). Following Gould (1988) individuals are understood to be social beings in the sense that individual self-development both occurs in the context of social relations and characteristically involves engagement in collective activities directed towards collective as well as individual ends. This engagement is mediated by cultural understandings that frame the expression of agency (Pugh and Thompson, 1999). The self, who acts, is thus 'the relational self', a term coined by Virginia Held. It is used by Frazer and Lacey as a way of expressing our 'empirical and logical interdependence' and of collapsing the 'individual/community dichotomy', which underpins the separation of liberal and civic republican/communitarian formulations of citizenship (1993, p. 178). Moreover, a strong web of citizenship rights, stretching well beyond formal civil and political rights, is essential if each individual is to develop her true potential.

The thread of human agency is of particular significance in the weaving of the rich tapestry of women's citizenship. Gould, for instance, has used it as the basis for feminist claims for equal rights: 'if each human being is regarded as an agent with a capacity for free choice and self-development', there can be no grounds for one gender to have a greater right to exercise this capacity than another and domination of one group by another constitutes a denial of the conditions of equal agency. Women's full freedom therefore lies in their ability to participate in the control of 'the economic and social conditions of their lives, as well as freedom from discrimination and domination' (1984, pp. 5–6). In this formulation, the notion of agency is put to the service of women's equal rights as citizens. It is also of importance from a feminist perspective in recasting women as active citizens, within the frame of politics, past and present. It has been one of the great achievements of feminist scholarship to illuminate the record of women's involvement in political struggle, thereby restoring them to the stage from the wings of history. As Chandra Mohanty observes, women's absence from traditional historical representations should not be confused with their actual absence as historical actors. She also makes the case for 'historicizing and locating political agency' as an antidote to universalist formulations of gender oppression beneath which other social divisions are submerged.[47]

Citizenship as the expression of agency can contribute to the recasting of women as political actors. Increasingly it is being recognised that the construction of 'woman' as victim can be damaging both politically and psychologically. The point has been made from very different political perspectives by bell hooks and Naomi Wolf (1993). The former calls for women to unite 'on the basis of shared strengths and resources' rather than 'shared victimisation'. 'Women who are exploited and oppressed daily', she argues, 'cannot afford to relinquish the belief that they exercise some measure of control, however relative, over their lives. They cannot afford to see themselves solely as "victims" because their survival depends on continued exercise of whatever personal powers they possess'.[48]

Support for this kind of argument can be found in recent critiques of the previously dominant welfare paradigm which, in its concern to avoid *blaming* the victims, has tended to pathologise and homogenise them as victims instead, thereby neglecting the 'role of creative human agency' (Titterton, 1992, p. 1). An alternative emergent paradigm emphasises people's capacity 'to be active agents in shaping their lives, experiencing, acting upon and reconstituting the outcomes of welfare policies', albeit within structural constraints (Williams *et al.*, 1999, p. 2; see also Mann and Deacon; 1999). It also incorporates new models of the life-course, which illuminate the ways in which 'women construct and can change their lives' despite the structural constraints they face (Monk and Katz, 1993, p. 22).

As will be clear from the earlier discussion, not all expressions of agency constitute citizenship. Doyal and Gough make a useful distinction between simple autonomy as expressed through agency and 'the higher degrees of critical autonomy which are entailed by democratic participation in the political process at whatever level' (1991, p. 68; see also Introduction). Translating into the language of citizenship, while we can distinguish between simple agency and citizenship agency, they are nevertheless intertwined, acting upon each other. To act as a citizen requires first a sense of agency, the belief that one can act; acting as a citizen, especially collectively, in turn fosters that sense of agency. Thus, agency is not simply about the capacity to choose and act but it is also about a conscious capacity, which is important to the individual's self-identity. As Susan Bickford writes 'identity is a personal and political force open to active re-creation through our words and actions' (1997, p. 124). The development of a conscious sense of agency, at both the personal and political level, is crucial to women's sense of themselves as full and active citizens on their own and in alliance with others.

An important element here is self-esteem. Susan James criticises the tacit and unproblematised assumption in liberal citizenship theory of citizens' emotional independence, which enables them to speak in their own voice. To speak in one's own voice and put forward one's own views in the polity, requires, she proposes, 'self-esteem – a stable sense of one's own separate identity and a confidence that one is worthy to participate in political life' (1992, p. 60). The particular value attached to self-esteem and respect by Black women is underlined by Collins (1991). Morris makes the same point with regard to disabled women. The greater impediments to the development of women's self-esteem (recognising the impact of differences such as 'race', class, poverty, disability and sexuality) act as a further brake on their ability to develop their full potential as citizens.

Small-scale political action at the neighbourhood level can be important in helping to strengthen women's self-esteem, particularly in the case of disadvantaged women. This, as argued already, is one reason why such action should be recognised as citizenship (provided it is not at the expense of other people's rights as citizens), with an emphasis on the importance of process. While recognising the dangers of romanticisation of what can be frustrating and exhausting work, political participation, in whatever sphere, contributes to the identification of 'women as political beings' (hooks, 1984, p. 127). It helps to build a sense of political competence which, as Pateman (1989) argues, is a necessary condition of active citizenship. Examples abound from around the world. For instance, accounts of women's struggle for human and citizenship rights in Guatemala describe how participation in collective political practices has built their 'citizenship capacity' (Blacklock and Macdonald, 1998, p. 151; Fonseca, 1998). Pateman adds the qualification that it is not a sufficient condition, for such participation needs to be worthwhile, in that it needs to be located in democratic structures (where they exist). This does not necessarily mean that the action has to be successful, for the very act of coming together to express one's political voice can help to build up women's self-esteem and sense of themselves as political agents. Agency thereby embodies 'a transformative' capacity which has been vital in the development of women's citizenship (Eduards, 1994, p. 181).

Behind this point, lies a particular conception of power, articulated by Nancy Hartsock as 'related to energy, capacity, and potential' (1985, p. 210). A similar distinction is made by Giddens who identifies two notions of power: the 'hierarchical', which describes the ability of a group or individual to exert their will over others, and the 'generative' which is about 'self-actualisation' (1991, pp. 211–14). Feminists have used Giddens' formulation to argue for a conception of power that links women's agency to oppressive structural relations so as to avoid, on the one hand, blaming women for the inequalities that disadvantage them and, on the other, casting them as passive victims.[49] Similarly, Black feminist thought has been characterised by Collins as bringing together notions of power as energy and as domination, with the former being harnessed by 'creative acts of resistance' against the latter (1991, p. 223). Black women's organising is, according to Julia Sudbury, fuelled by the belief that they 'can assert their agency and "claim back our power" in opposing the structures of dominance which shape our lives' (1998, p. 235).

Wolf has helped to popularise ideas of women's potency with her criticisms of their traditional 'power illiteracy' and call for a new 'psychology of female power'. The 'genderquake', which she identifies, 'demands that women begin to see themselves as potential agents of change with many resources, rather than as helpless victims' and as responsible for making choices as well as claiming rights (1993, p. 57). The optimism of Wolf's treatise is refreshing but, in her desire to combat the (somewhat exaggerated) negativities of 'victim feminism' she has discounted the extent to which many women (and in particular 'minority group' women) still are the victims of discriminatory and oppressive male-dominated political, economic and social institutions. People can be, at the same time, both the subordinate objects of hierarchical power relations and subjects who are agents in their own lives, capable of exercising power in the generative sense. The feminist citizenship project developed here aims to give due account to the agency of different groups of women, while identifying also the public and private structures, gender cultures and power relations that continue to deny them their rightful place as full citizens.[50] Wolf's individualistic approach also downplays the importance of collective struggle. Ultimately, in order to achieve change, the expression of individual agency needs to be translated into collective action (Collins, 1991). It is when individual agents 'engage in common activities, oriented to common ... ends' that they are acting quintessentially as citizens (Gould, 1988, p. 71). Oldfield (1990), while characterising citizens as autonomous individual agents, emphasises that in acting as citizens they must have regard to their fellow citizens with whom they stand in a relationship of mutual dependence.

For Oldfield, we are talking here of citizenship participation as political obligation. Marquand (1991), likewise, poses the question as to whether the justification of rights on grounds of agency does not place an obligation on the citizen to exercise that agency. I have already distanced myself from the civic republican response that it does; its implicit assumption that all citizens are more or less equally well placed to fulfil such an obligation bears little relationship to the realities of many women's as compared with many men's lives. However, I am conscious that there is a potential weakness in my argument. I have stressed that political participation is a vital element of citizenship on the one hand but that it should not be regarded as obligatory on the other. Where, you might ask, does that leave those women (and men) who, for whatever reasons of choice or constraint, including severe disability, frailty or chronic illness, do not participate in politics, at whatever level? Do they not deserve the accolade of citizenship? Are they somehow lesser citizens? For the same reason that I would not want to cast political participation as an obligation, I would not want to use it as a measuring rod of citizenship against which many women might, yet again, fall short. Yet, this appears to contradict the emphasis I have placed upon it. In trying to resolve this apparent contradiction for myself, I find myself distinguishing between two formulations: to be a citizen and to act as a citizen, thereby bringing together Oldfield's bifurcation of citizenship as a status and as a practice.[51] To be a citizen, in the legal and sociological sense, means to enjoy the rights of citizenship necessary for agency and social and political participation. To act as a citizen involves fulfilling the full potential of the status. Those who do not fulfil that potential do not cease to be citizens; moreover, in practice participation tends to be more of a continuum than an all or nothing affair and people might participate more or less at different points in the life-course.

Conclusion

This chapter has attempted to provide the first pieces towards a theoretical framework for thinking about citizenship and in particular women's citizenship. Drawing on the broad citizenship traditions of liberalism and civic republicanism (and with reference to the latter's communitarian cousin), it has used the notion of human agency to synthesise critically the two. Citizenship is thus conceptualised here both as a status, carrying a wide range of rights, and as a practice, involving political participation, broadly defined. Obligations and responsibilities straddle the status-practice divide. Both as a practice and in the relationship between practice and rights, citizenship can be understood as a dynamic process. The stance adopted in reinterpreting the two citizenship traditions has been an inclusive one. Yet, citizenship has been criticised as an intrinsically exclusive concept, which draws boundaries between those who do and do not belong as full members of the citizenship community. The next two chapters engage with the difficulties that this raises for an inclusive feminist citizenship project.

2
Inclusion or Exclusion?

Inclusion and exclusion represent the two sides of citizenship's membership coin. Whereas much of the literature on citizenship has traditionally focused on its inclusionary face, more radical contemporary writings tend to portray citizenship as a force for exclusion. This and the next chapter examine the exclusionary tensions inherent in the concept of citizenship and how they operate at different levels to create non- or partial citizens. These non- or partial citizens can be characterised as 'those who are excluded from without' and 'those who are excluded from within' specific citizenship communities or nation-states (Yeatman, 1994, p. 80). The former are the subject of this chapter; the latter of Chapter 3.

Traditionally, citizenship theory, following Marshall, has tended to concentrate on the processes of inclusion/exclusion within the boundaries drawn and regulated by nation-states. This has provided only a partial picture, as a more recent migration-oriented citizenship literature, upon which this chapter draws, demonstrates.[1] It is therefore necessary to incorporate the perspectives of those moving, or attempting to move, between nation-states and of non-citizen residents. At the same time, the status of the nation-state, caught in a pincer movement between the forces of globalisation and localism/regionalism, is itself being questioned. These are the two threads running through this chapter, leading up to a discussion of ways in which a more inclusive approach to citizenship in both the national and international spheres might be developed in an attempt to address the contradiction between citizenship's inclusionary claims and its exclusionary force. In particular, I consider the potential of international human rights agreements combined with a nascent global citizenship infrastructure as a political tool for 'outsiders' at the gates of citizenship. One implication of this discussion is that a feminist citizenship theory and praxis must be internationalist in its outlook and scope.

Inclusion/exclusion

Critical citizenship theory has put the spotlight on the symbiotic processes of inclusion and exclusion, which form the kernel of citizenship as a concept and a practice. Whether the focus is the nation-state or the community, or particular groups within these localities, boundaries and allocative processes serve to include and exclude simultaneously. These boundaries operate both as visible physical borders and as less tangible structural and symbolic barriers (Wiener, 1999). The patterns of inclusion/exclusion they create are gendered and racialised, albeit in ways which reflect specific national, cultural and historical contexts (Fulbrook and Cesarani, 1996; Saraceno, 1997). These patterns in turn generate differential opportunities for and constraints upon the exercise of agency (Lutz, 1997).

Exclusion and inclusion operate at both a legal and sociological level through 'formal' and 'substantive' modes of citizenship. The former denotes the legal status of membership of a state, as symbolised by possession of a passport, the latter the possession of rights and duties within a state.[2] Certain rights and duties can apply to those who are not formal citizens. At the same time substantive citizenship, in the sense of 'full and equal rights and opportunities' does not automatically follow from formal, as the experience of New Commonwealth immigrants to Britain exemplifies. Racial discrimination, harassment and violence are themselves exclusionary processes that undermine the substantive citizenship of Black citizens and residents.[3]

Thus at both the legal and sociological level, exclusion and inclusion represent more of a continuum than an absolute dichotomy (Castles and Davidson, 2000). Within nation-states, different groups enjoy different degrees of substantive citizenship, for social divisions and poverty are corrosive of full citizenship. This is the context in which social exclusion has become a central theme in the social policy of the European Commission. Similarly, the rights associated with residence in and membership of a state can be seen as more of a hierarchy than a sharp division between citizens and non-citizens. This, in turn, creates a hierarchy of non-citizen residents at the bottom of which stand 'illegal' immigrants. The treatment of the different groups of non-citizen residents operates as something of a litmus test for the degree of inclusiveness of substantive citizenship in any particular society (Dahrendorf, 1989).

However, for those physically excluded from a territory, exclusion does operate as an absolute. In an era of extensive migration across an economically polarised world, the boundary-staking functions of citizenship as a legal status have become more prominent. Citizenship has thus been described as 'a conspiracy against outsiders' (Hindess, 1999, p. 67). Boundaries are also now being drawn at the supranational level of the European Union, culturally as well as physically.[4] As Nira Yuval-Davis notes, the right to enter, or remain, in a country is a critical issue for citizenship. 'Constructing boundaries according to various inclusionary and exclusionary criteria, which relate to ethnic and racial divisions as well as class and gender divisions, is one of the main arenas of struggle concerning citizenship that remain completely outside the agenda of Marshallian theories of citizenship' (1991a, p. 61).

The 'age of migration'

It is an arena that has taken on increasing significance as migration flows have accelerated, in what has been dubbed the international 'age of migration', characterised by the globalisation, acceleration, differentiation, feminisation and growing politicisation of migration (Castles and Miller, 1998). Migration has been expanding in terms both of its overall volume and of the number of countries affected. In Western Europe, postwar immigration has been marked by its magnitude and its diversity, embracing ex-colonial subjects, 'temporary' migrant workers from the South and subsequently their families, and, increasingly, refugees and asylum-seekers and 'illegal' immigrants. In this section, we examine the operation of the boundaries they face, with particular attention to gender perspectives.

The migrant as a gendered subject

A growing proportion of migrants are women: it is estimated they account for around half of both international migration and the refugee population.[5] Castles and Miller acknowledge that 'women play an increasing role in all regions and all types of migration' and that 'the migrant is a gendered subject' (1998, pp. 9 and 34). Yet, the 'gendered subject' makes only an intermittent appearance in their subsequent analysis (albeit a notably more prominent one than in the first edition of their influential work). The mainstream migration literature, and also policy discussion, still tends to assume that migrants are primarily male and to adopt models of migration based on male experiences (Kofman *et al.*, 2000). Insofar as the mainstream literature recognises the part played by women, it casts them as the dependants of male migrants, ignoring the significant minority of women who have migrated as workers in their own right and the contribution that they make to their countries of destination and origin (*ibid.*; Gibson *et al.*, 2001). In the context of gendered labour markets, female immigrant labour may be recruited for particular kinds of jobs.[6] The construction of women as dependants also informs immigration and nationality laws and the discourses surrounding them. Thus, even where ostensibly gender-neutral, the laws governing immigration can be indirectly discriminatory in their effect. Moreover, because of their disadvantaged economic position, women can be particularly harshly affected by the application of racialised immigration laws.[7]

There has, though, been growing recognition in some quarters, including the United Nations and European Commission, of the particular needs and vulnerabilities of migrant women both as workers and dependants, partly thanks to pressure from Black and migrant women's groups (Hoskyns, 1996). A Communication from the Commission acknowledges that:

> The existing legislation on migrants has been drafted on the assumption that, generally, migrant workers are men, and tends to see migrant women as dependent spouses. Women arriving in their host countries as dependants following family reunification experience greater problems than their husbands already settled in the country, in procuring work permits, and in extending these to the full range of occupations (COM(88)743, 1988, quoted in Knocke, 1995, p. 230).

Fortress first world

A key element in the 'age of migration' is the growing economic gulf between countries of immigration and emigration, compounded by the impact of globalisation. Yeatman portrays migration to the 'affluent citizenship communities of the "first world"' as 'claims on global redistribution of citizen status' (1994, p. 80). However, it is a distinctly second-class citizen status which is achieved when migrants are exploited economically as a reserve army of labour and are denied full substantive and/or formal citizenship rights.[8] Moreover, 'the affluent citizenship communities of the "first world"' are resisting these claims. In the late twentieth century, tighter, increasingly racist and discriminatory, immigration controls typified the reactions even of nations that traditionally welcomed immigrants, such as the US, Canada and Australia, to mounting migration. In a number of European countries, the basic civil right of family reunion has been eroded in law.[9] More recently, concerns about the implications of demographic trends for labour supply in industrialised countries have reawakened an interest in encouraging limited economic migration, provided that it is strictly regulated.[10]

The boundary-staking functions of immigration laws in modern welfare states have always been intimately connected to regulation of access to welfare provisions; indeed, residence qualifications for welfare pre-date the welfare state (Pierson, 1998). In recent years, a battery of exclusionary rules has been added to such residence tests in a number of European countries so as to limit immigrants' access to welfare (Fekete, 1997). In some cases, this reflects the advances of the far right in some of the most affluent countries, such as Denmark (Geddes, 2002). The political pressure to restrict, or even remove, the welfare rights of non-citizens has become particularly acute in the US. In 1994, the state of California passed Proposition 187 in order to bar illegal immigrants from publicly funded education and social services and non-emergency health care, despite the reliance of many citizens on their labour and the fact that many pay taxes (Morris, 1994). Although overturned in the courts as unconstitutional, its main objectives were subsequently promoted in federal legislation, passed in 1996, which, *inter alia*, removed from legally resident aliens (with limited exceptions) the right to most welfare benefits and services (www.clasp.org).

At European level, the 'First' World's exclusionary stance is symbolised by the image of 'Fortress Europe', or more accurately 'fortress Western Europe, defending its own economy, putting up the shutters to "outsiders" and maintaining surveillance of the "outsiders" within' (Simpson, 1993, p. 92). Strict external border controls; measures to restrict immigration and the rights and number of refugees and asylum-seekers admitted; provisions for the swift expulsion of unwanted aliens, all backed up by a comprehensive computer network, constitute the key pillars in the ramparts of Fortress Europe.[11] The construction of a cordon sanitaire around the EU has made possible the abolition of most internal border controls in the name of free movement within it, which, with concomitant employment, social and political rights, comprises a key ingredient of European citizenship. As such, it is a right confined to citizens of the EU and members of their families.[12] The relaxation of internal border controls has been paralleled by the intensification of controls within borders, through the use of identity cards and passport checks. The main objects of such controls are those who 'carry their passports on their faces' regardless of whether or not they are *bona fide* residents or even of their place of birth (Sivanandan, 1993). The more such internal checks are applied to Black residents and citizens of the EU, the more compromised are their substantive citizenship rights and their status as citizens or legitimate residents.

Fortress Europe thus contributes to the exclusionary side of citizenship and helps to feed the expression of racist attitudes and practices (which are also gendered phenomena) with regard not only to 'outsiders' but to racialised minorities inside its walls also. In doing so, the dividing line drawn between citizens and foreigners is creating stronger cultural and symbolic as well as actual borders between Europeans and non-Europeans; between 'us' and 'them', for which read White and Non-White. Here we have a more subtle form of exclusion 'at the level of ideas, an exclusion of those who do not conform to the image that the new Europe has of itself. This image, holds, implicitly if not always explicitly, that to be European is to be white, Christian and holding to a Eurocentric view of the world, and that to be other than this is to be "Other", to be outside'.[13]

The gates of admission

A double set of actual boundaries is operated by nation-states, controlling admission first to their territories and second to full or partial membership, with its associated rights and obligations. Refugees, asylum-seekers, would-be immigrants and migrant workers face a common set of 'gates', albeit differently constructed. These regulate first their admission, second their right of domicile and their residence status, which governs access to social and civil rights, and finally their access to formal citizenship, and the political rights it entails, through either naturalisation or, where it is permitted, dual citizenship. The exception are those migrants who held the citizenship of the host country as members of former colonies, a particularly significant group in Britain, France and the Netherlands. Again, analyses of movements through the three gates tend to be ungendered, reflecting inaccurate assumptions about the typical male migrant.

At the bottom of the hierarchy created by this set of gates stand 'illegal' or more accurately 'irregular' immigrants, whose numbers and significance have been growing in the wake of more stringent immigration and asylum legislation. A common response has been ever tougher controls in an attempt to prevent their entry or continued stay. Exploited in the labour market, they lack any formal citizenship rights and are likely to make only limited claims on welfare services because of their precarious status in the face of possible deportation. As a consequence, they live on the margins of society, vulnerable to intense poverty.[14] Above them are the asylum-seekers, refugees and temporary or 'guest' workers who lack long-term residence rights and enjoy only limited social and economic rights and who may be subject to specific political and employment restrictions. The exact nature of their rights varies and the gap between formal and substantive rights can be particularly wide. Moreover, there has been a general tendency to restrict the welfare rights of asylum-seekers pending resolution of their application.[15] This reflects a generally more exclusionary and hostile stance towards asylum-seekers, as they form a growing proportion of migrants overall. This stance has also resulted in higher barriers against admission and, for those who nevertheless surmount them, a decline in recognition of formal refugee status, with damaging implications for access to rights (Faist, 1997).

Women refugees and asylum-seekers face 'gender-based discrimination and gender-specific violence and exploitation' at all stages of their flight (UN, 1995a, p. 637). Nevertheless, many have played a crucial role in refugee communities and in some cases their migration has enhanced their economic independence and has led to a gain in their power and status.[16] The position of female guestworkers can also be especially precarious, for their jobs, which are their passport to residence, have been more susceptible to industrial restructuring. They represent a particularly vulnerable and 'flexible' workforce, often incorporated into the bottom of sexually and racially segregated labour markets. Where they have migrated on their husband's work permit, they are rendered totally dependent upon him for their residence rights, with serious implications in cases of domestic violence.

From denizen to citizen

Once inside the first gate of admission, it is the next gate to permanent residence that is of greatest significance from the perspective of civil and social citizenship rights. Yet, since the mid-1980s, a growing proportion of migrants are unable to move beyond this first gate and remain economically and politically insecure and without clear legal rights (Faist, 1997; Castles and Davidson, 2000). Indeed, in some cases the gap between the rights available inside the first and subsequent gates has widened, with gendered implications (Kofman and Sales, 1998; Kofman *et al.*, 2000). For migrants, social and civil rights typically precede political rights, in contrast to the Marshallian evolutionary model in which social rights represent the final stage (Soysal, 1994). Tomas Hammar divides those without formal citizenship in their country of residence into 'denizens' 'with a legal and permanent residence status' and others with only temporary rights of residence (1990, p. 15). Denizens normally enjoy full social and civil rights.[17] Therefore, from the perspective of socioeconomic life-chances, once a foreigner has taken up residence, it is the admission to denizenship rather than formal citizenship that really counts. However, residence in some cases remains conditional and insecure (Morris, 1997, 2000; Schuster and Solomos, 2002); and the fragility of denizens' civil rights was underlined in both the US and the UK as normal rights governing arrest and trial were rescinded post-September 11 (Stephens, 2001). The withdrawal of certain social rights from denizens in the US also indicates that denizenship is a less secure status than citizenship.

As Chapter 1 made clear, citizenship is not just a matter of social and legal rights; it is also about political rights and participation. With the exception of voting rights in local elections in some countries, denizens are denied the basic political right of the vote (although this does not necessarily spell political inactivity).[18] The implications are spelt out by William Rogers Brubaker:

> But if citizenship status is not a decisive determinant of immigrants' life chances, it remains a crucial determinant of their place in the polity and, more broadly, of the general character of politics in the countries of post-war immigration. This is not to imply that non-citizen immigrants are politically mute. Nor is it to attribute miraculous virtues to universal suffrage ... it is simply to recall the obvious: the fact that the exclusion or self-exclusion of immigrants from formal citizenship is tantamount to the disfranchisement of a significant fraction of the population, and of a much higher fraction of the manual working class; and that the interests of disfranchised groups do not count for much in the political process (1990, p. 385).

This has damaging implications for democracy. The three main, not mutually exclusive, solutions are: the extension of full political rights to denizens; the liberalisation of naturalisation laws and greater acceptance by states of dual citizenship. The first, proposed by Hammar (1990), seems unlikely given the opposition that has been voiced to even local voting rights in some countries. He therefore favours the liberalisation of naturalisation laws as the best route to full political inclusion. So too does Joseph Carens (1989), on the grounds that membership and the social ties it creates carries with it a moral right to formal citizenship for all those resident in a state for any significant length of time (together with their children). He includes irregular immigrants and those (mainly women) admitted as family members, once they have firmly established themselves in a society. While naturalisation rates vary between countries, they are, with a very few exceptions, extremely low. This reflects both the difficulties of entering this last gate to citizenship but also the reluctance of many to do so, if it means renouncing their original citizenship. For this reason, there is strong support in the migration literature for more general acceptance by states of dual citizenship, which is becoming more common.[19] This, Rainer Bauböck suggests, could represent 'the political expression of multiple membership of different societies' (1991, p. 41).

Citizenship and cultural rights as symbol

The stance taken by a state towards access to formal citizenship also has symbolic importance as a signifier of an inclusive or exclusive understanding of membership and national belonging. The status of large numbers of people resident in states of which they are not legally citizens raises a series of question marks over the meaning of citizenship in a world where migratory pressures are likely to intensify. The more inclusionary the response, whether it be at the level of citizenship rights or at that of acceptance of 'the other' as a fellow citizen with cultural rights, the better will citizenship match up to its universalistic claims. Carens thus argues forcefully that to require cultural assimilation as a precondition of citizenship is a violation of the liberal–democratic 'principles of toleration and respect for diversity' and calls into question the equal status of existing minority group citizens (1989, p. 38).

This raises the important issue of the relationship between citizenship and cultural identity of which women are often the icons.[20] Marshall's conceptualisation of citizenship emphasised the right to a full share 'in the social heritage' and, in his discussion of the rights and duties associated with education, he argued that a community that enforces the duty 'to improve and civilise oneself' in the interests of its 'social health' 'has begun to realise that its culture is an organic unity and its civilisation a national heritage' (1950, pp. 8, 11, 26). In a world where significant minorities do not share in the 'national heritage' of the country in which they live or where that heritage is contested as between indigenous and settler peoples and where cultural diversity is now the norm, a tension arises between the notion of a common cultural standard, implicit or explicit in traditional formulations of citizenship, and the realities of a pluralist society. This tension lies at the heart of contemporary theorisation around the concept of 'cultural citizenship', defined by Jan Pakulski in terms of:

> the right to be 'different', to re-value stigmatised identities, to embrace openly and legitimately hitherto marginalised lifestyles and to propagate them without

hindrance. The national community, in other words, is defined not only in formal-legal, political, and socioeconomic dimensions, but also increasingly in a sociocultural one. Full citizenship involves a right to full cultural participation and undistorted representation (1997, p. 83).[21]

In contexts of ethnic diversity, in particular, this right has been framed in terms of claims to 'multi-cultural citizenship', which challenge the traditional citizenship template of cultural homogeneity. According to Stephen Castles, multi-cultural citizenship 'combines the principle of universality of rights with the demand for differential treatment for groups which have differing values, interests and needs'. Citizens are thus seen 'simultaneously as having *equal rights as individuals and different needs and wants as members of groups with specific characteristics and social situations*' (1994, pp. 10, 15, emphasis in original). Key elements are linguistic and cultural rights or 'rights of recognition', which denote equality of respect, which in turn enhances human dignity and agency.[22] Fears that recognition of minority cultural rights will erode the ties of common citizenship and undermine responsible democratic citizenship are countered with the argument that, on the contrary, it should 'actually strengthen solidarity and promote political stability, by removing the barriers and exclusions which prevent minorities from wholeheartedly embracing political institutions'.[23]

There are, though, other problems with a multi-cultural model of citizenship. First, it runs the risk of essentialising and freezing cultural differences and of treating cultural groups as homogeneous and closed, ignoring, for instance, gender, sexuality, class and age differences and the fluid nature of the boundaries between collectivities and the realities of cultural hybridity. Thus crucial questions about who has the power to interpret and enforce cultural norms and membership are often glossed over.[24] In his treatise on multi-cultural citizenship, Will Kymlicka (1995) suggests an answer to some of these difficulties by distinguishing between minority rights that promote the interests of 'minority groups' in relation to the majority and those that allow 'minority groups' to impose restrictions on their own members in the name of traditional authorities and practices. Support for the former but not the latter, he argues, helps to ensure not just equality between groups but freedom and equality within groups.[25] Second, there is a danger that the multi-cultural model can embody superficial liberal toleration of diversity, confined to the 'private sphere', rather than genuine acceptance and recognition of such diversity in the 'public'.[26] However, again, there is a potential tension between the principle of public acknowledgement of minority cultures and that of recognition of the differences within them; a tension that has come to the surface in the UK over the issue of single-sex education in separate Muslim schools.[27]

The notion of 'trans-culturality', which captures the heterogeneity and inter-penetration of cultures and which neither reduces people to fixed cultural groups nor ignores (hybrid) cultural identities, has been put forward as a possible way of avoiding some of these pitfalls.[28] Both it and multi-culturalism, for all its limitations, represent an attempt at formulating an inclusive response to the challenge to citizenship created by migration and pluralist societies. However, as racism and xenophobia have reemerged on a significant scale in both Europe and the US, a more exclusive populist model of citizenship, rooted in a common culture and identity, has gained ground. Racist expressions of nationalism, together with the growing force of religious fundamentalisms, pose a serious threat to the development of a genuinely inclusive multi-cultural or trans-cultural model of citizenship.

The nation-state under pressure

The Black and migrant experience has been one of a number of factors that have contributed to a new critical focus on the defining legal and sociological link between citizenship and the nation-state – 'the entity to which the language of citizenship refers, and within which the claims of citizenship, community and participation are made'.[29] Today the nation-state is being squeezed simultaneously by pressures from both within and without, from overlapping globalising and localising forces, which are explored briefly in this section.[30] The link with citizenship was effectively forged during the nineteenth century, when the nation-state emerged as the basic political and economic unit of the modern world, steadily expanding its scope and powers until the second half of the twentieth century. 'As an institutional and social-psychological reality, the nation-state is a distinctive way of organising and experiencing political and social membership' (Brubaker, 1990, p. 380). Through its link with citizenship, it constructs the legal and ideological parameters of inclusion and exclusion (Taylor, 1989). The nature of that link varies between countries, reflecting their different paths towards and understandings of nationhood.[31] Nevertheless, underlying it, there remains a 'powerfully similar... complex articulation of nation with culture and "race"', institutionalised in different ways through the boundaries around citizenship (Williams 1995a, p. 143).

This articulation has contributed to the 'myth of the nation' as coterminous with what have never been, in fact, ethnically or culturally homogeneous nation-states. Anthias and Yuval-Davis have challenged the conventional assumptions of national homogeneity which have served to conflate the nation with the nation-state.[32] They have also drawn attention to the crucial role played by women in the reproduction of nations. This includes not only biological reproduction (which may be encouraged or discouraged at different times and for different groups of women according to the 'national interest') and the transmission of culture in early childhood, but also women's position as symbols of the nation, its spirit and honour, to be defended in war.[33] While women are often active participants in national-ist struggles in many Third World contexts, they can also be marginalised in the role of reproducers of male citizens by the politics of nationalism.

Pressures from within

It is the politics of nationalism that is the source of one of the internal pressure points on the nation-state. The increasingly prominent reassertion of nationalist claims within and across nation-state boundaries in the late twentieth century, most notably but by no means solely in Eastern Europe and the former Soviet Union, has contributed to the disintegration of existing nation-states and the reconstitution of new ones where nation is more closely linked to state. This, often violent, process of fragmentation is resiting rather than dismantling the boundaries of inclusion and exclusion – at its most extreme in the name of 'ethnic cleansing' (Young, 1993). The construction of citizenship in the new emergent states has, in places, been built on the violation of women's most basic rights. As symbols of 'the other', they have been vulnerable to sexual assault and rape in the civil wars that have marked the break-up of some nation-states, most notably the former Yugoslavia where many women have also opposed nationalisms and campaigned for peace.[34]

Western nation-states are also coming under pressure from nationalist forces demanding various degrees of autonomy, or even independence, for example in Quebec, Scotland, Corsica and the Basque country. These pressures fuel and coincide with a growing impetus towards the devolution of some of the powers of the nation-state to regional and local level. The extent to which power has been claimed by regional governments varies considerably between the member states of the European Union but there is a clear movement towards such a devolution in the establishment, under the Maastricht Treaty, of a Committee for the Regions and in the growing purchase of the idea of a 'Europe of the Regions'. Regional governments are also playing an increasingly significant role in India and some Latin American countries.[35] Some citizenship theorists see a 'Europe of the Regions' as providing the most promising avenue for the devel-opment of citizenship in the EU context, as nation-states are forced to cede some of their power to subsidiary layers of government. As one of a number of layers of authority in the EU, Elizabeth Meehan, for instance, believes regional government opens up greater possibilities for citizenship participation. This, together with an emphasis on local government's importance, echoes the concern among some of the early proponents of civic republicanism, such as Hegel and de Tocqueville, that there should be scope for the exercise of citizen-ship at a level below that of the state (Oldfield, 1990). This is of particular importance for women, and other marginalised groups such as people in poverty, who have traditionally found it easier to participate politically locally than nationally.

Pressures from without

Such calls for the devolution of political power need to be understood in the context of the centrifugal forces pulling power away from nation-states. The development of supranational institutions, most notably the EU, represents one of the external pressures on the nation-state (the others being economic and ecological), although it should not be forgotten that the EU is very much a union of nation-states which have ceded to it a number of their powers. It has been described as a 'hybrid polity', in which supra-national, national and regional levels of governance are interlocked (Delanty, 1998). The idea of European citizenship has been promoted by the European Commission since the mid-1980s as a means of building a 'Euro-polity' and of capturing the loyalty of EU citizens to it (Wiener, 1999). The status of 'Citizens of the Union' was formally enshrined in the Maastricht Treaty, which granted to these citizens the right to vote in local government and European Parliament elections in their country of residence, regardless of their nationality. European citizenship, Yasemin Soysal suggests, represents 'postnational membership in its most elaborate legal form' (1994, p. 148; see also Delanty 1998, 2000). Nevertheless, nationality continues to act as a passport to European citizenship and it is, as we have seen, an exclusive form of postnational membership which shuts out non-citizen residents: a citizenship for Europeans rather than for all those living in Europe.[36]

The meaning, potential and limitations of the status and ideal of European citizenship, together with the ability to act as citizens at European level, have been explored by a number of citizenship theorists.[37] Meehan, for instance, draws parallels between the development of EU citizenship and that of nation-states, although, as she points out, the trajectory of the evolution of civil, political and social rights is rather different (1993a). In her writings about women's citizenship in the EU, she warns of the limitations of a citizenship that is largely tied to the interests of paid workers and that involves remote political institutions, while at the same time suggesting that the EU 'as a potential force for equal citizenship should not be dismissed'.[38] The potential value of EU citizenship to women depends in part on factors such as 'race', class and sexual orientation. It is also viewed differently in different member states. Thus, for example, whereas British women have gained a number of important social rights as a result of membership, Scandinavian women have feared an erosion of the rights they already enjoy (Hobson, 1999; Gould, 2001). The progressive potential of the EU has been strengthened by article 13 of the 1997 Amsterdam Treaty, which permits the Council of Ministers to 'take appropriate action to combat discrimination based on sex, racial or ethnic origin, religion or belief, disability, age or sexual orientation'. This has resulted in one directive on equal treatment in employment, covering all specified grounds of discrimination, and another on equal treatment irrespective of racial or ethnic origin in a number of spheres, together with a general action programme to combat discrimination.

Carl F. Stychin suggests that the EU has facilitated 'a fairly active form of citizenship around sexuality' and sexual orientation, contributing to the kind of synthesis between rights and participation explored in the previous chapter (2001, p. 298).

More generally, what the EU promises for the future will depend, in part, on the development of its political institutions and on the effects of increased economic and monetary integration.[39] This, in turn, depends, in part, on wider global economic forces, which brings us to another set of exogenous pressures on the nation-state associated with globalisation. This represents a shorthand for a number of related processes that together are internationalising the scope of economic, political and social activity; accelerating the mobility of capital, information and (some) people; and deepening the interconnectedness between nation-states. While the fact of the interconnectedness of nation-states is not new, the contemporary nature of its patterns and dynamics arguably is. Thus, despite disagreement as to how globalisation is to be understood, it is widely acknowledged to be 'an agent for economic, social and political transformation'.[40]

Changes in the global economy have been facilitated by the globalisation of information and communication networks through which information, like money, flows above and through national boundaries. Giddens indeed suggests that globalisation is primarily 'about the transformation of time and space' through instantaneous global communication and mass transportation (1994b, p. 22. 1994a). According to John Keane, this 'restructuring of communicative space' fragments and creates new dimensions to the notion of a public sphere outside the confines of the nation-state. While Keane's image of a 'mosaic' of public spheres may offer exciting prospects for the exercise of citizenship at transnational level, market-led technological development has a tendency to aggravate the exclusion from full citizenship of disadvantaged groups, without access to advanced means of communication.[41] Moreover, reports of sexual harassment and racism on the Internet suggest that processes of exclusion seep into ever-more sophisticated channels.

In the same way that capital and information flows are no respecters of national boundaries, so too do pollution and environmental degradation pose a threat that cannot be contained within them. The implications for citizenship partially bypass the nation-state, as the necessity of action at both the local and transnational levels is emphasised.[42] Notions of ecological citizenship, as well as the impact of international economic forces, raise urgent questions about the ability of nation-states to respond collectively at a global level.

Beyond the nation-state?

The developments outlined so far mean that our understanding of citizenship can no longer be confined within the boundaries set by nation-states. In this section, we consider the potential for a conception of citizenship that transcends national boundaries and whether, through its relationship to international human rights agreements and institutions, it is possible to strengthen citizenship's inclusionary side. The most comprehensive statement of the ways in which 'national citizenship is losing ground to new forms of citizenship, which derive their legitimacy from deterritorialized notions of persons' rights', is that elaborated by Soysal under the rubric of 'post-national citizenship'.[43]

In the face of the migratory momentum and the global economic forces, of which it is partly a product, the status of the nation-state is now at issue. The dawn of the age of migration and globalisation is being heralded by some, such as Horsman and Marshall (1994), as marking the dusk of the age of the nation-state. Others, most notably, Hirst and Thompson (1999), suggest that the obituaries are premature. In making sense of this debate, it is helpful to bear in mind the distinction between 'sovereignty', the power and undisputed right of the state to make and enforce law and policy within its territory, and 'autonomy', the state's actual capacity to achieve goals and policies once set (Held, 1989, 1991b). While the degree of autonomy exercised by nation-states is a matter of dispute, (subject to the powers they have ceded to supranational agencies and international law) they retain their sovereignty, albeit within more constricting limits than previously.

Indeed, one response to the age of migration has been a more determined (even if not always successful) assertion of sovereignty by nation-states in their capacity as gate-keepers, aided by technological developments, which have increased their powers of surveillance generally and over immigrant groups in particular.[44] Thus the freedom and power of capital to roam the globe is not matched by that of labour (Massey, 1995; von Bredow, 1998). Within constraints created by both international agreements and economic pressures (Sassen, 1998), nation states continue to regulate access to territory, jobs and welfare (even if, in practice, growing numbers are penetrating their defences). Moreover, while globalisation may have eroded the autonomy of nation-states, they can still use their sovereign powers to mitigate its impact on their members through the economic instruments and social policies at their disposal.[45] Hirst and Thompson conclude that 'nation-states are now simply one class of powers and political agencies in a complex system of power from world to local levels, but they have a centrality because of their relationship to territory and population' (1999, p. 275). Thus, it is accepted, even by sceptics of the full-blown globalisation thesis such as Hirst and Thompson, that the exercise of the sovereignty of nation-states in their capacity as the gate-keepers of citizenship has to be understood now in a global setting. This, Anthony McGrew suggests, calls for a rethinking of 'our understanding of the modern political community' (1992, p. 94).

The global citizen

This rethinking is leading a number of social and political theorists to argue for the development of an analysis and a politics of citizenship at a global or transnational level.[46] Although thinking on the subject is still at a fairly rudimentary level, the notion of a world community, of the 'cosmopolis' or city of the universe, is an ancient one which can be traced back to Greece in the fourth and fifth centuries BC and to earlier Eastern civilisations (Heater, 1990). An historical perspective reminds us that the umbilical cord between citizenship and nation-states pertains to a specific historical period and can therefore be cut, shrunk or stretched to embrace a variety of geographical entities. The elasticity of the tie between citizenship and the nation-state is underlined by those who favour the idea of a multi-layered citizenship, operating on several frontiers from the local to the global, in which people can express multiple and overlapping loyalties and identities.[47] Within this multi-layered framework, the development of a notion of global or cosmopolitan citizenship must also address the values that would underpin it and the institutions and channels – governmental and non-governmental – through which it would be exercised. A key issue is whether it is possible to transcribe at the international level the values of responsibility, individual rights and democracy associated with nation-state citizenship and in so doing promote the inclusionary over the exclusionary side of citizenship's coin.

Richard Falk suggests that there are at least four levels at which citizenship can be envisaged beyond the confines of the nation-state, from which emerge a number of models of the global citizen. One, an overwhelmingly male model, is very much a product of the forces of economic globalisation: a member of a 'kind of homogenized elite global culture' with little or no allegiance to any one country but, at the same time, lacking 'any global civic sense of responsibility' (1994, pp. 134–5). The danger is that this elite group, enjoying considerable economic power and status, opts out of citizenship at the national level without contributing to its development at the global. It is thus debatable whether it is appropriate to label them global citizens at all, even though they might see themselves as such. Indeed, Christopher Lasch (1995) dismisses as a 'higher form of parochialism' the cosmopolitanism of an international elite, which is divorced from the principles and practice of citizenship. In contrast, each of Falk's other models – those operating at the global level as reformers, managers of the global order or activists – is underpinned explicitly or implicitly by some notion of rights and responsibilities transcending the nation-state. Described as 'the globalisation of rights and responsibilities' (Pianta, 2001, p. 170), it is this that, I would argue, is the essence of any global conceptualisation of citizenship.

Responsibilities and rights from a global perspective

It is accepted by a number of citizenship theorists that principles of distributive justice together with ecological imperatives demand an internationalist interpretation of citizenship obligations in the context of global economic and physical interdependence.[48] In the words of J.K. Galbraith, 'the responsibility for economic and social well-being is general, transnational' (1996, p. 2). Concern for human suffering, he argues, cannot stop at national frontiers. Social policy analysts concerned to understand and combat poverty at the international level take a similar position. The case for 'a socially responsible globalization', as part of an emergent global social policy, is being propounded. This would involve projecting on to the global level 'the policies of social redistribution, social regulation and social empowerment that governments do when engaging in social policy nationally'.[49]

In the political arena, the UNDP has warned that the growing gulf between rich and poor countries can only be tackled by 'a new international solidarity'. It is seeking 'a new framework of development cooperation that brings humanity together through a more equitable sharing of global economic opportunities and responsibilities'.[50] Although the exercise of such obligations has to be channelled primarily through national governments and other institutions, as the main political actors at international level, there is still scope for individuals to see themselves as citizens of the planet, with a 'sense of global responsibility' (UNDP, 1999, p. 101) and to act accordingly. The responsible use of environmental resources is one obvious example (Isin and Woods, 1999; Faulks, 2000). John Urry additionally suggests that the individual's global responsibilities might include educating herself about 'the state of the globe', demonstration of a cosmopolitan stance and persuading others 'that they should also seek to act on part of the globe as a whole which is suffering collectively' (1999, p. 267). Such action, I would argue, would include active support for the international redistribution of resources through governments and international agencies. Indeed, Doyal and Gough ascribe to those in the First World, as beneficiaries of the world order, a 'duty to participate in some way in organisations with feasible strategies for challenging those world politico-economic structures which deny millions their most basic needs' (1991, p. 294).

This injunction reflects the belief that, in an economically divided world in which poor nations and their peoples have been and continue to be exploited by rich, citizenship must be internationalist, if it is not to perpetuate these processes of domination and exclusion. Kathleen Jones similarly sketches a feminist stance that 'stresses the global parameters of the responsible citizen's obligations' (1994, p. 269; see also Hutchings, 1999). Globalisation as both a process and an ideology means that 'citizenship needs to be rethought as a possible tool for feminist use within a global frame' (Pettman, 1999; Yuval-Davis and Werbner, 1999). The importance for a feminist politics of citizenship of placing citizenship in a global context is underlined by the evidence of the ways in which women in the poorer nations, as the managers of poverty and as suppliers of cheap and 'flexible' labour, tend to bear the greater burden of the impact of the policies of the richer nations and of the international economic institutions such as the IMF which represent their interests.[51] The UNDP notes also that, on the human development index, 'men generally fare better than women on almost every socio-economic indicator'. It argues for a new development paradigm that 'enables all individuals to enlarge their human capabilities to the full and to put those capabilities to their best use in all fields – economic, social, cultural and political'. Such a paradigm recognises that 'not much can be achieved without a dramatic improvement in the status of women and the opening of all economic opportunities to women'.[52] The ability of all women to realise their full potential in society is also emphasised in the Declaration from the 1995 UN Conference on Women.

Implicit in these UN statements is a notion of human agency, tying together rights and obligations at an international level, in parallel with the link at national level outlined in Chapter 1. This is made explicit by both Gould and Parry. The former, in exploring the implications of her theory of democracy at the international level, promotes 'a cosmopolitan perspective, which asserts the universal equality of all humans as agents and as bearers of human rights. Such universality therefore transcends national borders' (1988, p. 323). Thus she suggests that her central principle of justice – 'the equal right of all individuals as agents to the conditions of their self-development' – might, subject to certain qualifications, apply at the international as well as the national level. Parry similarly upholds the right to relief of those, typically in the Third World, who may face starvation, on the grounds of their 'right to the necessary conditions of agency' (1991, p. 178, citing Gewirth, 1982). This right imposes, via governments, a strong duty on the better-off as human agents to provide assistance in recognition of the agency of others.

'Freedom to develop and realize one's human potential' is, according to the UNDP (2000, p. 1), one of the goals of human rights. Both cosmopolitans (such as Charles Jones, 1999) and opponents of cosmopolitanism (such as David Miller, 2000) posit human rights as the foundation stone of global justice. Making the link with citizenship, Oliver and Heater distinguish between traditional citizenship linked to nationality and 'new citizenship [which] recognises the existence of human rights outside the context of the state' (1994, p. 195). They do not, though, explore the difficult questions raised by the relationship between the two. One formulation of this relationship is that supplied by Bauböck. First, the right to citizenship of an identifiable state is itself a basic human right. Second, human rights and citizenship rights share a common language: human rights represent both the 'cornerstone' of citizenship rights and 'a universalized form of citizenship, transcending boundaries of state membership' (1994, p. 247; 1991). As such they are increasingly acting as a reference point for feminists claiming human rights as women's rights, reflected most notably in the Declaration from the UN Women's Conference. Manisha Desai suggests that, thanks to the international women's human rights movement, 'from being a discourse of international agencies, academics, and some committed activists, human rights have become a "power tool" available to thousands of grassroots groups for local organizing'.[53]

It might be argued that, once rights are detached from the context of the state, the discourse of human rights becomes more appropriate than that of citizenship (Turner, 1993, 2000). This is especially the case, when human rights are defined broadly as in the 1966 UN International Covenant on Economic, Social and Cultural Rights. This asserts that 'the ideal of free human beings enjoying freedom from fear and want can only be achieved if conditions are created whereby everyone may enjoy his [sic] economic, social and cultural rights, as well as his civil and political rights'. Despite the secondary status often accorded the former, the indivisibility of the different strands of human rights and of the struggles to achieve them has been emphasised by the UNDP (2000) amongst others.

Delanty defines human rights as 'basic ethical rights that all individuals enjoy by virtue of their common humanity, whereas citizenship rights are specific to a political community' (2000, p. 69). The notion of the 'right to have rights' can, in some ways, be understood as translating the ethical into the political. Although human rights reside in individuals *qua* humans rather than *qua* citizens (with the exception of the right to political participation), arguably citizenship rights derive ultimately from human rights as the necessary condition for human agency. Thus they could be said to represent the specific interpretation and allocation by individual nation-states of the more abstract, unconditional and universalisable human rights.[54] Despite the erosion of their autonomy, nation-states are likely to remain the main source of citizenship rights for the foreseeable future. Subject to the dictates of basic human rights (and the constraints of inter-governmental, quasi-supranational institutions such as the EU), it is for individual governments to determine the contents of and conditions attached to citizenship rights in the context of specific cultures and available resources in line with the principles of self-determination and cultural pluralism.[55] As argued above, the framework of global citizenship helps to focus on the responsibilities of the more affluent nation-states towards those in the 'developing world' that lack the resources to translate human rights, as defined in the UN Covenant, into effective citizenship rights. There is therefore a good case for retaining the discourse of citizenship, while recognising that its roots, in that of human rights, come nearer to the surface when we move outside the confines of the nation-state.

There is, though, a tension between the dictates of human rights and the right of nation-states to exercise sovereignty in the control of access to their territories. Here, universal human rights and more narrowly circumscribed citizenship (and residence) rights can, and often do, come into conflict with each other. By the same token, the discourse of human rights represents a resource for migrants and asylum-seekers (who are thereby constituted as claims-makers under international law), counterpoised against the exclusionary boundaries around citizenship and membership drawn by individual nation-states.[56] Human rights thereby provide a potential tool for sculpting a more inclusionary model of citizenship.

Global governance

The effectiveness of this tool does, though, depend on the existence of international laws and institutions through which it can be deployed. International law prescribes certain rights and duties which transcend national laws.[57] What is lacking is a robust infrastructure of global citizenship incorporating institutions with the power to enforce such rights and duties. The case has been made by the UNDP for strengthening the international human rights machinery and for promoting the 'acceptance of human responsibilities and obligations' at a global level (1999, p. 98; 2000). The need for action is underlined by the increasingly exclusionary stance taken by many Western countries to refugees and asylum-seekers who are, in any case, protected by only a limited set of rights. These regulate the status of those accepted as refugees and forbid 'refoulement' (the return of asylum-seekers to a country where they are in danger). There is no enforceable right to asylum as such and those rights that do exist have been subject to infringement and reinterpretation and are not properly monitored by the UN.[58] The need for more effective rights and for international regulation of asylum-seeking and of migration generally, in this 'age of migration', forms part of the case for the development of stronger institutions of global citizenship.[59]

Another major plank in this case is the growing disparity between the democratically unaccountable power of the institutions of global capitalism (both private and public), such as the multi-national corporations, the IMF and the World Bank, and that of the existing institutions of global citizenship.[60] If the members of the poorer countries of the 'developing world' are to enjoy the social and economic rights enshrined in the UN Covenant, this imbalance of power will have to be addressed. Demands are growing for more concerted international action on poverty and global inequalities and stronger international labour standards; in response, elements of the emergence of a more 'socially responsible globalization' among international organisations have been discerned (Deacon, 2001).

A third, inter-connected, plank is the ecological imperative. The Intergovernmental Panel on Climate Change has demonstrated that it is the poor of the world who are being hit hardest by global warming (*The*

Independent, 12 July 2001). Acknowledging the disproportionate responsibility of industrial countries for environmental problems faced by the 'global
commons', the World Bank argues that 'flexible mechanisms that transfer
resources from rich to poor countries are central to any solution of global
environmental problems' (1999, p. 88). Giddens and Hutton make an
urgent case for 'a global environmental protection agency' (2000, p. 221; see
also Giddens, 2000). This echoes the position of a number of environmental
organisations pressing for transnational political action in the name of global
citizenship, as reflected in the Rio Declaration after the 1992 UN Earth
Summit. As Howard Newby argues, 'global governance of global resources
will require new institutions of democratic accountability if the rights of all
global citizens are not to be infringed' (1996, p. 214).

Falk is among those who emphasise the importance of democratic
accountability for the development of an infrastructure of global citizenship:

> Citizenship is tied to democracy, and global citizenship should in some way be tied
> to global democracy, at least to a process of democratization that extends some
> notion of rights, representation and accountability to the operations of international
> institutions, and gives some opportunity to the peoples whose lives are being regu-
> lated to participate in the selection of leaders (1994, p. 128; see also Young, 2000).

The principle of democratic accountability is the central demand of an international Charter for Global Democracy, launched in 1999; key to realising this
principle is the idea of 'global governance'. This is defined by Halliday as 'the
institutions for managing relations between states across a range of issues, from
security to human rights and the environment'. Such institutions already exist;
the challenge Halliday maintains is 'how to make this governance system more
effective, more just, and more responsive to the changing international situation' (2000, p. 19). In his exploration of the potential for a 'cosmopolitan
model of democracy' (defined as 'a system of democratic governance which
arises from and is adapted to the diverse conditions and interconnections of
different peoples and nations'), Held contrasts such a notion of global governance with the idea of an integrated world government. The former refers to
political co-operation and the development of 'cosmopolitan democratic law'
(which *inter alia* would regulate the free-market and trade system) through a
web of international bodies (complemented by devolved local autonomy); the
latter to a 'a supranational state which has a monopoly of coercive and legislative power' which, he argues, carries the threat of global tyranny rather than
the promise of global democracy.[61]

The notion of effective and just global governance has been promoted by
the UNDP and by the Commission on Global Governance and is increasingly becoming common currency among activists and scholars.[62] Some may
dismiss it as utopian, given the current state of international affairs and the
reluctance of many governments to challenge the power of global capital.

Nevertheless, there is arguably an urgent imperative, born of both self-interest and morality, to adopt 'a politics of impossibility based on ... attitudes of necessity' (Falk, 1994, p. 132). In a sketch of 'a global governance for the twenty-first century', Jan Tinbergen, a former economics Nobel Prize winner, points out that 'the idealists of today often turn out to be the realists of tomorrow' (UNDP, 1994, p. 88). Indeed, it is striking the extent to which such ideas are being seriously discussed at the turn of the twenty-first century in the face of international financial instability, global terrorism and growing concern about global inequalities. One concrete example is the growing support for an international tax on foreign exchange transactions (called the Tobin Tax after its originator), which, many NGOs and global activists argue, could finance an attack on world poverty.[63]

Global civil society

NGOs and global activists are promoting the cause of global governance more generally as representatives of a nascent global civil society: an expanding web of organisations and networks spun across national borders around issues of common concern. By the turn of the twenty-first century, there were already over 20, 000 transnational civic networks active on the global stage (Anheier *et al.*, 2001; Edwards, 2001, p. 4). Their impact on international institutions and agreements and on the development of global governance has been considerable (Gaventa, 2001). Membership ranges from the increasingly professionalised international NGOs (INGOs) to the increasingly prominent loose coalition of international social movements from both North and South who constitute a 'counter-hegemonic globalisation' of protest, from below against hegemonic top-down processes of globalisation.[64] An example of the two strands of global civil society coming together is the campaign for debt relief, spearheaded by the 'global advocacy movement' Jubilee 2000 (Collins *et al.*, 2001, p. 135; Desai and Said, 2001). This has since spawned the Jubilee International Movement for Economic and Social Justice, which aims to build 'an organised, global citizens movement'.[65]

Falk paints the image of 'a citizen pilgrim ... on a pilgrimage that loosens spatial connections' in the non-violent struggle for a better world for future generations. He suggests that 'traditional citizenship is being challenged and remoulded' by this transnational activism (1996, p. 24; 1994, p. 138; Harvey 1998). Nevertheless, he warns that it is 'premature to proclaim the existence of transnational "citizenry" in the absence of institutional participatory machinery' (2000, p. 14). Alternatively, it could be argued that the very *practice* of global citizen action is creating such a citizenry, carving out its own arenas of participation where necessary through what Martin Albrow terms 'performative citizenship' (Albrow, 1996, pp. 175–7; Gaventa, 2001).

Giddens stresses the significance of global activism in the promotion of 'dialogic democracy', a public arena in which controversial issues can be pursued through a process of dialogue (1994a, b). A dialogic global citizenship requires global public spheres and institutional fora (Linklater, 1998; Delanty, 2000). The UN summits of the 1990s provided such fora and the contribution of a huge number of NGOs to their deliberations can be seen as an exercise in 'dialogic democracy'. It was broadened out further by the medium of the internet, which, despite inequalities of access, has proved a potent tool in the hands of global movements.[66] Although the era of such megaconferences appears to be past (in part because of some national governments' unhappiness about the effective use made of them by global civil society), they played an important role in stimulating transnational networking (Florini, 2001; Pianta, 2001).

This was particularly true for women's organisations and lobbies who seized this 'global political opportunity structure' to develop new and existing transnational networks and alliances (Berkovitch and Moghadam, 1999, p. 286), including the international women's human rights movement. Their strength was, in turn, demonstrated by the UN summits: women's networks helped to shape the agenda and outcome of the 1993 Vienna Conference on Human Rights, the 1994 Cairo Conference on Population and Development and the 1995 Beijing World Conference on Women.[67] At regional level also, women are networking across national borders.[68] As at the national level, women are more active and more prominent in the networks of global civil society than in the more formal global institutions such as the UN, which has been criticised for its failure to promote women to senior levels within the organisation. To the extent that it is through international civil society that individuals can best act as global citizens, women are helping to shape the meaning of global citizenship and arguably are having more impact than at national level in some countries. However, as at the national level, this does not provide an alibi for their exclusion from the actual and potential arenas of global power. Also the effectiveness and accountability of global action and alliances depend on strong links with local and national tiers of political action; global civil society cannot afford to become disconnected from its roots (Suarez Toro, 1995; Edwards and Gaventa, 2001).

Shifting the boundaries of exclusion/inclusion

A multi-layered analysis, such as I have attempted in this chapter, begins to free the concept of citizenship from the confines of the nation-state without losing sight of the continued power of the nation-state to delineate and control (even if not always successfully) the boundaries of exclusion. The right of free movement has been identified by Hardt and Negri as the 'ultimate demand for global citizenship' (2000, p. 400). Bauböck (1994) likewise proposes that a universal immigration right should be a long-term target against which shorter-term policies should be measured. Indeed, despite increased hostility to immigrants and asylum-seekers in many countries, the case for the dismantling of immigration controls can increasingly be heard on both the right and the left, reflecting economic as well as global justice arguments.[69] Yet, nation states' jealous guarding of their powers of sovereignty makes the complete dismantling of immigration and asylum controls, together with the relaxation of citizenship requirements, unlikely. Thus the boundaries of exclusion are likely to continue to operate to some extent in a world of scarcity and conflict (von Bredow, 1998; Whitaker, 1998). As Yeatman warns, 'all that can be done is to substitute a new order of inclusions and exclusions', which may nevertheless, she claims, 'mean a substantive step in respect of correcting particular wrongs' (1994, p. ix). The challenge then is how to use international human rights law and the development of an infrastructure of global citizenship to substitute a more just 'order of inclusions and exclusions', in the name of global citizenship rights and responsibilities.

Such an order would need to be informed by a set of principles governing admission to membership and formal citizenship of nation-states (and now the EU) through the three gates that regulate entry, residence rights and citizenship. What might be the principles that would underpin a more just 'new order of inclusions and exclusions'? I would suggest the following: non-discrimination so that the rules governing access at any of the gates do not disadvantage particular groups; observance of basic human rights, governing, in particular, the situation of refugees, asylum-seekers and the family members of existing citizens or residents; the recognition of the autonomous legal status of all individuals regardless of gender or marital status; internationalism in the sense of a recognition of the obligations placed on industrialised nations faced by asylum-seekers and migrants in an economically polarised world; trans-culturality, in which cultural differences are publicly affirmed but it is recognised that cultures are fluid and hybrid and that neither majority nor minority groups are homogeneous.[70] The first three could be formally enshrined in international law; the last two would be guiding rather than enforceable in status. In terms of formal citizenship laws, these principles, together with that of democracy, would imply the need for easy access to citizenship through naturalisation, complemented by the right to dual citizenship, for all established residents. Similarly, at the level of the EU, they suggest endorsement of the demands of immigrant, refugee and other groups that European citizenship should be extended to all legal residents in the EU, regardless of their actual nationality (Dummett, 1991).

Moving up to the global layer of citizenship, there needs to be more effective international regulation of such matters, especially in the case of refugees and asylum-seekers with particular reference to the discrimination and disadvantage faced by women. More fundamentally, a fairer world economic order, in which poorer societies have a real say, would provide the most effective brake on the migratory momentum in the longer term. Castles and Miller spell out what this might mean:

> restricting the international weapons trade, altering the terms of trade between the North and the South, and changing world financial systems so that they encourage a real transfer of resources from the rich to the poor countries, rather than the other way round, as at present. It would also mean basing developmental assistance programmes on criteria of human rights, environmental protection, ecological sustainability and social equity (1998, p. 293; see also Dirks, 1998).

Implicit in their agenda is a notion of global citizenship as explored in this chapter. If the rights and obligations of citizenship are to be in any way meaningful at an international level, work has to begin on the construction of a set of democratic institutions, which would constitute the infrastructure of global citizenship, drawing on the ideas emanating from bodies such as the UN and the Commission on Global Governance. Even if idealistic, increasingly such ideas are being promoted through existing international fora and the various UN summits of the 1990s could be seen as global 'prefigurative political forms', bringing together governments and representatives of global civil society in recognition of the interdependence of nations.[71] When, at the 1995 Copenhagen Social Summit, the UN Secretary-General spoke of the 'duty' of the UN towards 'the wretched of the earth' and of the need 'to mobilise world public opinion' over a long timescale, he was, in effect, appealing to a global citizenry.

Conclusion

This chapter has been informed by the recognition that a feminist theory and politics of citizenship must embrace an internationalist agenda of global justice. This immediately highlights the exclusionary force of citizenship towards an increasingly significant body of outsiders in what has been dubbed 'the age of migration'. It also throws into relief the role of the nation-state, the body from which citizenship derives in modern times, in regulating the boundaries of exclusion. This role is being executed with increasing aggressiveness in the North and West at a time when the power of the nation-state is otherwise being curtailed by pressures from both within and without. These two factors – the threat to the nation-state's position yet its continued power to exclude outsiders from residence and citizenship – pulling in opposite directions, have led some to reject the notion of citizenship as unhelpful.

I have tried to address this position in two ways. First, I have suggested that the changing position of the nation-state in the face of globalisation points to the need for a multi-layered understanding of citizenship which embraces the notion of global citizenship. This in turn provides the framework for dealing with the second objection. International human rights law, enforced by more effective institutions of global governance, could subject nation-states' exclusionary powers to an internationally agreed set of principles including that of non-discrimination. This would furnish 'outsiders', and in particular refugees and asylum-seekers, with a potentially powerful tool. Scepticism among some feminists about the value of citizenship as a theoretical and political project is not, however, confined to the treatment of 'outsiders'. It is as 'insiders' also that many women and members of 'minority groups' experience citizenship, in its substantive sense, as exclusion. This is the subject of the next chapter.

3

A Differentiated Universalism

Feminist political theorists have exposed the ways in which women's long-standing exclusion from the theory and practice of citizenship, in both its liberal and republican clothes, has been far from accidental. The universalist cloak of the abstract, disembodied individual has been cast aside to reveal a definitely male citizen and a white, heterosexual, non-disabled one at that. This is the starting point for this chapter. The focus then widens as the category woman is itself (temporarily) deconstructed to underline the ways in which women's exclusion from citizenship is mediated by other social divisions such as class, 'race', disability, sexuality and age. This, it will be argued, does not invalidate the project of engendering citizenship. It does, though, demonstrate the need for 'a conception of citizenship which would accommodate all social cleavages simultaneously' (Leca, 1992, p. 30). While attempts to elaborate such a conception demonstrate the difficulties, I will argue that this is the direction citizenship theory has to take, in relation to citizenship both as a status and a practice, if it is to match up to its inclusionary and universalist claims. Thus, rejecting the 'false universalism' of traditional citizenship theory does not mean abandoning citizenship as a universalist goal. Instead, we can aspire to a universalism that stands in creative tension to diversity and difference and that challenges the divisions and exclusionary inequalities, which can stem from diversity.[1] Such a *differentiated universalism* provides a theoretical underpinning for an inclusive notion of universal citizenship 'defined through and across difference' (Alexander and Mohanty, 1997, p. xxxi).

Women's historical exclusion from citizenship

The ostensible gender-neutrality of the term 'citizenship' disguises the gender divisions constructed in its name, both historically and today. For much of history, ancient and modern, women were denied the formal status and rights of citizens. In ancient Greece, they lived outside citizenship's boundaries, together with slaves. Slavery is, indeed, how the legal status of women was described by John Stuart Mill and Mary Wollstonecraft and by many feminists subsequently.[2] However, in the context of Black slavery, which itself left a deep stain on the history of US citizenship, hooks has condemned the insensitivity of those who appropriated 'the horror of the slave experience to enhance their own cause'.[3]

As late as the nineteenth century, a married woman did not exist as an independent individual under the common law doctrine of coverture, which meant that she lived under the 'cover' of her husband who, as head of household, enjoyed the status of civil citizenship. Thus, until the enactment of Married Women's Property Acts (in the mid-nineteenth century in the US and the late nineteenth in the UK), followed by a series of other measures, all fought for intensely, a married woman could not, without her husband's consent, own property or make contracts – key elements in the understanding of citizenship at that time. Free access to education and employment and even the custody of her own children were rights denied to her. Coverture also gave a man unconditional conjugal rights to his wife's body, a restriction of women's civil rights that continued until the late twentieth century in many countries and still exists in some. There are numerous other examples of delay in extending civil rights. For instance, in the US, women were excluded from jury service even after they had won the vote; in many countries, including the UK, female citizens enjoyed inferior rights under nationality and immigration laws and married women did not exist as individuals for taxation purposes until late in the twentieth century. In some non-Western societies women still remain legal minors, denied full civil rights (or deprived of rights won earlier).[4] In the Muslim world the right to education, in particular, has been identified as a 'litmus test' of female citizenship.[5]

Ursula Vogel emphasises the historical significance of women's, or more specifically married women's, exclusion from the rights and duties of civil law because, until the extension of the franchise beyond the propertied classes, it was civil rather than political rights that conferred the status of citizen. The historical legacy has been to contribute to an image of women as incapable of true citizenship. Moreover, she argues, women did not simply stand outside civil society but were connected to it through a relationship of 'dependence and subordination', which then provided the model of indirect citizenship that was to inform the composition of women's social citizenship rights (Vogel, 1988, 1994, p. 76).

It has, though, been the extended struggle for the franchise, well into the twentieth century in some cases, that has stood as the symbol of women's more general fight to be admitted into the citizenry. Even active involvement in revolutionary and nationalist movements did not guarantee their subsequent endorsement as full political citizens. The classic example is the French Revolution in which Olympe de Gouge's impassioned Declaration of the Rights of Woman and the Citizeness fell on largely deaf male ears.

Nevertheless, women's mobilisation in this and other struggles sowed the seeds for their later battles for their own political rights and the gains from participation in more recent nationalist struggles have generally been greater. In post-colonial societies women typically won the vote at the same time as men, although it does not follow that they thereby became equal political citizens with them.[6]

It is not possible to identify a single temporal sequence or model for women's acquisition of the different elements of citizenship, as these reflect differing priorities in the context of specific citizenship regimes.[7] In many Western societies, they achieved political rights before full civil rights, a fact that is conveniently glossed over in Marshall's evolutionary model in which civil rights, according each individual equal status before the law, form the platform upon which political and social rights could then be built. Marshall's preoccupation with the relationship between citizenship and social class (the title of his classic essay) blinded him to the significance of gender (and other) divisions for the history and contemporary practice of citizenship. A similar myopia often impairs contemporary critiques of Marshall and is typical of much of the contemporary political discourse around citizenship in which a mantle of invisibility cloaks women.[8]

The exile of the female

Where the cloak of invisibility is set aside, it is usually to treat the history of women's exclusion from citizenship as no more than an historical aberration or mistake, now more or less effectively remedied. Thus, for instance, Oldfield claims that, it does not 'require too much imagination ... to extend the concept of "citizen" to include women. Machiavelli apart, there is nothing aggressively male in the civic-republican conception of the citizen, even if one takes on board the fact that that conception included the idea of the "citizen-soldier"'(1990, p. 159). It has been one of the major contributions of feminist scholarship to illuminate the way in which the civic-republican conception of the citizen *was* 'aggressively male', so that the exclusion of the female (only partially rectified by women's formal incorporation in the twentieth century), far from being an aberration, was integral to the theory and practice of citizenship in both the republican and liberal traditions. In the republican tradition, the active participation of male citizens was predicated on the exclusion of women who sustained that participation by their labour in the 'private' sphere. In the liberal tradition, the legal subordination of married women under coverture (as well as the legal classification of slaves as property in the US) was, Fraser and Gordon argue, more than a simple matter of exclusion: it helped 'to define civil citizenship, for it was by protecting, subsuming and even owning others that white male property owners and family heads became citizens'.[9]

In some ways, though, such examples are simply the surface manifestations of a much deeper 'epistemological deficit' (Benhabib, 1992), whereby
the seemingly gender-neutral concept of citizenship was and is profoundly
gendered in a way that 'malestream' theorists such as Oldfield have simply
failed to grasp. Thus not only women's historical exclusion but also the
nature of their contemporary inclusion is imbued with the stain of gendered
assumptions. The arguments used to justify women's exclusion may have
varied through time and place but they have in common an essentialist categorisation of men and women's qualities and capacities. The weave of the
epistemological cloak, which has both hidden the man lurking behind the
gender-neutral citizen and rendered invisible woman's absence, is so tight
that it is difficult to disentangle the separate threads out of which it is fabri-
cated. Central to the pattern, though, are two intertwined constructs: the
abstract, disembodied individual on whose shoulders the cloak of citizenship
sits and the public–private divide which has facilitated the relegation to the
'private' sphere of all the functions and qualities deemed incompatible with
the exercise of citizenship in the 'public'. Running through both these constructs is a set of dichotomies, saturated with gendered implications and associations, which permeates the very fabric of citizenship. They can be
characterised as follows:

Public, male, citizen	Private, female, non–citizen
Abstract,disembodied, mind	Particular, embodied, rooted in nature
Rational, able to apply dispassionate reason and standards of justice	Emotional, irrational, subject to desire and passion; unable to apply standards of justice
Impartial, concerned with public interest	Partial, preoccupied with private, domestic concerns
Independent, active, heroic and strong	Dependent, passive, weak
Upholding the realm of freedom, of the human	Maintaining the realm of necessity, of the natural and repetitious

In both liberal and republican traditions the citizen is represented by the abstract, disembodied, individual; the former tradition tries to ignore particularity and the latter to transcend it. Feminist theorists have exposed the way
in which abstraction has served to hide the essentially male characteristics of
the individual *qua* citizen. Thus the qualities of impartiality, rationality, independence and political agency, which the citizen is expected to demonstrate,
turn out to be male qualities in the binary thinking that informs traditional
citizenship theory. In a classic double bind, women are banished to the

private realm of the family, either physically or figuratively, because they do not display such qualities and because of their association with that realm, they are deemed incapable of developing them. Their contribution as reproducers and carers in the domestic sphere is then devalued as 'the merely natural and repetitious' in contrast to the 'human', identified with the public male (Held, V., 1993, p. 45). The way in which the citizen represents the more visible and valued 'male' characteristics is obscured by the false universalism of the abstract, disembodied individual.

This individual stands and acts in the public sphere as the representative of the household which he heads through the hierarchical institution of marriage, the locus of male citizens' power over female non-citizens. At different times in history, he can be seen as the citizen-owner of property or labour and as the citizen-soldier, a more overtly masculinist incarnation of the citizen as hero and defender of the nation, as symbolised by woman. The warrior-hero has left a particularly marked imprint on the template of citizenship, reflecting both citizenship's earlier close association with the right and duty to bear arms and the contribution to the construction of masculinity of the ideal of the warrior-hero against which women were measured as physically weak and incapable.[10]

The disembodied public citizen

It is not only the supposed weakness of women's bodies that has disqualified them from citizenship. More fundamentally still it has been the very identification of women with the body, nature and sexuality, feared as a threat to the political order, that has rendered them ineligible. In the masculine citizenship community, writes Hartsock, 'bodies and their appetites and desires are given no legitimate place. The body and its desires are treated as loathsome, even inhuman, things that must be overcome if a man is to remain powerful and free ... individuals must separate themselves from and conquer the feelings and desires of the body'.[11] It is only male individuals who are deemed capable of such transcendence; women as sexual beings and as bearers of children are not. In the case of Black women, the debasement of the body has been compounded by racist stereotypes; disabled bodies are, conversely, 'reduced to their biological (lack of) functioning; as deficient' (Meekosha, 1998, p. 170).

Male disassociation from the body and its disruptive and dangerous demands was made possible by the latter's association with the female, banished to the private realm of the household and family, who then symbolised all that citizenship had to transcend. Not only did the private sphere become the repository of a disturbing sexuality, but, as the locus of reproduction and labour, it represented the realm of 'necessity' upon which the classical public realm of political freedom depended. The history of women's exclusion from citizenship in Western societies is thus intimately linked with their relegation to the private side of the public–private dichotomy. This relegation operates both as discourse and, for some women at some times and in some places, as physical exile from the public sphere, notwithstanding the fact that some women have become political leaders.[12] In Western political thought the public–private dichotomy stands in for the whole catalogue of binary oppositions, listed above, which are constitutive of citizenship, as traditionally conceived, and through which those qualities attributed to the private sphere and to the women who inhabit it are deemed antithetical to citizenship.

The continued power of this deeply gendered dichotomy has meant that women's formal admission to citizenship has been on different terms to those enjoyed by men. Moreover, on entering the public sphere they have not been able simply to shed the sexualised and familialised skin that bound them in the private. The question of women's inclusion in the public realm is not a simple numerical one but involves more complex issues concerning their status as 'other', the 'carriers of qualities that are both feared and denied'.[13] Different from the abstract individual *qua* citizen, women enter public space as *embodied* individuals; their citizenship can be jeopardised by sexual violence and its threat, sexual harassment and pornographic or derogatory sexual representations. Women's bodily experiences still tend to be 'constructed as problematic, abnormal, or outwith the realm of politics', as 'a barrier to citizenship', against the norm of male bodily experience which is taken for granted (Frazer and Lacey, 1993, p. 124).

This brings us back to the longstanding male bias in much political theory, which has spelt a continued indifference to women's past exclusion from formal citizenship and their present exclusion from, or at best partial and precarious inclusion into, substantive citizenship. This partly stems from a preoccupation with the public sphere as the stuff of politics and a dismissal of whatever occurs in the domestic private sphere as irrelevant. In this way the 'patriarchal separation' (Pateman,1989, p. 183) between the two disappears out of the focus of what constitutes political theory. It becomes, instead, a boundary around it, the fixing of which is nevertheless a political act. Indifference to the question of women's citizenship also betrays a more general masculine norm in political theory masquerading as universalism so that women are either assumed uncritically to be incorporated in the form of a false gender-neutrality or they are simply forgotten; either way they are effectively invisible.[14]

Diversity, division and difference

Thanks to feminist scholarship, the veil of universalism has been lifted to make visible the female non-citizen who stood outside it and to reveal the male citizen lurking beneath it. Jeff Hearn, from the perspective of critical studies on men, argues that 'to gender citizenship more fully ... [means] making the theorizing of men more critical and more explicit' (2001, p. 248), but in a manner that simultaneously decentres men, while also acknowledging socially structured differentiations amongst them (see also Carver, 1996).

The challenge to political theory's false universalism has now been matched by a similar challenge to the false universalism of the category 'woman' (and 'man'), which also helps to underline that women's exile from the community of impartial, disembodied citizens has been paralleled in some ways by that of other groups, which, of course, also include women. Further groups defined as 'other' by dominant groups and identified, in different ways, with the body and its demands have included Black peoples, disabled and older people, gays and lesbians, each regarded as 'unable to attain the impersonal, rational and disembodied practices of the modal citizen' (Yeatman, 1994, p. 84). Young observes how, in nineteenth-century discourse, groups such as women, Blacks, Jews and homosexuals were interchangeable in their sexualised categorisation and that the early American republicans defined civilised republican life in opposition to the uncultivated passion and wild nature which they identified with the 'red and black people in their territories' and with women outside the domestic realm.[15] Meekosha extends the embodied analysis to cover disabled people, arguing that 'bodily control or fear of difference and allusions to uncivilized nature must be seen as common themes in the history of oppressed peoples' (1998, p. 176; Begum, 1992).

Groups that do not conform to the universal norm established by the White, able-bodied, heterosexual male still represent 'the other' whose claim to citizenship is insecure. Among women, those oppressed because of their 'race' or ethnicity, their age, sexual orientation or bodily impairment are particularly vulnerable to objectification and vilification, in some cases as sexualised, in others as de-sexed bodies, with echoes of earlier bodily prejudices.[16] Such negative forms of embodiment can serve to make these women feel particularly unwelcome and out of place in the public sphere. Jenny Morris, for instance, tells how, as a disabled woman, she knows 'that each entry into the public world will be dominated by stares, by condescension, by pity and by hostility', by 'messages from the non-disabled world that we are not wanted, that we are considered less than human' (1991, pp. 25–6). This prejudice, she argues, is more a reaction to physical difference than to physical limitations. Davina Cooper writes that lesbians and gays are defined in such sexual terms 'that even their mere presence is erotically saturated. The threat of contamination means no space where others are present can be safe', prompting her to pose the question as to whether the private sphere then shrinks to the bedroom in face of fears associated with, for example, lesbian parenting (1993, p. 209; Hubbard, 2001).

The deconstruction of the unitary woman

The challenge to the false universalism of the category 'woman' has come from two main sources: from on the one hand, the theoretical advance of post-structuralism and on the other, from Black and other groups of women whose identities and interests have been ignored, marginalised or subsumed under the category 'woman'. This category has been shown to be representative of dominant groups of women in the same way that the abstract individual of traditional political theory has been representative of dominant groups of men. Although the nature of these two dimensions of the challenge has been very different, their impact on feminist theory has been mutually reinforcing.[17] Post-structuralism's rejection of any 'essentialist' categories, which deny the multiple and fluid identities that, it is argued, make up each individual, goes much further than a simple recognition and celebration of diversity. In its deconstruction of all such categories, it subverts the very notion of 'woman' or 'women'. Nevertheless, in its 'weaker' forms, post-structuralism or postmodernism has been espoused by some feminists who still believe that women exist but who have either revealed or acknowledged the falseness of an abstract, unitary construction of womanhood that represents all women. Jones, for instance, provides a helpful conceptualisation of gender as 'a space whose occupation we negotiate' and experience in different ways, rather than a rigidly determining 'identity card'.[18]

It has been Black feminists who have taken the lead in unmasking the particular women embodied in the old unitary figure, as they exposed the white prism through which the category 'woman' has been constructed by White feminists. This exposure has taken a number of forms including the identification of the ways in which the interests and concerns of Black women do not necessarily coincide with those highlighted by White feminists as important for all women. Black feminists have pointed out that White is itself a 'racial' category which bestows privilege and that White feminists have, since the last century, contributed to the oppression, economic exploitation and exclusion from citizenship of Black women. Some White feminists have responded by acknowledging that women's status as victims of male oppression does not constitute an alibi for our simultaneous status as the bearers of White privilege and that this involves recognition of our own agency as oppressors, even if often unwitting.[19]

A further criticism has been the tendency to homogenise groups regarded as 'other', for instance in the creation of what Mohanty terms 'a composite, singular "third-world" woman' who is denied all agency (1988, p. 62). In turn Razia Aziz (1992) has pointed out how Black feminists have similarly homogenised White women as middle class while characterising Black women as typically working class, in both cases denying the reality of class differences. Although class has always been a critical fault line running through the category 'woman' and class divisions have been a recurrent theme in historical accounts of women's struggles, it is often omitted from theoretical discussions of difference.[20] Yet today, in a number of countries, class divisions are widening among both Black and White women.

Aziz also warns that the understandable adoption of the label Black in the face of racism runs the risk of suppressing the differences that exist among those so labelled, some of whom, such as British people of South Asian descent, may not identify themselves as such. She points to the significance for Muslim women of growing fundamentalist tendencies (although these are not, as she points out, confined to Muslim communities). Religious and cultural differences are an increasingly significant target of racism and have figured prominently in a number of contemporary conflicts from Northern Ireland to the former Yugoslavia.[21]

The challenge of Black feminists has been followed by similar challenges from lesbians and disabled feminists to the conventional construction of womanhood. The 'ideology of heterosexuality' has shaped this construction around the image of the 'normal' heterosexual woman so that, until recently, lesbians have remained invisible. The template for the identikit citizen is not only sexist but also heterosexist, so that lesbians are at best 'marginal citizens'. As members of 'sexual minorities', lesbian and gay rights activists have been fighting for full citizenship status as gays and lesbians as opposed to asexual citizens who may enjoy formal equality. In most countries, their legal status is circumscribed. Moreover, although gay and lesbian rights activism represents a form of active citizenship, it is often still difficult for lesbians and gays to 'come out' in the formal political system. Homophobic attitudes and (sometimes violent) practices create an atmosphere that is inimical to the full enjoyment of citizenship rights.[22]

As noted in the Introduction, the paradigm of citizenship has been adopted by the disabled people's movement in their struggle against social, economic and political exclusion. Disabled feminists have highlighted the way in which implicitly it is a male paradigm that has been embraced, even though women represent the majority of disabled people. According to Morris, 'while the disabled people's movement has made important gains in recent years for all disabled people, it has tended to treat women's concerns as particular or marginal' (1996, p. 9). Their main criticisms, though, have been directed at feminism itself which, even as it began to take on board the criticisms of Black women, continued to ignore the perspective of disabled women whose citizenship is compromised both as women and as disabled people. Indeed, Morris has illuminated the way in which feminist research in the area of care had constructed the category 'woman' so as to exclude disabled women.[23]

The same applies, she argues, to the treatment of older women in feminist theory and research. This criticism has been developed and addressed by Arber and Ginn (1991, 1995) and Bernard and Meade (1993) in the British context, which the latter contrast with North America where the position of older women has not been subject to the same neglect. The main focus of Arber and Ginn's 1991 study is the nature of the greater constraints on active community participation faced by older women in comparison with men in the context of 'ageist stereotypes' of older people, which are 'particularly negative and demeaning' with regard to women, who form the majority of older people (p. 6). Bernard and Meade's collection of essays aims to counter such stereotypes and to present a picture of older women as active 'skilful survivors' and potential political actors.[24] Dulcie Groves (1994), who has been the exception to the rule in British feminist social policy in her longstanding concern with the position of older women, has developed these issues from the viewpoint of older women's citizenship, a viewpoint which, she observes, is largely lacking from the citizenship literature.

Age is also relevant for citizenship at the other end of the life span. Marshall referred to education as 'trying to stimulate the growth of citizens in the making' (1950, p. 25; Arnot and Dillabough, 2000). Youth represents a time of negotiation of transitions to the rights and responsibilities of adult citizenship within structural constraints (a process that has been made harder for many young people in the face of a changing labour market). Until they reach the age of majority, young people are not formal citizens with the right to vote and full independent legal status; initially social rights of citizenship accrue to them indirectly through the adults responsible for their care and for their development as future citizens. Nevertheless, the adoption of the UN Convention on the Rights of the Child has signalled an 'explicit recognition that children have civil and political rights, in addition to the more generally accepted rights to protection and provision' and that 'children's lack of effective voice in the political, judicial and administrative systems that impinge on their lives renders them peculiarly vulnerable to exploitation, abuse, and neglect' (Children's Rights Development Unit, 1994, p. 3).[25] Of course, as the Convention recognises, the ability of children to exercise such rights is a function of their 'evolving capacities' as they begin the journey through their life-course. One group of children who could be said to have demonstrated at least some of the capacities for citizenship through their exercise of some of its responsibilities, often to the detriment of the rights enshrined in the UN Convention, are those providing 'community' care for a parent or relative. Their existence in a number of Western European countries has only recently been (partially) recognised.[26]

Increasingly age differences, and their implications for citizenship, are being theorised within the framework of a life-course perspective, 'concerned with the movement of individuals over their own lives and through historical time'.[27] The deployment of this perspective in feminist analysis could be said to represent a third strand in the challenge to a simplistic, unitary notion of 'woman'. Feminist geographers, Pratt and Hanson, for instance, argue for the inclusion of changes over a woman's life-course in feminist discussion about difference as a way of emphasising women's agency. A life-course approach, they argue, can incorporate 'both the diversity of women's experiences and social change' and illuminate how 'the category woman is created and recreated in different ways throughout even a single woman's life' (1993, p. 30).

Averting the dangers of deconstruction

In developing this account of the different strands of the deconstruction of the category 'woman', I am conscious of a number of dangers. The first, and most fundamental for my own project, is that if woman is simply deconstructed and left in fragments, there is no woman left to be a citizen. A number of feminist commentators, sympathetic to the case for the deconstruction of the unified woman, have nevertheless warned of the political dangers of taking the process too far, for recognition that the category woman is not unitary does not render it meaningless (Jones, 1993; Maynard, 1994).

A number of Black feminists have argued that, provided the differences between women are fully acknowledged (too often they have not been), they do not preclude solidarity between them on the basis of those interests they still share as women. Central to these interests is exclusion from full citizenship, as the patterns of entry to the gateways to the various sectors of the public sphere remain profoundly gendered. They thus stem not from any necessary shared identity or attributes among women but from common structural constraints, which may themselves be experienced differently. At the same time, the recognition that we occupy multiple identities does not have to invalidate the notion of women's political agency. Even Denise Riley, who has deconstructed 'women' out of existence, accepts that this is compatible with 'a politics of "as if they existed"'.[28] I therefore agree with Jones that 'the strategic deployment of generalizations about women are necessary to the feminist political project' (1993, p. 13). On the same grounds, I would argue that the deconstruction of the category 'woman' has not invalidated the project of 're-gendering' citizenship although it does mean that it has to be conceived of as part of a wider project of differentiating citizenship.

The second danger is that, in separating out the fragments in order to highlight the different ways in which gender divisions are in turn framed by other sources of diversity and division, the result can be to give the impression of either a random set of disconnected inequalities or a kind of Russian doll in which they fit neatly into each other in the, now discredited, notion of a 'hierarchy of oppression'. In order to avoid this outcome, it is important to emphasise the interrelationships between the different sources of oppression, that these inter-relationships can be either mutually reinforcing or contradictory, and that they can shift over time. Where these sources of oppression do coincide the relationship is better described as multiplicative rather than additive.[29]

Finally, for many, to deconstruct woman is to celebrate diversity rather than illuminate oppression. While there is room for such celebration, a preoccupation with and delight in diversity for its own sake, shorn of any political edge, runs the risk of losing sight of the power relations that shape the significance of diversity when it translates into divisions and their associated axes of advantage/disadvantage and domination/subordination.[30] Indeed, 'managing diversity' has become a management tool which effectively obscures the reality of discrimination (Bacchi, 1996). Recognising these dangers, Mouffe has posited a radical pluralism which she distinguishes from postmodernism, as commonly articulated, on the basis that the former keeps sight of the power relations between the fragments of deconstruction and discriminates between legitimate diversity and illegitimate division grounded in inequality (1992a, 1993a).

The challenge of diversity and difference for citizenship

Mouffe is one of a number of radical political theorists whose work is helping to rearticulate the meaning of citizenship within the framework of an appreciation of diversity and recognition of difference (although she does so from a position that argues that 'sexual difference should become effectively non-pertinent' [1992b, p. 376]). Perhaps the most thorough attempt at such a rearticulation though has been that made by Iris Young (1987, 1989, 1990a, b, 1993, 2000). Using her work as a starting point, and then drawing on notions of a 'politics of difference' and 'transversal politics', I will discuss the challenge that difference and diversity pose for citizenship, first as a practice and then as a status. First, though, we should heed Phillips' warning that 'if difference is attached only to the marginal, their citizenship is still second class'. Instead we need to recognise that 'all of us are different in many different ways, and that being "different" is the norm' (2000, p. 41).

The first stage in Young's thesis, as originally articulated, is a critique of the ideal of impartiality and a unified polity. This, as noted in Chapter 1, she rejects on the grounds that it promotes the particular standpoint of the privileged as if it were a universal standpoint, thereby legitimating their privilege and invalidating as partial the viewpoints of the oppressed. Instead, she argues that 'a conception of justice which challenges institutional domination and oppression should offer a vision of a heterogeneous public that acknowledges and affirms group differences' (1990a, p. 10). She makes the case for a 'politics of group assertion' which 'takes as a basic principle that members of oppressed groups need separate organisations that exclude others, especially those from more privileged groups' (p. 167). To achieve this, 'a democratic public should', she contends, 'provide mechanisms for the effective recognition and representation of the distinct voices and perspectives of those of its constituent groups that are oppressed or disadvantaged' (p. 184). More specifically, these mechanisms should support the self-organisation of groups; group generation of policy proposals in institutionalised contexts which require decision-makers to have regard to them; and group veto power regarding specific policies which affect any group directly.

Young's work has been of immense value but the critiques of her proposals from those sympathetic to her general position underscore some of the difficulties in elaborating a group-differentiated conception of citizenship. Phillips has, for instance, argued that group representation is not the answer to the problems of democracy and difference for three main reasons: the difficulties of establishing which groups are most pertinent to political identity; the dangers of freezing identities and of 'group closure' so that change and the development of wider solidarities are blocked; and the near impossibility of achieving accountability.[31] Mouffe (1992b) is similarly critical of what she regards as an essentialist notion of groups which takes as given and unchangeable group identities and interests. She also finds problematic Young's conception of a group as displaying a clear, comprehensive identity and way of life. This, she suggests, may be appropriate in the case of certain groups, such as Native Americans, but not when it comes to the other examples given, such as women, old people, disabled people, working-class people and lesbians and gay men. In the last case, her criticisms are echoed by Angelia Wilson who, while she recognises a certain appeal in Young's notion of groups who define themselves according to a sense of affinity, retorts that 'the essentialism' required by a group-defined identity of this kind 'is simply beyond the reach of a lesbian, gay and bisexual "community" which has fundamental internal differences' (1993, p. 187).

Young, in fact, does acknowledge the fluidity and internal differentiation of groups and emphasises in her later work that her notion of a (primarily structural) politics of difference is not to be confused with that of a (primarily cultural) politics of identity. Thus groups are not constituted by the substantive attributes of their members but relationally; they are differentiated by 'cultural forms, practices, special needs or capacities, structures of power or privilege' (2000, p. 90). She appeals to the notion of 'social perspective', reflecting experiences derived from differential social positioning, as the basis for ensuring the representation of groups whose perspectives are generally marginalised in decision-making. Individuals, she notes, interpret society 'from a multiplicity of social group perspectives', which 'may intersect to constitute a distinctive hybrid perspective' such as that of Black women (p. 139). She also acknowledges that mechanisms to promote group representation need to be sufficiently flexible so as not to rigidify groups and group relations.

Yet, it is difficult to see how such mechanisms can genuinely capture the fluidity and differentiation of groups so that we still face what amounts to a Catch-22 summed up by Aziz: that the very assertion of a difference tends to create 'fixed and oppositional categories which can result in another version of the suppression of difference' (1992, pp. 299–300). It also runs the risk of causing fragmentation. The Greater London Council (GLC)'s attempt to empower marginalised groups, through the pursuit of a politics appealing to their differences, has been held up as a cautionary tale that exemplifies the difficulties with Young's approach. While recognising the GLC's achievements, Cain and Yuval-Davis warn that it 'created a politics of fragmentation and divisiveness', as groups (with overlapping memberships) competed with each other for resources and individuals were identified solely in terms of their group membership(s).[32]

Such fragmentation can serve to marginalise further already marginalised groups. Thus, for instance, Margaret Lloyd suggests that disabled women might do better to work with non-disabled women and disabled men to get their concerns accepted as '*central*, to both disability and feminist agendas' than to pursue a separatist strategy. For Black disabled women, she continues, 'achieving centrality within feminist, black and disability agendas may be the way out of the trap of fragmentation, marginalisation or absorption' (1992, p. 219, emphasis in original). Nevertheless, as she recognises, it is no easy way out (becoming more difficult the more multi-faceted is the experience of oppression) and she argues that 'it is another form of oppression for an already marginalised minority to struggle with it alone'. Her account of disability politics highlights the constant tension between on the one hand the dangers of fragmentation, which can leave the weakest fragments isolated and ignored, and on the other the tendency towards the subordination of 'minority group' interests within the articulation of those of larger groups.

A politics of solidarity in difference

If a politics based on group identity is to avoid these outcomes, it has to be rooted in a broader commitment to solidarity, premised on recognition of difference rather than on sameness and able to move beyond fragmentary identity politics (Dean, 1996, 1997; Young, 2000). At one level, this involves acknowledgement of a commonality of interests with the potential to unite the fragments. It has been described by Yeatman as a 'politics of difference', which involves 'a readiness on the part of any one emancipatory movement to show how its particular interest in contesting oppression links into and supports the interests of other movements in contesting different kinds of oppression' (Yeatman, 1993, p. 231). While far from easy, there are countless examples around the world of women forging bonds of solidarity across their differences in the pursuit of specific common goals.[33]

At a theoretical level, it is possible to draw out from the rich literature in this area a number of elements that would constitute such a 'politics of solidarity in difference'.[34] Adopting 'an impure, eclectic, neopragmatist approach' (Fraser, 1995, p.158), these ingredients are derived from theorists influenced by different theoretical paradigms – Habermasian and post-structuralist. As Jodie Dean (1996) observes, recent theorising has been probing the points of congruence between these philosophical positions previously treated as incompatible.

The first element, which underpins the others, is derived from Mouffe (1992a and b; 1993b). She asserts the need for some kind of 'framework agreement' of political values or 'grammar of political conduct' in order to provide the foundations for citizen engagement. This, she suggests, is more compatible with modern democratic pluralism than the notion of a 'common good' enshrined in traditional civic republicanism. The key features of this political syntax are a commitment to valuing difference and to dialogue. The point of the commitment to the value of difference, Yeatman emphasises, is not simply liberal respect for the 'minority' voice which is all too often not heard, but to build in difference to the very fabric of the political project. Such a politics of difference, she argues, requires both 'an inclusive politics of voice and representation'.[35]

It also requires a non-essentialist conceptualisation of the political subject as made up of manifold, fluid, identities that mirror the multiple differentiation of groups. In the words of the poet June Jordan 'every single one of us is more than whatever race we represent and more than whatever gender category we fall into. We have other kinds of allegiances, other kinds of dreams' (Parmar, 1989, p. 61). Which identities individuals choose to identify with politically can not be taken either as a given or as static. Political identities emerge and are expressed through an ongoing social process of individual and collective 'identity formation'.[36] A group-differentiated politics, which asks the individual to identify with just one aspect of her identity, runs the same risk of fragmentation at the individual as at the group level:

> As a Black lesbian feminist comfortable with the many different ingredients of my identity, and a woman committed to racial and sexual freedom from oppression, I find I am constantly being encouraged to pluck out some one aspect of myself and present this as the meaningful whole, eclipsing or denying the other parts of my self. But this is a destructive and fragmenting way to live (Lorde in Crowley and Himmelweit, 1992, p. 52).

The female citizen as occupant of multiple identities represents one strand in Sarvasy and Siim's sketch of a 'feminist pluralistic notion of citizenship', which also incorporates the differences that exist between women and the plurality of the sites of women's participation as citizens (1994). Their emphasis on a plurality of sites of citizenship participation is important also in relation to the remaining plank of the framework agreement of a politics of solidarity in difference: a commitment to dialogue. This commitment has been expressed under a number of rubrics most notably 'dialogic', 'deliberative' or 'communicative' democracy.[37] Underlying them is Habermas's notion of a 'communicative ethic' which emphasises the crucial role of free and open public communication and deliberation between citizens as the basis of democratic political legitimation. This has been deployed critically by a number of feminist political theorists who envisage such public dialogue as the framework for the articulation of difference in which diverse voices, particularly those normally excluded from public discourse, have an equal right to be heard. Unlike Habermas himself, for them the point of such dialogue is not to arrive at agreement on 'the' general interest. Instead, the aim is to promote the development of views and the exercise of judgement, having taken account of different viewpoints. The very *process* of dialogue, encouraging greater understanding, is important in itself (Dean, 1996; Delanty, 1997b).

Dean (1996, 1997) develops this position in a statement of a 'feminist solidarity of difference', which attempts to move beyond both identity politics and short-term 'tactical solidarities'. She seeks an inclusive 'reflective solidarity' in which 'openness to difference ... lets our disagreements provide the basis for connection' (1996, p. 17) and in which the differences that create barriers in identity politics are transformed 'into resources for connections' (1997, p. 260). As well as dialogue with others, 'reflective solidarity' requires self-reflection. She suggests that 'a reflective attitude' towards the rights and duties associated with citizenship helps us to realise 'that citizenship in a pluralist society requires support for the other in her difference' (1996, p. 142).

A commitment to dialogue is also premised on the belief that it enables new positions to emerge as other viewpoints are taken account of. The importance of dialogue in which 'each group becomes better able to consider other groups' standpoints without relinquishing the uniqueness of its own standpoint or suppressing other groups' partial perspectives' is emphasised by Collins (1991, p. 236) as typical of Afrocentric feminist thought. Drawing on the work of a group of Italian feminists, Yuval-Davis calls this a process of 'rooting' and 'shifting', in which participants remain rooted in their own identities and values but at the same time are willing to shift views in dialogue with those with other identities and values. This she suggests represents a 'transversal' dialogue or politics (1994, 1997a and b, 1999).

How to turn such theoretical ideals into practical realities is, of course, another question. As Yuval-Davis warns, there are some situations in which conflicting interests are not reconcilable in this way and, by and large, political systems do not provide the time and space for such dialogue. Moreover, there is a tendency to underestimate the difficulties some groups, in particular the poor and economically marginalised, would have in entering the dialogue in the first place. Nevertheless, we can point to examples which show that such a transversal politics is possible. To take just two from conflict areas: during the period of transition to the new South Africa, a Women's National Coalition was formed which represented an 'extraordinary convergence of women across geographical, racial, class, religious, and political lines' and 'a forum through which women who harbored deep animosities could also identify common concerns' (Kemp *et al.*, 1995, pp. 150–1). Through a process of dialogue and negotiation and despite fissures and disagreements, as noted in the introduction, the Coalition drafted a Women's Charter for Effective Equality which gave women in their diversity a voice in the writing of the new constitution, thereby injecting it with 'a gendered understanding of citizenship' (Seidman, 1999, p. 302; McEwan, 2000).

My second example comes from Northern Ireland. Elizabeth Porter has described the attempt to pursue a politics of solidarity in difference by the Northern Ireland Women's Coalition. Through a process of dialogue, the Coalition has provided a space in which different identities can be named and different voices heard in an attempt to promote women's presence in Northern Ireland's excessively male-dominated politics. Acknowledging women's multiple identities, this space has been used to create 'a middle ground between commonality and difference', that is 'a strong position that respects diversity, makes space for different forms of individuality, and seeks ground for commonality' (Porter, 1997, pp. 91–2). Porter draws the lesson that 'dialogue across difference requires equality, negotiable identities, solidarity and respect', together with recognition of 'listening [as] an active practice of citizenship' (2000, p. 160). In a statement, which captures something of the essence of transversal politics, the Coalition itself observes that 'we have found that you learn more if you stand in other people's shoes. Our principles of inclusion, equality and human rights help us to do that' (NIWC, undated, p. 12).

Transversal politics is tough, often involving 'enormous personal journeys' (Porter, 1997, p. 87). Also drawing on women's projects in Northern Ireland, as well as in Bosnia and Israel, Cynthia Cockburn (1996b) has pointed to the value of a clear practical focus and a sensitivity in defining agendas. In each of these projects, there was an explicit commitment to working with the 'other' and to affirming difference. This was combined with an acknowledgement of differences within each group and of the fluidity of ethnic identities, together with a willingness to look outwards. For instance, in Belfast, links were made with women in the local Indian and Chinese communities. Cockburn's description of the work of Belfast women's centres, in an essay, called 'Different together', provides a good example of transversal politics in action:

> Individually women hold on to their political identities – some long for a united Ireland, others feel deeply threatened by the idea. But they have identified a commonality in being women, being community based and being angry at injustice and inequality, that allows them to affirm and even welcome this and other kinds of difference (1996a, p. 46).[38]

A pluralist politics of community

The 'community' to which Cockburn refers represents the arena in which women are often most able to act as citizens. It has for some time been identified as the site for much feminist activism. It can both offer a *space* for women to interpret and negotiate their own varying needs and represent their *place*, a place that they largely create: the outer boundaries of their real or ideological restriction to the domestic sphere.[39] It has also been framed as the locus of resistance to racism: described by Mirza and Reay in relation to Black women's community action as 'a "third space" of radical opposition', embracing 'unity and difference' (2000a, p. 70; 2000b, p. 540). As commonly used, though, the notion of 'community' is at odds with the pluralist approach to citizenship politics that I have been describing. This is exemplified by the attempt by communitarians to revive the idea of a community of common values and collective responsibility as the fount of individual obligation and the glue that holds society together.[40] Counterpoised to the narrow, competitive individualism that marked the dominant philosophy of the 1980s, it is not surprising that the notion of community has a resonance for many people. An appeal to community asserts a public interest beyond individual self-interest in recognition of the fact that people are social creatures who live in a condition of mutual interdependence. The problem arises in 'determining which or whose community of interest we may be talking about' (Yeatman, 1994, p. 93).

This question is suppressed by conventional conceptualisations of community which treat it as a natural organic whole with given boundaries in which people enjoy a sense of belonging and a commitment to those with shared interests, positions or goals. The sense of cosy inclusiveness and unity thereby engendered simultaneously 'generates borders, dichotomies and exclusions', serving to exclude or oppress those deemed to be different and repressing, in the name of homogeneity, those differences that do exist.[41] At the level of both the national and more localised communities, the consequence is that the divisions of power and opportunity and the conflicts of interest which in fact characterise them are obscured in the name of the ideal of a set of common values and a common interest that favours the more powerful. The majority thereby tend to be signified by '*the* community' while minorities are effectively excluded through the particularisation of their specific communities, as in 'the Black community' or 'the gay community' (Cohen, 1997). 'Community', as an image, is detached from the socioeconomic and political structures that shape and bound actual communities so that the sociological reality and the ideological ideal become confused.[42]

Thus, as presently constituted the ideal of community would appear inimical to the kind of politics of difference with which an inclusive approach to citizenship needs to engage. Does this have to be the case, or is it possible to link citizenship to a notion of community that explicitly distances itself from false and dangerous assumptions about a unity of interests? Young is sceptical: given that 'most articulations of the ideal of community carry the urge to unity', she suggests that to appropriate it for a politics of difference would simply be confusing (1990b, p. 320). She may be right; nevertheless it is unlikely that the word is going to be expunged from the lexicon of citizen-ship, given its central position in the traditional canons and its value as an antidote to liberal individualism and as a locus for women's activism and both feminist and anti-racist politics. Moreover, 'principles of mutual respect and co-operation' and bonds of solidarity forged within particular communi-ties can (ideally, if not always in practice) provide a foundation for a wider politics of solidarity in difference (Little and Hughes, 1999). Therefore there is a case for attempting to promote an alternative, pluralist, conception of community. Instead of obscuring diversity, division and difference, this con-ception would place them centre stage and would be seen as 'multiple and open' rather than 'fixed and eternal', and as an arena in which a transversal politics can be played out.[43]

It is a conception that gives due recognition to the citizenship and agency of marginalised groups. For all the difficulties with any politics of difference that appeals to group identities, it is a politics that emphasises the agency of oppressed and marginalised groups. Yeatman's 'politics of voice and representation' is being developed by such groups to make visible their exclusion from full citizenship. The importance for women's citizenship of the idea of human agency takes on particular significance in the context of a politics of difference. This is brought out by Aziz who argues that 'in making a history that takes black women as its *subjects* and *agents*, not its *victims*, black women have challenged feminism with a project of the kind that is arguably dear to all feminists'. In the same volume, Mani expresses concern at the tendency, noted earlier, for 'Third World' women to be 'consistently represented in Eurocentric discourses as lacking agency ... as primarily beings who are passive and acted upon'.[44]

Disabled women have likewise challenged their construction as passive victims, rather than as agents struggling against discrimination and preju-dice, in some feminist writings. The same applies to stereotypical images of older women and to popular representations of disabled people in the media and by some charities, which have come under increasing attack from disabled people for representing them as objects of pity, thereby denying them human agency. Similarly, there are dangers in the conven-tional approach to poverty research which portrays people in poverty as helpless victims which is then, again, replicated in media representations. At the same time, though, we need to avoid creating a new source of divi-sion between the image of an idealised actor and that of an even more stigmatised victim.[45] An emphasis on the agency of subordinated groups can, also, as Mani warns, be misrepresented. It is important, therefore, to distinguish between agency on the one hand and responsibility for one's own subordinate position on the other. As argued in Chapter 1, people can be, at the same time, both agents in their own lives and the victims of oppression or inequality. This brings us to the implications of diversity, division and difference for citizenship rights.

Citizenship rights: the universal and the particular

At one level, citizenship rights are represented as essentially abstract and universal and therefore not very amenable to a politics of difference. Nevertheless, it is possible to distinguish two, complementary, approaches to the incorporation of diversity and difference into the conceptualisation of citizenship rights – without sacrificing the principle of common and equal rights which in itself is necessary for the accommodation of difference. As Bauböck argues, 'the basic requirement of political justice is to provide all members of society with a comprehensive bundle of citizenship rights that takes into account their different social positions and group affiliations but enables them to see themselves as equal individual members of the polity'.[46] Indeed, Dean makes the point that it is because of our differences that rights, with their claim to universality, are necessary to guarantee 'that each, because of her very particularity, is valued and her differences secured' (1996, p. 87).

The first approach is to recognise that rights can be particularised to take account of the situation of specific groups both in the 'reactive' sense of counteracting past and present disadvantages that may undermine their position as citizens and in the 'proactive' sense of affirming diversity, particularly with regard to cultural and linguistic rights.[47] Examples of the former are affirmative action programmes, which recognise that the mere absence of discrimination is not sufficient to redress the balance of disadvantage faced by members of certain groups such as women and Black people, and the kind of wide-ranging disability discrimination legislation well established in the US. The latter goes beyond the outlawing of specific acts of discrimination to require that 'reasonable accommodation' is made to enable disabled people to participate fully in the public sphere. Thus, for instance, in the case of employment this may include, where appropriate, the acquisition or modification of equipment and the provision of qualified readers and interpreters (Bynoe, 1991; Silvers, 1997).

Multi-cultural language policies which give official recognition to the languages of significant minority ethnic groups, as in Australia and Sweden, and which represent the multi-cultural model of citizenship discussed in Chapter 2, are one example of 'proactive' minority rights. According to Castles, the Australian multi-cultural model has shown that it is possible to combine a universal guarantee of basic rights regardless of origin with specific rights upholding cultural difference, although that model is now under challenge to incorporate more effectively the interests of Australia's aboriginal peoples.[48] The specific political and legal rights enjoyed by indigenous American Indians in parallel with their rights as US citizens provide another example of 'proactive' minority rights. Such a rearticulation is, however, politically charged as can be seen in the US where the growth of the Hispanic community has led to pressures for English to be declared the official language and where there is a growing backlash against affirmative action programmes for women and people of colour. Moreover, in countries, such as France, which subscribe to an ideology of individual assimilation (albeit not realised in practice) rather than group recognition, there is considerable resistance to any specific rights which, it is argued, could serve further to stigmatise difference.[49]

The second approach, advocated by Taylor, is to anchor citizenship rights in a notion of need on the basis that need 'can be seen as dynamic and differentiated, as against the universal and abstract basis of rights'.[50] This helps to highlight the relationship between needs and rights, or what Nancy Fraser calls the 'politics of needs interpretation'. This involves a process of 'claims-making' (Drover and Kerans, 1993) through a series of struggles over the legitimation of 'competing needs discourses', the interpretation of needs and their translation into rights (1987, 1989). The disability rights movement provides a good example of a political challenge to orthodox needs interpretations. It has also underlined the dangers of disconnecting a needs from a rights discourse: in the UK, it is argued that an earlier shift of emphasis from the rights to the needs of disabled people opened the way for the professional domination of welfare provision and 'a retreat from active to passive citizenship' (Oliver and Barnes, 1991, p. 8).

Taylor's formulation is thus useful in opening up the political dynamics of the relationship between needs and rights in citizenship struggles. However, his distinction between needs as differentiated and rights as abstract and universal is something of an oversimplification. Rights, as we have seen, can be differentiated on a group basis. Doyal and Gough's theory of needs, upon which he draws, is, as Taylor himself notes, rooted in a universalistic understanding of basic human needs which are then subject to different cultural and historical interpretations. Doyal and Gough do, nevertheless, accept that oppressed groups will have additional needs so that 'there is a place in any politics of need for a politics of difference'.[51] What this discussion suggests is that both needs and rights need to be understood as tiered, embracing both the universal and the differentiated, and standing in a dynamic relationship to each other through the 'politics of needs interpretation'.

Living with the tension between the universal and particular

Having discussed the challenge of diversity and difference for citizenship, the question remains as to whether a concept originally predicated on the very exclusion of women can be reformulated so as satisfactorily to include women, rather than just add them on; and whether, in doing so, it can give full recognition to the different and shifting identities that women simultaneously hold. These are aspects of a broader question posed by Hall and Held as to whether there is an 'irreconcilable tension' between, on the one hand, the ideals of equality and universality embodied in the very idea of the citizen and, on the other, the 'variety of particular and specific needs, of diverse sites and practices which constitute the modern political subject' (1989, pp. 176–7). The exposure of the partial nature of the ideal of universality enshrined in the traditional conceptualisation of citizenship, together with postmodernism's anti-universalising thrust, might suggest that citizenship is irredeemably tainted by its universalist roots. Nevertheless, in the same way that I argued earlier that the deconstruction of the category woman does not invalidate a feminist citizenship project, so, as implied already, I believe that the critique of universalism does not mean that its claims should be totally abandoned. The political dangers of jettisoning gender as a political category are matched by those of rejecting universalism out of hand.

In support of this claim, it is helpful to note the distinction made by Young between universality as impartiality 'in the sense of the adoption of a general point of view that leaves behind particular affiliations, feelings, commitments, and desires', which she rejects as a fiction, and the 'universality of moral commitment' to the equal moral worth and participation and inclusion of all persons.[52] It is in this latter sense that citizenship cannot be divorced from its universalist roots. Riley, for instance, while recognising the dangers in a claim to universal citizenship which masks real differences, points out that 'importantly, it also possesses the strength of its own idealism. Because of its claim to universality, such an ideal can form the basis for arguments for participation by everyone, as well as for entitlements and responsibilities for all ... Citizenship as a theory sets out a claim and an egalitarian promise'.[53] Without the promise of the universal, against which the denial of full and genuine citizenship to women and 'minority groups' can be measured and claims for inclusion can be directed, the concept of citizenship loses its political force. It is precisely because of its intrinsically universalist 'emancipatory potential' that it has a resonance for many (Vogel, 1988, p. 157). I therefore believe that the citizenship ideal is still worth pursuing from a feminist perspective, despite all the difficulties associated with it.

A creative tension

This still leaves the problem of whether the citizenship ideal can at the same time accommodate the particularity it was originally supposed to transcend. Vogel is sceptical on the grounds that 'it is difficult to imagine that one could graft upon it substantive assumptions about particularity without rendering it meaningless for political theory and ineffective for political practice' (1988, p. 157). Nevertheless, such imaginings are arguably the stuff of much contemporary radical political theory which is attempting to 'particularise' the universal in the search for 'a new kind of articulation between the universal and the particular'.[54] Such a re-articulation is necessary, Ernesto Laclau argues, because both are 'ineradicable dimensions in the making of political identities' and the universal creates 'chains of equivalence in an otherwise purely differential world' (1996, pp. viii, 57).

From within feminism Benhabib and Dean offer possible theoretical formulations. The former provides a 'post-Enlightenment defence of universalism', a potentially feminist universalism which would recognise gender and the specificity of context. She conceptualises it as an 'interactive universalism [which] acknowledges the plurality of modes of being human, and differences among humans, without endorsing all these pluralities and differences as morally and politically valid' (1992, pp. 3, 153). Dean suggests a 'discursive universalism' that 'enables us to move beyond the opposition between universal and particular to account for the diversity that is always part of universality' and that a truly inclusive universality has to acknowledge. The emphasis here is on the '*processes* of reaching understanding', on the basis of what we have in common, alongside recognition of our differences (1996, pp. 143, 162, emphasis in original).

Such processes have been crucial to the work of the international women's human rights movement. Through networking at local, national and international levels, it has, according to Charlotte Bunch, 'developed a model that affirms the universality of human rights while respecting the diversity of particular experiences'. This has reflected a belief in 'building links among women committed to a common vision of rights but diverse in terms of race, ethnicity, class, religion, sexual orientation, culture, and geography'. The movement is thus, claims Dorothy Thomas, 'demonstrating that universal human rights and the principle of difference can readily accommodate each other'.[55] While the ease of such accommodation should not be exaggerated, the kind of transversal 'grammar of political conduct' discussed above, which sets the ground rules for engagement, can facilitate the process of achieving it, across differences of both identity/social location and viewpoints. At the same time, appeals to universal human rights are increasingly being used to frame particularistic citizenship claims grounded in difference. Soysal (1994, 2001) cites the example of the arguments used to assert the right of French Muslim schoolgirls to cover their head in schools. Another illustration is the demands of disabled people for the achievement of equal citizenship and human rights, through the assertion of disability as a particular social and political category rather than through its negation in the name of the equality they are seeking (Barton, 1996; Marks, 2001).

The disabled people's movement exemplifies the ways in which struggles for social justice increasingly draw on a discourse of a cultural politics of recognition of difference as well as the more traditional discourse of a socioeconomic politics of redistribution.[56] At a theoretical level, the integration of the two exemplifies one of a number of attempts to reconcile the insights of postmodernism with a clear anti-oppressive moral standpoint through the vehicle of a theory of social justice. Jane Flax (1992, p. 205), for instance, suggests that one element of justice, understood as an ongoing process rather than a pre-given standard, is 'the reconciliation of diversities into a restored but new unity'. Claims to justice are thereby framed in terms of difference rather than sameness; indeed, she points out, it is because of the differences between people that justice is an issue.

One of the most concerted attempts to re-think justice in such terms is provided by the edited volume *Principled Positions*, which aspires to reconnect the deconstruction of identities to 'a theory of social justice'. In her introduction, Judith Squires observes that the contributors move beyond the increasingly monotonous postmodernist celebration of diversity to contemplate how difference can be accommodated politically, and oppression and injustice challenged. This, she contends, requires 'a clearly formed and articulated set of values, ethical standpoints and evaluative criteria' (1993, p. 9). For instance, David Harvey concludes that universality, while unavoidable, 'must be construed in dialectical relation with particularity. Each defines the other in such a way as to make the universality criterion always open to negotiation through the particularities of difference'. It is, he claims, the task of progressive politics to find a powerful and persuasive way of 'relating the universal and the particular in the drive to define social justice from the standpoint of the oppressed' (1993, p. 116). A theme running through the volume, and one that echoes my earlier point, is the need to cultivate human solidarity as a means of 'constructing bonds across the chasm of difference'.[57] Helpful here is Dean's notion of 'reflective solidarity', discussed earlier, which 'projects a universalist ideal urging the inclusion of our concrete differences' in order to 'break through the opposition between difference and universality' (1996, pp. 142 and 10).

This discussion suggests that although the tension between universalism and diversity cannot be erased, this does not mean that they are 'irreconcilable', as reconciliation does not have to mean the suppression of opposites. Tension can be creative, pointing the way to what we might term a *differentiated universalism* in which the achievement of the universal is contingent upon attention to difference. In the same way that, in Chapter 1, I proposed a critical synthesis of the two main historical traditions of citizenship, so I believe that it is a dynamic synthesis of the universal and the particular, as encapsulated in the notion of a differentiated universalism, that offers the way forward for a feminist formulation of citizenship. If the notion of citizenship is to be of theoretical and political value to women, in all their diversity, it has to integrate both universalist and pluralist perspectives in addressing the central issue of exclusion from citizenship. That said, the difficulties are not to be underestimated. At the political level, the task is to promote the voice and citizenship claims of marginalised groups, both insiders and outsiders, without provoking an exclusionary backlash from dominant groups who currently hold the citadels of citizenship. At the theoretical level, the challenge is to pursue a pluralist, feminist conception of citizenship without slipping back into a false universalism within the gender categories and to maintain a truly differentiated analysis which does not degenerate into tokenism.

Conclusion

In examining the exclusionary tensions that have served to perpetuate women's exile as a group from full citizenship, this chapter has emphasised the need to locate a gendered analysis within the wider framework of diversity and the divisions and exclusionary inequalities that can flow from it. This then raised the question of whether it is possible to reconcile such a framework with the universalism that lies at the heart of citizenship. In relation to citizenship as a practice, this reconciliation was attempted through the notions of a politics of solidarity in difference and a pluralist politics of community. With regard to citizenship as a status, it was argued that citizenship rights can be articulated in particularist as well as universalist terms. The tension between universalism and diversity or particularity thus emerges as a creative one which, I have suggested, can be characterised as a *differentiated universalism*. The synthetic approach adopted is developed further in the next chapter, which considers some of the key dilemmas raised by feminist theory for the construction of a woman-friendly and 'gender-inclusive' notion of citizenship.

4

Beyond Dichotomy

Women's exclusion from citizenship has, both historically and today, elicited two main responses: either to demand inclusion on the same terms as men, as equal, supposedly 'gender-neutral', citizens, or to press the case for the recasting of citizenship's premises so as to accommodate women's particular interests and acknowledge them as 'gender-differentiated' citizens. The conclusions reached in the previous chapter regarding the need for a pluralistic approach to citizenship, which embodies a differentiated universalism, raise a serious question mark over the former strategy. Yet the alternative likewise runs the risk of suppressing the differences between women and experience suggests that it is problematic. This chapter lays the groundwork for a consideration of the potential for a feminist conceptualisation and practice of citizenship that attempts to synthesise the two approaches, within the pluralist framework developed in the previous chapter. It argues that such a synthesis opens up the possibility of a woman-friendly, 'gender-inclusive' model of citizenship and that this should be our goal.

It does so through an exploration of a number of key debates in feminist theory that illuminate the nature of the dilemmas involved in the construction of such a conceptualisation. Central to these debates and to the difficulties in incorporating women in their diversity into the theory and practice of citizenship is the longstanding conflict between women's demands for inclusion based upon their equality with or their difference from men. This is commonly summed up as the 'equality *vs.* difference' dilemma. The characterisation of this conflict by Karen Offen (1988) as 'relational' *vs.* 'individualist' feminism helps to illuminate how it overlaps with the related controversies explored in this chapter. These revolve around the competing claims of an 'ethic of care' and an 'ethic of justice' and the value of independence as opposed to that of interdependence. Relational feminism emphasises women's rights *as women* and their contributions in the context of non-hierarchical relationships. An emphasis on the values of care and human interdependence flow from this stance. Individualist feminism, in contrast, prioritises the individual, her rights and her quest for personal independence or autonomy. The emphasis is on a more abstract notion of justice. Offen's own conclusion from her historical analysis – that contemporary feminism needs to draw on the strengths of both currents – supports the argument I develop here: a feminist reinterpretation of citizenship can best be approached by treating each of these oppositions as potentially complementary rather than as mutually exclusive alternatives.

This means, once again, problematising the binary thinking that underpins these dichotomies and that forces our conceptual and political choices into rigid and separate compartments. The deconstruction of dichotomy, to reveal the ways in which each side of a binary division implies and reflects the other, is one of post-structuralism's key tools.[1] The binary thinking it challenges has been one of the linchpins of Western thought since Aristotle and Plato, in contrast to Eastern thought, which has better understood the inter-relationships between opposites. Today, the principles of Eastern thought are being advanced under the rubric of 'fuzzy logic' which, on the principle that everything is a matter of degree, replaces bivalence with multivalence, that is, an assumption that there are not just two values or options in any situation. Bart Kosko sums up fuzzy logic as a label for a family of ideas: 'shades of gray, blurred boundary, gray area, balanced opposites, both true and false, contradiction, reasonable not logical', which has an ancient ancestry (1993, p. 67).

Within contemporary feminist writings, as Barrett and Phillips observe, 'the critique of dichotomies, of dualisms, of falsely either/or alternatives, has become a major theme'. The feminist diagnosis of binary thinking's harmful effects highlights the ways in which it promotes a logic of subordination, domination and hierarchy within which one side of the binary line is valued at the expense of the other and relations of exclusion are legitimated, as illustrated in the previous chapter. Moreover, it encourages essentialism and homogenisation, the objectification of the 'other' and the polarisation of debate, forcing what may be inappropriate either/or choices, thereby distorting the untidy realities of human experience.[2]

A gender-neutral or gender-differentiated citizenship?

The most fundamental either/or choice that has faced feminist theorists and activists pressing women's claims as citizens is whether our aim in seeking to 're-gender' citizenship is an ostensibly gender-neutral or an explicitly gender-differentiated model. Under the former, gender would be irrelevant to the allocation and exercise of citizenship rights and obligations. It would thus accord women equal citizenship rights with men and enable them to participate as their equals in the public sphere. The latter would, in contrast, recognise women's particular concerns and contribution and value their responsibilities in the private sphere.[3]

The dangers of pursuing the chimera of a gender-neutral citizenship ideal have been pointed out by various feminist political theorists. Vogel, for instance, dismisses as 'futile' any attempt to insert women into 'the ready-made, gender-neutral spaces of traditional conceptions of citizenship' which, as we have seen in the previous chapter, simply do not exist.[4] To do so, would be to require women, as the price of their admission to citizenship, to adapt to a template fashioned in a male image and would be to ignore the manner in which the body politic denies the body female. In this way the issue of women's citizenship is treated as purely quantitative, relating to their presence or absence in the citizen ranks, rather than as a qualitative one concerning the very nature of citizenship. To force women into the mould created by male citizenship paradigms could stunt and contort the process of self-development identified in Chapter 1 as pivotal to human agency and citizenship.

The alternative of an explicitly gender-differentiated citizenship runs the risk of sinking into the sands of an essentialism which, in lauding women's (read mothers') essential nature and values, ignores the differences between women and serves to trap them in the private sphere. This could then reinforce their economic dependence and political marginalisation. Moreover, historical analysis shows how such maternalist discourses can all too easily be misappropriated to the advantage of men and that it has proved very difficult to win recognition of the value of caring work in the construction of social citizenship rights.[5]

Pateman sums up the difficulties, which have for centuries faced women in their fight for full citizenship, as 'Wollstonecraft's dilemma':

> On the one hand they have demanded that the ideal of citizenship be extended to them, and the liberal-feminist agenda for a 'gender-neutral' social world is the logical conclusion of one form of this demand. On the other, women have also insisted, often simultaneously, as did Mary Wollstonecraft, that *as women* they have specific capacities, talents, needs and concerns, so that the expression of their citizenship will be differentiated from that of men. Their unpaid work providing welfare could be seen, as Wollstonecraft saw women's tasks as mothers, as women's work *as citizens*, just as their husbands' paid work is central to men's citizenship (1989, pp. 196–7, emphasis in original).

The dilemma today, Pateman continues, lies in the mutual incompatibility of these two routes to citizenship. The patriarchal welfare state permits only two options: either women conform to the male citizenship model or they continue with their tasks as carers, which are not and cannot be valued by that model. Pateman's conceptualisation of the dilemma is theoretically illuminating but, on the face of it, politically paralysing, for it appears to block off both of the two main approaches to citizenship. However, she does suggest a possible way through the impasse which takes as a starting point

the allocation of responsibility for the welfare of all citizens and which prob-
lematises men's relationship to citizenship, issues to which I will return.

So, while clearly there is a tension between two routes that point in different directions, are they necessarily incompatible in the sense that the outcomes identified by Pateman are the only paths that can be derived from
them? My argument is that they are not: we will have to continue straddling
both routes, through the construction of a number of criss-crossing paths, if
we are to redraw the map of citizenship so as satisfactorily to include women
in their diversity, without fettering them in the chains of essentialism. My
aim is to find ways of moving beyond the dichotomies that underpin the different routes to citizenship encapsulated in Wollstonecraft's dilemma, in
search of a synthetic 'gender-inclusive' model. These dichotomies run
through the theoretical and political dilemmas that have confronted, and
often divided, feminists fighting for full citizenship as both a status and a
practice. This chapter's review of the dichotomies at a theoretical level will
provide a framework for the subsequent more policy-oriented discussion.

Beyond equality *vs.* difference

The demands for women's inclusion into citizenship based on either their
equality with men or their difference from them have run like two currents
through the stream of feminist theory and politics since the late eighteenth
century. Tracing the writings of early feminist thinkers, Valerie Bryson
observes how 'the claim that men and women are morally and intellectually
equal had coexisted with the idea that women were the custodians of sexual
purity, temperance and traditional values', which qualities, it was argued,
should be reflected in the practice of citizenship.[6] She sums up the core ideas
underpinning the feminist equality stance as:

> the belief that women are individuals possessed of reason, that as such they are
> entitled to full human rights, and that they should therefore be free to choose
> their role in life and explore their full potential in equal competition with men. In
> accordance with these principles, earlier liberal feminists demanded the right to
> education, employment, property and the vote; their goal became full legal and
> political equality with men ... (1992, p. 159).

An exposition of the difference current is less straightforward, for it encompasses a variety of theoretical and political perspectives. This somewhat oversimplified account will merely attempt a summary so as to situate
my own position on equality/difference and on the related debate around
the ethics of care and justice. The focus on 'difference', which unites the
perspectives classified as difference or relational feminism, derives primarily
from women's capacity to bear children and their nurture of them. From

this has stemmed a maternalist politics which, in different contexts, has focused on improving the material conditions of women as mothers and on enhancing their political position and projecting their values into political life as a legitimate basis for women's citizenship from a position of moral superiority. Maternalist discourses 'that exalted women's capacity to mother and applied to society as a whole the values they attached to that role: care, nurturance and morality' played an important role in the early development of state welfare in a number of countries.[7] Contemporary feminist exponents of women's difference share 'an emancipatory vision that defends the moral (or subversive) possibilities of women's role as reproducer, nurturer, and preserver of vulnerable human life', often linking this to a broader pacifist and ecological politics.[8]

It is possible to distinguish a continuum between stronger and weaker forms of difference feminism on the basis of two distinctions. The first is whether the primary concern is with women's material *contribution* through their maternal responsibilities or with their supposed distinctive *qualities* and *values*. The second is whether the source of such different qualities and values is attributed to biology, psychoanalytic explanations or social conditioning and position. Thus, at one end of the continuum would be those whose theoretical and political reference point is a belief in the *essential* difference between women and men; at the other, can be placed those who focus more on the theoretical and political implications of the caring (not just maternal) responsibilities shouldered by women. While agreeing that the qualities and values typically labelled female should be recognised and valued alongside their dominant male counterparts, the latter do not accept that either set are to be attributed respectively and exclusively to women and men. It is from this weaker end of the spectrum that I make the case for collapsing what I shall argue is a false difference–equality dichotomy.

The relative dominance of the difference and equality models has varied according to time and place. The fact that they have come into direct conflict with each other at particular historical moments, for instance in twentieth-century debates around policy issues such as protective legislation and maternity rights, has tended to obscure the interplay between them.[9] Thus, the common representation of the history of feminism as irredeemably polarised between the two positions has been questioned by a number of contemporary feminists.[10]

Collapsing the dichotomy

Indeed, increasingly the dichotomous pairing of the two is being challenged as representing a logical, conceptual and political misconstruction.[11] Equality and difference are not incompatible; they only become so if equality is understood to mean sameness (as distinct from a principle that reflects what we have in common as human beings). In fact, the very notion of equality implies differences to be discounted or taken into account so that, despite them, people are treated as equals for specific purposes.[12] Equality and difference are, therefore, better understood as simultaneously incommensurate and complementary rather than antagonistic. The opposite of equality is *inequality*.[13] To posit it as difference disguises the relations of subordination, hierarchy and consequent disadvantage and injustice, which underlie the dichotomy, and serves to distort the political choices open to us.

The equality–difference divide also serves to suppress the differences within the categories of woman and man (as well as those 'transgendered identities' that cut across them).[14] Instead, Zillah Eisenstein argues for the pluralisation of difference to mean diversity rather than 'homogeneous duality'. In the search for 'a meaningful notion of equality that does not preclude differences and is not simply based in sameness', she proposes a 'radical pluralist methodology' which takes diversity as its starting point, while also recognising similarities. In this way, the false connections between equality and sameness on the one hand and between difference and inequality on the other are severed (1988, pp. 8, 35). This, Squires argues, represents a 'transformative rather than integrative' project (2001, p. 12).

Eisenstein is also one of a number of critics who reject the equality–difference straitjacket on the grounds that it assumes a male yardstick against which the female is measured. 'In neither instance does the female body displace the silent privileging of the male body', a male body which is implicitly White, middle-class, heterosexual and non-disabled.[15] From this asymmetrical relationship are derived the relations of hierarchy, domination and subordination which the dichotomy masks. 'When men and women are treated the same, it means women being treated as if they were men; when men and women are treated differently, the man remains the norm, against which the woman is peculiar, lacking, different' (Phillips, 1993, p. 45; Sevenhuijsen, 1998). This norm is predicated on an implicit conception of men as abstract individuals free of family responsibilities so that, conveniently, the experiences and qualities associated with such responsibilities are, of the essence, 'different'.

The problem, therefore, does not lie in either 'equality' or 'difference' as such, neither of which feminists can afford to discard, but in their misrepresentation as opposites (which is not to say that each is not capable of being interpreted in ways that are problematic for women's citizenship). 'How then', Joan Scott asks, 'do we recognise and use notions of sexual difference and yet make arguments for equality?' The answer, she suggests, lies in 'the unmasking of the power relationships constructed by posing equality as the antithesis of difference and the refusal of its consequent construction of political choices' (1988, p. 44).

Reconstruction

If equality *and* difference are to be reconstructed so that they open up rather than close off political choices, one inference, which Scott draws, is the need to recognise the contingent and specific nature of any political claims. Thus, her interpretation of the chequered history of the equality–difference debate is that there are certain political situations and historical moments when it makes sense to emphasise women's citizenship claims with reference to arguments associated with 'difference' (but avoiding the pitfalls of essentialism); there are others when arguments associated with 'equality' are likely to have more purchase (but avoiding the denial of women's specificity). Once it is recognised that women and men are both similar and different, the key test in any situation is which strategy will better address women's political, social and economic disadvantage.[16]

Conversely, a difference-based measure, such as protective legislation, can be used either to discriminate against women or to enhance their position and their progress towards equality. This reflects both changing political circumstances and also the policy implications of the differences between women. In other words, different groups of women may be affected differently by a particular measure so that at any moment the relative merits of an emphasis on equality or difference have to be judged from a number of perspectives. It is also an example of the tension that can exist between what Maxine Molyneux (1984) has termed 'practical' and 'strategic gender interests', where the former involve concrete measures to improve women's immediate situation and the latter address the more fundamental and longer term changes needed to achieve women's emancipation. Again, the relative political merits of equality and difference arguments can reflect a delicate balancing of practical and strategic gender interests.

Scott sees the resolution of the equality–difference dilemma as lying in a two-step process of deconstruction. The first step, she posits, is:

> the systematic criticism of the operations of categorical difference, the exposure of the kinds of exclusions and inclusions – the hierarchies – it constructs, and a refusal of their ultimate 'truth'. A refusal, however, not in the name of an equality that implies sameness or identity, but rather (and this is the second move) in the name of an equality that rests on differences – differences that confound, disrupt, and render ambiguous the meaning of any fixed binary opposition (1988, p. 48).

There have been various other suggestions as to how we can avoid getting stuck in the political cul-de-sac into which the equality *vs.* difference debate leads us. Mainly these focus on the reconceptualisation of what is meant by equality. Fraser, for instance, who is sceptical of strategies that try either to sidestep or embrace the dilemma, bases her own attempt to spring its trap on a multi-dimensional notion of gender equity, drawing on both sides of the equality–difference debate.[17] This, she suggests, permits a more fine-grained analysis which can identify the tensions between different strategies for equality and thereby better address them. Another approach is that of parity or equivalence, the essence of which is recognition of sexual difference on the one hand and the according of equal value on the other (see Cockburn, 1991; Cornell, 1992).

Synthesis

In a similar vein and writing explicitly in the context of citizenship, Wendy Sarvasy argues for a synthesis of equality and difference, possibly through 'the redefinition of equality as comparable treatment' (1992, p. 356). At the same time, difference, as 'represented by care and service work, has to be freed from the unequal power relations' that usually underpin such work (1997, p. 69). She takes inspiration from a group of North American post-suffrage feminists who 'groped for a theoretical and practical synthesis of equality and difference as the basis for women's citizenship and as the defining characteristic of public policies in a feminist welfare state' (p. 330). They developed a conception of 'the feminist-citizen-mother who performed a role both gender differentiated and equal' (p. 358). This 'citizen-mother' would be validated in her role but would not be confined to it; she would be a citizen in her own right, both politically and economically independent. The kind of argument put forward by the British post-suffrage feminist Eleanor Rathbone for family endowment was not dissimilar.[18]

Sarvasy describes three steps in what she terms 'a feminist method of synthesis': 'the uncovering of the negative aspects of gender differences as substantive gender inequality, the proposing of public policy remedies that embodied a new relationship between equality and difference, and the drawing out of the emancipatory potential of gender difference within a new context of greater substantive and formal gender equality' (p. 359). This process, she suggests, could help to resolve the tension between equality and difference and to distinguish policies that, in the name of difference, reinforce traditional gender relations from those based on the feminist potential of gender difference. However, to make such a distinction in practice might be more difficult than this suggests; as noted already, some policies can be contradictory in their outcome, which is where Fraser's more fine-grained analysis and Molyneux's 'practical/strategic' gender interests distinction could both be useful.[19]

Nevertheless, Sarvasy's formulation of a possible method of synthesis is helpful when thinking about the policy dilemmas around women's social citizenship rights. Also helpful is Carol Bacchi's thesis that a false choice between equal and different treatment diverts attention from the more fundamental issues of 'social responsibility for basic human needs such as childbearing and child nurture' (1991, pp. 83–4). However, this does not mean, I would argue, reducing women's claims to citizenship to those that derive from their position as the bearers and nurturers of children (and carers of adults). More generally, Bacchi proposes, in place of the supposedly abstract male model implicit in the equality–difference choice, 'a social model which includes women in the human standard' (1990, p. 266). Such a standard would take into account the actual needs and everyday commitments of women and men, recognising that they have responsibilities to children and others in need of care.

This discussion of the perennial equality–difference dilemma leads me to two main conclusions that underpin the 'gender-inclusive' model of citizenship proposed here. The first, as suggested already, is that we can only escape the straitjacket the dilemma imposes by breaking out of the binary oppositions that form the substance of that straitjacket, thereby reconstructing both equality and difference within the framework of diversity explored in the previous chapter. This also parallels the argument in that chapter in favour of a synthesis between universalism and particularity. The second is that this reconstruction must take as a touchstone the creation of the conditions that facilitate the meeting of human need and the exercise of caring responsibilities in such a way as to ensure that all individuals can develop and flourish as citizens. In this way, difference is incorporated into strategies for gender equity without reference to potentially essentialist notions of women's qualities and nature.

Beyond an ethic of justice *vs.* an ethic of care

Care as a practice and as a moral orientation or set of values associated with the practice stands on one side of another theoretical opposition, that between an ethic of care and of justice. The counterpoising of an ethic of justice, derived from abstract, universal individual rights, with that of an ethic of care, grounded in specific contextual relationships, parallels and has its roots in the equality *vs.* difference dilemma. At the same time, it reflects the tension between the universal and the particular and provides a different perspective on the debate about rights and responsibilities discussed in Chapter 1. I will explore the meaning of each ethic in turn as the basis for my argument that a more inclusive or woman-friendly model of citizenship needs to incorporate both.

The term 'ethic of care' (or responsibility), as distinguished from an 'ethic of justice' (or rights), was first coined by Carol Gilligan (1982) to describe what she believed to be two different modes of moral reasoning reflected typically in feminine and masculine thought. The moral reasoning associated with an ethic of care is contextual and particular in that it emphasises the responsibilities that stem from specific relationships in concrete circumstances and it addresses specific needs through a process of empathy and the 'activity of care' (see also Sevenhuijsen, 1998). In contrast, the dominant 'masculine' ethic of justice takes as its reference point the universal, abstract dictates of fairness and impartiality, the formal rules that derive from them and the rights they entail. Gilligan is thus, in effect, valorising the female, private side of the set of dichotomies described in the previous chapter.

Gilligan's formulation, which has been enormously influential, has been subject to various interpretations and criticisms and put to various uses. It has been drawn on heavily by contemporary maternalist feminists who have equated the ethic of care with women's particular (superior) moral perspective. Such an association has, at the same time, prompted criticisms of essentialism on the basis that Gilligan's research treated women as a homogeneous group, speaking with a single 'different voice', regardless of their particular historical or cultural situation.[20] Collins, while also critical of Gilligan's construction of a generic White middle-class woman, nevertheless herself draws on an 'ethic of caring', which values personal expressiveness, emotions and empathy, in the construction of an alternative Afrocentric feminist epistemology. In Collins' formulation, the ethic of caring represents an element of African-American culture in which Black men share (1991; see also Harding, 1987).

De-gendering the care ethic

This is consistent with the stance taken by a number of care theorists, most notably Joan Tronto, who has questioned the attribution of the ethics of care and justice to women and men respectively. Indeed, Gilligan herself has repudiated any absolute gender difference, even though her work has all too easily lent itself to such a reading by generalising uncritically about women. Tronto argues against a simple gender equation on both scientific and strategic grounds and points out that eighteenth-century Scottish Enlightenment thinkers, such as Hume, attributed to men the very moral qualities today associated with women. The gendering of care reflects not innate psychological characteristics but the gendered division of labour in which women do more caring.[21]

Tronto herself has developed thinking about an ethic of care in a different direction, explicitly disassociating it from notions of 'women's morality' and instead insisting on the central importance of contextualising it politically. In her richly textured book, she makes 'a political argument for an ethic of care' in a world 'where the daily caring of people for each other is a valued premise of human existence': the creation and sustenance of an ethic of care requires 'a political commitment to value care and to reshape institutions to reflect that changed value' (1993, pp. x, 178). Care is described as a practice and a process involving the four phases of: caring about or noticing the need for care; taking care of or assuming responsibility for care; care-giving and care-receiving. It can, she asserts 'serve as both a moral value and as a basis for the political achievement of a good society' (p. 9). At both an individual and societal level, the quality of care accomplished serves as a critical standard. From the four phases of the activity of care, Tronto derives and expounds four ethical elements of care – 'attentiveness, responsibility, competence, and responsiveness' (p. 127) – which together comprise her formulation of an ethic of care. How caring responsibilities are best met, taking account of the needs of both care-givers and care-receivers, represents the central moral question addressed by an ethic of care.

Politically, this question exemplifies the process of 'needs interpretation', at both a collective and individual level. This point is underlined by Selma Sevenhuijsen who also introduces the idea of 'judging with care' through which the values derived from an ethic of care can be applied to the process of balancing equality and individual differences, which she regards as the principal task of citizenship (1998, p. 15). Both Tronto and Sevenhuijsen emphasise the importance to these processes of an ability to adopt the standpoint of others, particularly that of relatively powerless groups or individuals, which has also been characterised as essential to a 'transversal politics' of difference. Sevenhuijsen differentiates the capacity to put one's self in another's position in this way from the self-sacrifice that typically can undermine women's autonomy. The values of reciprocity, equality, trust, respect for difference(s) and the promotion of self-respect, which distinguish an ethic of care, are not to be confused with the relations that can derive from a situation of 'compulsory altruism'. The latter deprives both care-givers and recipients of choice as to how needs are to be met and reinforces patterns of enforced dependency.[22] In the iron grip of compulsory altruism's velvet glove care relations are distorted. This is corrosive of the citizenship of both the providers and receivers of care, to the particular detriment of women in both instances. If this outcome is to be avoided, thereby enabling the theory and practice of citizenship to be enriched by the values and insights associated with an ethic of care, the latter has to be tempered by the more conventional ethic of justice or rights to which it is frequently opposed.

An ethic of justice and rights

I have already asserted the importance of rights to citizenship, both generally and with respect to women and 'minority groups', and have noted how the value of social justice is being reasserted in some quarters in an attempt to reconcile the political claims of radical pluralism and universalism. Here, I shall build on those arguments to support my case for an approach to citizenship that embraces both ethics.

A forceful denunciation of the application of the language of care to citizenship has been made by Michael Ignatieff in the British context:

> The language of citizenship is not properly about compassion at all, since compassion is a private virtue which cannot be legislated or enforced. The practice of citizenship is about ensuring everyone the entitlements necessary to the exercise of their liberty. As a political question, welfare is about rights, not caring ... The pell-mell retreat from the language of justice to the language of caring is perhaps the most worrying sign of the contemporary decadence of the language of citizenship ... (1989, p. 72).

Ignatieff's argument, predicated on a conventional public–private split, makes no reference to feminist perspectives on citizenship, thereby ignoring the possibility of a political bilingualism that incorporates both justice and caring. Nevertheless, it does make a powerful case for retaining the language of rights and justice in the lexicon of citizenship. From a different perspective to that of Ignatieff's, namely the citizenship of disabled people, a similar hostility has been expressed to what is perceived as a subversion of a rights by a care discourse. Morris, for instance, cites the struggle waged by those committed to the promotion of disabled people's citizenship rights against 'the ideology of caring' which, she argues, undermines their independence and autonomy (1993a; Wood, 1991). Anita Silvers warns that 'substituting the ethics of caring for the ethics of equality threatens an even more oppressive paternalism' (1997, p. 33; Shakespeare, 2000).

Within mainstream feminist theory itself, there is an important tradition that emphasises justice and that today, in some cases, extends beyond the limits of conventional liberal feminism with which this tradition is most closely associated. Oversimplifying, it is possible to identify two, sometimes overlapping, strands of feminist justice arguments that focus respectively on patterns of distribution and on relations of domination and oppression. Examples of those writing within the distributive framework are Tove Stang Dahl and Susan Moller Okin. Dahl identifies justice as an essential element of 'women's law', arguing for its applicability to 'the distribution of benefits and evils between the two sexes' in public and private spheres and, in particular, the unjust distribution of money, time and work. A more equitable distribution of each of these resources is a prerequisite for women's liberation: their freedom from oppression and freedom to pursue their 'self-determination and self-realization' (1987, pp. 89–90).

Okin's main purpose is to apply the principles of distributive justice (especially as developed by the liberal political philosopher John Rawls) to the family which normally lies outside the purlieus of liberal justice theorists. She does so on the grounds that justice in the private sphere of the family is necessary for women's equality in the public spheres of the economy and *polis* and to afford them the same opportunities as men to develop their capacities. She also argues that the 'just family' can help instil in children a commitment to the principles of justice necessary to their socialisation into citizenship in a just society. For example, she questions what children learn about fairness in households where women undertake the bulk of domestic work on top of a full-time job or where men use a traditional sexual division of labour to dominate women (1989, 1994).

Young, while accepting the place of the distributional paradigm in a comprehensive theory of justice, asserts that such a theory must also go beyond it for two main reasons. First, by focusing attention on the distribution of material goods and social positions, it tends to divert attention from the institutional and structural contexts that shape the distributional patterns. Second, when extended to non-material goods, such as power or self-respect, the distributional paradigm fails to capture their dynamic quality as a function of social relations and processes. Instead of a concept of social justice that treats people primarily as the possessors and consumers of goods, she suggests a paradigm that addresses relations of domination and oppression, thereby addressing people as actors. In this formulation, justice refers to the 'institutional conditions necessary for the development and exercise of individual capacities and collective communication and cooperation'.[23] A more dynamic notion of justice to counter the domination that characterises gender relations is also proposed by Flax (1992). Interestingly, her conceptualisation of justice as a process, incorporating reconciliation of diversities; reciprocity; recognition of others' standpoints; and judgement, bears some resemblance to the qualities associated with an ethic of care by Tronto and Sevenhuijsen.

Uniting the ethics

This suggests that rather than setting care and justice against each other as mutually exclusive ethics, they need to be seen as potentially complementary, each reinforcing and thereby transforming and strengthening the other. Gilligan herself, it has been suggested by Flanagan and Jackson, 'shifts between the ideas that the two ethics are incompatible alternatives to each other but are both adequate from a normative point of view; that they are complements of one another involved in some sort of tense interplay; and that each is deficient without the other and thus ought to be integrated'. Their own view is that there are neither logical nor psychological reasons why the ethics of care and justice cannot be applied to the same problem, even if they may sometimes conflict.[24]

This position is echoed increasingly, and indeed more positively, by feminists writing respectively from within both the care and justice paradigms. Thus, from within the latter, Okin suggests that the best theorising about justice 'has integral to it the notions of care and empathy, of thinking of the interests and well-being of others who may be very different from ourselves' (1989, p. 15). Likewise, from within the care paradigm, Tronto is at pains to make clear that she is not setting up an ethic of care in opposition to one of justice. She recognises the importance of rights to the protection of oppressed individuals and suggests that care has to be tied in to a theory of justice in order to address the conflicts of interest and imbalance of power that can arise between the providers and recipients of care in a context of inequality; to adjudicate as to which needs have priority; and to guard against the dangers of 'parochialism' whereby individuals can be indifferent to the needs of others than those for whom they themselves care. A standard of justice is also necessary, she recognises, in order to assess the distribution of care tasks and benefits and its relationship to patterns of power, in other words to disconnect care from 'compulsory altruism'. Even Virginia Held, who writes from an explicitly maternalist standpoint, concedes the dangers for women's equality of a morality grounded in an ethic of care alone and that caring relationships need to be underpinned by a 'floor of justice'. 'So', she concludes, 'an ethic of care, essential as a component of morality and perhaps even as a framework, seems deficient if taken as an exclusive preoccupation or one which fails to make room for justice'.[25]

This position is not to be confused with the argument that they should be regarded as appropriate to separate spheres, with an ethic of justice governing the public and an ethic of care the private sphere. Such a position effectively marginalises the care ethic and contains its implications for political morality on the one hand and denies the relevance of principles of justice for domestic relations on the other. The point of arguing for a synthesis of the two is that, in combining what may appear at first sight to be incompatible principles, each acts on the other to create together a more powerful dual ethic, which promotes the citizenship of women in their diversity in both public and private spheres.

(In)dependence, autonomy and interdependence

The synthesis of the ethics of care and of justice also helps us to rethink the trichotomy of dependence, independence and interdependence. It does so by providing a framework within which due recognition can be given to the interdependence that is quintessential to human relationships – and, in particular, those involving the giving and receipt of care – while not losing the cutting edge of the longstanding feminist critique of women's economic dependence upon men and the negation of rights and autonomy that it entails. Historically, independence has been construed as a prerequisite for citizenship and today, as we saw in Chapter 1, a number of political and social theorists appeal to the broader notion of autonomy in their advocacy of democratic and social citizenship.[26] Prominent among these is Albert

Weale, who claims that the principle of autonomy 'asserts that all persons are entitled to respect as deliberative and purposive agents capable of formulating their own projects, and that as part of this respect there is a governmental obligation to bring into being or preserve the conditions in which this autonomy can be realised'.[27] This is precisely what has been missing in a construction of citizenship that is indifferent to the dependency of women. For many feminists, therefore, the ideal of autonomy and agency has been at the centre of the struggle against exclusion from full citizenship, whether that struggle has been waged in the name of equality or difference.

This stance is now being contested by some feminists from the perspective of the care ethic, as negating the value of human interdependence as expressed, in particular, through the care relationship. Thus, the opposition in this debate lies not so much between dependence and independence, with interdependence representing the synthesis (though that argument is part of the debate), but between dependence and independence on the one hand and interdependence on the other. Central to this debate is the issue of women's *economic* (in)dependence, which in turn needs to be related to *physical* and *emotional* independence, which are also significant in the construction of women as autonomous citizens. Implicit here is a distinction drawn by Young between independence as autonomy (the ability to make and act upon one's choices) and as self-sufficiency ('not needing help or support from anyone in meeting one's needs and carrying out one's life plans') (1995, p. 548). Autonomy, provided it is not misinterpreted as the kind of atomistic individualism implicated in the notion of self-sufficiency, far from being incompatible with the recognition of interdependence, is, I shall argue, the precondition for genuine, non-exploitative, interdependence.

Economic (in)dependence

Despite the fact that the new social liberalism tradition, within which Marshall was writing, placed great emphasis on autonomy as a condition of citizenship, the implications for women were ignored. Thus, one of the criticisms that has been made of Marshall's work is his failure to treat as problematic the relationship between citizenship and economic dependence within the family in the same way that he did the relationship between citizenship and social class (Pascall, 1997). Yet the issue of women's financial independence was central to early twentieth-century campaigns for their social and economic welfare in the industrialised world. Earlier still, the case for women's economic independence, through their ability 'to earn their own subsistence, independent of men' as 'enlightened citizens' had been made back in 1792 by Wollstonecraft. More than two centuries later many women still do not enjoy genuine economic independence. This case has therefore continued to motivate campaigns for women's social and economic citizenship rights and to inform feminist analysis.[28] The importance of women's economic (in)dependence has also been stressed from a Third World perspective, particularly in the context of development programmes which have, until recently, targeted men.[29]

The emphasis placed upon the question of women's economic (in)dependence has, though, been challenged on a number of counts. First, is the argument that dependency is a racialised concept in the context both of US debates about welfare and feminist analysis of women's position in the family. Black feminists have been critical of the preoccupation with the issue of economic dependence in much White feminist writing, pointing out, for example, that it ignores the fact that many African-Caribbean women have long known economic independence, albeit typically in low-paid employment.[30] This is an important corrective although it does not mean that economic independence is not valued by Black women. Collins, for instance, suggests that 'the linking of economic self-sufficiency as one critical dimension of self-reliance with the demand for respect permeates Black feminist thought'. Research also points to the importance to many Black and Asian women of an independent wage.[31]

Moreover, it is only the more privileged women who are totally immune against the discourse of women's economic dependence, which still governs the general position of women in the labour market, a position still characterised by relatively low pay and poor conditions. This means that, even though a growing proportion of women are in the labour market for most of their adult years, their rewards from it are not necessarily sufficient to guarantee economic independence.[32] Thus women generally are caught in a vicious circle in which a discourse of economic dependence is fuelled by their economic marginalisation which is, in part, a function of the discourse of female economic dependence. As Glendinning and Millar (1987) have observed, this discourse or ideology, which underpins the sexual division of labour, does not simply describe the economic circumstances of many women, it also generates and legitimates gender inequality inside and outside the home. For immigrant women, this is reinforced by immigration laws that construct them as dependants.

The discourse can be particularly damaging to the interests of disabled women, where it interacts with a similar discourse that casts disabled people as dependants. The image of the dependent disabled woman is particularly powerful, but disability generally is equated with dependence. Morris points to a double confusion at work. First, the dependence created by disabling physical and socioeconomic environments is erroneously treated as an inevitable consequence of impairment. Second, disabled people's reliance on others for help with the tasks of daily living is confused with dependence whereas, according to the independent living movement, independence stems from the ability to control the assistance required. The dependence that results from the lack of such control is, Morris argues, corrosive of disabled people's rights as citizens. Its origin lies, in part, in the economic dependence which all too often accompanies disability and which also undermines the reciprocity which, she claims, characterises most relationships between disabled people and those providing them with support.[33]

Morris is not challenging the discourse of (in)dependence as such, but the inappropriate manner in which it is used to label disabled people to the detriment of their citizenship status.[34] There is, though, as suggested already, a strand of feminism that does question it as individualistic and gendered. This, the argument goes, is to the detriment of women who are associated with devalued dependence in opposition to a conception of independence that reflects masculine attributes and capacities and that conflates autonomy and self-sufficiency. In equating dependence with weakness and incapacity for citizenship, the reality of the human life-course, during which we all experience different degrees of dependence and independence, is denied.[35]

Interdependence

Such arguments point to a potential contradiction. On the one hand are the demands for women's autonomy and economic independence as essential to their citizenship; on the other is a rejection of what has been identified as a false dichotomy between dependence and independence in favour of notions of interdependence. This interdependence governs relationships at both the individual and societal level and between paid employment and unpaid care in the home.[36] It is, though, obscured by artificial distinctions between the economically 'independent' and 'dependent' where the former's ability to work in the marketplace rests on the latter's unpaid work in the home.[37] Fraser and Gordon suggest a feminist response in an essay which unpicks the ideological underpinnings of the concept of dependency and which sketches the beginnings of 'an alternative semantics premised on the inescapable fact of human interdependence'. The solution, they argue, is to revalue the devalued side of the dichotomy: that is 'to rehabilitate dependency as a normal, even valuable, human quality'. However, they recognise that this needs to be done cautiously, given that 'dependence' on welfare can reduce self-esteem and autonomy.[38]

I would argue for a similar caution in the rehabilitation of dependency in the context of the family for similar reasons. Moreover, in this context, there is a danger of losing sight of what Fraser and Gordon themselves earlier refer to as 'dependency as a social relation of subordination' (1994a, p. 21). The unequal power relationship that underpins women's economic dependence upon men means that the interdependence of which it is a part is skewed in men's favour. It is not surprising therefore that the other element of the equation – men's dependence on women for care and servicing, which facilitates their own independence as workers and citizens – is conveniently obscured. Uncritical usage of the language of interdependence runs the risk of disguising these underlying unequal relationships of dependence and independence.

Part of the feminist project has to be to distinguish between the different kinds of dependence involved in this relationship of interdependence. Fraser and Gordon suggest a differentiation between what they term 'socially necessary' and 'surplus' dependence.[39] The former represents the need for care which is 'an inescapable feature of the human condition'; the latter, in contrast, 'is rooted in unjust and potentially remediable social institutions' (p. 24). The goal would be to eliminate the 'surplus' dependency which currently adheres to the care-giving involved in the 'socially necessary' dependency. Their vision is that economic dependence should no longer be the price tag attached to care. From the perspective of disabled and older people in need of support, the elimination of the 'surplus' dependency, which derives from disabling environments, would similarly help to disentangle their inescapable physical needs from a relationship of dependence.

Fraser elsewhere highlights exploitable forms of dependency as antithetical to gender equity. Exploitable dependency is characterised as an asymmetrical relationship in which the subordinate party depends on the other party for a needed resource over which the latter has discretionary control. A key test is how easily the subordinate party can withdraw from the relationship.[40] Relationships of economic dependence carry the seeds of exploitation because of the asymmetrical nature of the interdependence of which they form a part. Thus, working to minimise economic dependence does not mean the destruction of interdependence.[41] The implications for the citizenship of both women and men are significant; one way of illuminating the nature of the link is to problematise not just women's economic dependence but also men's independence. Men's independence is built on the freedom from the caring responsibilities that contribute to women's dependence. Thus, Bettina Cass maintains that public policy should be identifying not women's dependence as the problematic but men's independence, 'with the negation of welfare that it implies and which is its consequence'(1994, p. 114; see also Pateman, 1989). Moreover, to the extent that men's citizenship has traditionally been constructed through their role as defenders of and economic providers for their families, this has also been predicated on women's dependence and is now seen by some as threatened by women's assertions of independence.[42]

Private vs. public economic dependency

While agreeing with Cass on the need to put the spotlight on men's independence from caring responsibilities, I would nevertheless argue that the continued economic dependence of many women, and the discourse which sustains it, does not thereby cease to be a problem for their position as citizens and therefore for public policy. Indeed, it is arguably taking on renewed importance in those countries where public policy is attempting to shift economic dependence back from the public to the private sphere. Similarly, in the former socialist countries the locus of dependency has shifted from public to private patriarchy as many women were evicted from the labour market and the social infrastructure, which supported their labour market participation, was largely dismantled.[43]

It has been argued that the earlier shift of dependency from the private to public sphere, as women became workers and claimants in the emergent welfare states, did little more than shift the exercise of male power on to a new stage.[44] This viewpoint is reinforced if wage-labour itself is seen as involving dependence on the (largely male) owners of capital and other employers. This thesis is not lightly dismissed for it underlines the unequal terms on which women engage with the state and labour market. However it disregards the potentially positive implications for women's citizenship of this engagement. It also loses sight of the particularly oppressive nature of private forms of economic dependence in which economic subordination can undermine emotional and physical autonomy. Economic dependence on even a woman-unfriendly state or labour market is more conducive to women's autonomy than one-to-one economic dependence on a man. However inadequate and oppressive the nature of state provision, it potentially offers women more rights and control than uncertain dependence on male patronage. The 'dependency' relationship involved is also a more impersonal one, even if the process of claiming can be humiliating, particularly for Black women. I shall argue that the poverty, relative powerlessness and erosion of emotional and physical autonomy that economic dependence on a man can spell mean that autonomy and economic independence have to be central to women's claims for full citizenship, albeit in the context of the weave of the interdependencies of human relationships.

The relationship between autonomy or human freedom and economic independence is explored in Dahl's treatise on feminist jurisprudence. Within a framework of the central values underlying 'women's law' – those of justice, freedom and dignity – she argues that 'a minimum amount of money for oneself is a necessary prerequisite for personal freedom, self-determination and self-realisation' (1987, p. 91). Conversely, economic dependency is portrayed as the negation of freedom. From a human rights perspective, women's economic dependence on men is, she contends, 'a moral problem, both on an individual and a societal level' (p. 97). Dahl thus argues that 'access to one's own money should be considered a minimum welfare requirement in a monetary economy ... An independent income of one's own is a prerequisite for participation in and enjoyment of life, privately as well as publicly. Lack of money, on the other hand, gives a person little freedom of movement and a feeling of powerlessness' (p. 111).

Poverty and power

Dahl's account points us to the relationship between economic dependence and women's poverty. The economist A. B. Atkinson observes that, if poverty is conceptualised in relation to a 'right to a minimum level of resources', 'we may question whether the dependency of one partner, typically the woman, on the other, is acceptable' (1991, pp. 9, 10). Stephen Jenkins develops this to suggest that a feminist conception of poverty 'concerns the individual right to a minimum degree of potential economic independence' (1991, p. 464). Both the actuality and the discourse of women's economic dependence serve to make them more vulnerable than men to poverty. The longstanding failure to recognise the family as an important site of distribution, reflected in the typical measurement of poverty at the level of the family or household, means that the poverty of some women, fully or partially economically dependent on men, remains invisible (see Lister, 1992, 1995b).

The distribution of resources (including work and time as well as money) within the family is partly a function of power relationships which, in turn, reflect to some extent the relative economic resources that each partner commands. The strength of the link between a woman's command over an independent income and economic contribution to the household and her relative power within it is underlined in the context of both the US and a range of Third World countries in Rae Lesser Blumberg's edited volume, which explores the 'triple overlap' between gender, family and economy. UK research has demonstrated how the unequal power relationship, typical of full or partial economic dependence, is experienced by many women as a lack of control over resources, a lack of rights and a sense of obligation and deference.[45]

This power relationship has been analysed using Hirschman's framework of 'exit' and 'voice' in which 'exit' refers to the possibility of opting out of an unsatisfactory situation and 'voice' to the ability to change it. Access to an independent income from either the labour market or the state strengthens women's voice and their opportunities for exit. Underlining the interaction between public and private influences, Barbara Hobson suggests that Hirschman's model,

> when applied to the bargaining position of men and women in families, implies the following conditions: (1) the more dependent, the weaker the voice; (2) the lower the earnings potential, the fewer the exit possibilities; (3) the fewer the exit possibilities, the weaker the voice. The dynamics of power and dependency in the family resemble a two-way mirror: a woman's position in the market economy affects her bargaining position in the household; and a woman's position in the household (how unwaged work is divided) affects her earnings and potential earnings in the labour market.[46]

Physical and emotional (in)dependence

This two-way mirror has implications also for women's physical autonomy for, as Jan Pahl observes, a 'husband's exercise of the power of the purse and the force of the fist' can coincide.[47] Where economic dependence deprives women of voice and closes off their exit, they can all too easily become trapped in violent and abusive relationships, which can in turn sap women's autonomy and self-esteem. This is particularly true of disabled women.[48]

The autonomy which has traditionally been understood as a prerequisite of political citizenship embraces not just economic but also physical independence, that is, freedom from 'bodily violation, or the threat of it' and freedom to control one's own body.[49] In a feminist critique of the UN Declaration of Human Rights, Helen Holmes deplores the omission of an explicit right to bodily integrity, noting that back in 1906 an Illinois appellate court declared that such a right was 'a free citizen's first and greatest right' (1984, p. 256). At the heart of civil citizenship rights, it has a particular significance for female citizens whose identification with the body, as we saw in the previous chapter, has traditionally been regarded as a disqualification from full citizenship. Issues such as male violence and rape, pornography, sexual harassment and reproductive rights all, therefore, have ramifications for the question of women's citizenship, often with particular implications for disabled, lesbian and Black women.

Male violence inside and outside the home, together with the fear it creates, serves to undermine women's position as citizens. If women cannot move and act freely in the public sphere and/or are intimidated in the private sphere because of the threat of violence, then their ability to act as citizens is curtailed, as is that of Black and gay men as well as women, in the face of racist and homophobic violence.[50] Where women have fled their country to escape sexual violence, the lack of recognition of the right to bodily integrity in international human rights law has served to deny them refugee status in many countries (Bhabha and Shutter, 1994). Women's freedom in the workplace and the political arena can also be circumscribed by sexual harassment which serves to silence and subordinate women and thereby jeopardise their status as effective actors on the public stage.[51] This status is also threatened by pornographic representations of women, representations which, reflecting the sexualised racism referred to in Chapter 3, are also often racialised. Nicola Lacey draws on the radical feminist analysis of pornography (while distancing herself from the legalistic prohibitionist political strategies derived from it) to argue that 'the private consumption of pornography inevitably impacts on the public status of women – on women's citizenship' by infringing women's autonomy.[52] There is, though, a thin dividing line between an anti-pornography stance that upholds women's sexual autonomy and one that casts women as passive victims of male sexuality rather than active sexual actors.

Of importance here is the question of self-esteem which according to Susan James (1992), as we saw in Chapter 1, represents emotional independence. This, she interprets, not like traditional citizenship theorists as impartiality, but as a confidence in one's own separate identity and abilities, without which effective citizenship participation is difficult. Self-esteem has tended to be more problematic for women than men, reflecting their socialisation and subordination in both private and public spheres, and also for stigmatised 'minority groups'. We can see here a vicious, and potentially virtuous circle, in which lack of economic and/or physical independence undermines emotional independence and self-esteem, thereby acting as a brake on women's capacity to act as political citizens. However, by breaking into the circle at any point, it is possible to reverse it so that, for instance, informal political action can enhance self-esteem, which in turn can strengthen women's position within the family thereby making it easier for them to assert their economic or physical independence (which in turn affect each other).

Relational autonomy

James suggests that her approach helps to defuse the tension between citizenship as independence and citizenship as care embedded in relationships of dependency, for emotional independence is hardly incompatible with an ethic of care; indeed most proponents of the latter emphasise its importance, if care is not to degenerate into self-sacrifice. I would broaden the point to argue that none of the elements of citizenship autonomy propounded here is necessarily incompatible with an ethic of care. To quote Seyla Benhabib:

> A coherent sense of self is attained with the successful integration of autonomy and solidarity, or with the right mix of justice and care. Justice and autonomy alone cannot sustain and nourish the web of narratives in which human beings' sense of selfhood unfolds; but solidarity and care alone cannot raise the self to the level not only of being the subject but also the author of a coherent life-story.[53]

This returns us to Virginia Held's notion of the 'relational self' introduced in the discussion of human agency in Chapter 1. The autonomous self does not have to be set in opposition to notions of interdependence and reciprocity, provided that it is understood that this autonomy, and the agency that derives from it, is only made possible by the human relationships that nourish it and the social infrastructure that supports it (Dagger, 1997; Porter, 2001). Moreover, as noted already, we all enjoy different mixes of autonomy and dependence at different stages of the life-course, for both represent a continuum rather than an absolute. Thus, as Eisenstein writes, we need to differentiate women's struggle for independence from men from 'the ideology of liberal individualism that posits the isolated, competitive individual'.[54] If citizenship is to be understood as involving relationships of interdependence, it is crucial that these relationships are not distorted by the denial of women's autonomy and by the inequalities of power that characterise relationships of dependency. True interdependence between individual women and men will not be possible so long as the economic and power relationships underpinning their interdependence are so unequal.

Across the binary divides

At the outset of this chapter, I questioned the binary thinking that pushes us into the political and theoretical cul-de-sac of a choice between an ostensibly gender-neutral and an explicitly gender-differentiated model of citizenship as the way forward for women in their diversity. It is, of course, easier to state the problems with dualistic thinking than to find a way to move beyond it, given the power of its grip on Western thought and language. The identification by feminists of the false dichotomies characteristic of orthodox masculine Western thought can all too easily slip into a simple reversal of the value attached to the two sides of the binary divide. Some, though, would argue that this is a necessary phase in the process of deconstruction, given that this process has to start from within the very binary categories it aims to subvert and the need to illuminate the hierarchical relations involved (see Cornell, 1991; Coole, 1993). The challenge is to avoid stalling at the point of substitution of one subordinated category for another. The other main options are the transcendence or synthesis of the dualistic categories; and these are not necessarily mutually exclusive.

The conceptualisation of difference as plural and relational rather than oppositional provides an example of an attempt to transcend the conventional dualistic construction of difference. Thus, as argued in this chapter, equality and difference represent a false dichotomy, for the two are not incompatible. Instead, equal citizenship has to embrace difference, understood pluralistically and difference cannot afford to be divorced from equality. This combination of universalistic and particularist arguments exemplifies the principle of differentiated universalism proposed earlier. In the same way, an ethic of justice, which provides the compass for the equality approach, is enriched if it combines with an ethic of care; an ethic of care, without an ethic of justice, can perpetuate the exploitative gendering of care relationships. In a dialectical relationship with each other, the two are thereby transformed. Underlying these two dichotomies are two different images of the ideal citizen. One is the independent citizen of traditional political theory; the other is the citizen who locates herself within the valued bonds of human interdependence. Again, such dualistic thinking is unhelpful. To idealise one or other of the images runs the risk of obscuring the symbiotic relationship between them; in particular the way in which unequal power relations distort interdependence, creating asymmetrical relations of dependence and independence, to the detriment of those cast as dependants. A more balanced approach is needed which recognises that the achievement of genuine human interdependence and individual autonomy in each case requires the other.

Through a process of subversion of the three dichotomies, I have tried to point to how we can transcend the binary thinking that underpins them. As in earlier chapters, I am attempting to deploy the tool of critical synthesis in order to move beyond a static dualism. I thereby hope to open up the possibility of a more dynamic, dialectical relationship between the two sides of this key set of theoretical stances which trap us into either an ostensibly gender-neutral or an explicitly gender-differentiated model of citizenship, neither of which is satisfactory on its own. Instead, our goal should be a 'gender-inclusive' model, which draws on elements of both but which is circumscribed by neither. While it is difficult to shake off the habits of dualistic thinking completely, the aim has been at the very least to loosen its grip so as to avoid the distortion of reality and of political choices within which it can trap us. More prosaically, it is a matter of asserting our right to think in terms of both/and rather than be confined within the straitjacket of either/or.

Conclusion

This chapter has explored three related theoretical dichotomies, which together contribute to the construction of either an ostensibly gender-neutral or an explicitly gender-differentiated model of citizenship. Both models pose problems. In each case, I have argued that the dichotomies are, in different ways, misleading and unhelpful. Thus, it is not a question of having to opt for a claim to full citizenship based on *either* women's equality with *or* difference from men; inspired by an ethic of *either* justice *or* care; premised on an ideal of *either* the independent *or* interdependent citizen. Instead, we need to shake off the shackles of such binary thinking. This enables us first to illuminate the ways in which each side of these dichotomies depends on the other and second to move beyond them through a process of subversion, transcendence or critical synthesis to construct a 'gender-inclusive' model of citizenship. In the next chapter, I will extend this analysis to the public–private dichotomy, which, as observed earlier, constitutes the foundation stone of the masculine construction of citizenship.

Part II

Across the Public–Private Divide: Policy, Practice and Politics

5
Private–Public: the Barriers to Citizenship

The historical centrality of the public–private divide to the exclusion of women from citizenship in both theory and practice was underlined in Chapter 3. I will now develop the argument, first at a theoretical level and then by illustrating some of the practical implications for women's citizenship today. My starting point is the ideological nature of the traditional gendered construction of a rigid separation of the 'public' from the 'private' which underpins the dichotomies explored in the previous chapter. As in that chapter, I will challenge the binary thinking that disguises the symbiotic relationship between the two sides of the divide in which each side defines the other. From there I will suggest three ways in which the public–private split needs to be rethought, if it is no longer to act as both a theoretical and a practical barrier to women's citizenship. This theoretical argument provides the basis for an examination of the impact of the interaction between the public and the private on women's material position as citizens. It is, I shall argue, within both the public and the private spheres and the interrelationship between the two, as governed in particular by the sexual division of labour and time, that the practical barriers to women's citizenship lie. Moreover, both women and men's citizenship would be enriched, if the value to citizenship of caring responsibilities in the private sphere were acknowledged and if those responsibilities were shared more equitably between the sexes.

Contesting the public–private divide

The distinction between 'public' and 'private' has a number of connotations. These include, most importantly, the separation of state and market sectors with regard to the economy and the provision of welfare services on the one hand and the 'patriarchal separation', which divides off the domestic or intimate sphere on the other (Pateman 1988, p. 13; 1989; p. 183). It is the patriarchal separation that concerns us here. Lacey suggests a further

119

distinction between public and private spheres and values. The latter refers to the sexualised dichotomy, discussed in Chapter 3, which constructs the 'private' and the female attributes associated with it as inimical to citizenship. The notion of public and private spheres is itself divided into descriptive and normative claims. The descriptive claim of a private family, unsullied by state regulation, within which women are confined and from which men, who instead inhabit the public realm, are absent is a distortion. The reality is more complex: direct and indirect state regulation of the family; easy male passage between private and public spheres and the, albeit more difficult, entry of growing numbers of women into the public (Lacey, 1993; see also Dahlerup, 1987). This has not, however, been an obstacle to the normative claims made on behalf of a private, unregulated family as the bastion of individual freedom nor to the sexualised values that support these claims, to the benefit of men.

It is this ideological construction of the public–private divide that is pivotal to the feminist reinterpretation of citizenship. By treating as irrelevant for citizenship whatever occurs in the private sphere, the dominant public–private discourse erects what Tronto (1993) describes as a 'moral boundary' between the family and the 'political'. This is then used to justify non-intervention to address injustice or oppression within the family and to deny the significance of the care and domestic service upon which the public exercise of citizenship has always depended. The ideological construction of the public–private divide thereby contributes to the opposition of justice and care and to the convenient camouflaging of men's dependence upon women for care and servicing.

Rearticulating the public–private split

One response to a construction that has served to sustain the position and power of male citizens in this way has been to call for the complete dissolution of the two categories in the face of what is seen as the ubiquitous nature of male power. However, apart from a small minority, such as the radical feminist Kate Millett, most feminists explicitly distance themselves from such a position. Instead, they argue for a rearticulation of the public and private, and of the relationship between the two, as necessary to the understanding and achievement of women's citizenship.[1] Three main elements of this rearticulation can be identified. The first involves the deconstruction of the sexualised values associated with public and private so that it is the gendered quality of the distinction and of the attributes associated with each of the spheres that is dissolved, rather than the distinction itself. According to Siim, this is beginning to happen in Scandinavia where the public–private divide 'has lost some of its gendered meaning' (1994, p. 298, 1999, 2000). Secondly, as demonstrated in the second half of this chapter, the rigid ideological separation between the two is rejected in acknowledgement of the myriad ways in which the public and private impact upon each other, thereby illuminating and challenging the oppressive and unequal gender relations that ensue. Thirdly, recognition has to be given to the changing nature of the boundaries between public and private. It is this last aspect which is the focus of the first half of the chapter.

It is emphasised by Jean Bethke Elshtain who, in her review of the treatment of public and private in the history of Western political thought, takes an otherwise rather different position to that set out here with regard to the nature of the rearticulation needed. In opposition to the feminist slogan that 'the personal is political', she argues for their separation in defence of the autonomy of the private realm of the family and the intimate human relationships therein against the encroachment of the political. Drawing on a somewhat idealised vision of the family, which largely denies the evidence of the ways in which it acts as a key site of male oppression, she calls for the reaffirmation of the private familial sphere and the values associated with it.[2] Feminists, who do not share Elshtain's rather sanguine view of the family, tend to be wary nevertheless of equating recognition of the political nature of the 'private' with a green light for unlimited state intervention. This is a point of particular importance for Black women who do not necessarily experience the public–private divide in the same way as White.

Moreover, most feminists would probably acknowledge the value to women as well as men of an area of privacy (Okin, 1998). Dean, for example, argues for privacy to be understood as 'a boundary' that 'secures decisional autonomy, inviolate personality, and bodily integrity' (1996, p. 130). This boundary, she suggests, can be used by women in the public sphere as protection against sexualised forms of harassment, which are thereby identified as inappropriate. Young sees a good practical and theoretical case for maintaining a public–private distinction, provided it is not construed as a hierarchical opposition. She suggests that, instead of defining the private as that which is excluded by the public, it should be understood as 'that aspect of his or her life and activity that any person has the right to exclude from others. The private in this sense is not what public institutions exclude, but what the individual chooses to withdraw from public view' (1990a, pp. 119–20; 1987). This is helpful but it does leave open the question as to which individuals have the power to make their choices stick. For example, some men would like to keep from public view the issue of domestic violence or marital rape. In other words, it is not only public institutions that have tried to define as 'private' that which it has been in women's interests to define as matters of public concern. Definitions and boundaries of public–private, and the ability to enforce them, reflect gendered power relations in both public and private spheres.[3]

The key point, therefore, is that the public–private divide has to be seen as an essentially contested construction. The crucial question is: who has the power to decide where the line is to be drawn in any particular situation on any particular issue? Indeed, it has been one of feminism's achievements that it has, in some countries at least, succeeded in shifting the boundaries between public and private on a number of important issues such as marital rape and domestic violence as well as the area of sexuality more generally.[4] Nevertheless, the legal boundaries ultimately have to be drawn through (still largely male-dominated) parliaments or courts, so that much depends on the openness of these institutions to women's demands which may not necessarily be unanimous.[5]

A shifting construction: time, place and power

The contested nature of the line between public and private is one reason why it cannot be treated as a fixed given. Another is that its positioning and meanings are historically and culturally specific and reflect different state forms.[6] Yuval-Davis (1991a, 1992) illustrates the point with reference on the one hand to Third World countries where the penetration of the modern state, especially in rural areas, is still quite limited and on the other to the intrusiveness of the state in the former communist societies of Central/Eastern Europe. With regard to the latter, Barbara Einhorn contrasts the Western feminist interpretation of the public–private dichotomy with Central and Eastern European women's idealisation of the private sphere 'as both haven from and site of resistance to the long arm of the state ... in opposition to the over-politicised and didactic, exhortatory nature of the public sphere'.[7] An insight into how women and men might react differently to the notion of public and private under a totalitarian regime is provided in *Wild Swans*. Writing of her mother's difficulties with the Party, Jung Chang observes how her mother felt let down that her father would not express his support for her even in private: 'My father's devotion to communism was absolute; he felt he had to speak the same language in private, even to his wife, that he did in public. My mother was much more flexible; her commitment was tempered by both reason and emotion. She gave a space to the private; my father did not' (1991, p. 138).

The fluid nature of the public–private divide can be illustrated within societies as well as between them, for the line can be drawn in different places for different groups according to the amount of power they can yield. Increasingly, the 'private' is being lauded over the 'public' and the privileged are retreating into private fortresses, most notably in North and South America, leaving a devalued public space behind them, although the power they yield is still very public.[8] In contrast, homeless people living on the streets in other people's public space are afforded little or no privacy. Likewise, the penetration of the private is particularly marked for those claiming social assistance for whom there is little privacy in the face of a state that can require exposure of the most intimate details of their lives.

The privacy of disabled people is also often treated with little respect. Morris observes how 'non-disabled people feel that our differentness gives them the right to invade our privacy and make judgements about our lives ... Our physical difference makes our bodies public property', subject to the demeaning impact of the stare (1991, p. 29; Meekosha, 1998). Lesbians and gays, on the other hand, are expected to confine the expression of their sexuality to the private sphere so as not to contaminate the public, which is identified with the heterosexual side of what is a sexualised as well as a gendered divide. Such restrictions are, though, increasingly under challenge through, for instance, Gay Pride marches and the emergence of 'gay and lesbian public spheres', which exemplify the existence of 'multiple, hierarchically layered and contested public spheres'. The alternative cultures developed here 'leak', in turn, into the wider dominant public sphere.[9]

An illustration of an explicit challenge to the public–private divide is provided by Kerreen Reiger's account of Australian mothers' campaigns to breastfeed in public (2000). Another example of how the relatively powerless can subvert the public–private divide is the claiming by working-class women of 'private' space, for example the kitchen table, as the locus of their politicisation, from which they might plan campaigns around 'public' policy issues that affect them. According to Susan Hyatt, activism of this kind is to be understood less as a process of movement from private to public spheres than as the expression of a realisation of the extent to which 'private' space has been penetrated by the public and political.[10] This is illustrated by the protests of White working-class women in the US against toxic waste disposal. Celene Krauss observes that pollution forced them 'to examine their assumptions about the family as a private haven, separate from the public arena....Women's politicization around toxic waste protests led them to transform their traditional beliefs into resources of opposition which enabled them to enter the public arena and challenge its legitimacy, breaking down the public/private distinction' (1998, p. 138).

At a global level, campaigning networks have highlighted the implications of the public–private split for the lack of rights enjoyed by, mainly female, homeworkers. They expose the ways in which the public sphere of the economy has infiltrated and shaped the domestic space of these women and they make public a form of exploitation which has, until relatively recently, been hidden behind a domestic front door marked 'private'. Homeworking, which in its more exploitative forms, is most common among minority ethnic and poor working-class women, is one example of public and private merging in these women's homes, often with damaging consequences for health and family relations. Childminding provides another example.[11]

Similarly the public–private split blurs for women in domestic service as one woman's private sphere can become another woman's public. Evelyn N. Glenn has made this point in the US with regard to both working-class White women and 'racial ethnic women'.[12] The difference between the two, she suggests, is that racial ethnic women expect to subordinate their own domestic role to the servicing and care of their White employer's family. In a number of countries, access to the public sphere for better off women in dual-earner families increasingly is being facilitated by the employment of poorer women in the former's private sphere (Anderson, 2000). This then becomes part of these poorer women's public sphere. Thus, both historically and today, the situation of White middle-class women has benefited from that of Black and White working-class (and increasingly migrant) women in a way that disrupts the public–private divide for the latter groups.

Glenn is also one of a number of Black writers who have underlined how the scope and construction of the private family sphere can differ as between Black and White women. Thus, she argues that, 'under conditions of economic insecurity, scarce resources, and cultural assault', Black women have historically needed to draw on a wider domestic kinship network for goods and services. In the words of Collins, the survival strategies of poor African-American families have created 'fluid public/private boundaries'. In fact, similar patterns can be discerned in some White working-class communities where women's 'survival networks', both historically and today, can cut across arbitrary public–private divisions.[13] The construction of the family as not just a source of sexual oppression but also a site of protection from and resistance to racial oppression, in some cases under threat from divisive immigration laws, has also served as an important corrective to conventional White feminist thinking about the public–private divide. While not ignoring conflict within the family, Glenn argues that this becomes secondary in a situation in which the family can provide a bulwark against racist oppression, exploitation and 'the atomizing effects of poverty' (Glenn, 1991, p. 194). A parallel can be seen here with women's experience of the family under totalitarian regimes.

A political divide

What this discussion adds up to is that the public–private divide cannot be treated as a given. Rather, it has to be seen as a shifting political construction under constant renegotiation, which reflects both historical and cultural contexts as well as the relative power of different social groups. The struggle to control its meaning and positioning is central to the project of re-gendering citizenship. The implications for citizenship have been understood for some time by the few and ignored by the many. In the eighteenth and nineteenth centuries Wollstonecraft and Mill both made the link between women's exclusion from citizenship and their position in the private sphere. Contemporary feminist scholars take the argument further to challenge the sexual division of labour which is seen as holding the 'master key' to the door that governs entry to the public sphere for women and men. They have also illuminated how the work of caring, which moulds women's relationship to citizenship, cuts across public–private boundaries.

Yet, all too often, prominent male citizenship theorists either ignore or discount these insights or reassert a rigid separation of public and private as constitutive of citizenship. Bryan Turner, for example, in his 'outline of a theory of citizenship', of which one axis is the division between public and private space, is completely silent on the gender implications of this division. John Pocock has warned that dissolution of the public–private divide could mean the dissolution of citizenship itself.[14] Marquand (1991) has responded to the feminist case by arguing that it is unreasonable to expect the notion of citizenship to address questions concerning the 'private' sphere of the home and family. This last example underlines how the dichotomisation of public and private serves to rule out of political bounds those impediments to women's citizenship that are located in the private sphere.

It is to these that I now turn in order to illustrate the point that women and men experience a different relationship to the private and public spheres as well as differential ease of passage between the two. While separating out the two spheres for the purposes of analysis, I hope to illuminate the considerable interpenetration between them and how the keys to women's citizenship lie in the nature of the interaction of the public and private. I start from the private side of the divide, partly in order to counteract the tendency in 'malestream' citizenship theory to ignore it and partly to emphasise its continued profound impact on women's citizenship in many societies, even if its grip might be weakening in Scandinavian countries such as Denmark (Siim, 1994, 1999, 2000).

Autonomy undermined or promoted at the public–private intersection

While my main focus will be the domestic division of labour and time, I will first draw out the relevance of a number of aspects of my earlier discussion of (in)dependence and autonomy in both their physical and economic guise. These help to illustrate the ways in which women's citizenship is inhibited, but also can be promoted, at the intersections of the public and the private.

Bodily integrity

The issue of bodily integrity, more than any other, exemplifies how what have traditionally been construed as quintessentially 'private' matters, are, in fact, preconditions of women's full and free access to the public sphere. Critical to bodily integrity are reproductive rights, embracing contraception, abortion and reproductive health. Their importance to women's autonomy, equality and democratic participation has been a key tenet of modern feminism and has now been given official recognition by bodies such as the United Nations.[15] Without such rights women cannot take control of their bodies or their lives; their agency, and hence their citizenship, is profoundly compromised. As group-specific rights essential to women's ability to enjoy full and equal universal citizenship, reproductive rights embody the principle of differentiated universalism proposed in Chapter 3.

Sheila Shaver (1993/94) develops the notion of reproductive rights as a form of citizenship, entailing the traditional triad of civil, political and social rights. In an analysis of abortion rights in liberal welfare states, she distinguishes between, on the one hand, Britain and Australia, where access to legal abortion is treated as 'a medical entitlement', albeit not an unconditional one, and on the other the US and Canada where it has been won as a 'body right'. The latter has proved more vulnerable to anti-abortion mobilisation (O'Connor *et al.*, 1999). Also, as Shaver points out, as this 'body right' is expressed primarily through the medical market, the right to abortion has at the same time been prejudiced by the denial of the social right to the services necessary to exercise it. Women with money are thereby privileged over those without. This has led Catherine MacKinnon to argue that 'women were granted the abortion right as a private privilege, not as a public right' (1989, p. 192). Even in countries such as Britain, with a universal public health service, the right, under certain conditions, to a publicly funded abortion can in practice be undermined because of pressure on overstretched services.

Thus, as Pippa Norris (1987) points out, because of the distinction that has to be made between *de jure* and *de facto* women's rights, one has to examine the ease with which women can exercise their reproductive rights as well as the rights themselves when assessing how effective they are in promoting women's autonomy. Norris's own survey suggests that, by the mid-1980s, considerable advances had been made in many countries towards the achievement of women's sexual autonomy as a result of the development of both reproductive rights and the services to underpin them. However, there are still many countries, particularly in the Third World and in Eastern/Central Europe, where women's autonomy is undermined because 'their reproductive health is not protected, and their reproductive rights are not guaranteed'.[16] In some others, abortion rights already won have either been lost or are under threat in the face of a backlash, particularly virulent in the US. In the former Communist countries of Eastern/Central Europe there has been increased 'restriction of women's control over their own reproductive well-being' and the subordination of their reproductive health to nationalist and pro-natalist aspirations, reflecting 'diverse religious, economic and political processes'.[17]

There are also some groups of women whose autonomy has not necessarily been promoted by certain reproductive rights, which have been deployed to deny them the choice of motherhood. The unrestricted fertility of poor and/or Black women has sometimes been seen as problematic. Such women have, on occasion, been 'encouraged' to be sterilised or injected with the long-term contraceptive Depo Provera and women with learning difficulties can be sterilised without their direct consent. For disabled women the issue can be the right to have children in the face of prejudiced attitudes.[18] Moreover, the assumption that the diagnosis of foetal impairment automatically justifies an abortion has been attacked by Morris (1991) as a denial of the right to life, never mind citizenship, raising difficult issues for feminist abortion politics. Power may also be exercised over which women may choose motherhood, so as to reinforce dominant discourses about sexuality, by restricting the access of lesbians to infertility treatment and donor insemination (Carabine, 1992, 1996; Richardson, 1993).

As indicated earlier, another threat to women's bodily integrity is male violence and harassment in both private and public spheres. Again, we can see how public and private interact to the detriment of women's citizenship. Even though they are as likely to encounter violence in the private as in the public sphere, women's fear of male violence constrains their freedom in the latter. An atmosphere of violence in the public sphere, such as in Northern Ireland, can be reflected in particularly brutal violence in the private.[19] Although feminists have achieved some success in placing domestic violence on the public policy agenda, there is still a reluctance among many states to recognise such violence and other infringements of bodily integrity as human rights violations in the context of granting refugee status. Likewise, women's political resistance to such violations tends not to be acknowledged as such. Both reflect a traditional preoccupation in human rights law with 'public' rather than 'private' actions. Women fleeing domestic persecution, unprotected by their government, have rarely been granted refugee status. This is beginning to change, as the US, Canada, Australia and the UK have moved to acknowledge the right to refugee status of women fleeing sexual persecution, including by non-state agents. Nevertheless, Heaven Crawley argues that protection under the Refugee Convention is still undermined by 'the continuing tendency among decision makers to allow a public/private dichotomy to engender the determination process as a whole' (2000, p. 20).[20] Ironically, at the same time immigration laws can require, particularly female, migrants to expose intimate details about their private lives.

While clearly there is considerable progress to be made, the claims made by women, and also lesbians and gays, for sexual autonomy have helped to loosen the rigid partition between public and private, giving rise to the notion of 'sexual citizenship'. The politics of sexual citizenship are both promoting the citizenship status of 'sexual minorities' who do not conform to the patterns of institutionalised 'hegemonic heterosexuality' (Richardson, 1998, p. 83) and articulating new claims to 'sexual rights', understood as 'a set of rights to sexual expression and consumption' (Richardson, 2000a,

p. 107). Jeffrey Weeks heralds the 'sexual citizen' as 'a harbinger of a new politics of intimacy and everyday life'.[21]

Ken Plummer 'provisionally' identifies this new politics as a politics of 'intimate citizenship' (2001). This he defines as 'a cluster of emerging concerns over the rights to choose what we do with our bodies, our feelings, our identities, our relationships, our genders, our eroticisms and our representations' (1995, p. 17). Broader than, but encompassing notions of reproductive rights and of sexual and gendered citizenship, 'intimate citizenship', according to Plummer, serves 'as a sensitising concept which sets about analysing a plurality of public discourses and stories about how to live the personal life' (2001, p. 238). It thus extends our understanding of citizenship responsibilities as well as rights, thereby feeding back into and expanding traditional conceptions of citizenship, to illuminate the most intimate corners of the private sphere. At the same time it projects the intimate on to the global canvas, through, for example, trans-national campaigns for sexual rights. The term nicely captures how citizenship's territory extends beyond the conventional public sphere so that our understanding of public citizenship as both status and practice has to be grounded in an understanding of its roots in intimate citizenship. However, following the distinction made in Chapter 1, I would argue that intimate citizenship only constitutes a sphere of citizenship *practice* when its claims are made in the public sphere(s). In other words, I would see 'the intimate' as the proper object of citizenship struggles but not as the locus in which those struggles take place, which is not to deny the political nature of conflict within the intimate sphere nor the relevance of that conflict for the capacity to act and claim rights as a citizen.

Economic (in)dependence

Linking the physical and economic dimensions of autonomy as a precondition of citizenship is the issue of mobility both between and within societies.[22] According to Doreen Massey 'the limitation on women's mobility, in terms both of identity and space, has been in some cultural contexts a crucial means of subordination' (1994, p. 179). Within societies, mobility can represent access to key spaces in the public sphere. An important medium is transport. Research in the UK shows that women, and in particular disabled women and African-Caribbean women, are less likely than men to have a driving license and to own or have independent access to a car. This can have important implications for women's confidence in going out after dark, particularly in the case of Black women who may also fear racist attacks.[23] The central importance of public transport to women's access to the public sphere has been underlined by Hamilton and Jenkins: 'transport is an essential part of women's lives: it determines access to a wide range of resources including employment, child care, education, health and the political process'.[24] The question of transport is particularly vital for women on low incomes, whose 'time poverty' is compounded by poor public transport (Turner and Grieco, 2000), and for women living in rural areas. A study in Northern Ireland found a degree of 'mobility deprivation' which 'has a huge impact on rural women's quality of life' (Kilmurray, 1991). Lack of mobility can limit severely rural women's opportunities for economic and political involvement when these are located at a distance from their homes.

For disabled and older women, whose mobility is impaired by an inaccessible physical environment, the constraints on public participation are that much greater. Disabled women have voiced particular concern about personal safety issues associated with transport difficulties (Ellis, 1995). British research has shown how even the most basic right of political citizenship – the vote – can effectively be denied to disabled people. More generally the autonomy of disabled people, the majority of whom are women, is systematically undermined in those countries that have failed to create the conditions necessary to promote their independent living and their effective citizenship.[25]

Migrant women's autonomy is particularly vulnerable at the intersection of the public and private, even though for many women migration may ultimately open the way to greater personal autonomy and economic independence.[26] As indicated previously, under immigration laws, they tend to be cast as economic and legal dependants without separate public status, with implications for their rights of entry and subsequent social, legal and economic rights. This makes them vulnerable to economic and sexual exploitation and to possible deportation. This, in turn, can have the effect of locking them into violent marriages where their right to stay in a country derives from their relationship to their husband. The position in much of Western Europe is summed up in a report to the European Parliament:

> The dependency of women on men – husbands or other family members – in immigration policy is encouraged by the restriction of rights for newly arrived spouses and by governments' attempts to limit family reunification ... As most black and migrant women today gain entry on the basis of family reunification, they gain their rights to residency indirectly. It is usually a few years before they can enter the job market; obtaining social security and insurance benefits, too, is dependent on a husband's legal status ... Women are coerced to 'toe the line' [by, sometimes violent, husbands] by the threat of deportation at any moment during the transitory time between arrival and finally getting full residency.[27]

In the British context, an Equal Opportunities Commission report argues that the construction by immigration law of women as dependants has served to reinforce that dependency by undermining their labour market position.[28] This represents in more extreme form the more general longstanding construction of women as the actual or potential dependants of male breadwinning citizen heads of household: another example of how the private affects the public. If women are constructed as the economic dependants of men, confined more or less to the private sphere, key aspects of their relationship to citizenship tend to be mediated through those men who enter the public sphere on their behalf. The power of the discourse of economic dependency is such that it can, as observed earlier, shape the lives of, for instance, lesbian or African-Caribbean female heads of household. Moreover, it continues to frame women's access to the labour market and to social rights even when total economic dependence is no longer the norm (Sørensen and McLanahan, 1987).

The sexual division of labour, responsibility and time

The construction of women as dependants is closely linked to the sexual division of labour, which governs the relationship of both women and men in heterosexual couples to the public sphere. It also structures the relationship of both women and men to time which is, itself, a crucial resource for citizenship as both a status and a practice. A wide range of literature from the countries of the First, Second and Third Worlds attests to the ubiquity of a sexual division of labour which, while different in its details in different contexts, is characterised by the allocation to women of the unpaid domestic tasks of housework and childcare (the tasks of reproduction), whether or not they are also engaged in paid employment (the sphere of production). A four-nation study of East and West, for instance, concluded that, variations notwithstanding, the one constant finding was that 'the primary burden of domestic labour falls upon wives' (Stockman *et al.*, 1995). While I will draw primarily on evidence from Europe and North America, it should be noted that for women in Third World countries the physical toll of domestic work, particularly when combined with work outside the home, can be immense.[29] Emphasis on the ways in which women worldwide are caught within the web of the sexual division of labour should not, however, be interpreted to mean that its impact and meaning is necessarily the same in all contexts (Mohanty, 1988).

There is some disagreement in the burgeoning literature on the domestic division of labour as to how, or even whether, it is responding to changes in male and female paid employment patterns, partly reflecting methodological problems with comparisons of different surveys. On balance, the picture painted by research in Western Europe and the US is one of some movement but without any fundamental disturbance of the traditional skewed pattern of responsibilities in the domestic sphere. The conclusion reached by Warde and Hetherington (1993) from their own study, together with a research review, is that there has been very little change overall in the unequal contributions of women and men over the previous two decades. Drawing primarily on research in the US, Blumberg underlines the 'extent to which housework is the aspect of family life most resistant to changes in the woman's economic and labour force position' (1991, p. 9). In the UK context, surveys suggest that the limited increase in male involvement in a range of household tasks has lagged well behind changes in attitudes in this area.[30] The evidence generally regarding the effect of male unemployment on the domestic division of labour is mixed, but on the basis of a review of UK and US research, Lydia Morris concludes that 'there is little evidence of any renegotiation of gender roles'.[31]

In the former Communist regimes women's full-time participation in paid work was not reflected in any increase in male participation in unpaid domestic work. The result was a heavy double burden of paid and unpaid work, exacerbated by the strains of shopping in 'shortage economies'. Although, officially, women were deemed full and equal economic and political citizens, their heavy domestic duties spelled a different reality.[32] Since then, the gender disparity in the overall work burden has, if anything, increased (UNDP, 1999; Pascall and Manning, 2000). In Western Europe, the European Commission observes that 'the greater commitment of women to paid work has not been accompanied by any significant redistribution of household labour, with women performing more than 80% of household tasks in all but the Nordic Member States, Sweden and [perhaps surprisingly] the United Kingdom' (European Communities, 2000).[33] The evidence from many countries suggests that to the extent that men's share of routine domestic work has risen in the face of female (full-time) employment, it reflects more the reduction in women's input than the (smaller) increase in men's.[34] The time men spend looking after children has increased, but the time women spend has increased even more (Sullivan and Gershuny, 2001).

A relatively optimistic reading of the changes that are occurring can be found in the work of Oriel Sullivan and Jonathan Gershuny. The former argues, in relation to the period 1975 to 1997, that the increase in men's participation in domestic work has been 'significant' and that there has been 'a clear reduction in gender inequality in the performance of some of the normatively feminine-associated tasks'. Nevertheless, she concedes that the change 'is clearly slow, and the outcome is still highly unequal' (2000, p. 451). Gershuny (2000) posits a model of 'lagged adaptation' on the part of men to women's labour market participation, as they gradually transfer a small amount of their time from paid work to unpaid domestic tasks. Rubery *et al.*, however, suggest that the adaptation 'may remain partial and incomplete' (1998, p. 201).

To the extent that research does reveal an increase in male participation in domestic work, it suggests a tendency to cream off the more enjoyable tasks. Moreover, most importantly, women retain the overall responsibility for housework and childcare, for patching together the 'crazy quilt' which keeps the household going, while men tend simply to contribute assistance, sometimes on an *ad hoc* basis.[35] Thus, the time, responsibility and energy (physical and emotional) that women have to devote to the household is open-ended in a way that is rare still for men, with implications for women's health and for their freedom to act as citizens in the public sphere.[36]

The lack of boundaries around unpaid domestic work is particularly marked where care is provided for adults, an aspect of the domestic division of labour which tends to be ignored in time-use studies (Land, 1991). With the exception of spouse care, women predominate among those providing care in the home for adults and, in particular, among those providing the most intensive care. Research demonstrates the hard, time-consuming work, often requiring constant presence, that is involved.[37] Analysis of the British General Household Survey shows that a third of female co-resident carers were working a total of 100 hours or more a week compared with a fifth of male carers (Arber and Ginn, 1995). For disabled women themselves, caring and domestic tasks can be doubly time-consuming.

Time as a resource for citizenship

Time is a highly gendered commodity that impacts on and is mediated by the public–private divide (Glucksman, 1998; Pillinger, 2000). Although time-budget studies suggest some convergence in the overall hours – paid and unpaid combined – worked by women and men in the West, there is still a strong perception that for many women the total workload is both higher and less easily containable because of the open-ended and fragmented nature of domestic work and the responsibility for it.[38] This tends to leave them more susceptible to 'time poverty', often reflected in tiredness among women with caring responsibilities, especially if also working full-time, as Black women are more likely to be in the UK.[39] For disabled women, the strain can be even harder. The time-consuming and time-fragmenting nature of women's domestic work has implications for their leisure time (Deem, 1996), which, in turn, can shade into their domestic work (Siranni and Negrey, 2000). (Indeed, the British *Social Trends* survey discusses household tasks under the heading of 'home-based leisure activities'.) Even in retirement, women's association with domestic work can continue to constrain their ability to exercise their 'citizenship in the third age' (Gilleard and Higgs, 2000, p. 49).

Fraser (1994) highlights the distribution of leisure time as a crucial dimension of gender equity. What is at issue is not only the actual gendered division of time (in terms of quality as well as quantity, reflecting the degree to which it is fragmented), but also the relationship between and value accorded public and private uses of time (Balbo and Nowotny, 1986; Hernes, 1987). Paid work offers rewards and opportunities that unpaid work does not (Bryson, 2000; Gershuny 2000). Likewise, the differential treatment of time devoted to unpaid care and paid work by social security systems impedes women's access to social citizenship rights.[40] Time is also itself a resource that either constrains or facilitates choices in a highly gendered way. It is a resource that has profound implications for the ability of women and men to act as citizens in the public sphere and to pursue the process of self-development identified earlier as critical to effective citizenship.[41]

It is important to emphasise that it is men as well as women's citizenship that is at issue here. On the one hand, formal equality for women in the public sphere, in its economic, social and political manifestations, is undermined by the weight of their responsibilities in the private. Their fragmented lives are out of sync with the demands of public citizenship; their opportunities for self-development are infringed by the demands of domestic time. On the other hand, men are privileged by this situation in a way that gives them a headstart over women in the public sphere and that enables them to maintain their power over women inside and outside the home. Janet Chafetz describes the vicious circle, criss-crossing the public–private divide, thereby set in motion: 'Male power at the macro level sustains a gender division of labour that supports male micro power, which, in turn, further reinforces that division of labour and therefore male macro power'. The process is sustained, she argues, by men's 'definitional power' which, in legitimising the sexual division of labour at an ideological level, serves to obscure and to perpetuate gender inequalities.[42] The advantage that men gain over women is a collective one which can affect even those women living without men, such as lesbians and lone mothers, who are not personally caught up in the sexual division of domestic labour. To the extent that men are serviced by women and that the public sphere of the economy and the polis is organised on the presumption that they are, men operate with a competitive advantage over women.[43] Lone mothers can be particularly disadvantaged without even the limited time contribution from fathers in two-parent families.[44]

For women with money (which includes very few lone mothers) time poverty can be relieved to a greater or lesser extent by buying the time of other women, which has become an increasingly common strategy in recent years in a number of countries.[45] Generally, as noted earlier, it is the time and labour of poor women and, in many countries, of predominately Black and/or migrant women that is being bought, creating a complex nexus of gender, class and racialised relations and disrupting conventional public–private boundaries. Private domestic work has become the main source of employment of migrant women in Europe (Anderson, 1997; Kofman *et al.*, 2000). From a wider perspective, Arlie Hochschild (2000) identifies a series of 'global care chains' forged by global capitalism (see also Williams, 2001). These involve three sets of care-providers: the migrant woman herself, the woman who cares for her children back home and the third who cares for the latter's children. The racial dimension is emphasised by the European Women's Lobby:

> Black and migrant women's organizations point out that, as white women improve their situation through campaigning and social change, some of the roles that they leave behind are being filled by black and migrant women. As a result, many white women across a range of EU Member States have black and migrant women nannies, maid servants, cleaners and domestics (1995, p. 268).

The cleavage that this can create between Black and White women's status as citizens has been particularly visible in North America, illuminating the ways in which the racialised and gendered dimensions of the division of labour re-inforce each other. In a study of the racialised practices of Canadian domestic placement agencies, Bakan and Stasiulis illustrate how they act as effective gatekeepers to female migrant labour seeking domestic positions as a means of entry. They argue that: 'the increasing demand for in-home child care in de-veloped capitalist states and the similarly increasing but highly regulated supply of Third World migrant women together work to structure and mediate citizenship rights across and within national boundaries'.[46] By virtue of their employment in the private spheres of other women, who are thereby freed to participate in the public sphere and enjoy its associated rights, migrant women themselves are 'rendered largely invisible' and unprotected by citizenship rights (Stasiulis and Bakan, 1997, p. 132; Anderson, 1997, 2000).

As it is women who usually organise and pay for substitute care and domestic work as part of their general organisational responsibilities, while continuing to undertake some of their traditional tasks, this strategy rein-forces rather than challenges the domestic sexual division of labour (Gregson and Lowe,1994a, b; Anderson, 1997, 2000). Men's domestic absenteeism remains undisturbed. Moreover, this particular private resolution of the problem of time poverty (as opposed to one that tackles the sexual division of domestic labour head on) is, by definition, open only to those who can afford it. Where pay and conditions are poor, it is at the expense of less privi-leged women.

This underlines the importance of public support for the care of children and others as a key element in the equation of women's citizenship. The quality and quantity of such public support impacts on women's 'private' responsibilities. Public provision is crucial, in particular, in addressing class differentials and the needs of lone parents. It can also mitigate the burden created by the impact of the sexual division of labour. Cross-national research suggests that the extent to which the domestic division of labour impedes women's entry to, and progress in, the public sphere is affected by the nature of the public provisions available.[47] Thus, for instance, in their comparison of the gendered division of labour in Australia and Finland, Bryson *et al.* observe that the well-developed childcare provisions in the latter country 'not only underpin far higher levels of paid labour than in Australia, but also effectively reduce the burden of unpaid work' (1994, p. 124). Finnish women's gender position is, they argue, modified by their rights as citizens. For Southern European women, the brake on their participation in the public sphere, created by a highly gendered sexual division of labour, is generally more marked in the absence of a decent social infrastructure of support.[48]

Public provision does not, though, of itself, strike out the competitive advantage which the domestic division of labour gives to men, for housework still has to be done and children still need to be cared for outside of working hours.[49] Therefore the importance of an extensive and high quality social infrastructure of support notwithstanding, neither private nor public strategies to reduce the impact of the sexual domestic division of labour obviate the need to tackle directly the domestic division of labour and of responsibility itself. Until this happens, women's ability to enjoy full and equal access to the polity and to the labour market, together with the social rights that derive from the latter, will be compromised. Men meanwhile continue to abscond from their 'private' obligations as citizens, thereby freeing them to develop as public citizens.

The same conclusion has been reached by a number of feminist theorists.[50] It has also informed thinking at the European policy level.[51] A declaration on equality between women and men in political and public life from a European Ministerial Conference made the explicit link with citizenship, endorsing 'the view that *de facto* equality between women and men in the world of work, in the family and other areas of life, will not come about without the full sharing between women and men of the duties and responsibilities that democratic citizenship implies' (1986). Cass has developed the point, turning the argument on its head with the claim that men should not be 'accorded full citizenship if they do not fulfil their responsibilities for caregiving work'.[52] Of course, another issue is how they fulfil those responsibilities. Unfortunately, we cannot assume that men's participation in the family is always a blessing. Men may not have a monopoly on violence and sexual abuse within the family, but there can be no doubt that they are its main perpetrators. The evidence about the extent of violence and abuse suggests a degree of caution is in order when claiming greater male involvement in parenting as 'the' solution, although research does suggest that men who are more involved in the process of care from early on are less likely to be perpetrators.[53] For some women there is also the fear that they may lose what power they have in the private sphere without gaining power in the public and that, in the event of divorce, they may then lose their children.[54] Nevertheless, as an EC report, which acknowledges such fears, concludes, '*increasing men's participation in the care of children is important for women, children and men themselves.* Men's increased participation is a condition of equality for women in the labour market'.[55]

The reference to the importance for children and men themselves, as well as for women, serves as a reminder that care should not simply be regarded as an impediment to public citizenship, thereby denying the value of care itself to citizenship.[56] Indeed, Hirschmann argues, from a standpoint of care as central to citizenship obligation, that 'starting from an assumption of connection and obligation allows the claim that men must also care for children to enter public and political discourse' (1996, p. 172). Sevenhuijsen draws the policy implication that 'government should see its primary task as enabling men to build intimate and caring relationships with women and children, by making this possible in terms of time, space and material resources' (1998, p. 111).

As this advice indicates, the fulfilment of men's care responsibilities is not simply a matter of private choices (see Chapter 7). The citizenship of women and men is constructed through the interaction of the public and the private. Social, economic and cultural constraints can make it difficult even for those who are committed to making changes in the domestic sphere. Nevertheless, the balance of the evidence suggests that, so far, it is women who have been doing more of the changing. If the private side of the domestic division of labour does not adequately accommodate the changes taking place in the public side, women will continue to suffer time poverty, with possible implications for their health and for their ability to participate as active political citizens; witness the experience of many Central and Eastern European women under the former regimes (Einhorn, 1993; *Social Politics*, 1995).

'One hand tied behind us'

The pivotal role of the sexual division of labour in constraining women's opportunities as political citizens was highlighted some years ago by Stacey and Price who maintained that 'as long as the attitudes to women's status and obligations and the division of labour in the home remain unchanged, it is difficult to believe that gender will be irrelevant to politics' (1981, p. 151). Key here are men's attitudes towards their partners' proper roles and responsibilities. Cross-national research indicates that men can actively impede women's participation in politics of any kind.[57] One woman community activist has spoken of men's resentment of their partners' community involvement, resulting sometimes in emotional and physical intimidation (Haq, 1994). There are echoes here of the difficulties encountered a century ago by the suffragette Hannah Mitchell, who wrote, 'No cause can be won between dinner and tea, and most of us who were married had to work with one hand tied behind us, so to speak ... domestic unhappiness, the price many of us paid for our opinions and activities, was a very bitter thing' (1977, p. 130).

Time has been identified as a critical resource for both formal and informal forms of politics; lack of it constrains the exercise of women's political citizenship.[58] Although men's formal paid work hours tend to be longer, they have greater freedom over how they spend their time outside those hours than do women who, as observed already, cannot clock on and off from their caring responsibilities. It is not just a matter of the amount of time but also of being able to control the availability of one's time. This is one reason why, as we shall see, participation in informal rather than formal forms of politics is easier for women. Moreover, longer hours in the workplace can also shade into more political activities whereas women's political participation is more likely to take place in unpaid time and separate from the workplace. This is exemplified, in particular, by the greater ease with which men can involve themselves in trade union activities.[59]

A series of political and academic studies of women's political participation in a number of countries has identified the domestic division of labour as a critical brake, particularly in the case of mothers of young children.[60] In her overview of women and politics, Vicky Randall concludes that 'women's responsibility for small children is perhaps the key constraint on the "supply" of women for leading political positions, determining both the age at which they become available and the qualifications they bring' (1987, p. 323). Care of older people is also likely to place restrictions on political activity. Randall's thesis has received support from a large-scale and detailed study of political participation in Britain. Although this found that overall the gender gap was modest, it was substantial for married (although not lone) parents during early to middle age, when married women with children 'are the least participatory relative to men in the same circumstances' (Parry *et al.*, 1992, p. 147).

Phillips (1991), too, places great emphasis on the role of the sexual division of labour in 'engendering democracy'. However, she argues against a determinist link between it and the level of women's representation in political elites, noting that there will always be some women who overcome the obstacles. Nevertheless, her argument is that if we take a broader view of democratic participation than just elite representation, then it is key to women and men's political equality. Moreover, women should not have to face such obstacles and make such sacrifices in their personal lives in order to be full political citizens.

Phillips also points to the progress made in the Scandinavian countries without the achievement of equality in the domestic division of labour. Siim (1994, 1999, 2000), on the basis of empirical evidence of current trends in women's political participation in Denmark, argues that motherhood is no longer a barrier to Danish women's active political citizenship. From a theoretical perspective, it is her view that an overemphasis on the sexual division of labour runs the risk of underestimating women's potential as political agents and the independent impact of politics itself. I would certainly agree that one should not discount factors in the political system itself in terms of both their direct and indirect impact on women's political participation, for this underlines again the interaction between public and private. Nor would I want to deny women's potential as political agents. Nevertheless, it is arguable that what has happened in Denmark is evidence in support of a link (albeit, I agree, not a deterministic one) between domestic labour and women's political involvement. The imbalance in the sexual division of labour is not quite as marked as in many countries, and there is a much better infrastructure of public support for caring work. This in turn has facilitated women's labour market participation.

The economic key to women's citizenship

The significance for women's citizenship of their labour market position is, in part, a reflection of the extent to which paid employment has replaced military service as the 'key to citizenship'.[61] It is the key to financial independence (full or partial) both directly through the wage and indirectly through the social citizenship rights linked to employment status which still tend to reflect male employment patterns. Paid work (outside the home) represents an important locus of social participation, which many women value, as well as a source of self-esteem, which, as argued earlier, is important for the fulfilment of women's potential as citizens.[62] Although the evidence with regard to the relationship between women's labour market and political participation is mixed and does not point to any automatic link, paid work outside the home can also encourage politicisation and open up political processes and the wider 'public' sphere (particularly through trade unions). It can also provide access to the kinds of skills needed for advancement in conventional forms of politics.[63] Thus paid work can be important as a route to both social citizenship rights and active political citizenship.[64]

The interaction of the private and public is especially important in understanding women's economic position. On the one hand, the sexual division of labour in the private sphere means that women and men enter the labour market on very different terms. British longitudinal research has, for instance, attributed a decline during marriage in women's occupational status relative to their husbands' to the gendered domestic division of labour.[65] On the other hand, labour market structures and processes, which still by and large disadvantage women relative to men, feed back into the private sphere. The domestic division of labour is reinforced by the labour market's economic logic, which encourages the prioritisation of male paid work as more profitable to the family as a whole.[66] Conversely, women's labour market participation can translate into greater power and financial equality within the home (Crompton, 1997; Laurie and Gershuny, 2000). Commentators vary in the relative weight they give to the public and private obstacles to women's economic advancement.[67] What matters here though is the fact and nature of their interaction, which is in turn, as noted earlier, influenced by public policies and provisions.

The level and character of women's labour market participation is, therefore, a product of both 'supply' and 'demand' factors. On the face of it, the increased demand for female labour, translated into higher female economic activity rates in the post-Second World War era, might seem to suggest that women now enjoy a much firmer economic base upon which to construct their citizenship. While this is to some extent true, it would be misleading to overstate the degree of progress made. The historical data suggest that, in terms of actual hours devoted to paid work, the increase in women's economic activity has been exaggerated as, until the late 1980s at least, full-time employment was replaced by part-time in a number of countries.[68] This reflected both the demands of employers and the domestic constraints imposed on women for whom part-time work represents an attempt to juggle the demands of paid and unpaid work, usually after a period of absence from the labour market after a child's birth.[69] Where both parents work full-time, research suggests that fathers rely on mothers' flexibility, hard work and sacrifices to negotiate the competing demands of family responsibilities and the workplace.[70] Male employment patterns thereby once more both sustain and are sustained by the domestic division of labour.

Although children only inhibit labour market participation for a limited phase of the life-course, their impact on women's economic position is often long term (Rake, 2000). Moreover, care of older people also acts as a constraint. A significant minority of women is combining care with paid employment, often with great difficulty and involving very long hours of work. At the same time, a number of studies have demonstrated the 'depressing effect of caring responsibilities on the level and nature of the labour force participation of carers', especially those providing the more intensive forms of care.[71] In some cases, the demands of male partners or adult children for servicing, mean that women continue to work part-time, even after children have grown up.[72]

Part-time work is largely a female phenomenon, although the proportion of women working part-time varies considerably between countries as do the number of part-time hours worked.[73] The association of part-time work with women on the one hand and with inferior pay and employment conditions on the other means that it all too often spells labour market marginalisation, and associated exclusion from social rights, for many women.[74] This marginalisation is aggravated by the lack of prospects for training and advancement associated with part-time work and the long-term impact it can have on women's economic status.[75] Part-time work, moreover, rarely provides women with sufficient resources to promote genuine economic independence and shift the imbalance of domestic economic power. Despite this, research suggests that, in some countries, many women prefer part-time to full-time work, reflecting the unequal burden of domestic work. The point is that the problem lies not in part-time work *per se*, but in the low status attached to it, the conditions under which it is frequently performed and the fact that it is women who have to 'choose' it because of the constraints upon their time.[76]

Female part-time workers' economic marginalisation reflects, in particularly acute form, the broader vertical and horizontal segregation that characterises women's employment in countries throughout the world. The tendency is for women and men to work in different sectors of the labour market and for the former to be less likely to move into the upper reaches of job hierarchies. This tendency persists worldwide, with 'new contours of seg-regration' emerging even as some old ones dissolve and women do break into higher level jobs.[77] Gender segregation also spells greater vulnerability to unemployment in most countries (with a few exceptions, including the UK) and to low pay, as women's average wages continue to lag behind those of men.[78] Disabled women and some groups of minority ethnic women are particularly at risk of low pay.[79]

The gender pay gap derives from women's position in both public and private spheres and the assumptions that underpin the relationship between the two. The wage itself, both, historically and today, is, in Joan Acker's words, 'a gendered phenomenon' (1988, p. 480). The ideology of the family wage, earned by a male breadwinner to support his family, still runs deep so that even where women's earnings are making a substantial contribution to household income, there is a tendency to devalue them and to treat them as marginal.[80] Women's economic opportunities are shaped by the ideology, irrespective of the presence or absence of a 'male breadwinner' capable of earning a family wage, with implications for their ability to earn their financial independence. If women are constructed as secondary earners, it makes it more difficult for those women who have to support themselves (and any dependants) to do so.

One of the most marked recent labour market trends is, however, a growing occupational class cleavage within the female workforce as success-ful, better-educated, 'career' women (who may nevertheless find their advance checked by a 'glass ceiling') and part-time, low-paid female workers increasingly occupy different employment worlds.[81] Employment and occu-pational class status is only one source of divisions within the female work-force. Minority ethnic and migrant women may experience racialised as well as gendered forms of job segregation and tend to be more vulnerable to unemployment.[82] For many Asian and migrant women, full-time work takes the form of homework which is associated with particularly low pay and lack of employment rights.[83] There is some evidence also that Black women are more likely to experience sexual harassment in the workplace (Doyal, 1990; Murrell, 1996). Sexual harassment is widespread; it can shade into racial and homophobic harassment.[84] Discrimination on grounds of 'race', disability or sexual orientation can compound gender discrimination, which is still preva-lent, as well as divisions between women themselves.[85]

The poverty gender gap

At its most acute, women's inferior economic position translates into what has been dubbed 'the feminisation of poverty', although their vulnerability to poverty is not a novel phenomenon (Lewis and Piachaud, 1992). Women's position in the private sphere of the home and the public sphere of the labour market, and consequently in welfare systems, meshed together in the web of the discourse of female economic dependency, spells an increased risk of poverty in most countries. In North and South, East and West, poverty is more likely to wear a female than a male face, although to a rather lesser extent in Scandinavia. According to the UN, 'the majority of the world's 1.3 billion people living in poverty are women'.[86] As the price of caring responsibilities, poverty tends to be most prevalent among lone mothers, most notably in the UK and US. Racially disadvantaged and disabled women, are particularly vulnerable.[87] The economic disadvantages which women face during their working lives then feed into inferior pensions and poverty in old age.[88]

To the extent that official statistics reveal the gender poverty gap, they tend to underestimate it because estimates, which take the family or household as the basic unit of measurement, are unable to take account of the hidden poverty that can result when income is not distributed fairly within the family.[89] Moreover, women's financial poverty interacts with their time poverty, as they take on the main burden of managing poverty and debt and of mediating with welfare institutions, as part of their general responsibility for money and household management in low-income households. Women thus act as the shock-absorbers of poverty, with implications for their mental and physical health (Payne, S., 1991; Graham, 1993).

Poverty is corrosive of citizenship both as a status and a practice, undermining rights and the ability to fulfil the potential of citizenship.[90] As one woman contributing to a published discussion on women and poverty observes, 'being poor has a negative impact on your self-image and self-assertiveness. It also saps your energy.' Nevertheless, she points to the women on her estate who are trying to assert their needs and 'build networks of mutual support' (Stone, 1986). Even though women on low incomes often play a leading role in community-based politics, generally the obstacles to political participation are harder to overcome for those without money than those with (Ward, 1986; Phillips, 1999). The combination of time and financial poverty means that the political handicaps tend to be greater for poor women than poor men at every level and more markedly the higher up the hierarchy of power one moves.

Conclusion

The significance of the traditional construction of rigidly separated public–private spheres for women's citizenship has been the focus of this chapter. The intention has been to argue not for the dissolution of a public–private distinction but for its rearticulation. This rearticulation involves the de-gendering of the meaning of the public–private divide;

acknowledgement of the ways in which its two sides interact with each other; and recognition of its fluid and political nature. This helps to illuminate the different relationships that men and women (and different groups of each) have to the public and private spheres and to the paths between the two, to the advantage of men's citizenship claims and the disadvantage of women's.

I have used two main examples to illustrate the implications for women's citizenship. The first concerned the ways in which women's autonomy, articulated both as bodily integrity and economic independence, can be undermined (or promoted) through the interpenetration of public and private. The politics and theory of public citizenship, as traditionally understood, cannot therefore be divorced from the tendrils of 'intimate citizenship' with which it is intertwined. The second centred on the sexual division of unpaid work and time within the private sphere of the home which, it was argued, moulds female and male access routes to the public sphere, and in particular to the labour market which holds the key to many social citizenship rights. At the same time, the domestic division of labour and time, together with the overall level of 'private' caring responsibilities, can itself be shaped by employment practices and government policies and by the extent to which these practices and policies acknowledge and value care as itself an expression of citizenship. The extent of its impact on women's access to the public sphere therefore differs between societies and between different groups of women. While the fact of the interaction between public and private is a constant, the nature of that interaction and its effects are not, varying both between and within societies and over time. The implications for women's citizenship, both as a status and a practice, will be explored in greater depth, from a policy perspective, in the next two chapters.

6

Women's Political Citizenship: Different and Equal

The theoretical dichotomies, explored in the previous two chapters, are reflected in dilemmas of policy, practice and politics, which face women fighting for full inclusion in citizenship as both a status and a practice. It is citizenship as a practice that is the focus of this chapter. To reframe in the political arena the question posed in Chapter 4: is the objective to acknowledge *difference* through the development of concepts and practices of citizenship that take into account the dominant sexual division of labour within the private sphere and that value women's continued caring role within it? Or is it to promote *equality* by challenging the conditions, in both private and public spheres, that curtail women's rights and opportunities as political citizens? Alternatively, following the theoretical position I have outlined, is it possible to promote women's political citizenship by developing policies and practices that draw on both approaches?

My starting point is a brief overview of women's participation in formal and informal politics. I then consider whether the kind of maternalist arguments discussed in Chapter 4 are helpful to the understanding and construction of women's political citizenship. The case is made for recognition of women's informal political participation as a *different* form of political citizenship. On its own, though, there is a danger that 'different' spells 'unequal and marginal'. I therefore also make the case for opening up formal politics to women in their diversity and for improving the links between formal and informal modes of politics, so as to promote women's *equal* political citizenship. Thus, by arguing for a combination of strategies that straddle the theoretical dichotomies explored earlier, I hope to point the way towards a more woman-friendly political citizenship.

The masculine sphere of formal politics

The gap between women's formal political status and their actual power in the formal political sphere is summed up in the Human Development Report 1995: 'political space belongs to all citizens, but men monopolize it' (UNDP, 1995, p. 41). According to the Inter-Parliamentary Union, women held, on average, only 14 per cent of parliamentary seats at the end of 2001 (IPU, 2001). Progress has been greatest in the Nordic countries where the figure was 39 per cent. Representation at government level is even lower: globally, in 1998, only 8 per cent of government ministers were female (UN, 2000). In the EU, about a quarter of all government ministers were women, with Sweden the sole country to achieve gender parity but Denmark not far behind (European Database, 2000). In much of the EU, women's representation is even lower at local/regional level, with the UK, France and Italy standing out as exceptions (Henig and Henig, 2001; Squires and Wickham-Jones, 2001).

At supra-national level, the parliamentary figures look slightly better. After the 1999 European elections, women represented 31 per cent of the European Parliament compared with an average of 16.4 per cent for the national parliaments within the EU (IPU, 2001). There is a strong commitment within the EC to increase women's participation in political decision-making. Progress has, however, been uneven: the upper echelons of the EC's own decision-making structures remain male-dominated and Black and migrant women remain largely outside them.[1] Parallel to women's under-representation in the upper echelons of formal politics, is a similar, or sometimes even more marked, under-representation in other theatres of power and influence such as corporate bodies, trade unions, companies and the judiciary.[2] The same applies at the level of the global institutions discussed in Chapter 2.

Depressing as the facts and figures of women's political representation are, they do represent some advance. In the preface to the second edition of her study of women and politics, Randall notes that during the five years since the first edition, there had been, with some exceptions, 'steady if unspectacular progress ... in women's rates of representation in both summit political bodies and those political arenas and related occupations that feed them' (1987, p. xi). Since then, though, progress has been uneven. According to the IPU, the turn of the twenty-first century was marked by increases in the number of women winning parliamentary seats world-wide. Progress has been particularly notable in parts of the south. As against that, there have been some serious setbacks, particularly in the former Communist societies, despite women's active involvement in the struggles for democracy.[3] This is symptomatic of a wider pattern in which women's active involvement in transitions to democracy is not subsequently rewarded by real political power. An exception is the new South Africa where, even though they are still very much under-represented, women have increased their political presence and influence significantly since the end of apartheid.[4]

Women's experience in many of the new democracies underlines the distinction that has to be made between the level of women's political representation and of their political activity. There has been a tendency in the past to read off one from the other so that the conventional wisdom has been that women are less interested than men in fulfilling their potential as political citizens. Whatever the position in the past, the contemporary evidence suggests that any gender gap in political activity, from the vote to more active forms of political participation, is, in many countries, modest and by no means constant.[5] Thus, increasingly, the issue of women's political citizenship is less of a quantitative one and more to do with its status and visibility. The constraints on women's political activity outlined in the previous chapter, combined with barriers in the political system itself, still serve to depress their political potential so that much of what they do do is marginalised. That so many women overcome these constraints, at least to some extent, is a testimony to their commitment (not necessarily conscious) to the ideals of political citizenship.

The feminine sphere of informal politics

This commitment is particularly marked in the sphere of informal politics, which embraces both local community-based action and national and international 'new social movements'. The invisibility of much of women's political activism is, in part, a reflection of the tendency to define politics within the narrow terms of the masculine sphere of formal politics. Once such a restrictive definition is abandoned, it has become almost an alternative conventional wisdom that informal politics represents a more feminised political sphere. At first sight this belief appears not to be born out by research into general political participation, which does not, in fact, reveal a greater propensity amongst women than men to engage in informal and protest politics. Yet, studies and more journalistic accounts, which start from the other end of looking at local community action itself, all tend to support the conclusion of a European study that 'women are often a *driving force in local action*'.[6] I suspect that the disjunction arises from the fact that the kind of unstructured and fluid activism highlighted by more localised studies escapes the net of even relatively broadly trawled research into political participation. Norris (1991) makes a similar point but then downplays its significance in reaching her conclusion, based primarily on evidence about participation in protest rather than local community politics, that there is no real gender gap here. Following on from my argument in Chapter 1 that such community activities do nevertheless constitute an important form of political citizenship, I will concentrate here on this dimension of informal politics. The distinction I am drawing is not, however, a hard and fast one, for locally based community action can easily shade into the kind of protest politics which are more likely to be identified in studies of political participation.

There is perhaps a danger of idealising women's community activism, often born of deprivation and disadvantage and sometimes exhausting, dispiriting and burdensome (Mayo, 1994). Moreover, not all such action is necessarily progressive in intent. Nevertheless, the picture that emerges from a variety of accounts is that of a rich and inspiring nexus of citizenship-enhancing activities. A number of British studies have painted a vivid portrait of working-class women organising around issues of daily life, often unsupported by men. The pattern is evident in different configurations worldwide.[7] 'Minority group' women, who are virtually completely absent as one ascends the formal power hierarchy, which favours the privileged on every score, are often, like working-class women, nevertheless politically active. Black (and some other) feminists have drawn attention to the long history of Black women's resistance and have challenged the cultural stereotypes of Asian women as passive.[8] In her study of Black women's organisations, Julia Sudbury uses an explicitly broad definition of politics, rooted in Black women activists' 'everyday theorising', to highlight the extent and range of their political activity. She identifies six arenas: the individual, the family and the Black community, as well as 'those which engage with mainstream power structures: the local, the national and the international' (1998, pp. 225 and 60). Women are also active in the disability and gay and lesbian movements and in campaigns around 'grey power' (for instance, through the Older Women's Network, Europe), despite a tendency for male domination to assert itself in protest just as in establishment politics.[9] More generally, when formal management or paid employment positions emerge, or a protest campaign shifts to the national level, there is an observed tendency for men to take over.[10]

Northern Ireland provides a particularly telling example of the contrast between women's traditional invisibility and lack of power in formal politics and the force of their presence in working-class communities. The independent Opsahl Commission received many examples of how working-class women, both in women's groups and wider community groups, were working within and across communities, to improve conditions and in particular the opportunities open to young people. One witness, for instance, drew the Commission's attention to 'the phenomenal contribution of local women's groups in terms of keeping hope alive within and between divided communities'.[11] Cockburn describes how Northern Irish women's community activism has 'signified politics with a small 'p' mobilizing and challenging big-P Politics as it is normally done', as well as transforming many women's lives (1998, pp. 59–60).

Hyatt has coined the term 'accidental activism' to describe the process through which 'women who previously did not see themselves as in any way political are becoming advocates for social change' (1992a, p. 6). A similar process of '"becoming" an activist' is portrayed in Krauss' study of mothers involved in toxic waste protests, after discovering the impact on their families' health: 'propelled into the public arena in defense of their children, they ultimately challenged government, corporations, experts, husbands and their own insecurities as working-class women' (1998, pp. 134 and 130). Such accidental activists are, Hyatt suggests, the 'active citizens' of deprived communities. Beatrix Campbell likewise paints a portrait of women in 'Britain's dangerous places' as 'a model of active citizenship', maintaining informal networks and community services and generally sustaining 'the personal, public and political lives of these neighbourhoods' (1993, p. 321; 1995). In doing so, she argues, they have broken down the boundaries between private and public space, as they challenge young men's, often threatening, occupation of the latter.

A different politics?

It is primarily (but not solely) as mothers that these women have transgressed the public–private divide in their struggle to protect their families and communities. A cross-national study is typical in its finding that 'concern with the care, health and education of children is a unifying thread' running through women's local action (Chanan, 1992, p. 86). A similar point has been made in relation to African-American women whose community activism has often been prompted by concern for their own children and those in the extended family and community (Collins, 1991; Roberts, 1995). 'Activist mothering' is the term used by Naples to describe the stance taken by the female community workers she studied in the US: 'political activism as a central component of mothering and community caretaking of those who are not part of one's defined household or family'. She illustrates how 'women draw on traditional female identities to justify taking revolutionary actions to improve their communities and the lives of their families', while in the process defying 'the dominant definition of motherhood as emphasizing work performed within the private sphere of the family'. This is especially true of the African-American women and Latinas for whom activist mothering includes the struggle against racism (1998a, pp. 11 and 22; 1998b). Similarly Krauss describes how White working-class mothers' protest against toxic waste was spurred by a traditional understanding of the role of motherhood as 'protector of the family and community'. Yet, in the process 'they developed a public, more politicized ideology of motherhood that became a resource to fight gender and class oppression' and they 'discovered the power they wield as mothers to bring moral issues to the public', exposing the destructive impact of social policies on their children (1998, pp. 140, 148 and 142).

There is a parallel here with the Madres (Mothers) of the Plaza de Mayo in Argentina, and similar groups in other Latin American countries, who occupied public space to protest against the disappearance of their children and husbands. Their powerful protest was made explicitly as mothers and not as women; it was as mothers, fighting to preserve their families, that they felt justified in taking over public political space. In doing so, they 'politicised motherhood' and subverted the boundaries and meanings of the public/private divide'.[12] Behind the self-conscious projection of a traditional maternal role, some of those involved developed more 'expansive', shifting and contested understandings of motherhood, more akin to Naples' 'activist mothering' than traditional maternalism (Stephen, 2001, p. 58; Craske, 1998).

The example of the Madres of the Plaza de Mayo has, nevertheless, been used to effect by contemporary maternalists such as Sarah Ruddick in order to illustrate the potential political force of 'maternal thinking' or values. As observed in Chapter 4, maternalist arguments have been used historically by women to promote both their social and political citizenship. Within the political sphere, two broad approaches can be discerned. The first was to argue for women's accession to full political citizenship on the grounds of the qualities and gifts that they could bring as mothers. The need to preserve those very same qualities as part of women's philanthropic mission was, however, also used to justify opposition to female suffrage.[13] Such arguments were closer to the other strand in maternalist thought, that of republican motherhood under which motherhood was deemed the equivalent of a male civic republicanism grounded in active political participation and the ability to bear arms.[14] Motherhood represented the epitome of difference, for only women, as mothers, could bear the next generation of citizens. However, it was a racialised difference in that typically it was White and not Black women's motherhood which was valued, although African-American women developed their own maternalist arguments.[15]

Within contemporary feminism, Elshtain's work perhaps comes closest to representing the second strand of maternalism. She celebrates mothering and asserts the primacy, dignity and purpose of the private familial sphere in the context of an 'ethical polity', imbued with its values. This is then counterpoised to 'an ideal of citizenship and civic virtue that features a citizenry grimly going about their collective duty, or an elite band of citizens in their "public space" cut off from a world that includes most of the rest of us' (1981, p. 351). Elshtain's idealisation of the private familial sphere and affirmation of a rigid public–private divide is incompatible with my own position.[16] Moreover, an approach that, even if implicitly, promotes motherhood *per se* as a vehicle for political citizenship runs the danger of consolidating women's political marginalisation. As Pateman (1992) observes, women were, in effect, incorporated into the political order on this basis and were thereby subordinated to men. Lip service might be paid to the importance of mothering but political power (including the power to shape the conditions under which mothering takes place) would remain in the hands of the true political citizens. At the same time, the impetus for women's actual political representation would be undermined, while the traditional sexual division of labour would be legitimised.

The other strand in maternalism, which emphasises the qualities that women as mothers can bring to politics, is best exemplified today by Ruddick's notion of 'maternal thinking'. Although Ruddick herself applies the notion to mothers' potential contribution to peace politics rather than explicitly to citizenship, others such as Elshtain and Pnina Werbner have made a more direct connection. The latter argues that 'political mother-hood's' strength has been to define human qualities such as compassion as 'equally foundational in the legitimation of the political community' and in the embodiment of the citizenship ideal (1999, p. 227). Ruddick identifies as a possible 'agent of political change' 'a women's politics of resistance [which] affirms obligations traditionally assigned to women and calls on the commu-nity to respect them ... In the name of womanly duties that they have assumed and that their communities expect of them, they resist' policies or actions that interfere with the fulfilment of these duties (1989, pp. 223–4). The Madres are the prime example of such a politics of resistance.

Ruddick sums up 'maternal thinking' as 'the intellectual capacities [a mother] develops, the judgements she makes, the metaphysical attitudes she assumes, the values she affirms'. This 'maternal perspective' is developed by mothers 'acting in the interests of preservation and growth'. Elsewhere, she writes that 'nonvio-lent action, the ideals of renunciation, resistance and peacekeeping, govern maternal practice'. These attributes and values, she argues, need to infuse the public sphere in the interests of our children and of peace. Mothers, she con-tends, 'might bring to *any* politics capacities honed in their work – for example, attentiveness, realism and a welcoming attitude toward change'.[17] Ruddick is, in all her writings, careful to make clear that maternal thinking is more of an ideal against which mothers measure themselves (and often fall short) than an actual achievement, so that she explicitly distances herself from claims of female moral superiority. She also, rather confusingly, denies that it is the sole preserve of actual mothers (or even parents), even though it arises out of actual child-rearing practices and even though she believes that women, as daughters, expe-rience maternal thinking differently from men. Thus, she suggests that men can be mothers but because 'in most cultures the womanly and the maternal are conceptually and politically linked', it follows that 'to elucidate maternal think-ing is also to elucidate a "woman's way of knowing"' (1989, p. 41). Thus, for all her provisos, it is difficult not to read her thesis for the incorporation of maternal thinking into the political arena as an idealisation of the mother–child relationship, which is then offered as a political model. As such it has been the subject of considerable criticism.

The critique of maternal thinking as the key to a feminist model of citizen-ship has been spearheaded by Dietz who argues that 'women are not uniquely identified by maternal thinking, nor does maternal thinking necessarily promote the kind of democratic politics social feminism purports to foster'. Indeed, she suggests that the opposite is true in that the inequalities of power and exclusiveness associated with the mother–child relationship are inimical to the principles underlying democratic citizenship.[18] Lynne Segal makes a similar point, noting how parents frequently appeal to their children's interests to justify class and race privilege. She is also critical of the essentialising tendencies and the association with pacifist values of what she dubs 'maternal revivalism' (1987, p. 145). In privileging the status of motherhood, maternal thinking is in danger of exaggerating the differences between men and women and of minimising the differences between women themselves.[19] While it is true that the majority of women do experience motherhood, it is not necessarily their only or even primary defining characteristic, particularly once their children have grown up. Other forms of caregiving can also provide the impetus for collective action (Hooyman and Gonyea, 1995). Moreover, as argued in Chapter 3, identities are multiple and shifting and motherhood represents but one identity, the power of which varies over the life-course.

Furthermore, a growing minority is choosing not to have children and to the extent that lesbians are less likely than heterosexual women to choose and be able to pursue motherhood, a narrow maternalism promotes heterosexist assumptions (Carabine, 1992). The Icelandic Women's Alliance, for example, in its espousal of maternalism, has tended to sideline childless women and, in particular, lesbians. Its essentialist celebration of women's superiority, while initially liberating, has, some would argue, been limiting and divisive in the long run (Björnsdóttir and Kristmundsdóttir, 1995). In situations of conflict, a narrow maternalist politics can render vulnerable other women who take political action as *women* (Pettman, 1998). Yet, at the same time as it privileges mothers over other women, maternal thinking also runs the danger of marginalising mothers politically within the existing sexual division of labour, in the name of promoting their values. Naples, for instance, suggests that by appealing 'to their identities as mothers and community caretakers', the community workers she interviewed 'did circumscribe their self-presentation as political actors, thus limiting their efficacy in the formal political arena (1998b, p. 299). This is also one of the lessons drawn by a number of feminist commentators sympathetic to the stand taken by the Madres of the Plaza de Mayo and similar groups. The moral power they exerted as mothers so successfully did not translate into equivalent political power as democratic structures were re-established.[20]

Beyond maternalism

It is for reasons such as these, that a number of feminists, sympathetic to some of the values promoted by maternalism, are now arguing for a non-maternalistic conceptualisation of difference in politics around the broader notion of care and an ethic of care, discussed in Chapter 4. Diemut Bubeck (1995b), for instance, describes care as a resource for political citizenship on the grounds that private concerns, values, skills and understandings can all enhance public practices. This was a common theme emerging from Fiona Mackay's interviews with female Scottish local politicians. They spoke of the transferability to and positive impact on the political arena of 'the practical strategies and intellectual skills which arise from the practice of caring such as attentiveness, connectedness, responsibility and reciprocity'. Mackay suggests that Sevenhuijsen's notion of 'judging with care', in which political judgement is informed by such values and practices, offers a potential lever for introducing an ethic of care into the formal political arena. Central to such judging, Sevenhuijsen argues, is the balancing of the demands of equality with human individuality and diversity.[21] Others have argued also that such a broader conceptualisation can better accommodate difference and diversity in rethinking citizenship (Sarvasy, 1994; Sarvasy and Siim, 1994). By shedding some of the tenets of maternalism as such, this looser interpretation of this strand of maternalism represents the weaker end of the spectrum of difference feminism. Broadened out to embrace an ethic of care, in combination with that of justice, rather than confined to 'maternal' values, it points to a possible formulation of a politics that values women's experiences and attributes without essentialising them.

The picture I am painting is that of an informal politics in which women are the primary actors, operating at the interstices of the public and the private, motivated often initially by personal, domestic concerns, frequently, but not necessarily, affecting their children. These concerns propel them to move into the public sphere to work with others, especially if public policies are impinging on their private space.[22] As they express in the public arena needs that derive from their various caring responsibilities and campaign for change and new rights, they are, in effect, giving practical expression to the synthesis of the ethics of care and justice explored in the previous chapter. As they make public experiences of sexual oppression and domestic violence, previously quintessentially private, they are contributing to the construction of notions of 'intimate citizenship', again subverting the public–private divide. Through such activities they become active citizens in the 'politics of needs interpretation' (Fraser, 1987), forging practices of 'everyday-life citizenship' (Joaquim, 1998, p. 79). Indeed, in Denmark a new term 'everyday makers' has been coined to refer to '(women) citizens actively engaged in politics in relation to local everyday life problems' (Siim, 2000, p. 165).

At the same time, they are forging a different way of doing politics – generally less hierarchical, more participatory and committed to democratic practices, more informal. Often they are also trying to inject enjoyment and fun into the political process as a way of generating energy and harnessing enthusiasm.[23] This is not an argument for women's inherent political superiority.

Rather, again, it represents a position at the weak end of the difference spectrum (discussed in Chapter 4), in recognition of the approach that many women take to local political activism, reflecting their experiences rather than fixed character traits. At a time of growing disenchantment with conventional politics in many countries, there is growing recognition in some quarters of 'the need to overcome traditional modes of political organization both within and beyond the nation-state. The value of politics lies in the process as well as the result' (Miliband, 1994, p. 6). As the pioneers of alternative modes of political organisation, within and beyond the nation-state, women, working within the spaces where public and private worlds collide, are providing new role models for active political citizenship. In doing so, they are contributing to a more pluralist framework of citizenship, open to traditionally excluded groups.

The evidence from studies of women's community activism exemplifies and reinforces the case made in Chapter 1 for a broad definition of political citizenship, which embraces informal modes of politics. Their work on behalf of their families and communities feeds what Robert Putnam has dubbed 'the capillaries of community life' (1993, p. 41). At the same time, it can transform their own sense of themselves as political actors, individually and collectively, as they acquire new knowledge and skills. A prime example of both points is provided by the role played by women in British mining communities in the fight against pit closures. It was the women who sustained the communities through the long period of hardship and many were changed irrevocably as a result. Lovenduski and Randall were told in Wales that 'even though the battle was lost and the women returned to their kitchens – these were new women. Poems, songs and stories written by miners' wives and daughters as a result of the fearful events of the previous 12 months bear witness to their permanent politicisation'.[24] In Castleford, Yorkshire, some of the women set up a women's centre, which went on to provide degree-level education.

Education is another important focus for the exercise of women's citizenship. Its value to women themselves is underlined by Deprez and Butler (2001). They recount the story of women activists who campaigned for low income women's access to post-secondary education as part of Maine's welfare-to-work programme. A survey of women who benefited indicated that, for many, involvement in post-secondary education had enhanced their sense of self-esteem and independence and had changed their lives. Others point to women's role as citizens in enhancing the education of children. Siim, for instance, highlights citizen participation in schools and child-care facilities as a primary example of how, in Denmark, women are 'at least as active as men' in the '"small" democracy' of everyday life (2000, p. 137; 1998). Outside the formal school system, Mirza and Reay theorise the implications for citizenship of their exploratory study of Black supplementary schools in London, mainly run by women.[25] They argue that, through this work, Black women act as 'collective transformative agents' to create a '"third space" of strategic engagement', disruptive of the public–private divide. In this 'third space', 'Black women educators' acts of belonging and sustenance of community demonstrate new and inclusive forms of "real citizenship" that deserve to be recognised' (2000a, pp. 59 and 70).

The importance of women's activism to the construction of their political citizenship cannot be underestimated. However, it can only be part of the full citizenship equation for, on its own, a different politics runs the risk of being marginalised as an unequal politics. In the former Yugoslavia, for instance, the maternalist stance adopted by a women's peace group, symbolised by its name, Mothers for Peace, was challenged by a feminist group, Women in Black. The latter declared 'we wanted our presence to be visible, not to be seen as something "natural" as part of a woman's role'.[26] There is still a tendency to downgrade women's activism and to pigeonhole its politics of care as 'women's issues'. The danger is that the economic sexual division of labour, which this reflects, is then reinforced by a political sexual division of labour of formal and informal politics in which stereotypes about women's 'natural' contribution are reinforced. More fundamentally, women's political empowerment through informal politics is not the same thing as gaining power in the wider society, even though it can effect change at a local level and can achieve political influence, broadly defined (Dahlerup, 1986). The Northern Ireland Women's Coalition has pointed to how 'more and more women are breaking out of the mould of community politics ... into central spheres to which they have previously been peripheral' because 'no matter how successful one's community group is, its autonomy and its policy agenda are always limited' (Fearon, 1999, p. 160). The conclusion reached by Stacey and Price in their classic study of women and power, echoed in subsequent studies, therefore still holds good: 'if women wish to make changes in the societies they live in, they must seek and achieve power positions. It is essential that women should enter the political arena since the societies are all male dominated, for men certainly cannot be relied upon to initiate or carry through the necessary changes'.[27]

A more inclusive formal politics

My argument in this next section therefore is that, if political citizenship is to promote women's equality as well as their difference, women will also have to engage with the formal political system. The value of informal politics does not provide an alibi for the continued under-representation of women and 'minority groups' in the formal structures of power. A more inclusive formal politics will require changes in the formal political system itself so as to make it more open both to individual women and to the kinds of informal modes of politics in which many women will probably still prefer to participate.

The case for women's formal political participation and representation

First, though, I will examine the arguments upon which the case for women's increased political representation rests. Derived from the general literature on women and politics, they are important also to the case for women's inclusion as full political citizens. These arguments tend to cluster around three main propositions: that women constitute a political interest which should be represented in the decision-making process; that society will benefit from the attributes which women can bring to the formal political sphere; and that their gross under-representation is an affront to the ideals of democracy and justice. The first two coalesce around the discursively appealing particularist notion that women will 'make a difference', which was important, for instance, in mobilising women around the new Scottish Parliament (Mackay, 2001; Stephenson, 2001). The third appeals to universalist ideals.[28] Which form of appeal is more likely to be successful partly depends on the political and social context (Bacchi, 1996).

Implicit in the argument of Stacey and Price is an assumption that women have specific interests, different from, and potentially in conflict with, those of men, which need to be represented by women themselves in the decision-making process. Indirect representation of their interests by others is not sufficient. Phillips conceptualises this position as that of a 'politics of presence', which challenges, as inadequate on its own to overcome political exclusion, a faith in the representation of interests through a 'politics of ideas'. Women's perspectives need to be articulated directly in political debate and decision-making (1994, 1995). The case is spelt out by Anna Jónasdóttir who argues that women:

> must be visible politically as women, and be empowered to act in that capacity, because there is the continual possibility (not necessity) that they may have needs and attitudes on vital issues which differ from those of men. This does *not* imply that women have no needs and preferences in common with men. Nor does it imply that these differences only reflect biological distinctions, but it *does* imply, as extensive facts in contemporary Western societies also indicate, that women and men are beginning to constitute themselves as two basic societal corporations' (1988, p. 53, emphasis in original).

Jónasdóttir is, nevertheless, sensitive to some of the problems in representing women as a single interest group. Not only do women's 'objective' interests often differ on the basis of the dimensions of difference spelt out in Chapter 3, but also they do not necessarily subscribe to similar ideologies or share the same priorities just because they are women. This then raises questions such as how interests are constituted and articulated in the political process; which women's interests are being represented by female politicians; and what are the mechanisms of accountability through which these interests can be articulated.[29]

Following my argument in Chapter 3, there is a case for identifying women's shared exclusion from full citizenship as a common interest. This is consistent with Jónasdóttir's stance, which focuses on women's shared 'formal' interest in access to political power rather than on the content of any shared interests. Cockburn has taken the argument further by suggesting that questions of content are best described as 'women's concerns'. In this way, it is possible to identify 'issues that bear on women without in any way presupposing what position any given group of women would take on them' (1995, p. 69; 1996c). Thus, for instance, Siim (2000) notes that in Scandinavia women are not united in the position they take on child care policy. From a slightly different angle, Young (2000) deploys the notion of 'social perspective' to denote the ways in which our social situation shapes how we approach an issue, but makes clear that our social perspective does not determine the content of the position we take. Others have identified the sexual division of labour as a key source of conflict between the group interests of women and men (Sapiro, 1981; Lovenduski, 1986) and the continued impact of the domestic side of the division on women's access to power (Mackay, 2001). Beyond these broad statements of interest, it has to be recognised that not only will different groups of women have different priorities about women's concerns, but that these may come into conflict. The danger is that the interests and concerns of working-class, poor and 'minority group' women will continue to be marginalised, if it is primarily White middle-class women who are able to break into the male political citadel (Hoskyns and Rai, 1998). This does not mean, though, that there will not also be occasions when their interests and concerns coincide and when coalitions of interests can be constructed, as argued in Chapter 3. The point is that *a priori* assumptions about a commonality of concerns tend to reflect those of relatively powerful groups of women and therefore are always open to challenge.

To the extent that it is possible to identify a set of shared women's concerns in any situation, the twofold question then arises as to whether women in power (should) see it as their responsibility to represent them and as to what impact they are able to have. In other words, following Phillips, what are the implications for the policy-based 'politics of ideas' of women's political presence? The evidence with regard to the first question is, not surprisingly, mixed, reflecting different countries and contexts. A Canadian study suggests that feminist consciousness is a stronger predictor than gender of the views of parliamentary candidates on gender-related issues (Tremblay and Pelletier, 2000). Yet women who enter politics are by no means all feminists and many do not enter politics in order to fight for women's interests (Sapiro, 1981). Nevertheless, it is also the case that many do, for instance in Norway where there was a concerted feminist campaign to increase women's political representation in order to empower women as a group rather than simply to enhance the position of a number of individual women (Skjeie, 1993). Even here, though, the power of party allegiance has inhibited cross-party alliances between women. The grip of party discipline is particularly tight in the Westminster parliament. Thus, although a significant proportion of New Labour women MPs elected in 1997 identify themselves as feminists and as having a responsibility to articulate women's concerns, they have done so mainly behind the scenes rather than vote against the Government.[30] Earlier research by Norris and Lovenduski (1995) revealed a very modest gender influence in the stance of female politicians. They suggest that gender has had a greater impact on the actions and attitudes of politicians in the US where a growing gender gap in women's voting behaviour has meant a greater tendency to construct women as an interest group.[31]

One reason why even women sympathetic to feminism do not always want to be seen as speaking for women is the tendency in some countries for gender equality and 'women's issues', concerned with the sphere of reproduction, care and welfare, to be relegated to the second division of politics. This can be seen as damaging to the careers of ambitious women and also as reinforcing the notion that such issues do not need to concern men. Female politicians can thus face a double bind: even if they are willing to risk personal marginalisation by promoting 'women's issues', they might be seen as contributing to their political ghettoisation. On the other hand, to avoid identification with such issues can be interpreted as colluding with their second-class political status. Ironically, the politicisation of welfare in the face of neo-liberal assault has perhaps helped to ease this dilemma in some countries, as has the greater saliency of gender politics.

As to the impact that women are able to have on political agendas and outcomes, again the picture is mixed. Women politicians cannot necessarily achieve women-friendly policies, designed to promote women's concerns, even when they try to do so. Indeed, it has been suggested that in Australia and Canada their presence has been used as a smokescreen for policies harmful to women (Sawer, 2000; Tremblay and Pelletier, 2000). Nevertheless, the Scandinavian evidence (and increasingly that of other countries) does suggest that they can have some impact, especially on the political climate within which policies are developed.[32] According to Hege Skjeie, in Norway, 'within political life women now take an active part in creating those definitions of reality on which efforts to effect changes rest ... Women's inclusion is perceived as having caused changes in party attitudes on a wide range of political issues' (1993, p. 258). However, when it comes to actual policy prescriptions, there can be significant differences, reflecting party allegiances. Within the European Parliament, there is also some evidence that above-average female representation has had an impact (Hoskyns, 1996).

The lesson commonly drawn by observers is the need for a 'critical mass', if women are to have a real impact on the political arena and if their concerns are not to be marginalised. A 30 per cent participation threshold was suggested as critical by the UN Commission on the Status of Women. Drude Dahlerup has developed the argument to assert that it is 'critical acts', designed to improve the situation of women as a group, that are more important than a critical mass as such (1988). Nevertheless, the larger the critical mass of women, arguably the greater the scope for critical acts and the greater the likelihood that women will feel confident to exploit that scope. Also, the more likely it is that the mass will reflect a diversity of women's interests; whether it does or not will depend, in part, on the nature of the policies designed to increase women's political representation. Even if we have to treat the notion of the representation of women's interests and concerns by women with some scepticism, it is reasonable to suppose that there is a greater likelihood that they will be promoted in the formal political arena, if women are there than if they are not. If women are absent, their perspectives will not be adequately taken into account (Phillips, 2000; Young, 2000). As Phillips concludes, 'the crucial requirement is for women's political presence: which is not to say that only women can speak on "women's" issues, that women must speak only as a sex' (1991, p. 167). Indeed, while as a feminist I would hope that women who do gain power would see it as a vehicle to advance the interests and concerns of women more widely, thereby advancing the broader cause of female citizenship, I am also conscious of the dangers of requiring female politicians to carry a set of responsibilities not expected of their male counterparts (Phillips, 1991). Women members of the Scottish parliament have found that this can create a 'burden of, often contradictory, expectations', as they 'were expected to bring something new to politics, while at the same time proving that they were equal to men' (Stephenson, 2001, p. 205).

The critical mass argument is also used with reference to one element of the second strand of the case for women's political representation: that women's qualities and ways of working would help to change the culture of politics, thereby improving the political process. This thesis is propounded by the European Network of Experts 'Women in Decision-making':

> A balanced representation of women and men at all levels of decision-making guarantees better government. Because of their history as a group, women have their own and unique perspective. They have different values and ideas and behave differently. Increased participation of women in decision-making will create a new political culture and shed new light on how power should be exercised. Women attach great importance to the quality of contact between people. They are less individualistic than men (1994, p. 8).

Put so baldly, the argument is in danger of appealing to an essentialist construction of women as politically superior beings, an ideal to which real live female politicians do not necessarily conform. Nevertheless, there is some evidence to suggest that women do sometimes attempt to bring the more co-operative ways of working developed in informal politics into formal politics, thereby helping to create a more open political culture, which is in turn less hostile to women.[33] A good example is provided by the new legislative bodies in Scotland and Wales, which reflect women's attempts to create less combative political institutions: 'women have written optimistically about the new culture of politics that the influx of women has created' (although the less confrontational political culture has meant reduced media interest) (Stephenson, 2001, p. 200; Gill, 1999). Joyce McMillan writes of the seriousness with which many of the new female Scottish parliamentarians attempt to create 'a new style of politics' and of their consciousness of 'grassroots pressure to work in a more practical, problem-solving way and to avoid pointless party confrontation' (2001, p. 40). They demonstrate how a critical mass of women can bring their experience of a different politics to bear on the formal political sphere and the masculine political culture that permeates it. The tenacity of that culture, however, should not be underestimated, especially in the context of the Westminster model, which does not provide 'a safe space' within which to practice a different style of politics (Childs, 2002; Mackay, 2001).

Again, this argument can be interpreted as a weaker version of the maternalist thesis discussed earlier. Gould suggests that the attributes that women bring to politics, which she emphasises are historically contingent rather than essentially feminine, represent an important element in the 'democratic personality'. As such, she argues, if injected into the public sphere, they could lead to more participatory and co-operative forms of politics.[34] Bacchi contends, in similar vein, that 'it is possible to insist upon the necessity of "different" political values without suggesting that women embody them' (1990, p. 253). More broadly, it is argued that the experiences that women bring to politics are different to those that men bring, thereby helping to change the political agenda (even if not as radically as many would like), as witnessed, for example, in Norway and Scotland (Skjeie, 1993; Squires and Wickham-Jones, 2001). Again to quote the European Network report: 'Everyone in public and political life knows that, if women participate in decision-making, issues that have been neglected in the past suddenly surface' (1994, p. 8). These are primarily social issues, affecting the quality of family and community life, as well as more explicit gender equality issues. More neutrally, it is pointed out that the absence of a large tranche of the population reduces the talent available to public life.

While there are elements of the first two propositions that strengthen and help to popularise the general case to be made for women's political representation, they run the risk of setting women a set of standards over and above those applied to men in order to justify their claims for a political presence. Ultimately, therefore the case has to be underpinned by a universalist rather than a purely particularist argument. This derives from the equal rights of all members of a democracy to participate in the decisions of that democracy in the name of justice. This argument goes to the core of the case from the perspective of women's citizenship: women's equal participation at all levels of political decision-making is essential to their right 'to achieve full citizenship' (European Network, 1994, p. 7; EWL, 2001). According to Voet this is critical to 'active and sex-equal citizenship' (1998, Ch. 11). Moreover, the legitimacy and authority of a democracy is undermined if its institutions do not reflect the diversity of society, with implications also for the representation of 'minority groups' (Kymlicka, 1995; Norris and Lovenduski, 1995). According to Diane Sainsbury, Swedish women's success in increasing their political representation followed a switch of argument from that of the representation of a special interest to one that appealed to 'democratic principles and equal rights' while at the same time redefining 'women's issues' as party issues (1993b, p. 279). This change of strategy brought women and 'women's issues' into the mainstream of the political parties.

Opening up formal politics to women

The Swedish example underlines the important role played by women themselves in opening up formal politics to women in Scandinavia and more widely (Lovenduski and Norris, 1993). Denmark, Scotland and the US are examples of countries in which feminist groups have played a crucial role (Siim, 2000; Mackay, 2001; Bryson, 1999). In Sweden, women who had already acquired positions of power employed their political agency in the pursuit of carefully planned strategies to open up the political process to other women (Sainsbury, 1993b). The success of such strategies suggests that, the constraints on women's political participation in the private sphere notwithstanding, there is much that can be done to lower the barriers within the public political sphere itself which serve to exclude women. Randall (1987), who provides an overview of these barriers, concludes that they probably act as equally powerful deterrents as the sexual division of labour. Moreover, the two interact to maintain formal politics as a largely male preserve in most countries.

Norris and Lovenduski (1995) provide a threefold classification of strategies to change this: the meritocratic, affirmative action and radical models. The *meritocratic* model exemplifies a narrow technical equal opportunities approach. Useful and popular reforms they identify within this model are improved training programmes for potential female candidates (of particular value in 'developing' countries according to USAID [2000]) and help with personal campaign expenses. However, they also emphasise the model's limitations, as does the EC's White Paper on European Social Policy which states that 'experience now shows that formal equal opportunities alone do not automatically result in either equal treatment or proper representation of women at decision-making levels. Closer examination is required of the entrenched institutional and cultural barriers that inhibit or prevent the proportional representation of women in public and political bodies' (European Commission, 1994, pp. 43–4). It is these barriers that the affirmative action and radical models address.

The *affirmative action* model's main instruments are targets and quotas for women's representation at different stages of the recruitment process. It is the setting of quotas (either by law or internal party rules) that has proved particularly controversial, not least because they highlight that a woman's gain is a man's loss. Nevertheless, according to Squires and Wickham-Jones the comparative evidence shows that both legally imposed and internal party quotas 'have had an unambiguously positive impact on the level of women's representation' (2001, p. 46). The lesson drawn by the Human Development Report 1995 is that, while women's political advance is best promoted through broad-based economic, political and social change, 'numerical goals and timetables and affirmative action by states can provide a critical take-off point for accelerated progress' (UNDP, 1995, p. 109). Thus, despite the resentment quotas can generate and the unease that some women themselves feel about them (Mackay, 2001), there is a strong case for their transitional use as the most powerful tool available to redress the gross gender imbalance that continues to scar most political elites.[35]

A more fundamental strategy has been adopted in France where this imbalance has been particularly marked. In 2000 'parity' legislation was passed, requiring parties to present equal numbers of women and men on candidate lists for municipal, regional, European and Senate elections under the proportional system (but not for majoritarian Parliamentary elections). This resulted in a leap in the proportion of women elected to local councils from 22 to 47.5 per cent (Squires and Wickham-Jones, 2001).[36] Parity has divided French feminists, some of whom fear that it essentialises gender differences (Siim, 2000). In a comparison with Nordic quota systems, Skjeie and Siim argue that 'parity is both the means and the permanent goal', whereas quotas tend to be regarded as primarily a temporary 'means to equal citizenship' (2000, p. 355). They also suggest that parity is less easily linked than quotas to strategies to increase the representation of marginalised 'minority groups'.

Parity thus raises in more acute form a general difficulty with all such mechanisms designed to increase women's political representation. Once we move beyond the unitary category 'woman' and bear in mind the difficult questions raised by difference and diversity for political citizenship, their limitations become apparent. Many of the arguments for quotas to achieve gender parity could also be applied to the question of the proportional representation of 'minority groups' such as ethnic minorities and disabled people and arguably they should be.[37] However, we are then confronted with some of the same difficulties about the potential essentialising of group identities noted in Chapter 3 in relation to Young's proposals for a group-differentiated citizenship. There is no clear answer to such dilemmas, but they cannot be glossed over in an avowedly pluralist feminist citizenship politics. Phillips proposes as a working principle that 'when a particular characteristic has come to matter (meaning that it substantially dictates the fortunes of the people whom it defines) then there should be some mechanisms to ensure that group's proportional representation' (1991, p. 154). When the characteristic no longer 'matters', the mechanism would be withdrawn. However, Phillips herself recognises the problems in deciding what 'matters'; moreover, while this approach avoids freezing group identities for all time, it still, inevitably, separates them out along different axes of disadvantage.

Affirmative action policies need therefore to be framed with the knowledge that what is being affirmed is only one facet of group members' complex identities (Werbner, 1996). In her subsequent work, Phillips explores these dilemmas further and concludes that the most appropriate mechanisms for promoting a politics of presence will vary according to the nature of the excluded group.[38] With regard to women, she suggests the dilemma is less critical for, since they form such a large group, they will not be misconstrued as representing a single, undifferentiated, interest. However, this is perhaps to underestimate the tendency for White, middle-class, non-disabled, heterosexual women to rise to the surface of formal politics where they may be seen as speaking on behalf of 'women', so that 'the politics of presence' still remains an issue within the female constituency.

In some ways, an effective affirmative action approach would be more radical in its effects, in the sense of challenging the male power monopoly head on (and therefore more likely to face resistance), than would the strategies included under Norris and Lovenduski's third, *radical*, model. This involves, where necessary, reform of the electoral system and of parliamentary institutions and culture. The radicalism of such reforms lies in their wider implications for the political process. First, the voting system has been identified as a key variable in a number of cross-national studies: women are twice as likely to be elected under proportional representation (PR) than under a simple majority system and their chances are particularly high where there are party-lists and multi-member constituencies.[39] Such systems are also more conducive to the representation of 'minority groups', as they encourage an appeal to different sections of the electorate (Squires, 1999; Sawer, 2000).

The second prong of the radical reform model identified by Norris and Lovenduski addresses the running of the political system on the assumption that those who participate in it have no family responsibilities, to the obvious disadvantage of women. Their study found 'overwhelming bi-partisan support among candidates for improving childcare facilities in parliament, as well as changing the hours of parliamentary sittings' (1995, p. 247; Mackay,

2001). Recommendations for 'family-friendly' working hours and facilities have 'become standard in proposals to reduce obstacles to women's access to parliamentary careers' and to local government.[40] They have been taken on board in Scotland and Wales (Gill, 1999; Mackay, 2001). Parliamentary reform of this kind is one practical example of how politics can be reshaped to fit women rather than the other way round (Jones, 1988, 1993). However, it is important that, at the same time, it challenges the assumption that it is only women whose political lives must be tempered by their family commitments. Thus, for example, Georgina Ashworth suggests that such changes are important not just because they will make it easier for women to pursue a parliamentary career but also because they will set a good example by promoting 'better fathering and domestic sharing' (1992, p. 29).

It is not, though, only practical reforms that are needed to make political institutions more 'woman-friendly'. Research and experience suggest that women are also deterred from entering the political system by the masculinist, combative, alienating culture which often permeates it.[41] Where this is accentuated in a system, like the British one, run on two-party lines, electoral reform might help. However, in the longer term the best antidote to a masculinist culture is the 'critical mass' of women identified as essential earlier. At a more fundamental level, it involves the task set by Jones of stripping political authority of its masculinist connotations in the name of what she describes as 'compassionate authority' (1993).

Opening up formal to informal politics

Even if the formal political system is made more 'woman-friendly', it will only be a minority of politically active women who will be able to enter the political elites. Moreover, it is likely that many women will continue to prefer to engage with informal forms of politics, especially so long as the sexual division of labour ties them more closely than men to the private domestic sphere. However, as noted earlier, this important mode of political citizenship tends to be marginalised in both political theory and practice. The final element of the equation of a more woman-friendly construction of political citizenship is therefore to reconstruct the relationship between formal and informal political institutions and processes so that the former can be better grounded in and more accountable to the latter.

For feminists who enter the formal political arena, continued links with a vibrant wider women's movement outside help them to remain in touch with their feminist roots. Such links are important both in counteracting the pressures to conform with the institutions they set out to challenge and in promoting both accountability to and the influence of the wider women's movement on the formal political process, a lesson which Scandinavian feminists have applied.[42] Moreover, according to Skjeie and Siim, 'the key to more inclusive citizenship in Scandinavia undoubtedly has been the interaction of women's political mobilization "from below" – in social movements, voluntary organizations, and through feminist activism – with the political integration "from above" through political parties and institutions' (2000, p. 357).

At the same time, better links between informal and formal political institutions might encourage more women to make the transition from one to the other (Rooney and Woods, 1992). Opening up formal to informal modes of politics would serve to legitimate and enhance the latter as a form of political citizenship. As a group of women from North Belfast put it: 'We are involved with politics with a little "p" on the ground, but we get no recognition for it from the politicians who are involved in politics with a big "p". There needs to be recognition for those engaged in politics with a little "p"' (Pollak, 1993, p. 12). Likewise, participatory research in Scotland has identified a demand for the recognition of community action as an important element in Scottish politics (Gray, 1996). In both Northern Ireland and Scotland women have been instrumental in lowering some of the barriers between formal and informal politics (Russell *et al.*, 2002). In Northern Ireland it has been claimed that 'the gulf between women's under-representation in the formal political system and women's contribution to informal politics is literally being "bridged" through the rise of The Women's Coalition and The Women into Politics Programme' (Women into Politics website). Both have helped to overcome fear of politics with a big 'p'. The Coalition works across the formal/informal politics divide and was instrumental in the establishment of a Civic Forum as part of the Northern Ireland Agreement to provide 'a good avenue of communication between elected representatives and representatives of community-based organisations' (Fearon, 1999, p.138; Roulston and Davies, 2000). Likewise with the establishment of the Scottish Parliament, 'women campaigned for structures which would provide greater access to government and the policy-making process for individual women and diverse groups of women'. This contributed to the new parliament being charged with a 'responsibility to promote openness, participation and consultation' (Mackay, 2001, p. 214; McMillan, 2001).

The greater the under-representation of marginalised groups in the formal political arena, the more important it is that their voices can nevertheless be heard in that arena. Hilary Wainwright sees opening up formal politics as the pivotal mechanism for 'new forms of democracy' which, she argues, combine 'the representation of individual but socially and economically unequal citizens with the representation of groups through which citizens organize to overcome their unequal social position' (1991, p. 74). She proposes a partnership between formal political institutions and community groups or social movements which enable the latter to have an input into the political process at local and national level. Wainwright suggests that the women's committees established by the former Greater London Council and some other British local authorities provide an example of such a partnership. Through the use of open meetings, consultation exercises and co-options, these committees made a concerted effort to involve marginalised groups of women and thereby provide a link between them and local government.

Although an enthusiastic supporter, Wainwright has no illusions about some of the difficult problems the women's committees raised. In particular, she acknowledges how they became the forum for a divisive identity politics.[43] They also highlighted the difficulties associated with the representation of group interests, particularly by non-elected individuals who were not necessarily 'representative' of the communities on whose behalf they were expected to speak. Inevitably, they tended to draw on already established groups and networks, thereby marginalising even further those whose interests are not expressed in any organised way, in particular women living in poverty. Wendy Stokes (1995) suggests that this last difficulty could be addressed by a more proactive strategy of encouraging groups to organise around shared concerns. This might involve fairly intensive community development work deploying some of the lessons learned from user or citizen involvement schemes.[44] Lovenduski and Randall (1993) also draw attention to the dangers of such initiatives being marginalised within local government and their consequent inability to meet raised expectations. Nevertheless, they identify a number of achievements, not least the precedent set by such attempts to forge new relationships between formal and informal modes of politics. They were particularly important in placing on the local political agenda lesbian issues previously treated as 'private' (Cooper, 1992/3, 1993). In Scotland, where 'a belief in the permeability and amenability of the local state persists', they helped to effect real change (Breitenbach *et al.*, 1999).

More radical attempts at opening up formal politics through the development of participatory forms of democracy can be found in South America, most notably Brazil, where the Workers Party (PT) has developed participatory budgets and planning processes in municipalities in which it has held power. The flagship is Porto Alegre, where it is estimated that more than two thirds of city residents have had some involvement in the budget process since 1989 (*Red Pepper*, March 2001, p. 12). Institutions of community participation have been designed to 'establish a permanent mediation and interaction' between municipal administrative agencies and community organisations (Santos, 1998, p. 469). These experiments have been described as marking 'a break from the old idea of politics as exclusive negotiations between a lucky few' (Chavez, 1999, p. 21) and the 'emergence of a new type of citizen' through a process which 'begins to approximate 'a more genuinely democratic conception of the public sphere ' (Baierle, 1998, pp. 135 and 133).

Although women's participation is low in the more formalised structures of participation relative to that in community associations (Santos, 1998), Fiona Macaulay (1995) points to a number of positive implications for women. While the mechanisms vary between municipalities, with some more radical than others, a common pattern has been the establishment of a women's council or secretariat to provide channels for the articulation of the views of women's organisations in an advisory 'forum for the representatives of civil society'. She suggests that the municipal governments have 'responded to women's practical and strategic needs in a variety of ways' including through a central focus on the politics of everyday life, the decentralisation of services and attempts at the reappropriation of public space by women and other marginalised groups. In Santo André, for example, a feminist geographer was invited to draft a new city plan from a gendered perspective, which was then debated in a women's forum of some 800 women brought together from existing women's groups in the city.

Another attempt at breaking down some of the barriers between formal and informal politics, although in more conventional form, can be identified within the European Commission. Jane Pillinger details some of the ways in which the Commission 'has opened its doors to women' through, for instance, networking and practical support to women throughout the EU to set up networks and exchanges. According to Catherine Hoskyns, it is now possible to identify a fluid women's European policy network, albeit one biased towards more elite groups and with inadequate representation of 'minority group' women and women in poverty.[45] This has helped to keep the Commission in touch with (some) women organising outside the formal political arena, exemplifying the value to feminism of close links between those inside and outside the formal political structures.

Conclusion: towards a woman-friendly political citizenship

Kathleen Jones has formulated the dilemma facing a feminist rearticulation of political citizenship as 'how to recognise the political relevance of sexual differences and how to include these differences within definitions of political action and civic virtue without constructing sexually segregated norms of citizenship?' (1988, p. 18). In this chapter, building on my earlier argument in Chapter 1, I have attempted to resolve this dilemma by arguing for a threefold approach. This (i) defines 'political action and civic virtue' in a way that gives due value to the informal 'different' politics which are often the expression of women's political citizenship; (ii) nevertheless emphasises the importance of the representation of women in their diversity as equals in the institutional political arenas in which decisions are made, with implications for the routes into and the organisation and conduct of those arenas; and (iii) squares the circle by proposing a rearticulation of the relationship between formal and informal politics, so that those who opt for the latter can nevertheless influence the former and those who choose the former are not cut off from the concerns and demands articulated in the latter. In this way, I have tried to make clear that the politics of women's political citizenship is not just about the advance of a minority of women into the political elites dominated by men but about the genuine empowerment of a much wider group of female citizens. Both as a status and a practice, the political citizenship of women in their diversity would be enriched.

Central to this approach has been an appreciation of the pivotal position occupied by women at the interstices of the public and the private, often attempting to bring to bear on a politics of rights and justice, the concerns arising from an ethic of care. The interrelationship between public and private also underpins the strategies needed to free women to develop their potential as active political citizens. While this chapter has focused on the obstacles in the public sphere which hold women back, it has to be read in the context of the previous chapter which emphasised the changes needed in the private sphere, most notably in the sexual division of labour. Bridging the public and private are also the constraints discussed earlier on women's physical autonomy and mobility, both vital for political citizenship. 'Minority groups' such as Black women, disabled women and women in poverty face particular barriers, which social and public policy need to address.

This attempt to synthesise equality and difference in the construction of women's political citizenship will not satisfy those who argue for a more radical sexual differentiation of the construction of political citizenship nor those who believe that any reference to claims of women's political difference is dangerous. Nevertheless, it does attempt to steer a path that embraces both an equal rights stance and one that acknowledges the differences that mould men's and women's relationship to politics as well as the differences among women. In doing so, it is again challenging the dichotomous thinking that requires us to opt for one or other strategy and that separates formal from informal modes of politics. In drawing on both universalist and particularist arguments, it is applying the principle of differentiated universalism to the political sphere.

The approach advocated has attempted to address Jones's injunction that 'a polity that is friendly to women and the multiplicity of their interests must root its democracy in the experiences of women and transform the practice and concept of citizenship to fit these varied experiences, rather than simply transform women to accommodate the practice of citizenship as it traditionally has been defined' (1990, p. 811). Even though it argues that some women, at least, must engage with formal politics, it places the onus of change not on individual women, but on men and the political institutions, which they currently dominate. Men's grip on the levers of power in the formal political system and on access to these levers cannot be left undisturbed. The dilemmas I have raised need, therefore, to be presented as facing not so much individual women but the very nature of politics (and of the organisation of social and economic life) itself. To the extent that they challenge men's long-standing virtual monopoly of power, the resistance to change is not to be underestimated.

7

Women's Social Citizenship: Earning and Caring

The welfare state represents an important arena for the expression of women's citizenship both as a status and a practice. It stands as the focus of many of women's citizenship struggles and this chapter begins by sketching out women's role as actors on the welfare stage, both historically and today. It then considers the ambivalent nature of women's relationship to welfare states which, simultaneously, offer a route to independence for some women, yet all too often construct, sometimes the very same, women as the economic dependants of men. The nature of this relationship varies both according to the type of welfare state or regime and as between different groups of women.

The chapter goes on to explore a number of policy dilemmas around women's claim to social citizenship rights which reflect the theoretical dilemmas outlined earlier. These crystallise around the question: who is a social citizen? In other words, are women's claims to social citizenship rights best couched in the language of equality with men, around the 'male' model of citizen-the worker, or in the language of difference, around the 'female' model of citizen-the carer? Or is it possible to transcend the policy dilemma through a model of citizen the worker-carer, which embraces both women and men? More specifically, is the aim to change the nature of social citizenship rights so that earning is no longer privileged over caring in the allocation of these rights? Or is it to improve women's access to and position in the labour market so that they can compete on equal terms with men and can thereby gain the same employment-linked social citizenship rights? Alternatively, is it possible to develop policies and practices that draw on both approaches? These dilemmas are explored in relation to the care of both children and adults by looking at the potential for policies designed to alter the sexual division of labour on the one hand and the balance of public and private responsibility for caring on the other. Running through the chapter is the underlying question of the nature of citizenship responsibilities, raised

167

initially in Chapter 1, leading to a discussion of Citizen's Income and of lone parents' paid work obligations.

Women as actors on the political stage of the welfare state

Historically and today, the struggle for social citizenship rights has represented a key terrain for women as political actors. As campaigners, welfare providers and welfare recipients, they have played a pivotal role in welfare state development so that the welfare state has provided an important stage for the expression of women's political citizenship, underscoring its intersection with social citizenship. There is a substantial literature that illuminates the significant contribution made by women as campaigners to welfare state development, despite the fact that they stood outside the citadels of power. While there is some disagreement as to the extent of their tangible successes in different countries in the face of this power deficit, there is general agreement among feminist historians about the importance of their agency and their impact. Bock and Thane, for instance, in an overview of the development of Western European welfare states, suggest that, even though women campaigners failed to achieve many of their goals:

> democratic welfare states everywhere would look very different if their development had not coincided with the growth of women's movements and women's acquisition of citizenship rights – political as well as social rights. By working with and within other political and intellectual currents of the time as well as by insisting upon their own and unique contributions to society at large, they ensured that women's needs were incorporated into policymaking (1991, p. 15).

Koven and Michel similarly conclude, from their edited study of emergent welfare states in Europe, Australia and the US, that the fact that in most cases women ultimately lacked the political power to forge welfare states that embodied their own visions, does not diminish the significance of their achievements or legacy.[1] One country where they were relatively successful is Sweden. Hobson and Lindholm argue that feminist groups were able, in the 1930s, to seize the opportunity of a period of fluid and permeable politics to promote successfully 'policies that became the core of women's social citizenship in the Swedish welfare state' (1997, p. 498). More recently, they have been mobilising again in the face of the threat to some of the social citizenship rights they helped to achieve. This is but one example of how today, too, much of women's campaigning political activity centres on social (and reproductive) rights, often from a defensive stance.[2] In some cases, collective action to defend or extend social rights stems from women's position as clients of the welfare state. It is women who generally take the main responsibility for the processes of negotiation with welfare state institutions.[3] As argued in Chapter 1, such processes of negotiation can themselves signify a form of political citizenship. On balance, it can thus be said that welfare institutions have offered political resources to women as workers and clients or service users and served to mobilise them as political citizens.[4]

Growing demands for user involvement in the provision of welfare services take further the process of fusion between social and political citizenship. Through user involvement, the politics of needs interpretation can be opened up in a more democratic way to embrace the relatively powerless and to challenge the exclusive power of experts to define needs.[5] Siim suggests that, in Denmark, the strong emphasis on user participation in schools and child care institutions represents a new form of social citizenship that has empowered women by giving them new welfare and participatory rights as citizens vis-à-vis the state' (1993, p. 34; 1998, 2000).

On the other side of the welfare coin, women have also, in the past and today, played an important role as the providers of welfare. In the late nineteenth and early twentieth centuries, a significant number of women participated in the development of welfare services as paid and unpaid workers, representing, Jane Lewis suggests, the expression of 'their conceptualisation of the duties of citizenship'. This contributed to the association of women with matters social, bridging private and public spheres but still subscribing to a gendered division of caring labour.[6] It also in some cases accentuated class and racial divisions.[7] Nevertheless, as Bock and Thane argue, 'these women, together with the broader women's movement, created innovative welfare approaches – such as health visiting in Britain – that prepared the way for future social policies at large, for women's role in them and for a new vision of the relationship between the public and the private sphere' (1991, p. 2).

Sarvasy has used the example of one such innovative approach, pursued by American feminists in the early twentieth century, to make the case for 'citizen social service' as a form of political as well as social citizenship. These feminists attempted to develop a form of citizenship as democratic social service, explicitly distinguished from the traditional philanthropic model. The main example she provides is that of the community-based settlement house which combined social service with wider political participation in a manner that aimed to build a bridge across ethnic and class differences. Sarvasy sees this tradition kept alive today 'in tension with bureaucratic forms of social service' by immigrant communities, services for the homeless and welfare rights organisations (1994, p. 319; 1997). Contemporary examples can be found worldwide. For instance, in First, Second and Third World countries women have pioneered a wide range of alternative health projects that combine self-help and campaigning functions and espouse feminist principles of organising. At times of economic and social crisis, or state withdrawal, it is often women who mobilise to provide an alternative welfare system, performing in the public sphere their 'private' responsibilities such as cooking. Einhorn (1999) warns, though, in the context of East/Central Europe, that this can create a 'civil society trap' in which women's role is marginalised as humanitarian rather than political. In contrast, in Norway, Arnlaug Leira describes women who, in the absence of adequate state provision, have developed their own 'informal child-care economy' as 'change agents' in 'the social reconstruction of motherhood in everyday life'.[8] In these further examples of the interplay between social and political citizenship, the public–private divide is again being breached.

The two sides of the welfare state for women's social citizenship

Welfare states are deeply gendered institutions; in their various forms they can simultaneously strengthen women's citizenship and reinforce unequal gender relations.[9] A number of studies have emphasised the positive implications of the welfare state's role as a major employer of female labour for women's economic independence, agency and social and political citizenship.[10] Less positively, in Britain, Black immigrant women, recruited to fill some of the least desirable posts in the health service in the postwar period, were not at the same time constructed as social citizens with health needs of their own and they remain concentrated in lower grade jobs.[11] Moreover, the recruitment of women to care jobs in the public sector has tended to be to the lower rungs of the employment ladder and has served to reinforce labour market gender segregation and the gendered coding of such jobs. To the extent that women are concentrated in public employment, they are also particularly vulnerable at times of cutbacks in public services. Nevertheless, as a provider of both services and jobs, the welfare state has facilitated women's entry into the public sphere, thereby helping to promote their economic independence as waged workers. It has also, despite its patriarchal nature, to a greater or lesser extent helped to 'provide a basis for women's autonomous citizenship' by offering some women, most notably lone mothers, a benefit income of their own, independent of men.[12] This can be of particular value in the face of the domestic violence experienced by many lone mothers.[13] Tax-benefit systems in welfare states as different as Sweden and the UK serve to moderate the gender gap in resources, albeit to different degrees.[14]

At the same time, welfare states still tend to be constructed in men's image. In the US, the template has been identified by feminists as a 'two-track' or 'channel' gendered welfare system in which (i) individualised, labour-market related insurance programmes position primarily male recipients as rights-bearers and (ii) family-based means-tested assistance schemes clientise their primarily female recipients.[15] It is reinforced by the way in which military service as an expression of citizenship has been translated into a set of superior social citizenship rights enjoyed by men. This same template has been identified in rather weaker form in Western Europe, notable exceptions being Denmark and Sweden (Sainsbury 1993a, 1994, 1996; Nyberg, 2002). However, where social insurance programmes have been eroded and means-tested assistance extended the gendered pattern of benefit receipt has become more blurred.[16] The template is also modified where there exist non-contributory, non-means-tested (sometimes called categorical) benefits which are beneficial to women. It is often through such benefits that women's caring work is recognised, but in countries such as the UK they have tended to be paid at a lower level than their contributory counterparts. In her study of the British and German welfare states, Daly argues that it is an over-simplification to reduce the gendered patterning of benefit receipt to the social insurance/assistance dichotomy. Instead she suggests that the 'source or origin' of a claim (that is, derived from the labour market, need or family) offers a more fruitful avenue of analysis. The broad conclusion, nevertheless, remains the same in the sense that 'women's incomes and their income-related opportunities remain substantially inferior to those of men' (2000, p. 217).

This remains the case despite the enactment of a series of EU equality directives, which outlaw most forms of sex discrimination in social security schemes. Although an important step forward, it has become clear that equal treatment, defined as the removal of explicit sex discrimination, does not guarantee equal outcomes. Male employment patterns continue to be privileged by social security systems which consequently disadvantage women with interrupted employment histories and/or low-paid, part-time employment, although in some countries greater flexibility is shown in accommodating part-time workers within social insurance schemes.[17] One consequence, aggravated by the unequal gendered impact of private and fiscal welfare, is women's generally inferior pensions status in later life.[18]

It is one of the contradictions of welfare states that, while offering women a degree of economic independence in the ways already identified, they, simultaneously, tend to construct them as economic dependants, thereby undermining their economic independence. 'The failure to treat women as full and independent fellow citizens with men' was identified by contemporary feminists as a fundamental flaw in the Beveridge Plan (Abbott and Bompas, 1943, p. 18; see also Lister, 1994c). Women's dependence continues to be entrenched, particularly in (increasingly dominant) social assistance schemes which, even when gender-neutral, tend in practice to channel benefits through male 'heads of household'. Where this is the case, the social citizenship rights of married and cohabiting women are mediated by their male partners, so that, in practice, they cease to be genuine rights. In this way, means-tested benefits, pensions and tax credits fail to address, and can even aggravate, the problem of female hidden poverty identified earlier; even where they can be paid direct to the woman in a couple, because eligibility is typically based on the couple as the unit rather than the individual, it means that the eligibility test cannot detect any hidden poverty which results from the maldistribution of family resources. It can also act as a disincentive to the woman's employment.[19]

Gendered welfare regimes and the state

The pattern of benefit-induced female dependence is most marked in what Lewis (1992a) has dubbed strong 'male-breadwinner' states. Her critical analysis of Gøsta Esping-Andersen's influential typology of 'welfare regimes' has contributed to a growing feminist critique and development of his original model, which is striking for its lack of a systematic gender analysis. In an early intervention, Langan and Ostner (1991) point out that Esping-Andersen's use of the concept of 'decommodification' – 'the degree to which individuals, or families, can uphold a socially acceptable standard of living independently of market participation' (note the fusion of individuals and families here) – takes no account of gender differences.[20] This suggests that the concept of decommodification needs to be complemented by what we might call 'defamilialisation', if it is to provide a rounded measure of economic independence.[21] Welfare regimes might then also be characterised according to the degree to which individual adults can uphold a socially acceptable standard of living, independently of family relationships, either through paid work or through social security provisions and either inside or outside of a couple relationship. More broadly, feminist analysis has underlined the need to incorporate the dimension of women's economic (in)dependence into cross-national study of welfare states and regimes. Ann Orloff and Julia O'Connor both develop the notion of autonomy – economic and sexual – as a means of complementing the concept of decommodification. The emphasis is on the '*capacity* to form and maintain an autonomous household', that is 'the resources to choose household forms freely', thereby also enhancing women's voice and power *within* couple relationships (O' Connor *et al.*, 1999, p. 32, emphasis added). Bringing together the different dimensions of autonomy discussed in Chapter 4, Orloff suggests a generic measure of 'individuals' freedom from compulsion to enter into potentially oppressive relationships in a number of spheres'.[22]

A key danger with the individualised 'adult-worker' or 'citizen-worker' model, identified by Lewis as emerging from the ashes of the male-breadwinner template, is that it assumes a degree of financial autonomy among women that is, in many cases, yet to be achieved. This is particularly the case in countries like the UK where the norm is a 'one and a half earner' rather than dual earner household and where there does not exist an adequate social infrastructure to help meet the care needs that were assumed to be met by women within the private sphere under the male-breadwinner model.

Lewis contrasts two pioneers of the citizen-worker model: Sweden and the US. In the US it is not underpinned by a proper social infrastructure of care services and is 'embedded in a residual welfare system that often borders on the punitive, whereas in Sweden it is supported by an extensive range of care entitlements with respect to children and older people'.[23]

This contrast exemplifies how the growing feminist interest in cross-national analysis of welfare regimes reflects a shift away from the construction of the state as an inherently oppressive capitalist–patriarchal monolith (Borchorst, 1999). This does not mean a reversion to a liberal conception of the state as a neutral benevolent institution. Rather, it is recognised that feminists have to engage with the capitalist–patriarchal state to extend and defend women's citizenship rights (Dahlerup, 1994). As J. M. Barbalet observes from the mainstream, 'no matter how intense the struggle for citizenship rights, it is the state which ultimately grants them, and it may choose to do so even in the absence of such a struggle' (1988, p. 110). Where this has happened in the former regimes of eastern and central Europe, the social rights granted were not generally experienced as enhancing citizenship, leaving a legacy of suspicion of any form of state intervention. Nevertheless, there is some evidence, that, as women have experienced the full ramifications of the loss of these rights, a minority at least is coming to their defence.[24]

The state can thus be understood, not as a monolith, but as comprising a number of facets and as a site of struggle and of the expression of different social interests. As such, Pringle and Watson argue that it should be seen not as 'a coherent, if contradictory unity', but as an 'erratic and disconnected ... series of arenas' within which different interests and power relations are played out.[25] This means that states differ in the extent to which they can be characterised as promoting or subverting women's citizenship rights and autonomy. More broadly, Shirin M. Rai contrasts the European regulatory welfare state, which directly 'touches' the lives of many women, with the state in India and most of the Third World, where 'state institutions figure marginally' in most women's lives (1999, pp. 32–3). Moreover within individual states there are variations between the different spheres of citizenship and over time. In all parts of the world, we are witnessing processes of state transformation in the face of globalisation and marketisation, leading to the emergence in a number of countries of 'the neo-liberal state'.[26]

Perceptions of the state can also differ. Thus, for instance, Scandinavian feminist scholars, while acknowledging the very real achievements of the Nordic welfare states, tend to be more critical than their male counterparts and less starry-eyed than commentators from outside Scandinavia. It was, nevertheless, a feminist, Helga Hernes, who suggested that the Scandinavian and Nordic welfare states 'embody a state form that makes it possible to transform them into woman-friendly societies' (1987, p. 15). Of particular importance has been the development of a 'social services state'.[27] However, the 'woman-friendly' thesis has not been accepted uncritically. One source of contention has been that the development of women's social citizenship rights has not always been matched by that of some of the other rights necessary to promote women's physical autonomy and bodily integrity. More fundamentally, the very notion of a single benevolent Scandinavian model has been rejected as misleading by a number of feminist scholars.[28] The concept of 'woman-friendly' states exaggerates their beneficial impact, it is argued, and the more 'woman-friendly' institutions which support women's care work are also the most precarious in the face of budget cuts (Hobson *et al.*, 1995). Siim, while relatively optimistic and cognisant of the advances women have made, has nevertheless highlighted the contradictory nature of the Scandinavian welfare states, simultaneously patriarchal and in some ways empowering of women. One source of reservation on her part is that the notion of the 'woman-friendly' state glosses over the 'growing economic and political polarisation among women' (1993, p. 30, 1988).

Siim is referring mainly to a growing class polarisation, one which is even more marked in Anglo-Saxon societies such as the UK, the US and New Zealand. This polarisation intersects with other sources of division and in her later work, she draws attention to emergent inequalities in Denmark associated with increased immigration (Siim, 2000; Warren, 2000). Since women do not constitute a single, undifferentiated interest group, no one policy will necessarily represent a gain for all women. Different groups of women stand in different sets of relationships to the state (Misra and Akins, 1998). The characterisation of welfare states as racialised as well as patriarchal is of particular importance here.[29] Linda Gordon, for instance, reviewing African Americans' contribution to the development of public welfare in the US, comments that 'this history suggests how racially specific have been what whites regard as mainstream welfare proposals; how deeply our welfare debates have taken place within a uniquely white set of political, economic and familial assumptions' (1990, p. 25). In the British context, Amina Mama has identified Black women's particular relations to the welfare state. She argues that, rather than treat them as citizens, it has, 'through various ideological mechanisms and administrative practices', behaved 'punitively and coercively' towards marginalised groups such as Black women. This, she continues 'is evidenced most clearly in the differential service delivery to black people', underlining the importance for citizenship of the way in which welfare benefits and services are delivered.[30]

The everyday relations involved in negotiating with welfare institutions are thus not only gendered but also racialised. Black people's relationship to the state is, at the same time, framed by immigration laws both generally and through their links with welfare entitlements (see Chapters 2 and 5). The state is also 'sexualised', promoting heterosexual interests on the one hand (although not necessarily with consistent effect) and representing a site of struggle for lesbian and gay interests on the other.[31] Similarly, the relationship of women to the state will be mediated according to their age and whether they are disabled or not, and will vary over the life-course and, even within countries, according to their geographical location.

Who is a social citizen?

The heterogeneous nature of women's interests and of their relationship to the state is, as already suggested, one important reason for misgivings about framing women's claims to citizenship in maternalist terms. Women's various interests and identities *qua* women cannot be subsumed under the one interest and identity of motherhood. Nevertheless, motherhood looms large in the life-courses of many women so that both historically and today it does shape their relationship to citizenship. Maternalist claims to political citizenship, discussed in the previous chapter, have been paralleled by those to social citizenship which still have purchase in contemporary debates. Lisa D. Brush warns that, however appealing, maternalism is today 'fraught with danger for feminists'. Historically, while such claims 'sometimes won material and ideological benefits', they have also, sometimes simultaneously, 'displaced women's interests with children's demands, drawn feminists into alliances with racist and nationalist agendas and reinforced gender differences and women's subordination'. On balance, she concludes that they have failed to increase 'the value of mother work in either the market or social policy' and to place 'women on par with male soldiers and workers when it comes to the benefits of citizenship' (1996, pp. 446, 430–1, 453–4).

The gendered nature of the benefits of citizenship has been a focal point – explicitly or implicitly – of twentieth-century debates about women's relationship to emergent welfare states. Central to these early debates were the issues of maternal and child welfare, as women in a wide range of countries strove to translate their private responsibilities as mothers into public citizenship claims.[32] In the model of citizenship handed down from the classic theorists of the British welfare state, social rights derived from social functions. This, Susan Pederson observes, begged the question as to 'which forms of activity would properly be considered citizenship functions. If soldiering and working are to bring with them citizenship entitlements, will housekeeping or mothering do so as well?' There was a strong strand in early twentieth-century feminism that argued they should. The campaign for the endowment of motherhood appealed to a 'rhetoric of motherhood as national service', the ethical equivalent of military service, as a basis for social citizenship and economic independence. Similarly, in the US, the comparability of men's and women's separate services to the state as soldiers and mothers was an important argument in the debate there about the endowment of motherhood.[33]

Others, such as Ada Nield Chew in Britain, argued that participation in waged work was the key to women's economic independence. Eleanor

Rathbone, who helped to spearhead the British campaign for the endowment of motherhood (which reached fruition in the introduction of family allowances in 1945), attempted to synthesise the two positions: not only would the endowment of motherhood give recognition to the value of women's work in the home, but it would also encourage equal pay, by undermining the case for the family wage, thereby simultaneously increasing the value of their waged labour (Land, 1990; Lewis, 1994). In Sweden, in the 1930s, an accommodation was also achieved by using the frame of citizenship rather than maternalism to mobilise, successfully, a wide range of women, including the housewives association. Their goal was not only the defence of their right to paid employment as a citizenship right but also the extension of employment rights; even those organisations that promoted mothers' position in the home accepted the demand for the right to be in the labour market within the 'cognitive frame' of citizenship (Hobson and Lindholm, 1997).[34]

Citizen-the wage-earner vs. citizen-the carer

Attempts at accommodation not withstanding, the longstanding tension between these different approaches to women's social citizenship continues to haunt contemporary debates. Running through these debates, and intertwined with each other, are the dichotomies discussed in Chapter 4, most notably that between equality and difference. Today, the tension is conceptualised in terms of the social citizenship rights which accrue and should accrue respectively to citizen-the mother or carer and citizen-the worker or wage-earner or alternatively to citizen-the wage-earner and carer (Hernes, 1987, 1988). Whatever the welfare regime, citizen the-wage-earner tends to be privileged over citizen-the carer (Sainsbury, 1999). Leira has analysed how this is the case in even the more progressive Scandinavian welfare states, reflecting 'the hierarchy of work forms, which accords primacy to wage-work, however useless, over other forms of work, however useful'. She concludes that 'what is lacking is a concept of citizenship which recognises the importance of care to society'.[35] With the emergence of the 'adult-worker model' and in the face of demographic trends, the issue has taken on increased salience particularly in countries that do not provide adequate public care services. As Lewis notes, care work still has to be done; the question is by whom and 'on what terms' (2000, p. 61; 2001; Daly and Lewis, 2000). A key aspect of this question is how to provide the recognition and valorisation called for by Leira and others without locking women further into a private caring role which serves to exclude them from the power and influence that can derive from participation in the public sphere of the economy and the *polis*. Moreover, the very inadequacy of most benefits provided in recognition of care, reflecting the general devaluation of care work in both public and private spheres, raises a question mark over the fruitfulness of any political strategy that promotes women's 'difference' (Sainsbury, 1996; Lewis, 1997).

One minimalist path, that avoids such dilemmas, is to provide adequate protection of social insurance records during periods when people are out of the labour market providing care for either children or older or disabled people. The UK, Germany, France, Norway and Sweden have gone down this road, with varying degrees of generosity (Sainsbury, 1999; Leitner, 2001). This represents the bottom line of recognition of caring work in the allocation of social security rights. The next step up would be the provision of non-contributory (and non-means-tested) pensions, as in the Nordic countries, the Netherlands and New Zealand. This ensures that all women get a pension in their own right regardless of breaks in their employment record and of marital status – in effect a citizenship pension. Dahl argues that, through such pensions, 'old age liberates women financially' (1987, p. 121; see also Ginn *et al.*, 2001). However, their level tends to be relatively low and women generally rely disproportionately on the basic pension alone (Brocas *et al.*, 1990). To the extent that Dahl's claim is valid, it reflects the extent to which social security provisions fail to liberate women under pension age financially for the reasons outlined above. There is considerable scope for the reform of social insurance benefits and for extending and improving categorical benefits, for instance for disabled people, so as to break the link between social security entitlement and the male standard employment relationship, thereby, in particular, providing adequate protection for part-time workers.[36] Going further, both the Council of Europe and the European Commission have expressed strong support for the principle of individual-based social security benefits as the most promising mechanism for achieving substantive, rather than just formal, equal treatment. Such reforms would do much to promote the financial independence of unemployed, disabled and older women and to tackle the poverty which they experience. However, in practice the general trend has been towards increased reliance on means-tested assistance (Eardley *et al.*, 1996; Cox, 1998), which is not compatible with genuine individualisation.[37]

The real dilemma arises with regard to the nature of the recognition, if any, that should be given through direct cash payments to those at home providing care. In my own position, a tension exists between the value I want to place on unpaid care work as an expression of citizenship responsibility and the emphasis I give to the importance of women's labour market participation to their citizenship. Two contrasting viewpoints, which sum up this dilemma, can be found in the same edition of *Social Politics*. According to Trudie Knijn 'caring for children is a social activity as important as many other social activities and ... women should be allowed to claim the right to an income from that activity' (1994, p. 103; Knijn and Kremer, 1997). Cass, while agreeing that 'care-giving work should be legitimated and supported', warns that 'to do only this, however, would enshrine care-giving as women's work. If the social welfare system legitimated and (inadequately) financially supported women as care-givers, why should activists concerned with women's rights insist on more equitable participation of women in paid employment and, thus, more equitable participation of men in care-giving work?' (1994, pp. 110–11). In this contemporary variant of Wollstonecraft's dilemma, we are torn between wanting to validate and support, through some form of income maintenance provision, the caring work for which women still take the main responsibility in the private sphere and to liberate them from this gendered responsibility so that they can achieve economic and political autonomy in the public sphere. The former challenges the notion that only paid work represents a contribution to citizenship and avoids treating care solely as a barrier to citizenship rather than as an activity of value in its own right (Sevenhuijsen, 1998). Yet if the latter option is closed off, it is less likely that the various concerns of women as mothers and carers will be articulated in the public world of the *polis* and economy, thereby further weakening their position in the private sphere.

Pateman's exposition of Wollstonecraft's dilemma (discussed in Chapter 4), and her suggested way through it, provides a possible framework for the discussion of the policy dilemmas raised in relation to both types of care. She poses the question: 'what form must democratic citizenship take if a primary task of all citizens is to ensure that the welfare of each living generation of citizens is secured?' Part of her answer is that 'if women's knowledge of and expertise in welfare are to become part of their contribution as citizens, as women have demanded during the twentieth century, the opposition between men's independence and women's dependence has to be broken down, and a new understanding and practice of citizenship developed' (1989, pp. 203–4). Such an approach usefully encourages a shift in the focus of attention from women to men as well as to the wider societal responsibilities for children and others in need of care. In doing so, it throws further light on the gendered nature of the link between citizenship rights and citizenship obligations.

Shifting the sexual division of labour

The central importance of the sexual division of labour in constructing women and men's citizenship rights, responsibilities and opportunities was emphasised in Chapter 5. As argued there, changes in the sexual division of labour will require changes in both private behaviour and public policy. Building on the earlier discussion, which emphasised the former, we will now consider the public policy side of the equation. To what extent can public policy change men's behaviour and their relationship with the public and private spheres? Some have answered this question by asserting that caring work should be enforced as a public citizenship obligation just as paid work is. Taylor-Gooby (1991), for example, argues that it is the state's role to apply sanctions to those who do not undertake their fair share of unpaid care work. He leaves unclear though how sanctions could be applied and does not address the problems of both practice and principle involved in policing such an approach. A more collectivist strategy is a proposal that citizens' time should be taxed through an obligation to undertake unpaid work for the community by means of some kind of universal citizens' service (Lagergren, 1986; Bubeck, 1995a, b). In this way, it is argued, care becomes central to citizenship.

While such an approach would remove more of the responsibility for care from the private to the public sphere and encourage a different perspective on the meaning of citizenship obligation, it has a number of very real limitations. It is not axiomatic that it would, of itself, shift the sexual division of labour. The obligation on men to undertake some caring work in the public sphere might make them even more resistant to doing so in the private where, however good the citizens' service, some care work and most housework would still be undertaken; women meanwhile would be adding citizens' service to their lifetime burden of unpaid domestic work. At the same time, such a service could undermine the position of those engaging in paid caring work in the public sector, the great majority of whom are women. Moreover, turning responsibility into formal obligation might have the very opposite effect intended, engendering resentment rather than genuinely caring labour (Tronto, 1993; see also Folbre, 1995).

One alternative which has been proposed is a notion of 'careful citizenship' which guarantees the 'rights to time for care and to receive care'. This would comprise the rights to take time out of the labour market to care and to synchronise employment and care, as well as rights to elder and child care.[38] This is a helpful formulation, which puts centre stage the politics of time, but it raises questions about the balance between paid and unpaid work obligations and, again, it does not of itself necessarily shift the sexual division of labour. It could certainly, as I myself will argue, facilitate such a shift but, construed only as a right, it leaves men free to choose not to exercise it. This suggests that such a right needs to be backed up with measures that would, at least, 'encourage' men to exercise it and would construct domestic care and housework as a male responsibility (and in the case of care a privilege), even if it is not feasible to back up such a responsibility with sanctions.

It is just such a strategy that has been advocated by the EC. Indeed, the Council of Ministers has adopted a Recommendation on Child Care, which includes as an objective the encouragement 'with due respect for freedom of the individual, [of] increased participation by men (in the care and upbringing of children) in order to achieve a more equal sharing of parental responsibilities between men and women' (1992, Article 6). It is a strategy already adopted by some Scandinavian countries, albeit it has to be said, with only limited success hitherto. Nevertheless, there are lessons to be learned from their experiences and the strategy's symbolic importance should not be underestimated. The equal sharing of responsibility for paid and unpaid work between women and men is part of the official ideology of the Scandinavian countries. A Swedish Ministry of Labour sex equality document, for instance, states: 'To make it possible for both men and women to combine parenthood and gainful employment, a new view of the male role and a radical challenge in the organisation of working life are called for' (1988, p. 5). This willingness, at least in theory, to challenge men's role in the private sphere stands in stark contrast to the stance of more laissez-faire governments such as in the UK and US.

There have been three main, interlinked, strands to the Scandinavian strategy: parental leave; working time; and public education programmes. Paid parental leave in effect transforms domestic child care into a form of paid work (Jenson, 1997). Paid or unpaid, parental leave has, however, been described as offering mothers a 'poisoned chalice' from the perspective of the sexual division of labour, (Fagnani, 1999). An overview of provision in a number of European countries concludes that, in general, lengthy, un- or poorly paid periods of parental leave 'taken solely by women can be counter productive, through re-inforcing dependency and gendered roles in a way which, in the medium and longer term, is unhelpful to women, children and family life' (Cohen, 1999, p. 297). The lesson drawn by Bruning and Plantenga from another European analysis is that 'much depends on the political and socio-economic context and ... on the precise structuring of the measure'. They contrast the position in Germany and Austria where fathers' use of the leave is negligible and the structure weakens mothers' links to the labour market with that in Norway and Sweden where 'the involvement of men is relatively favourable' and leave is structured so as to emphasise mother's links with the labour market (1999, pp. 207 and 206).[39]

Absolutely key to their impact on the sexual division of labour are the ways in which parental leave schemes either encourage or discourage male use. If it is associated only with women it can weaken their labour market position (Hantrais and Letablier, 1997). Moreover evidence from a number of countries suggests that experience of parental leave may have a beneficial impact on men's subsequent involvement in child care (Moss and Deven, 1999). Sweden, Norway and Iceland have explicitly attempted to raise fathers' take-up since the mid-1990s, as it became clear that, although in theory a gender-neutral measure, in practice parental leave proved to be significantly gendered, with women the great majority of users.[40] In each case, the pivotal policy instrument has been the introduction of a 'daddy month' or 'quota', which earmarks a period of leave for the father that is not transferable to the mother. The symbolic significance of such quotas is emphasised by Leira (1998). Yet, assessment of their actual impact has been somewhat mixed, with some commentators placing greater emphasis on change and others on continuity in men's tradition-ally low use of the leave. In Sweden, an increase in the proportion of eligi-ble fathers taking parental leave to around half from fewer than a fifth in the early 1980s has not been matched by a similar increase in their share of the overall leave taken, which remains at just above a tenth (Hobson, 2001). Nevertheless, of children born in 1995, 77 per cent had a father who used the whole of the 'daddy month' (Björnberg, 2002). It has been suggested that a reduction in the wage-replacement rate for the parental leave payment and high unemployment have combined to depress fathers' overall take-up (Hobson *et al.*, 1995; Oláh, 1998).

In Iceland, in 2000, parental leave was extended to nine months, of which three months is reserved for the father, three for the mother and the remaining three to be shared as the couple decides. Over 90 per cent of entitled men are reported to take the leave (Hrafnsdóttir, 2002). In Norway where only about 5 per cent of fathers had previously taken parental leave, the quota 'triggered a rapid increase in take-up rates to approximately 70 per cent of eligible fathers'. This, Leira suggests, is con-tributing to 'changing the carer aspect of fatherhood' (1999, p. 285; Millar and Ridge, 2001). She also contends that the fact that the month is lost if the fathers do not use it greatly improves their position 'when negotiating with reluctant employers' (1998, p. 372). Bruning and Plantenga point to Norway as an example of how such policies 'can increase male involvement dramatically' (1999, p. 205). Sainsbury's inter-pretation of the Norwegian scheme is less positive. She suggests that the mother is still enshrined as 'natural caregiver whose rights are transferred to the father' (1999, pp. 92 and 94). In particular, the father's right to the 'daddy quota' is contingent on the mother's own entitlement to parental leave. It is important therefore, she argues, that the right is an individual one.

Research indicates that financial considerations continue to act as a significant deterrent to male use of parental leave. So long as men can command, on average, higher rewards from the labour market than women, this deterrent is likely to continue, although full or nearly full wage-replace-ment should diminish its impact.[41] However, it is not just a matter of financial considerations. Significant also is a workplace culture of male indis-pensability which constructs men's use of parental leave as inappropriate and which can reflect wider gendered cultural norms.[42] This points to the impor-tance of both changes in attitudes and the organisation of work, if men are to make full use of parental leave provisions and if male absenteeism from domestic work generally is to be reduced. The two are interlinked, for the necessary change in men's attitudes will have to be supported by changes in the workplace and a challenge to the traditional male model of employment and workplace culture.[43]

An important aspect of this challenge involves the issue of working time or conversely 'the time for care'. Again this is recognised in Sweden, where parents of under-seven-year-old children can work 'part-time' (that is six instead of eight hours a day), although once more it tends to be women who make use of this facility. An alternative 'combination scenario' has been adopted in the Netherlands to enable all citizens to combine work and care. A maximum working week of 32 hours for all is promoted in the name of 'the equal sharing of time, between paid and unpaid work as well as between women and men', although the strategy is undermined by inconsistencies in policy.[44] Nevertheless such strategies can have symbolic importance in legitimising the validity of a shorter working day. A culture of long, paid working hours can serve to constrain male participation in unpaid caring and domestic work while it also creates barriers to women's full integration and advancement in the workplace, thereby fuelling the vicious circle created by the sexual division of labour.

In the UK, where men's paid working hours are above the EU average, a study for the Equal Opportunities Commission has observed that 'there seems no way in which a style of work which involved such a long commitment to paid employment could be emulated by anyone who had a major responsibility for children'. The report suggests that the single most effective way of promoting equality might be to regulate the hours of paid work undertaken by men.[45] Although this would not automatically translate into an increase in the hours they devote to unpaid work, it could help, particularly if backed up by public education campaigns directed at men and boys. This points to an important role for education and media programmes in promoting change, as emphasised by a report of an international seminar on men as carers and as adopted in Sweden (EC Childcare Network, 1993; Moss and Deven, 1999).

The balance of public and private responsibility for care

Some feminists are critical of too great an emphasis on a fairer sexual division of responsibility for the provision of care as representing a privatised response that could undermine demands for better public provisions. The reason for such an emphasis was explained earlier. However, as was also made clear, it represents only one part of the overall equation, particularly in the case of lone-parent families; the other concerns the division of responsibility between individual families and the wider community, as expressed, primarily, through state provision.[46] This state provision can be aimed at enabling parents and other carers to take paid work or at providing financial support for them to provide care themselves at home. There are both similarities and differences in the policy issues raised by the care of children and of adults. In each case, policy has to address a need for financial support, appropriate services and/or time (Daly, 2002).

Children

The main public policy instruments deployed to support the care of children are publicly funded childcare, parental leave, temporary leave for family reasons and (in some countries) paid childcare leave. On the basis of different (though shifting) combinations of these policies, Bruning and Plantenga (1999) distinguish four broad models. The 'time' model, exemplified by Austria and Germany, offers parents of young children 'time to care' rather than services. The 'sequential' model, forged by Sweden, prioritises publicly funded childcare after a period of parental leave. The 'parallel' model, pioneered by Finland, offers parents a real choice between time and services. The 'facilitation of services' model prioritises childcare over parental leave. Although Denmark and France are cited as closest to this model, the balance in both is shifting towards the 'parallel' model, with a greater emphasis on time to care than previously. The clusters identified in a wider analysis of 14 OECD countries' policies to support the employment of mothers similarly did not mirror Esping-Andersen's welfare regime typology, referred to earlier. This study also emphasised the importance of the (in)compatibility of school and employment schedules (Gornick *et al.*, 1997).

The availability of affordable, good-quality childcare is essential to the realisation of opportunities to enter paid work or training. This is the case not only for pre-school children but also for younger schoolchildren during school holidays and after-school hours (which is often given insufficient priority). The EC Childcare Network has emphasised the need for childcare provisions to be responsive to the diversity that exists among families and in particular to the needs of 'minority groups' such as lone parents, minority ethnic families, families with a disabled child or parent and rural families.[47] The Network claims that, by the mid-1990s, new and imaginative types of provision were emerging but that inequalities in provision continued between and within member states (European Commission Network on Childcare, 1996). By the early twenty-first century, the general picture in the EU is one of movement towards universal formal pre-school provision for the over-threes, with France, Belgium, Italy, Denmark and the Netherlands all claiming over 90 per cent coverage. Provision for younger children is generally much lower, with only Denmark (the leader) and Sweden achieving more than 40 per cent coverage.[48] In some countries, such as Sweden, expansion has been at the expense of quality, as spending has not increased commensurately (Szebehely, 1998; Nyberg, 2001), although the Swedish Government is committed to the release of additional resources to enhance quality (Björnberg, 2002).

In the UK, relatively low coverage reflects the inheritance of a liberal philosophy, in which childcare is seen as the responsibility of the individual parent, and to a lesser extent the voluntary sector and employers, but not of the state (Randall, 2000). With the advent of the New Labour Government, there is, at last, recognition that childcare is, in part, a public responsibility, leading to a national childcare strategy and public investment. Nevertheless, according to the Daycare Trust 'for most families childcare is still too expensive and the gap between paying for and accessing affordable childcare provision is still too great' and provision remains 'highly fragmented and patchy' (2001, pp. 1 and 3). In contrast to the EU, the picture in Eastern/Central Europe is one of contraction (Pascall and Manning, 2000). The US continues to lag well behind, with public support for childcare, other than through tax credits, relatively rare and, though expanding, largely confined to welfare-to-work programmes (Meyers *et al.*, 1999; Orloff, 2002).

Daly identifies 'a trend in European welfare states towards a greater subsidization of parental caring of young children' (1997, p. 140; 2002). This confirms the earlier finding of Kamerman and Kahn (1991) of a qualitative policy shift in a number of countries from an emphasis on facilitating the labour market participation of the mothers of under-three-year-olds to one of extended leave provisions and targeted financial support. The impact on gender equity (and by implication women's position as citizens) is, they suggest, mixed, depending to a large extent on the motivations behind the policies and their precise nature.[49] They, and others, contrast by illustration the German model which, although officially gender-neutral, was, in effect, designed 'to support traditional gender roles within traditional husband–wife families', with the Swedish which they see as promoting gender equity (1991, p. 217; Lewis, 2000).

Sweden is often cited as an exemplar of the Nordic welfare states, which have made a real attempt to provide parents with 'time for care' through the synchronisation of paid work and caring responsibilities.[50] There is, though, no single monolithic Nordic model and Sweden stands out in its use of parental leave (and generous temporary leave for family reasons) to support working parents. Despite its apparently 'woman-friendly' persona, feminist commentators have expressed some ambivalence about the implications of this strategy for women's citizenship. On the credit side, Lewis and Åström describe the Swedish approach as one that treats women as citizen-workers and then grafts on their claims as mothers through parental leave schemes (which have extended steadily in length). This, they suggest, can be understood as an attempt to synthesise equality and difference claims 'by grafting the right to make a claim on the basis of difference onto a policy based on equal treatment'. Thus, 'the Swedish model guarantees that choosing to care will attract reasonable monetary award only so long as the carer has first undertaken to become a citizen worker' (1992, pp. 60, 80). Such a synthesis could be said to exemplify the philosophy underlying the 'gender-inclusive' model posited in Chapter 4. The downside of the Swedish approach, identified by Lewis and Åström among others, is that it has inadvertently served to reinforce the sexual division of labour and a highly sexually segregated labour market in a country that has lacked effective equal opportunities legislation (although this has recently been strengthened to comply with EU requirements). This again highlights the gendered impact of what was framed as gender-neutral legislation.

The lesson, from this and the earlier discussion of parental leave, would appear to be not to abandon the idea of parental leave, which *is* a means of placing value on the care of young children and of facilitating 'time for care'. Instead, as increasingly recognised in Sweden and the other Nordic states themselves, it must be made harder for men to evade taking at least a share of the leave. In addition, generous 'family-friendly' leave and childcare policies need to be backed up by effective equal opportunities and sex discrimination measures. These need to promote the interests of women *qua* women in the labour market while also addressing the specific barriers faced by particularly disadvantaged groups such as Black women and disabled women. That said, there remains the danger that so long as it is women who are more likely to take advantage of the bulk of parental leave, breaks from the labour market (where lengthy) will disadvantage women's position within it.[51] This danger becomes even greater under policies that provide a cash payment for those who stay at home to care for children after the end of any parental leave period, such as in Finland, Norway and France. Although the extent to which mothers make use of such allowances can depend on the adequacy of childcare provisions, unemployment levels and cultural factors, the fear remains that they will cement rather than loosen the traditional sexual division of labour, as they are seen as primarily for mothers. They may also widen class divisions as working class, less educated and lower paid women are more likely to take advantage of the allowance.[52]

An alternative approach would be to pay a benefit to all those raising children, after the end of any parental leave period. This would reduce the disincentive to mothers to take paid employment (although not remove it altogether). It would constitute recognition of the costs, including 'time-costs', incurred by raising children, regardless of the parents' employment status and as such could be construed as a citizenship benefit. However, such a universal benefit would be expensive and in the context of welfare state containment and increased emphasis on means-testing seems something of a pipe dream.

Adults

Similar dilemmas arise with regard to the increasingly debated question of payments to those caring for adults (either directly or via the care-recipient). These are becoming more common in the face of ageing populations and a widespread emphasis on the provision of care in the 'community' or home rather than in residential institutions, as part of a broader shift to 'welfare pluralism' and, in many cases, retrenchment in welfare services. They stand,

Daly and Lewis suggest 'almost always in the less generous league of benefits' (1999, p. 4). Leaving aside the question of payment for volunteers, the growing literature on payment for carers underlines some of the difficulties in developing an approach that enhances the citizenship not only of those providing care but also of those receiving it, in both cases, as noted earlier, the majority of whom are women.[53] The earlier theoretical synthesis of the ethics of care and justice will be drawn upon to help negotiate these difficulties.

Three main models of paying for care can be identified according to whether, first, the principle is one of social security wage replacement or wages for care undertaken (McLaughlin and Glendinning (1994) and, second, whether such wages are paid direct or 'routed' via direct payments to care users (Ungerson, 1997). Although unusual, the British carer's allowance provides an interesting example of the strengths and weaknesses of the social security approach to paying for care in a system that privileges wage-earning in the allocation of rights. The allowance is an income replacement benefit for those providing at least 35 hours a week of care and earning below a fixed limit. It is subject to neither a contribution nor means test; as such, it has been described as a citizenship approach that recognises the impact of caring on the ability to undertake paid work without policing the actual care work undertaken (Ungerson, 1992, 1997; Pascall, 1993). However, its status as an independent citizenship benefit is compromised by eligibility criteria that link it to the receipt or non-receipt of other benefits by the care recipient and by its payment at only 60 per cent of the equivalent adult contributory benefit rate, so as to preserve the social insurance principle. More generally, McLaughlin and Glendinning criticise the social security approach on the grounds that, while recognising the role of carers, it does not attempt to reward the actual work they perform although many perceive the allowance as such a payment.[54]

Whether the alternative model – that of payment for care undertaken, directly or indirectly, – provides a firmer underpinning of carers' citizenship is, however, debatable. A number of disadvantages of such a 'commodification' of care into a form of waged labour are highlighted in the literature: the relatively low rates of pay and lack of employment rights typical of such schemes which may undermine the bargaining position of those employed in the formal care sector; the increase in control over carers; and the dangers of increased professionalisation of care work, to the detriment of non-professional carers.[55] Clare Ungerson warns of the possible development of unregulated 'grey' labour markets, drawing on cheap female and migrant labour, particularly where payments are channelled through care-users, as increasingly demanded by the disabled people's movement (1994, 1995, 1996). This highlights but just one of a number of emergent divisions in the politics of care, as it becomes clear that no one form of payment best meets the varied interests of different groups of carers and of care-users and that different forms of payment have different implications for the power relationships between those involved.

A danger common to all forms of payment for care is that mentioned earlier with regard to payment for childcare: that by paying (mainly in practice) women to undertake care work in the private domain, it could serve to institutionalise further the sexual division of caring labour. Janet Finch, among others, has warned of this risk but qualifies her reservations with the observation 'that it would be wrong not to continue to press for more support for women who currently do take on unpaid caring with little or no financial or practical support for the sake of potential longer-term gains' (1990, p. 52). Thus, more limited short-term demands (Molyneux's 'practical' gender interests or concerns) need to be complemented by longer-term strategies that address the sexual division of labour in both the private and public spheres (an example of 'strategic' gender interests or concerns).

At the same time, short-term practical demands need to be framed so as to minimise any possible negative impact on longer-term strategic interests. Thus, for example, any scheme for providing financial support for carers should be sufficiently flexible to enable carers of working age to combine their caring work with paid work, if they so wish and, in fact, a significant number of carers do try to juggle the two. The case for the kind of 'time for care' policies discussed in relation to childcare applies as strongly here, but they are generally much less well developed (Daly, 2002). Examples of such policies include flexible working hours and care leave to enable those who do take time out to care to retain their longer term link with the labour market, as well as appropriate community support services and 'more care-friendly environments'.[56] There are, though, some who are critical of a strategy that prioritises carers' labour market participation, partly on the grounds that, once again, it denies the value for citizenship of unpaid care work. It also ignores the needs of carers over pension age and, if not combined with other measures, could increase women's overall (combined paid and unpaid) workload, as Arber and Ginn found.[57]

Ungerson concludes that it is fruitless trying to decide in general whether one approach or another to paying for care is in or against women's interests. Instead, she suggests that what is needed is a set of agreed criteria for judging whether any particular scheme is in the interests of all involved in the caring relationship, in particular those of women carers. While such a set of criteria would be useful, one should not underestimate the difficulty in reaching agreement, given, as she herself has subsequently acknowledged, the conflicts of interests involved (1992, 1994, 1995, 1997). A critical axis of conflict is that between those who provide and those who receive care; the latter's perspective having only been relatively recently recognised in the care literature. Indeed, some disabled people are challenging the very language of care and carers as carrying with it 'the notion of "dependent people"' and are arguing that the ideology of caring is incompatible with a commitment to disabled people's rights to be full and equal citizens (Morris, 1993a, p. 150, 1996; Wood, 1991).

In policy terms, they argue that demands for policies such as respite care to ease the 'burden' of caring can reinforce the construction of disabled people as dependants and ignore their needs and preferences (Keith and Morris, 1996). There is, too, an increasingly explicit conflict of interests between carers' lobbies pressing for adequate direct payments to carers in order to safeguard their financial independence and the growing demand among some disabled people for payments to be made to them so that they can pay for and thereby control the way in which their care needs are met.[58] Both sets of demands can be justified with reference to the autonomy and citizenship of the members of each group. As Keith argues, rather than polarise the needs of the two groups, 'both partners in the caring relationship are struggling for some degree of financial independence, to have a presence in the public world and to have some freedom of choice' (1992, p. 172; Croft, 1986). Similarly, McLaughlin and Glendinning acknowledge that the interests of members of neither group are best served by policies that create financial dependence on the other. Policies that combine some form of direct payments to informal carers with some scope for disabled and older people, who so wish, to negotiate and control their own 'care packages', over and above such payments, in the context of good service provision, might offer the possibility of balancing the citizenship rights of the two groups.

At a theoretical level, McLaughlin and Glendinning suggest the deployment of the notion of the ethic of care, thereby focusing on 'the terms and conditions under which we engage in caring relationships' (1994, p. 61). Tom Shakespeare (2000), while articulating the disability critique of care, nevertheless acknowledges the potential of the ethic of care as a corrective to the individualism and scope for exploitation of the independent living model. From this perspective, Tronto's answer to conflict in caring relationships, as observed earlier, is to connect the ethic of care back 'to a theory of justice and to be relentlessly democratic in its disposition', so that a balance is maintained between the perspectives and needs of care-givers and care-recipients (1993, p. 171). Thus, we have here a specific policy-relevant example of the general theoretical case for a synthesis between the ethics of care and justice. It exemplifies my point that this synthesis is necessary, if the practice of care and the conflicts it can generate are to be underwritten and mediated respectively by the social rights associated with citizenship. At the same time our understanding of those citizenship rights is enriched by an ethic of care.

This formulation helps to meet Ungerson's doubts about applying the 'public construct of citizenship' to the 'essentially private constructs of love and kinship' involved in care relations. In fact, Ungerson concludes her discussion by partially overcoming her own scepticism: she suggests that, in the context of high quality, reliable support services, which enable those who wish to remain in their own homes to do so, 'the private aspects of care – the parts that contain the love and watchfulness – can flourish within a public framework, underwritten by the collectively guaranteed provision of caring services by the state'. Moreover, more recently she has acknowledged the ways in which developments in paid care are blurring the boundaries between the public and the private.[59]

Citizen's income

An alternative route to payments for care, of both children and adults, is that provided by Citizen's Income (CI), under which every citizen would receive a 'small but guaranteed' tax-free payment, 'regardless of age, sex, race, creed, labour market or marital status' and, in its purist form, without any conditions or citizenship obligations attached. As the name implies, the principle underlying the scheme is that of 'a citizenship share in national income'.[60] From a gendered care perspective, this blanket universalism can be seen as both an attraction and a limitation. On the one hand, it would provide all women with an income in their own right, thereby promoting their financial independence, and it is much better suited to supporting part-time work than other models of social security. It would also, according to some advocates, provide recognition of women's unpaid work in the home (Miller, 1988; Parker, 1993). On the other hand, it would do so on a totally undiscriminating basis, providing the same recognition for basic housework as for care work. Thus, it does not value caring work *per se*, given that the same basic benefit would be paid regardless of actual care responsibilities undertaken.

Moreover, if not combined with measures aimed at tackling the sexual division of labour in the home and in the labour market it could inadvertently serve to reinforce it as well as men's economic advantage over women, if men simply added their higher wages to their CI payment while women's links with the labour market were weakened. Some CI supporters argue that it would, of itself, encourage a fairer sexual division of paid and unpaid work. This is not, however, axiomatic and Hermione Parker has also acknowledged that 'mothers with babies would tend to stay at home longer before going back to work', although the actual impact on female labour market participation would, she suggests, depend on the details of any scheme which was introduced (1991, pp. 43–4). In one of the few feminist defences of CI, McKay and VanEvery contend that arguments that it could cement the sexual division of labour are exaggerated, as an independent income would alter the conditions under which labour is divided between the sexes. They make the case for CI as suited to an increasingly 'postfamilial' society because it does not discriminate between family and household forms and they emphasise its potential to promote 'gender-neutral social rights of citizenship' (2000, pp. 281 and 267).

My own position with regard to the, increasingly popular, notion of a CI is one of ambivalence, reflecting in part the ambiguities around its likely gendered impact. Clearly, it has attractions and if one believes that notions of 'full' employment no longer have purchase because of global economic and technological developments, so that a limited amount of paid work would need to be shared around, then CI looks an even more attractive option (though whether it would then be affordable is another matter). But so long as employment continues to be the primary, direct or indirect, determinant of incomes, it is doubtful whether an income maintenance system that deliberately challenged the link between income and wages would command the necessary broadly based political support. That such support is crucial to the adoption of such a radical strategy has been acknowledged by at least some CI advocates such as David Purdy (1994). On balance, therefore, I do not see CI as providing the way forward, at present, but there is nevertheless a case for leaving it on the table as a possible longer-term option which should not then be pre-empted by shorter-term reforms. A possible intermediate step, which would meet the objection that CI does not recognise the value of care work as such, would be that of a 'Participation Income', proposed by Atkinson and endorsed by the British Commission on Social Justice, as a complement to the existing income maintenance scheme. Like CI, this would provide a non-means-tested benefit on an individual basis but it would have attached to it a condition of 'active citizenship'.[61]

Paid work as citizenship obligation: the case of lone parents

Arguments for both a Citizen's and a Participation Income scheme raise important questions about the nature of citizenship obligations addressed at the start of this book, for they attempt to cut the umbilical cord between social citizenship rights and paid employment. In doing so, there is a danger that CI, at least, upsets the reciprocal relationship between rights and obligations discussed in Chapter 1 (White, 1995, 2000). CI thus represents one extreme of a continuum relating to the degree of conditionality attached to social security benefits for those of working age, capable of paid employment. Despite the growing popularity in some quarters of CI as an idea, in many countries actual policy is moving in the opposite direction, reflecting the growing hold of the 'duties discourse' discussed in Chapter 1. This applies not only in the US, but has also been observed in the EU where 'the trend towards *conditional* rights in relation to welfare benefits, especially employment-related benefits has been marked' (Robbins, 1994, p. 41, emphasis in original; Lødemel and Trickey, 2001).

My concern here is with the *extensiveness* of work obligations and in particular whether the obligation to undertake paid work should apply to those caring for children, most notably lone parents. This underlines the gendered, and in the US context racialised, nature of this aspect of the question of work obligation. US policy, in its growing obsession with the welfare 'dependency' of, primarily Black, lone mothers, has increasingly expected the mothers of even very young children to be full-time workers.[62] While private female economic dependence on a man is deemed 'natural' and uncontroversial in two-parent families where the woman is engaged in unpaid caring work, the public dependency of lone mothers is stigmatised as symptomatic of a 'dependency culture'. New right thinking is, however, divided between sanctification of the market and motherhood (O'Connor *et al.*, 1999). For those who sanctify the market, the presence of children to be supported intensifies the work obligation; for those who sanctify motherhood, this position is anti-family and seen as further weakening the economic position of men as family breadwinners. According to George Gilder, for instance, one of women's key functions in the family is to tame men in the 'duties and disciplines of citizenship' which are partly developed through the latter's assumption of the breadwinner role.[63]

The trend in US policy represents one policy extreme. It is being echoed, albeit more weakly and in different forms, in some members of the EU. The dominant policy model of lone motherhood is increasingly one that prioritises wage-earning over full-time mothering.[64] The clearest example is provided by the Netherlands, where the policy presumption that lone mothers are exempt from the obligation to undertake paid work has been abandoned. From 1996, lone parents whose youngest child is aged five or older are, by law, expected to seek work although, in practice, use of discretion by officials has exempted around three-fifths from the requirement.[65] In contrast, despite the preoccupation with 'welfare dependency' of both Conservative and New Labour administrations, lone parents remain exempt from the paid work obligation in the UK. In the conflict between different strands of neo-conservatism, unlike in the US, the sanctity of motherhood won out over that of the market under the Conservatives. Under New Labour, there is much greater emphasis on lone mothers as workers, with the use of voluntary welfare-to-work schemes and compulsory work-focussed interviews. Nevertheless, the UK is unusual in that, for the time being at least, a lone parent can still claim social assistance, without being required to be available for work, until her youngest child is aged 16.[66] On the face of it, therefore, lone mothers might appear to enjoy a relatively privileged position in the UK, at least insofar as their right to care for their children full-time is underpinned by the (inferior) social citizenship right of social assistance.

Relative privilege is not, however, the picture that emerges from cross-national comparisons of poverty rates among lone parents. These show the UK as having one of the highest lone parent poverty rates in the Western world, with the Nordic countries the lowest. They also show that, in all countries, poverty rates are significantly lower among employed than non-employed lone mothers.[67] However, it does not follow from this that paid work alone is automatically the answer to lone parent families' poverty. 'In no country does employment provide full protection from the risk of poverty' (Kilkey and Bradshaw, 2001, p. 225); the wealth of literature that now exists points to both material–structural and cultural factors that mediate lone mothers relationship to employment and the impact of employment on their living standards.

A key factor is the kinds of jobs and wages available to lone mothers. US welfare policy has been considerably more successful in reducing the welfare rolls than in reducing poverty levels, as many mothers 'have simply moved from the ranks of the welfare poor to the working poor', struggling to survive on low wages.[68] As observed earlier, comparisons between the US and Sweden, which share high lone mother employment rates, are instructive. In contrast to the former's residual welfare system and lack of social infrastructure, Sweden supports employed lone mothers with cash, services and flexible employment practices, resulting in much lower poverty rates (Lewis, 2001; Nyberg, 2002). Policies that treat lone mothers as workers must not forget that they are also mothers. The evidence from both cross-national research and surveys of lone mothers' own preferences underlines that their ability to combine the two roles depends heavily on adequate financial support, a decent social infrastructure (most notably good quality, affordable child and after-school care) and flexible employment practices (such as paid time off to care for sick children and working hours that fit around the school day).[69] Important also are education and training policies that would strengthen lone mothers' longer term position in the labour market.[70]

Another key finding from cross-national research is that the success of policies designed to move lone mothers into the labour market depends in part on socio-cultural factors. Duncan and Edwards have suggested the notion of 'gendered moral rationalities' to describe 'collective and social understandings about what is the proper relationship between motherhood and paid work' (1999, p. 235). Dominant gendered moral rationalities vary between countries and also between social and ethnic groups within countries. The Netherlands provides an example of how a policy that goes against the grain of dominant gendered moral rationalities has been unsuccessful in its attempt to require lone mothers of school-age children to enter the labour market.[71] In contrast, in the US, where female labour market participation is the norm, there was remarkably little opposition to the harsh intensification of work obligations (Orloff, 2002).

The fierce resistance in the UK to any such policies reflects both dominant gendered moral rationalities (at least in relation to young children) and the barriers created by an inadequate social infrastructure and inflexible employment practices. In this context, it might be considered that there is a good case for maintaining the *status quo* on the grounds that compulsion would be unreasonable and could be counterproductive if, as seems likely, it were experienced as punitive. Certainly in the short to medium term the priority has to be remove these barriers, thereby enabling lone mothers to combine paid work and their family responsibilities with minimal stress. Moreover, in line with the case made earlier for recognition of care as a responsibility of citizenship and White's principle of 'fair reciprocity' (2000), discussed in Chapter 1, I would continue to defend the right of mothers (parents) of younger and of disabled children and of those caring for older or disabled people to be exempt from the obligation to be available for paid work (as well as argue for the necessary social provisions to enable those who so wish to combine paid and caring work).

That still leaves the question as to whether it is axiomatic that citizenship as care should trump citizenship as paid work for the mothers of older children if, and it is a big if, the necessary social, employment and training policies were in place. Provided also that adequate safeguards existed, such as an exemption for the first year of lone parenthood and to deal with children's behavioural problems such as truancy, it does not seem unreasonable for there to be an expectation that for lone mothers of older children paid work is part of what it means to be a mother.[72] Given the evidence, cited earlier, of how women's long-term economic position is damaged by lengthy withdrawal from the labour market and of growing class divisions in women's employment patterns, such a policy would arguably be in lone mothers' longer-term interests, strengthening their long-term economic security and autonomy. Whether or not an element of compulsion should then be considered would depend in part on the success of more voluntaristic policies in signalling such expectations.

A further argument in favour derives from 'the dilemma of having it both ways' posed by Hobson in a cross-national analysis of the position of 'solo mothers': is it realistic', she asks, to imagine a social policy regime that supports equally a mother's wage for caring that would allow her to form an autonomous household, and a system of services and provisions that would allow mothers to be integrated into working life?' (1994, p. 186). It would perhaps be easier to sustain the case for such a regime, if we take a dynamic approach and distinguish between the needs and interests of mothers of younger and of older children. In this way, we can then assert the right of mothers (and fathers) of young children, if they so wish, to care for their children full-time through the payment of adequate parental and social security benefits. At the same time, we can press for the kind of social infrastructure necessary to enable parents of older children (and younger, if they wish) to combine paid work and caring responsibilities, free from stress. Indeed, one of the lessons that Millar and Rowlingson (2001) draw from their cross-national review is that where a clear line is drawn requiring lone parents to be economically active when their children reach a certain age, an implicit contract sometimes emerges under which more generous benefits are provided for lone parents with younger children and better services and financial support for those in paid work.

Hobson describes solo mothers, who are highly disadvantaged on a number of scores, as a 'litmus test group' from the 'standpoint of justice and citizenship rights'; the kinds of state support solo mothers receive can be seen as a measure of the strength or weakness of the social rights of women with families. Conversely, her study and other cross-national evidence appear to indicate that it is in countries that provide the best support for mothers in two-parent families, particularly to combine paid work and caring, that lone mothers tend to fare best.[73]

Conclusion

My central concern in this chapter has been to find a balance between, on the one hand, due recognition of the value to citizenship of the work women do as mothers and carers in the private sphere and, on the other, the promotion of their right to participate on equal terms with men in the public sphere of the labour market. As currently constructed, it is the latter that provides a passport to social citizenship rights. I have therefore been seeking a policy balance that reflects the theoretical balance elaborated earlier. In particular, in various ways I have attempted to sketch a social policy approach that promotes women's independence in the context of relationships of interdependence; that combines the ethics of care and justice; and that, most fundamentally, promotes both women's equality and difference while acknowledging the diversity of women's concerns.

The route map for this approach lies, I have argued, through a combination of policies designed to shift the balance of responsibility for care between both women and men and individual families and the state. Thus, in the one case, policy would be deliberately attempting to change relations in the private sphere so as to improve women's position in the public sphere; in the other it would be shifting the boundaries of public and private responsibility for the care of children and adults. At the same time I have stressed the significance, both historically and today, of social citizenship not only as the locus of important rights but also as an arena for women's citizenship as practice. Echoing the conclusions of the previous chapter, until women in their diversity are the subjects and not just objects of social policy-making, their citizenship is likely to remain marginalised.

Conclusion: Towards a Feminist Theory and Praxis of Citizenship

In the Introduction I posed a twofold question: whether a concept, originally predicated on the very exclusion of women can be reformulated so as satisfactorily to include (and not simply) append them; and in doing so, whether it can give full recognition to the different and shifting identities that women simultaneously hold. In other words, is the very idea of a 'woman-friendly citizenship' contradictory both because citizenship is inherently woman-unfriendly and because the category 'woman' itself represents a false universalism which replicates that of traditional constructions of citizenship? When I started working on the issue of women's citizenship I was unsure as to the answer I would reach. As will have become clear, my conclusion was and remains that it is possible to conceive of a woman-friendly conceptualisation of citizenship at both the theoretical and policy level, for all its exclusionary and disciplinary tendencies. Citizenship, I believe, provides an invaluable strategic theoretical concept for the analysis of women's subordination and a potentially powerful political weapon in the struggle against it. Moreover, it throws a searching light on difference, despite its universalist roots.

In this Conclusion, I will first draw together the various elements of my argument that provide the building blocks for a feminist reconstruction of citizenship and highlight some key threads which interlace them. From this theoretical consolidation, I will reflect briefly on some of the implications for a feminist praxis and bring back into the equation a crucial dimension which has been more implicit than explicit hitherto: that of power.

A feminist citizenship theory: building blocks and threads

My starting point has been to reformulate and bring together the two great historical traditions of citizenship, those of civic republicanism and liberal rights, in a *critical synthesis*. Citizenship is thereby understood as both a *status*, carrying a set of rights including social and reproductive rights, and a

195

practice, involving political participation broadly defined so as to include the kind of informal politics in which women are more likely to engage. (Straddling the status–practice divide are obligations and responsibilities emphasised in the more recent communitarian tradition.) The relationship between the two elements is a dynamic one, fired by the notion of *human agency*, itself mediated by structure and culture. My reinterpretation of the two traditions has been informed by the principle of *inclusiveness*. More broadly, this principle involves strengthening the inclusive side of citizenship's membership coin while explicitly acknowledging, and as far as is possible challenging, its exclusionary side both within and at the borders of nation-states. In the latter case, this means that a feminist reconstruction of citizenship has to be *internationalist* and *multi-layered* in its thinking. It is only through such a perspective that we can address the limitations of citizenship which are thrown into relief in the face of growing numbers of migrants and asylum-seekers and of a nation-state under pressure from within and without.

A multi-layered conceptualisation of citizenship loosens its bonds with the nation-state, so that citizenship is defined over a spectrum that extends from the local through to the global. In particular, the notion of *global citizenship*, which reflects at the international level the rights and responsibilities associated with national citizenship, offers a tool to challenge, or at least temper, citizenship's exclusionary power. It does so in two main ways, both of which involve a link between citizenship and human rights. First, the framework of global citizenship encourages a focus on the responsibilities of the more affluent nation-states towards those that lack the resources to translate human rights (as defined by the UN to embrace economic, social and cultural rights) into effective citizenship rights. Second, international human rights law, if enforced by more effective institutions of global governance, could circumscribe nation-states' powers to exclude 'outsiders' by the implementation of an internationally agreed set of principles, including that of *non-discrimination*. Citizenship as practice is also being furthered at the international level by the embryonic growth of a *global civil society* through which social movements and non-governmental organisations can pursue their goals across national borders. As at the local level, women are playing an active role in this alternative forum for citizenship politics.

Within nation-states, the exclusion of women has been pivotal to the historical theoretical and political construction of citizenship. The appropriation of citizenship as a concept of potential value to feminism involves a number of steps. First, is the exposure of the ways in which, hidden under the cloak of a false universalism, this exclusion has been not accidental but integral to both historical traditions of citizenship. This then affects the terms on which women are today admitted to citizenship. Secondly, a similar challenge to the false universalism of the category woman means that a feminist reinterpretation of citizenship must integrate a gender analysis into a broader understanding of the significance of difference. The third step is to address the tension that exists between such an analysis grounded in difference and the universalism that stands at the heart of citizenship. If we see this tension as creative rather than destructive, it is possible to develop an enriched understanding of citizenship both as a status and a practice. The underlying principle that I suggest to guide us is that of a *'differentiated universalism'* which embodies the creative tension between universalism and particularity or difference.

This principle can then be applied to the terms upon which women's claims to citizenship are articulated. Typically, women have been faced with a choice between a universalistic claim based on the principle of their equality with men or a particularistic claim based on their difference from men. These represent on the one hand an ostensibly gender-neutral and on the other an explicitly gender-differentiated model of citizenship. In both cases it is a male standard against which women's citizenship is being measured and difference is conceptualised in binary rather than pluralistic terms. Overlapping oppositions are those between the universalistic ethic of justice and the particularistic ethic of care and between the ideals of independence and interdependence. In each case the either/or choices presented lead us into a theoretical and political cul-de-sac. A feminist approach needs therefore to embrace the dialectical relationship that exists between the two sides of each of these theoretical divides and, through a process of subversion and critical synthesis, reconstruct citizenship along pluralist and gender-inclusive lines. In place of the male standard, masquerading as universalism, citizenship will then embody a differentiated universalism that gives equal status to women and men in their diversity.

Underpinning these theoretical dichotomies, as well as women's exclusion from citizenship, has been the rigid gendered separation of public and private spheres. Within this separation, public and private have represented respectively universalism, justice and independence on the one hand and particularity, care and dependence on the other. The *rearticulation of this public–private divide* thus provides one of the keys to challenging women's exclusion at the level of both theory and praxis. This involves the disruption of its gendered meaning; recognition of the ways in which it is socially and politically constructed and therefore fluid rather than fixed; and acknowledgement of how in practice each side impacts on the other. The ways in which the gateways to citizenship for women and men are differently shaped by the interaction of public and private are thereby illuminated.

The rejection of the binary thinking that creates dichotomies such as these has been central to my attempt to refashion citizenship within a feminist framework. From the starting point of my critical synthesis of the two citizenship traditions in Chapter 1 through to my working out of some of the political and policy implications in Chapters 6 and 7, I have abjured either/or positions and choices in favour of the principles of fuzzy logic and critical synthesis. This approach has helped to open up the potential of citizenship for women, whereas the kind of either/or choices with which we have been traditionally faced tend to reinforce the exclusionary side of citizenship's coin and to limit our options for challenging it. A word of caution, is, however, in order. There are dangers in confusing fuzzy logic with woolly thinking. Elshtain, for instance, has dismissed those who sprinkle terms such as 'dialectical' 'like so many conceptual croutons' as evading stubborn theoretical dilemmas (1987, p. 155). I have tried to use the principles of dialectics as neither a substitute for critical analysis nor as an escape hatch into the apparent safety of the middle ground. In particular, in this Conclusion I want to stress that an appreciation of the differences within and between binary categories must not be at the expense of a gendered analysis of the power relations which still underpin them and which thereby serve to perpetuate women's exile as a group from full citizenship.

This emphasis on gendered power relations reflects another thread running through my argument. I have tried to balance an appreciation of the ways in which differences within the category 'woman' mediate women's relationship to citizenship while not abandoning the category altogether. To the extent that women, in their diversity, share a citizenship status which is, at best, marginal, it is appropriate to deploy the theoretical and political tool of gender. Such a strategic approach is summed up by Bacchi's advice that 'feminists must continue to insist upon the political relevance of "women" but contest interpretations and deployments of the category which minimize progressive developments for women and other outgroups' (1996, p. 13). In this way, while my central focus has been the ways in which citizenship's exclusionary face wears a gendered mask, the features of this mask also bear the imprint of other dimensions of exclusion. At the boundaries of the nation-state, 'outsiders' are excluded whatever their gender, although even here women can face an additional set of hurdles. Within nation-states, social divisions such as class, 'race', disability and sexuality interact with gender either to aggravate or modify its impact on women's citizenship status and potential.

This interaction is a dynamic one in which women themselves are helping to shape the contours of the interrelationships between their various identities. This brings me to my final thread: the emphasis I have placed on agency and process. In bringing together the two traditions of citizenship, I underlined how they stand in an ongoing dialectical relationship to each other. The citizenship rights, which enable people to act as agents and to express that agency in the arena of citizenship, are not fixed. They remain the object of political struggles to defend, reinterpret and extend them. Who is involved in those struggles, where they are placed in the political hierarchy and the political power and influence they can yield will help to determine the outcomes. A feminist theory of citizenship thus has to be knitted into a feminist praxis.

A feminist citizenship praxis

I have argued that citizenship as the expression of agency contributes to the recasting of women as actors on the political stage. Through an inclusive definition of political citizenship, women's 'accidental activism' in the interstices of the public and private spheres; their active participation in a nascent global civil society; and their contribution to the development of welfare citizenship come to be acknowledged and valued as acts of citizenship. At the same time, by linking agency and structure as mediated by culture, the frame of citizenship keeps in view the ways in which that political stage is still structured both materially and symbolically to disadvantage women. Thus, the shaking off of the stifling cloak of victimhood does not mean that women have ceased to be the victims of discriminatory and oppressive male-dominated political, economic and social institutions. This is not to say that all men are more powerful than all women but that the institutions (public and private), which hold the keys to citizenship in its various forms, are still by and large dominated by men. If women are to seize hold of those keys, we will have to fight for them and this will mean alliances that bridge the differences between women. A feminist praxis needs therefore to be rooted in a *politics of solidarity in difference* or what others have termed a 'transversal' politics or 'reflective solidarity'.

Such a politics is one example of how a feminist citizenship praxis has to ride the tension between the universal and the particular. It has to do so also in its use of citizenship as a yardstick or ideal. On the one hand, the universal principle at the heart of that ideal acts as a measure of the extent to which women in their diversity are being excluded from full citizenship and provides us with powerful arguments for inclusion. On the other hand, to the extent that that universalist principle in fact embodies masculine particularist interests, women will remain excluded or will be included only on male terms. At this point, some counsel rejection of citizenship in favour of a political tool more obviously friendly to women; others that we should abandon all pretensions at universalism. But in both cases, to do so would also be to lose something of real potential value to feminism. The first step, therefore, is to expose the *false* universalism of citizenship as traditionally conceived and the implications that flow from that. The second is to refashion the yardstick so that the universal and the particular are combined in an unbiased way: a differentiated instead of a false universalism.

A key issue in the refashioning of the yardstick is the value to be placed upon care for citizenship and the recognition of care as a political ideal and practice that transcends the public–private divide. The synthesis at a theoretical level of the ethics of care and justice needs to be complemented at a policy level. In the field of social citizenship, the privileging of citizen-the earner over citizen-the carer, even in those welfare states that have gone furthest in placing value on care in the construction of social citizenship, continues to spell second-class social citizenship rights for many women. However, addressing this bias faces feminist politics with a dilemma. If the balance is tipped too far in the opposite direction, there is a danger that, paradoxically, it could undermine women's longer-term citizenship position. Thus, for instance, cash payments to those who stay at home to care for children beyond the parental leave period, or very lengthy parental leave provisions themselves, run the risk of weakening women's position in the labour market in the long term. In these instances, policies that value difference threaten to do so at the expense of equality. Or, following Molyneux (1984), women's 'strategic' concerns might be damaged by policies that appear to address shorter-term 'practical' concerns.

What we need is a policy framework that is able to incorporate care as an expression of difference into the citizenship standard itself but in a way that does not undermine progress towards gender equality, thereby balancing practical and strategic gender interests. Rather than replace citizen-the earner with citizen-the carer, policy needs to create the conditions for a *'gender-inclusive'* citizenship through which citizen-the earner/carer and carer/earner can flourish. The relationship between the public and private spheres represents the fulcrum upon which this framework can be built. The goal is to shift the dynamic of the interaction between public and private from a vicious circle that undermines women's citizenship to a virtuous circle that promotes it. This means public policy has to acknowledge the constraints upon women's citizenship that derive from the 'private' sphere as well as those in the public sphere itself. A pivotal constraint, and therefore target for a feminist citizenship praxis, is the domestic *division of labour* which, I have argued, gives men a collective advantage over women in the public sphere. *Time* is a resource for citizenship, generally skewed in favour of men. Citizenship politics is therefore in part about the politics of time. It is a politics with implications for public policy which can use various levers, such as parental leave and public education, to encourage a shift in the domestic division of labour. But public policy can do no more than encourage and, ultimately, progress will require change of individual men. A fairer sexual division of labour would promote both equality and difference: it would enable women to enter the public sphere of citizenship on more equal terms with men while emphasising the importance of care responsibilities for citizenship and offering men a more balanced relationship to citizenship.

Highlighting the sexual division of labour as a strategic target does not mean that it is necessarily the primary obstacle to citizenship for all women. Nor can it on its own effect the switch from a vicious to virtuous circle of interaction between public and private even though it is one of the key points of entry into that circle. A feminist citizenship praxis thus, not surprisingly, has to operate on a number of fronts simultaneously. In the private sphere, the other political issue which I have highlighted is that of bodily and reproductive rights, *de jure* and *de facto*. Different groups of women may prioritise different aspects of these rights but it is in the interests of all women that we are able to enjoy bodily integrity and exercise effective control over our own bodies. Reproductive rights embody the principle of differentiated universalism in that they are rights specific to women, which are essential to our enjoyment of the universal citizenship ideal.

In the public sphere itself, the obstacles to women's citizenship, which interact with the domestic impediments, are to be found in the labour market, the (welfare) state and the *polis*. In both the labour market and the welfare state, the priority must be to combat female poverty and promote women's economic independence. Action in the labour market needs to address not only the gendered horizontal and vertical occupational segregation and pay gap, which characterise labour markets worldwide, but also the growing cleavages within the female labour force itself. For some women, gender interacts with divisions such as class and educational attainment, 'race' and disability to spell long-term economic marginalisation and poverty. The strengthening of women's labour market position is important also for their social citizenship rights. In the welfare state, a primary target is the gendered template according to which social citizenship rights are determined. This would be part of a broader redrawing of social citizenship so as to promote 'time for care' both through the right to take (limited) time out of the labour market to care and through policies to facilitate the synchronisation of employment and care. Key policy levers include parental and carers' leave and time-off for family reasons on the one hand and the availability of high quality, affordable care services on the other. Such policies would signify a more balanced sharing of responsibility for the care of children and adults between the state and individual families than exists in most countries. In the political sphere, the future development of women's citizenship depends on women, in their diversity, being actively involved, both through the formal and informal political systems, in the development of public policies. As Dahlerup puts it, feminists have 'to learn to live with the state' (1994, p. 117). This requires strategies appropriate to each country for increasing women's representation in formal power structures, with attention to the interests of 'minority group' women. These need to be complemented by mechanisms to make formal political systems more accessible to informal political groupings.

This is true at every level of politics from the sub-national and the national, through the regional to the international. A feminist praxis of citizenship committed to the principle of inclusion cannot stop at the borders of individual nation-states. The notion of global citizenship provides a possible framework for an internationalist feminist politics committed to a more just global economic order and to more inclusionary and non-discriminatory policies towards 'outsiders' at the borders of and inside nation-states. In both cases, women are particularly adversely affected by policies of exclusion and by the world economic order. Feminist interventions have already been critical in furthering understanding in international circles that 'human rights are women's rights'. It was women's international collective action that achieved the recognition in the 1993 Declaration of the UN Vienna World Conference on Human Rights that 'the human rights of women and of the girl-child are an inalienable, integral and indivisible part of universal human rights' (Amnesty International, 1995). The 1995 Beijing Declaration likewise bore the imprint of the global feminist networking that preceded it. In terms of both outcome and process, Beijing marked a milestone in the development of an on-going internationalist feminist citizenship praxis.

It is important to acknowledge when progress *is* made while at the same time not losing sight of the distance we still have to travel. In the words of Pippa Norris, we have 'to steer a difficult course between the Scylla of complacency and the Charybdis of cynicism' (1987, p. 147). On the one hand, to discount cynically the extent of change is to underestimate women's achievements as citizens in helping to bring about that change against so many odds. In so doing, we reinforce the image of women as passive victims rather than as active agents of change and contribute to a culture of defeatism. On the other hand, complacency about women's position today feeds the forces of 'post-feminist' backlash in a denial of the extent to which women as a group still enjoy inferior citizenship status. Moreover, in highlighting the ability of more privileged women to take the citizenship stage alongside men, it ignores the cross-cutting relations of super- and subordination which serve to create a gulf between these women and those who are less privileged because of their class, 'race', sexuality, disability or age. From the perspective of women in poverty, in particular, this gulf is widening in a number of countries.

The delicate balance between complacency and cynicism hinges in part on the question of power. It is a question that has been more implicit than explicit in my account of citizenship although it has surfaced in most chapters. From the perspective of power as self-realisation, my account of women as active citizens has emphasised their power or potential power. From the perspective of power as domination, the power of both nation-states and of dominant groups within nation-states to exclude both 'outsiders' and subordinate 'insider' groups from full citizenship has been a recurrent thread. This power has been exercised at a material level, on both sides of and across the public–private divide, through control over access to the range of citizenship rights. It has also been exercised discursively, most notably through the gendered demarcation of public and private spheres itself, which has underwritten the masculine bias at the heart of citizenship as traditionally conceived. The challenge for a feminist citizenship theory and praxis is to challenge this power, in both its material and discursive manifestations, in the name of the citizenship claims of women in their diversity at both national and international level.

Notes and References

Introduction

1. For a critique, see Lister (1990b); Walby (1994); Voet (1998).
2. See, for instance, Lehning and Weale (1997); European Commission (1998); Osler and Starkey (1999); Wiener (1999); Hansen (2000).
3. See the report of the UK Qualifications and Curriculum Authority (Crick, 1998), discussed by Osler (2000) and compared with citizenship education in France in Osler and Starkey (2001). For a general discussion of citizenship education, see Demaine and Entwistle (1996); Heater (1999); Pearce and Hallgarten (2000); Lister et al., 2001 and for a gendered perspective Arnot and Dillabough (2000).
4. Examples can be found in special issues of *Citizenship Studies* on Muslim communities (1999) and Hong Kong (2001) and in discussions of gender and citizenship in India (Huq, 2000); Zimbabwe (Nkiwane, 2000) and South Africa (Seidman, 1999; McEwan, 2000). Castles and Davidson (2000, p. 195), however, warn that the notion is 'problematic' in those countries in Asia and the Pacific where democracy and human rights are absent. Jones and Gaventa (2002) illustrate its emergence as an area of debate in development studies.
5. Alvarez et al. (1998, p. 2). See also Soares et al. (1995); *Social Politics* (1998); Marcos (1999); Vargas and Olea (1999); Molyneux (2000); Schild (2002); Peruzzotti (2002).
6. One of the most influential works of the 1990s in the UK, Will Hutton's *The State We're In* (1995), drew heavily on the language of citizenship.
7. See for instance Alvarez et al. (1998); *Critical Social Policy* (1998); Crouch et al., 2001.
8. The phrase was coined by Gallie (1956), cited in Vandenberg (2002) who discusses its relevance to citizenship.
9. Jones and Gaventa (2002, p. 19); see also Jones (1994); Hall et al. (1999). Bussemaker and Voet (1998) discuss vocabularies. Citizenship's contextual nature is also emphasised by Carens (2000), and by Molyneux (2007) and McEwan (2000) in the circumstances of Latin America and South Africa respectively.
10. Saraceno (1997, pp. 27, 32); Jenson and Phillips (2001, p. 72). The point is exemplified by empirical research in the US and UK, which discovered different understandings of citizenship rights, duties and identities in the two nations (Conover et al., 1991).

11. Increasingly, though, the course is being regarded as a right which, as such, should not be confined to male 'breadwinner' claimants (Bussemaker, personal communication prior to change of government in 2002).

12. *Guardian*, 4 April 1989. Under the primary purpose rule, since abolished by New Labour, a would-be immigrant spouse or fiancé had to prove that a marriage was not entered into primarily in order to obtain admission to the UK.

13. Turner (1990, p. 193). His criticism has been made by a number of commentators but rejected by others such as Held (1989). For a discussion, see Rees (1996), who defends Marshall against the charge of underplaying conflict on the grounds that this was an accurate depiction of the development of citizenship in Britain, a stance that is itself open to challenge.

14. Oliver (1993, p. 6; 1996). See also Bynoe *et al.* (1991); Keith (1992); Barton, (1993, 1996); Morris (1993a); Shakespeare (1993); Beresford (1999); Marks (2001); and for a more critical, feminist, perspective Meekosha and Dowse (1997); Monks (1999).

15. Stonewall (2001). For an overview of the literature see Lister (2002b).

16. The term 'minority group' is placed in inverted commas in acknowledgement of its problematic status (see Brah, 1996). Its usage here is not confined to racialised or ethnicised groups, but refers to all groups whose numerically minority position places them in a disadvantaged position vis-à-vis 'socio-economic and cultural relations of power' (Brah, 1996, p. 188)

17. Williams (1995b) and Williams, Popay and Oakley (1999); see also Deacon and Mann (1999) and Hoggett (2001). Examples of social policy analysis, which does combine agency and structure, can be found in Finch (1989); Finch and Mason (1993); Yeandle (1996); Leonard (1997); Duncan and Edwards (1999).

18. Roche (1992, p. 2); Turner (1993, p. ix); see also Fulbrook and Cesarani (1996, pp. 210–11).

Chapter 1

1. A history of the two citizenship traditions can be found in Heater (1990), Oliver and Heater (1994) and Falks (2000), and of the development of democracy in Held (1987). For an account of classical Graeco–Roman citizenship see Pockock (1992), with a feminist critique by Okin (1992). Mann (1987) and Turner (1990) provide a more theoretical cross-national historical analysis, which has been the subject of a feminist critique by Walby (1994).

2. Authors such as Miller (2000) and Delanty (2000) emphasise also the differences between different strands of communitarianism. For an exposition of a communitarian citizenship agenda, see Tam (1998); and for a more critical discussion from a feminist perspective, see Frazer and Lacey (1993); Kingdom (1996); Bussemaker and Voet (1998). The influence of communitarianism on New Labour is discussed by Lister (1998); Hughes and Little (1999); Heron (2001).

3. Riley (1992, p. 180). For an assessment of Marshall's contribution, see Bulmer and Rees (1996) and for a re-reading of Marshall's work, which suggests it contains two, not necessarily compatible, theories of citizenship, see Rees (1995a).

Marshall has, though, been less influential in Continental European countries, most notably Germany and France.

4. Kymlicka (2001, p. 26). Canada (Jenson and Phillips, 2001) and South Africa (McEwan, 2000) are examples of explicit attempts to build a national citizenship identity in the late twentieth century; the European Union is an example of an attempt to do so at the supra-national level, appealing to a shared European culture through an 'ethno-cultural citizenship discourse' (Hansen, 2000, p. 153; Wiener, 1999).

5. Examples from a burgeoning literature include Jones (1994); Turner (1997); Pakulski (1997); Alvarez *et al.* (1998); Hobson (1999); Isin and Wood (1999); Werbner and Yuval-Davis (1999); Hall (2000); Stevenson (2001).

6. For a legal exposition, see Gardner (1990) and for a sociological, Turner (1993, 1994) and Scott (1994).

7. See, for instance, Dagger (1997); Kymlicka and Norman (1994, 2000); McKinnon and Hampsher-Monk (2000) and for a discussion of the importance of a culture of citizenship, Crossley (2001).

8. The two different orientations to citizenship are not necessarily mutually exclusive. For example, it is not unusual for those on the right to combine a classical liberal conception of citizenship rights with an emphasis on the paid work obligations of poorer citizens, reflecting both ideas of contract (Scott, 1992) and the combination of neo-liberal and neo-conservative strands in new right thought (King, 1987).

9. For a discussion of the development of a different paradigm in the US, which excluded social rights, see Turner (1990); Shklar (1991) and Fraser and Gordon (1994b). In Germany, the earlier deployment of social rights by the state means that the notion of social citizenship is not now common currency.

10. Plant (1988, 1989, 1990, 1992). See also Held, V. (1993, pp. 176–7) for a similar argument from a feminist perspective. The new right's approach is discussed by King (1987) and Faulks (1998); a critical account of both Plant and the neo-liberal position can be found in Espada (1996).

11. Gould (1988, p. 32). See also Held, D. (1989, 1994); Taylor-Gooby (1991); Twine (1994). Narayan (1997a, p. 54), however, suggests that 'human dignity' rather than autonomy is a more helpful concept to 'ground both negative and positive rights as central to citizenship'.

12. See Expert Group on Fundamental Rights (1999); Ferguson (1999); UNDP (2000); Jones and Gaventa (2002).

13. Esping-Andersen (1990); Marshall (1950, p. 47); see also Lister (1990a).

14. Its value has been emphasised in, for example, Latin America (*Social Politics*, 1998; Alvarez *et al.*, 1998; Richards, 2000); Canada (Jenson and Phillips, 2001); South Africa (McEwan, 2000).

15. See, for instance, Gerhard (1997). The best known exposition of the liberal feminist position is Friedan's *The Feminist Mystique* (1963/1986). Feminists who have emphasised the importance of rights from a more radical position include Narayan (1997a); Sarvasy (1997); Siim (2000). For radical feminist and care theorist arguments against rights see MacKinnon (1989) and Noddings (1984) respectively; for a socialist and a postmodern perspective see Rowbotham (1989) and Ahmed (1998) respectively. For other feminist accounts of rights see Kingdom (1991); Smart (1989); Vogel (1988, p. 155); Hirschmann and Di

Stefano (1996, pp. 16–19); and for an overview see Bryson (1992, 1999); Voet (1998); Hobson and Lister (2002).

16. Marques-Pereira (1995); see also Shaver (1993/4). Feminist misgivings about rights discourses in general are, however, mirrored in more specific debates around reproductive rights (Yuval-Davis (1997a), drawing on Correa and Petchesky (1994); O'Connor, Orloff and Shaver (1999)). See Pakulski (1997) and Isin and Wood (1999) for a discussion of cultural and other new rights claims associated with recognition politics.

17. Held (1989, pp. 201–2, 1994, 1995). Turner has identified the emergence of environmental, aboriginal and cultural rights, in the context of the erosion of the Marshallian, national citizenship framework. These, he suggests, are underpinned by a 'generic right ... to ontological security' (2001, p. 206).

18. Ignatieff (1989); Roche (1992). See also Croft and Beresford (1989, 1992); Beresford and Croft (1993); Barnes (1997, 1999a); Siim (1998); Higgins (1999); Commission on Poverty, Participation and Power (2000); and for an international perspective, Cornwall and Gaventa (2000). This approach to the empowerment of welfare state users stands in contrast to that of the British Conservative Government under John Major, which introduced a Citizen's Charter exemplifying a consumerist, market-oriented conception of citizenship rights in which the citizen is transformed into a customer (see Taylor, 1991/2; Miller and Peroni, 1992). It also needs to be distinguished from those participatory approaches that frame users as 'market citizens' as part of neo-liberal modernisation programmes in the Southern hemisphere (Schild, 1998, 2000; Cornwall and Gaventa, 2002). Moreover, despite a growing emphasis on user-involvement in Northern welfare states, the development of a 'contract culture' as part of the marketisation of welfare, reflects the narrower classical liberal conception of rights. As services are contracted out to non-state providers, the rights involved are those of contract rather than rights against the state, with possible implications for both access to and the quality of services provided. I am grateful to Jane Lewis for this point. It has since been developed by Freedland, who argues that marketisation downgrades 'the citizen's voice in government, both by denying the directness of that voice and by commercializing the subject-matter of the discussion between citizen and government' (2001, p. 91).

19. 'Work-welfare' programmes are discussed by Coenen and Leisink (1993); King (1995); Peck (1998a, b); Theodore and Peck (1999); Peck and Theodore (2001); Lødemel and Trickey (2001); Saunders (2002).

20. White (2000, p. 507). King and Ward (1992) draw attention to how the language of contract has been deployed to justify the intensification of 'work-welfare' programmes in both the US and the UK (see also Naples, 1997; Jordan, 1998; Rosanvallon, 2000; Jayasuriya, 2001). In the UK, New Labour launched its welfare reform strategy under the overarching title of 'A New Contract for Welfare' (see Lister, 2001). For an overview of the arguments concerning work obligations, see Deacon (1997) and Kildal (1999a).

21. I am concerned here not with the logical relationship between rights and duties i.e. that one person's right creates a duty on someone else to respect it, but with the moral and political relationship between a person's right and that person's own performance of duties (Kildal, 1999b). Empirical research in the UK among welfare state users found considerable differences on the question of whether

access to health, social housing and unemployment benefits should be conditional upon responsible behaviour. The conclusion reached was that willingness to accept a link between welfare rights and responsibilities depends on the particular context (Dwyer, 2000).

22. The former argument can be found in Doyal and Gough (1991) and Held (1994). Different kinds of reciprocity are discussed by Fitzpatrick (2001).

23. For a critique of the Conservative exposition of active citizenship see Lister (1990a, b) and Faulks (1998) and for a gendered analysis of how 'everyday citizens' understand the term, see MacKian (1998).

24. The main examples are Australia and the Netherlands. The case is made by Leisink and Coenen (1993); Young (1995); Leisink (1997); Hirsch (1999); Lister (2001).

25. Levitas (1998) makes a feminist case against paid work obligations and White and Gardner the case for a new 'integrated conception of civic responsibility', which acknowledges 'the contributive status of care work' (2000, p. 105). The more philosophical argument about the nature of obligations and responsibilities can be found in Hirschmann (1996) and Sevenhuijsen (2000). Narayan (1997a) goes further and argues that even more expansive understandings of citizenship responsibility, which include care, are potentially exclusionary and damaging to citizenship, understood as connoting social standing and dignity.

26. For a discussion of ecological citizenship, see Giddens (1991); Weale (1991); Roche (1992); Twine (1994); Isin and Wood (1999); Faulks (2000).

27. See Roche (1992); Oliver and Heater (1994); van Steenbergen (1994); Jelin (2000); Dean (2001).

28. Of particular importance has been *The Human Condition* (1958). For a discussion of the significance of Arendt's contribution see d'Entrèves (1992).

29. See Jones and Jónasdóttir (1988); Evans *et al.* (1986); Pateman (1989); Bryson (1992, 1999); Phillips (1998); Corrin (1999).

30. Held (1987, pp. 275, 277, emphasis in original). He does, though, exclude from politics what he describes as 'the sphere of the intimate', a distinction that is implicitly challenged by Plummer's (1995, 2001) notion of intimate citizenship (see Chapter 5). His definition also excludes cultural recognition politics (Fraser, 1997).

31. See Morris (1991); Barton (1993, 1996); Oliver (1993, 1996); Shakespeare (1998).

32. Lord Melchett in *The Independent*, 1 August 1999; Heater (1990, p. 201). The circumstances in which civil disobedience constitutes 'good citizenship' are not easily determined in the abstract. Sparks excludes violent action in a democratic polity on the grounds that it is undemocratic because it collapses 'the space for collective debate and contestation' (1997, p. 84). It also fails to respect the citizenship rights of others. The question of when breaking the law is compatible with good citizenship is also discussed by Dagger (1997) and McKinnon (2000).

33. See Narayan (1997a, p. 59); and in the context of the South, McEwan (2000); Jones and Gaventa (2002).

34. Leca (1992, p. 21). See also Lowndes (1995); Young (2000, ch. 5). Civil society has been defined in a variety of ways. My own usage of the term is consistent with that provided by Adamson (1987/1988): 'the public space between large-scale bureaucratic structures of state and economy on the one hand, and the

private sphere of family, friendships, personality and intimacy on the other', provided it is understood that the public–private divide upon which it is premised is permeable and not fixed.

35. Meekosha and Dowse (1997) point out how the language and imagery of citizenship is imbued with a disablist 'hegemonic normalcy'; see also Breckenridge and Voglar (2001).

36. In divided societies like Northern Ireland, the distinction is particularly difficult to draw. Depending on how it is conducted, community action can either feed sectarianism or help to combat it (Lovett *et al.*, 1995).

37. See Coote and Pattullo (1990); Mayo (1994); the Northern Ireland Women and Citizenship Research Group (1995); Naples (1998a, c); Sudbury (1998).

38. Indeed, according to Kymlicka and Norman (1994) it is 'their emphasis on the intrinsic value of political participation for the participants themselves', as the highest form of human development, that distinguishes civic republicans from other proponents of participatory democracy.

39. Frazer and Lacey (1993, p. 196). See also Waltzer (1970, 1992); Phillips (1991); Oliver and Heater (1994).

40. Gould (1988, p. 209). See also Parry (1991) citing Gewirth (1982); and Bauböck (1994); Delanty (2000).

41. Mouffe (1992a, pp. 225, 227) citing Skinner (1984, 1992).

42. Isin and Wood (1999, p. ix); Dagnino (1998, p. 50); Baierle (1998, p. 123); Santos (2001). See also Lustiger-Thaler and Shragge (1993); Pakulski (1997); Tilly (1997) and endnote 14, p. 205.

43. Dagger (1997) likewise emphasises the compatibility of the traditions, pointing out how some of the most important political theorists historically drew on elements of both. He argues, however, that this compatibility requires that the rights-bearing individual is understood not as atomised and isolated, but as embedded in social relations. He proposes a 'republican liberalism' that 'promises to strengthen the appeal of duty, community and the common good while preserving the appeal of rights' (p. 5). He thus places greater emphasis on the communitarian streak in republicanism than on its appeal to civic participation. For him the link between liberalism and republicanism lies in autonomy, but an autonomy grounded in interdependence. The importance of combining the traditions has also been emphasised as 'crucial to the study of citizenship in sub-Saharan Africa' (Halisi *et al.*, 1998).

44. The point is made by Vincent (1991, p. 206) in his history of 'poor citizens'; see also Ignatieff (1989) and the arguments of those on the centre-left for a combination of state-guaranteed welfare rights and democratic accountability 'through bottom up participation in the range of welfare services' (The Sheffield Group, 1989, p. 269; also Harris, 1987; Taylor-Gooby, 1991; Barnes, 1997).

45. For an historical account of this interaction, as it has varied between countries, see Lewis (1980); Dale and Foster (1986); Hernes (1987); Riley (1988); Gordon (1990); Bock and Thane (1991); Sarvasy (1992); Koven and Michel (1993); Tilly (1997); Hobson (1999); Siim (2000); Sainsbury (2001).

46. See Giddens (1991); Doyal and Gough (1991); Twine (1994); Williams *et al.*, 1999.

47. Mohanty (1992, p. 75). For an example of such feminist scholarship, see Rowbotham (1974, 1992).

48. hooks (1984, p. 45); see also Morris (1993b); Alexander and Mohanty (1997); Mirza (1997); Sudbury (1998).

49. See Davis (1991) and Wolffensperger (1991). An alternative, Foucauldian, notion of power is deployed by Brown to warn against the dangers of 'a politics of *ressentiment*', which 'fixes the identities of the injured and the injuring' in an 'economy of perpetrator and victim' (1995, p. 27). This, Yeatman (1997, p. 146) describes, as a politics of reaction and identity-preservation rather than 'of social transformation that encourages ... a positive relationship to power'. However, she acknowledges that there are situations of systematic exploitation, such as where democratic institutions are lacking, where a 'politics of *ressentiment*' makes sense. More generally, Bickford argues that 'claims of "victimhood" and suffering' should not simply be dismissed as expressions of powerlessness, for they can also constitute a protest against the unjust exercise of power. As such they are also 'part of the languages of citizenship' (1997, p. 126; see also Dean, 1997).

50. The concept of 'gender culture' is taken from Pfau-Effinger, who defines it as norms and values concerning 'the desirable "correct" form of gender relations and of the division of labour between women and men' (1998, p. 150).

51. Jones (1994, p. 260) takes a similar approach in distinguishing between citizenship as identity and practice so that, when combined, 'as a practice, citizenship defines the action of those who have the identity of citizens'. Likewise, Kymlicka and Norman (1994, p. 353) argue that 'we should expect a theory of the good citizen to be relatively independent of the legal question of what it is to be a citizen, just as a theory of the good person is distinct from the metaphysical (or legal) question of what it is to be a person'. However, Kymlicka (2001, pp. 297–8) has subsequently argued that citizens do have an obligation to protest against injustice and 'to uphold just institutions'. The general point is also an important one when considering the citizenship status of those citizens, such as chronically ill, frail or very severely disabled people, whose capacity to exercise their citizenship obligations and rights is impaired, a problem for citizenship theory raised by Rees (1995b); Bulmer and Rees (1996); Monks (1999). Meekosha and Dowse describe 'capacity for citizenship' as 'a major hurdle in the liberation of people with disabilities' (1997, p. 65).

Chapter 2

1. See Brubaker (1989, 1990, 1992); Hammar (1990); Baldwin-Edwards (1991a, b); Cesarani and Fulbrook (1996); Morris (1997); Castles and Miller (1998); Castles and Davidson (2000); Kofman *et al.* (2000).

2. The distinction between formal and substantive citizenship is made by Hammer (1990, p. 3); that between legal and sociological by Moore (1993).

3. See Ginsburg (1989, 1994a); Bovenkerk *et al.* (1990); Cook (1993); Castles and Davidson (2000, ch. 5).

4. See Lutz (1997); Delanty (1997a); Hansen (2000); Fink *et al.* (2001).

5. UN (1995a); UNHCR (2001). The inadequacies of the published data are underlined by Kofman *et al.* (2000), who provide a thorough overview of female migration in Europe. A gendered analysis can also be found in Morokvasic

(1984, 1991, 1993); Buijs (1993); Bhabha and Shutter (1994); Knocke (1995); Lutz (1997); Ackers (1998); Ferreira *et al.* (1998); Anthias (2000).

6. Sassen (1998) argues that female migrants now constitute a key source of labour in the globalised economy. The domestic service and sex/marriage industries are among the sectors for which they are recruited (Bakan and Stasiulis (1995); European Women's Lobby (1995); Anderson (1997, 2000); Lutz (1997); Hochschild (2000); Kofman *et al.* (2000).

7. See Morokvasic (1991); Anthias (1992); Anthias and Yuval-Davis (1992); Bhabha and Shutter (1994); Freeman (1995); Knocke (1995); Sales and Gregory (1996); Lutz (1997); Kofman and Sales (1998); Harris (2000) and, in the context of intra-European migration, Ackers (1996, 1998).

8. The economic context of migration is discussed in Hammar (1990); Simpson (1993); Dirks (1998); Düvell and Jordan (1999). Paul (1991) and Morris (1994) characterise migrants as a reserve army of labour.

9. European Women's Lobby (1995). A general account of the tightening of immigration laws can be found in Horsman and Marshall (1994); Williams (1995a); Fekete (1997); Kofman *et al.* (2000). For the British situation, see, for an historical account, Cohen (1985, 1995) and Lewis (1998), and for contemporary developments, Gordon (1989, 1991); Foley and Nelles (1993); Bhabha and Shutter (1994); Morris (1998).

10. This, in turn, has led to concern in countries such as South Africa about the poaching of welfare professionals (*Guardian Society*, 6 June 2001, p. 7).

11. The nature of the European shutters and their erection by non-accountable inter-governmental agencies is discussed by Paul (1991); Bunyan (1993); Mitchell and Russell (1994); Gallagher (1995); Kveinen (2002). The implications of Fortress Europe for women are explored in European Women's Lobby (1995); Lutz (1997); Kofman and Sales (1998). The tensions and contradictions involved in EU migration policies are analysed by Morris (1997).

12. It is also a relatively elite group of Europeans who are best positioned to enjoy this right (Hansen, 2000). Moreover, Bhabha and Shutter (1994) point out how the extension of the right of free movement to certain non-EU, non-resident nationals who are members of EFTA, while longstanding resident non-EU nationals remain excluded, highlights the racialised nature of the hierarchy of rights that has been created. The ways in which the hierarchy is also gendered are explored by Ackers (1994, 1998) who discusses family-based free movement rights and the problems associated with cohabitation and separation or divorce, which mainly affect women. Social rights are portable within the EU for EU nationals in paid employment (and their children) with a derived right for their legally married spouses. Other migrants within the EU, including non-married partners, have only minimal social entitlements.

13. Gordon (1991, p. 84). The point about symbolic borders is made by Bhavnani (1993), Lutz (1997) and Brah (1993) who also discusses the gendered nature of racism. See also Ginsburg (1989, 1992, 1994a); Cook (1993); Hensen (2000), Marfleet (2001) and for a more general discussion of 'the other', Young (1993).

14. The term 'irregular' immigrants is suggested by Spencer (1994). For a discussion of their treatment, see Brubaker (1989); Baldwin-Edwards (1991b); Silverman (1992); Morris (1994); Fakete (1997); Castles and Miller (1998); Düvell and Jordan (1999).

15. See Brubaker (1989); Ginsburg (1992, 1994a); Fekete (1997); Whitaker (1998); Katz (2001). In the UK, there has been strong opposition to the progressive erosion under Conservative and New Labour governments of asylum-seekers' rights, culminating in the replacement of social security by humiliating and less generous vouchers (to be withdrawn in the face of protest). There has also been concern about the denial of the basic civil rights of those held in detention, often for long periods. *INexile*, the journal of the Refugee Council, is a good source of information.

16. See Camus-Jacques (1989); Buijs (1993); Kofman *et al.* (2000). For more detailed information about the difficulties faced by female refugees and asylum-seekers, see Bhabha and Shutter (1994); Peters and Wolper (1995); www.womenlobby.org/asylumcampaign.

17. This is at least the theory and for those, mainly women, admitted as family members, such rights may only be derived from those of their husbands (Knocke, 1995). This is one aspect of a more complex 'civic stratification' discussed by Morris (1997). Also, in virtually all states access to certain public sector jobs is excluded.

18. For information about local voting rights, see Miller (1989); Hammar (1990); Baldwin-Edwards (1991a, 1991b); Layton-Henry (1991). Miller (and also Samers, 1998) points to the extent of political activity among immigrant populations. Kofman *et al.* document political activity among female migrants, suggesting that 'constraints on participation in the formal political process have not prevented women from participating in other aspects of political citizenship through struggles to extend their rights and those of others' (2000, p. 190).

19. For an overview of and naturalisation rate estimates and policies see Brubaker (1989); Baldwin-Edwards (1991a, 1991b); Clarke *et al.* (1998); Castles and Davidson (2000). Dual citizenship is advocated by Carens (1989); Hammar (1990); Canefe (1998). Castles and Miller (1998) suggest measures, such as special representative bodies and voting rights for long-term residents, in the case of those who choose not to become citizens.

20. See Bhavnani (1993); Yuval-Davis and Anthias (1989); Yuval-Davis (1993, 1997a, b); Kosambi (1995).

21. This tension is discussed by Harris (1987); Miller (1987); Riley (1992). For a discussion of cultural citizenship and its associated politics see also Alvarez *et al.* (1998); Isin and Wood (1999); Perez-Bustillo (2000); Stevenson (2001).

22. Parekh argues that positive equality requires that the usual repertoire of citizenship rights should be extended to include cultural rights. These he defines as 'the rights an individual or a community requires to express, maintain and transmit their cultural identity' (2000, p. 211). For further elaboration on cultural rights see Pakulski (1997); Cowan *et al.* (2001); Stevenson (2001). Pakulski draws particular attention to 'Aboriginal rights', as do Dodds (1998) and Turner (2001). For a more general discussion of recognition and citizenship see Taylor (1992) and Isin and Wood (1999). Language raises some difficult issues, discussed by Carens (2000, pp. 77–87, 124–131). In a number of countries, new members are required to learn the official language. This could be seen as enforcing cultural assimilation, as evidenced in the outcry against the proposal, in a 2002 White Paper, that learning English should be made a condition of UK citizenship. But Macey (1995) points out that without knowledge of the official

language, members of a society are likely to be marginalised and excluded from full participation, a point acknowledged by multi-culturalists such as Carens (2000) and Kymlicka (2001) who support the recognition of minority ethnic languages. Where women are denied access to knowledge of the language by male members of their communities, this exclusion is exacerbated; indeed UK Home Office Ministers have cited the protection of minority ethnic women's civil rights in justification of the proposal.

23. Kymlicka (2001, p. 36); see also Carens (2000); Kymlicka and Norman (2000); Patten (2000); Tully (2000); and Parekh's (2000) treatise on multi-culturalism.

24. Raz (1994, p. 73, cited by Phillips, 1995, p. 18) argues that respect for different cultures must be conditional on, among other things, 'the right of individuals to abandon their cultural group'. The general problems with multi-culturalism are elaborated by Yuval-Davis (1991a, 1994, 1997a); Anthias and Yuval-Davis (1992); Silverman (1992); Bhavnani (1993); Knocke (1998).

25. Although, as Kymlicka himself acknowledges, such a distinction may be difficult to maintain in practice, it does offer a possible framework for addressing claims for 'minority group' rights whilst recognising different interests within groups. For an alternative formulation in relation to family law, see Shachar (2000).

26. This argument has been put by Parekh (1991) and Galeotti (1993), the latter in a discussion of the implications for citizenship of the French 'headscarf' controversy, in which three Muslim schoolgirls were banned from school so long as they refused to uncover their heads. She argues that 'equality of respect', which is crucial to citizenship, requires public recognition of collective identities and not just their private sufferance. For a discussion of the 'headscarf affair' as an example of a conflict between secularism and difference, see Silverman (1992, pp. 111–18); Favell (1998, pp. 173–193); and for a feminist perspective, Kofman and Sales (1992) and Gaspard (1998).

27. In a letter to the *Guardian* (22 July 1989), Southall Black Sisters and the Brent Asian Women's Refuge attacked the British Labour Party's support for separate Muslim schools as delivering them into 'the hands of male, conservative and religious forces within our communities, who deny us our right to live as we please'. Separate schools, they argued, 'seek to control the lives of women', leaving no space for questioning of issues around reproductive rights, domestic violence and women's position in the family.

28. See Ålund (1999a, b); Welsch (1999) and, for an account of culture as a contested process, Cowan *et al.* (2001). Isin and Wood (1999) prefer 'diasporic' to 'multi-cultural' citizenship, as suggestive of a more transformatory politics.

29. Held (1991a, p. 24). This link is also discussed by Anthias and Yuval-Davis (1992); Turner (1993); Castles and Davidson (2000); Delanty (2000); Faulks (2000). For an exposition of the legal relationship between citizenship and the nation-state, with particular reference to the UK, see Gardner (1990).

30. For a discussion of the impact on nation-state citizenship of these pressures, see Hobsbawm (1994); Horsman and Marshall (1994); Held (1995); Pettman (1999); Castles and Davidson (2000); Delanty (2000).

31. The two most common paths are exemplified by France and Germany, commonly described as *jus soli* and *jus sanguinis*. Brubaker summarises the contrast between the two as follows: 'While birth and residence in France automatically transform second-generation immigrants into citizens, birth and residence in

Germany have no bearing on citizenship. Vis-à-vis immigrants, the French citizenry is defined expansively, as a territorial community, the German citizenry restrictively, as a community of descent. These diverging definitions of the citizenry embody and express distinctive understandings of nationhood, state-centred and assimilationist in France, ethnocultural and "differentialist" in Germany' (1990, p. 379; 1992; for a critical appraisal, see Behnke, 1997). The Schröder Government has modified Germany's citizenship laws to take some account of birth and residence in the face of considerable right-wing resistance (Morris, 2000; Schuster and Solomos, 2002). A number of theorists have developed typologies of models or regimes to make sense of different nation-state approaches to migration, membership and citizenship (Castles and Miller, 1993; Soysal, 1994; Williams, 1995a; Kofman *et al.*, 2000).

32. Yuval-Davis and Anthias (1989); Anthias and Yuval-Davis (1992); Yuval-Davis (1993, 1997a). See also Horsman and Marshall (1994), who refer to the 'myth of the nation' (p. xviii); Castles and Davidson whose 'main thesis' is 'that a theory of citizenship for a global society must be based on the separation between nation and state' (2000, p. 24); and Delanty (2000).

33. See also Walby (1992); Pettman (1996); Cockburn (1998). Women's symbolic and actual role in the construction of the nation and nationalisms has similarly been highlighted by Williams (1989, 1995a) with particular reference to the development of social citizenship in the context of early twentieth-century British imperialism. That it is a heterosexual nation-state which women symbolise is underlined by Alexander (1994) and Richardson (1996).

34. See Amnesty International (1995); UN (1995b); Pettman (1996); Cockburn (1998).

35. For a discussion of regionalism see Meehan (1993a); Horsman and Marshall (1994); Taylor (1994).

36. This formulation is borrowed from Silverman (1992). The exclusive nature of EU citizenship has also been analysed by O'Leary (1996); Roche and van Berkel (1997); Hansen (2000); Kveinen (2002).

37. See for instance, Soysal (1994); Lehning and Weale (1997); Roche and van Berkel (1998); Delanty (1997a, 1998, 2000).

38. Meehan, (1993c, p. 195, 1993b). For a relatively positive interpretation of the EU's impact on equal opportunities, despite the legal constraints within which it operates, see Walby (1999), who argues this has been achieved mainly through legal regulation of employment, and Hantrais (2000). A more critical reading, which emphasises the narrow interpretation of equality underpinning EU sex equality law and many of the decisions of the European Court of Justice, is provided by Hervey and Shaw (1998).

39. Teague (1998, p. 117), for instance, warns that 'the road to monetary union paved by Europe's political elite spells bad news for already beleaguered welfare and employment systems'. Kiernan (1997) is critical of the EU's failure to defend social rights in the face of the pressures of globalisation.

40. Hutton and Giddens (2000, p. xi). See also Robertson (1990); McGrew (1992); Held (1991b, 1993); European Centre (1993); Mishra (1999); Pettman (1999); Clarke (2001), and for the argument that we are seeing the maturing of an international economy, rather than globalisation as such, Hirst and Thompson (1999).

41. Keane (1994). For a more critical assessment, which places greater emphasis on the 'digital divide' that exists within and between societies, see Murdock and Golding (1989, 2001); Golding (1994, 1996); Comor (1998); Golding and Murdock (2001); Tambini (2001b); Selwyn (2002).

42. The implications of environmental factors for nation-state citizenship are explored by Steward (1991); Weale (1991); Oliver and Heater (1994); Twine (1994); van Steenbergen (1994); Newby (1996); Jelin (2000); Shiva (2000).

43. Soysal (2001, p. 335; 1994; see also Sassen, 1998, Ch.2). Although her formulation has been influential, it has also been criticised for exaggerating the extent to which human rights have superseded national citizenship rights and for downplaying the importance of participatory political rights, which remain rooted in nation state citizenship (Delanty, 1997a; Faulks 2000; Kofman *et al.*, 2000; Schuster and Solomos, 2002).

44. See Hammar (1990); Allen and Macey (1991); Bovenkerk *et al.* (1991); Bunyan (1993); Fekete (1997); Kofman *et al.* (2000).

45. Mishra is among those who argue that nation states still have considerable autonomy in relation to economic and social policy and that the impact of globalisation is mediated by national policy approaches, reflecting different models of capitalism, but that globalisation can 'serve as a convenient rationalization for neoliberal policies' (1999, p. 103; see also Hirst and Thompson, 1999, ch. 6; Pierson, 2001; Sykes *et al.*, 2001).

46. Examples are: Turner (1990); Roche (1992); Dahrendorf (1994, 1996); Yuval-Davis and Werbner (1999); Delanty (2000); Faulks (2000). Baubōck (1994) prefers the notion of 'transnational' to that of global citizenship because of the suggestion of global governmental institutions implied by the latter. Transnational citizenship represents, he suggests, a means of expanding citizenship beyond national boundaries through the emergence of interstate citizenship such as in the EU and through the development of human rights as an element of international law. Soysal uses the term 'postnational' citizenship or membership to describe rights conferred by international human rights principles on every person regardless of their historical or cultural ties to a particular community. She sees it as co-existing with national citizenship in a 'mutually reinforcing and reconfiguring' relationship (2001, p. 340; 1994; see also Tambini, 2001a). The case against, as well as for, 'cosmopolitan citizenship' is elaborated in Hutchings and Dannreuther (1999). Here, Miller (1999, 2000), its most prominent opponent, argues that effective citizenship practice is only realisable within a bounded political community in relation to fellow citizens with whom one can identify.

47. The idea of citizenship as multi-layered or tiered has been put forward by, for instance, Heater (1990, 1999); Held (1991a, 1995); McGrew (1992); Parry (1991); Soysal (1994); Yuval-Davis (1997a, b); Cohen (1999); Delanty (2000). A more sceptical note is injected by Kofman (1995) who warns that some groups are better placed to move between the different layers than others.

48. See Heater (1990); Weale (1991); Baubōck (1994); Newby (1996); Young (2000). The principles of cosmopolitan justice and/or citizenship are also discussed by Nussbaum and Glover (1995); Linklater (1998, 1999); Jones (1999).

49. Deacon (2001, p. 67; 1997, 2000). See also Townsend (1993; 1995); Mishra (1999).

50. UNDP, 1996 as cited in the *Guardian*, 16 July 1996; 1994, p. 3; also 1999, 2000.

51. For a discussion of the impact of global economic policies upon women in poorer nations see Mitter (1986); Mosse (1993); Rowbotham (1995); Connelly (1996); Sparr (1996); Moghadam (1999a); Pettman (1999); and of feminist struggles in reponse: Peterson (1996); Moghadam (1999a, b); *Women's Studies International Forum* (1999).

52. UNDP (1994, pp. 96–7, 4); the *Human Development Report 1995* (UNDP, 1995) provides more detailed information on the basis of a 'gender-related development index' and 'gender empowerment measure'. The 1999 Report devotes a chapter to how 'globalization is putting a squeeze on care and caring labour' (UNDP, 1999, p. 77).

53. Desai (1999, p. 193). For a generally positive account of human rights as women's rights, see Amnesty International (1995); Peters and Wolper (1995); Coomaraswamy (1999); Nussbaum (1999); Bunch *et al.* (2001); Merry (2001). A more critical stance is taken by Grewal, who argues that 'human rights discourse often seems to take the place of ... historically contextualized analyses of women's lives' (1999, p. 346).

54. For a discussion of the relationship between human and citizenship rights, see Parry (1991), Soysal (1994) and Delanty (2000). The last two suggest that the distinction between citizenship and human rights is becoming blurred, as the latter increasingly can be claimed through national legal systems in a context of interleaving layers of legal jurisdiction. A legal perspective is provided by Gardner (1990) and Neff (1999).

55. Gould (1988, Chapter 12) discusses some of the debates such an approach raises, in particular the tension between the right of self-determination of nations and the dictates of human rights and international justice. The vexed question of the clash between universalist human rights discourses, emanating from the West, and arguments in favour of cultural relativism is discussed by, for instance, Delanty (2000) and Parekh (2000). Many advocates of universal human rights point out that, even though they 'have their roots in Western cultural traditions, ... UN human rights treaties themselves have been co-authored by and represent the priorities of the entire international community' (Van Ness, 1999, p. 9). Indeed, there now exist four regional human rights instruments: Inter-American, European, African and Arab (UNDP, 2000). Some base their advocacy of human rights on 'a notion of universalism as a continually changing, negotiated, and tentative definition of international human rights' (Van Ness, 1999, p. 11; see also Ferguson, 1999). Santos goes further when he supports the 'emancipatory potential of human rights politics', provided it is grounded in cross-cultural dialogue rather than 'false universalisms' (1999, pp. 215, 222; see also Blacklock and Macdonald, 1998). From the perspective of women's rights, the case for a 'critical universalism', which is nevertheless sensitive to history and tradition, is argued in Nussbaum and Glover (1995). Merry (2001) argues that the universalism/relativism dichotomy obscures the ways in which women activists across the globe appropriate the concept of human rights and tailor it to local conditions. Strong arguments for the universality of women's human rights are similarly put by Coomaraswamy (1999); Nussbaum (1999, 2000) and in Peters and Wolper (1995), where it is also pointed out that the dynamic nature of human rights

means that their interpretation has changed over time, for instance to include social and women's rights.

56. The implications of this tension are explored by Soysal (1994), Jordan (1997); Whitaker (1998) and Schuster and Solomos (2002). Soysal provides a rather optimistic account of its potential resolution through her notion of 'postnational' membership or citizenship, which has been challenged elsewhere (see, for instance, Kofman *et al.*, 2000). The value of universal human rights to immigrants, asylum-seekers and indigenous peoples is stressed by Sassen (1998), Bhabha (1999) and Hocking and Hocking (1998) respectively. Oswin (2001) provides an alternative, critical, view.

57. These international laws are explored by Held (1991b) and Gardner (1990). Most important are the UN International Bill of Rights, which comprises international treaties covering civil, political, social and economic as well as general human rights; the European Convention on Human Rights and the UN Geneva Convention on the Rights of Refugees. The establishment of an International Criminal Court, with power to try those accused of crimes against humanity, has been described as a 'momentous breakthrough ... towards a world order in which the rule of law might operate' (Lloyd, 1998, p. 28). However, a number of major states, including the US, have refused to become party to the statute (Thomas, 2001; Roberts, 2002).

58. See Loescher and Monahan (1989), Bauböck (1991) and, from the particular perspective of women, Bhabha and Shutter (1994); Peters and Wolper (1995); www.womenlobby.org. At the start of the twenty-first century, as asylum has become a heated political issue, there have been growing calls among politicians for a review of the Refugee Convention and even talk of quotas.

59. See Loescher and Monahan (1989); Bauböck (1991); Castles and Miller (1998); Halliday (2000).

60. See Held (1991b, 1995); McGrew (1992); Hobsbawm (1994); Horsman and Marshall (1994); Trend (1996); Giddens (1998, 2000); Grieve Smith (2000). Giddens and Hutton (2000) argue for a World Financial Authority to regulate financial markets and oversee international financial institutions and a World Central Bank to act as lender of last resort.

61. Held (1995, p. 140; 1991b, p. 208; 1993). See also Gould (1988); Giddens (1994a, 1998), Deacon (1997); Linklater (1998); Hirst and Thompson (1999); Young (2000). A more sceptical note about the possibility of democratising international institutions is sounded by Kymlicka (2001, pp. 323–6).

62. See UNDP (1994, 1999); Muetzelfeldt and Smith (2002). The Commission on Global Governance was chaired by the Prime Minister of Sweden and the former Secretary General of the Commonwealth Secretariat with a membership including a former president of the World Bank.

63. France has seen a popular campaign for the tax (Aguiton, 2001) and both the late President Mitterand and Prime Minister Jospin have voiced support. War on Want has organised a UK campaign (see www.tobintax.org.uk). In response to the financial turmoil following September 11, the EC initiated a study into its feasibility.

64. Santos (1999, 2001); see also Aziz (1999); Falk (2000); Hardt and Negri (2000); Starr (2001); Muetzelfeldt and Smith (2002). Anheier *et al.* (2001) point out that global civil society is most concentrated in North Western Europe,

followed by Latin America and sub-Saharan Africa and is relatively weak in North America and East and South Asia. An important milestone in 'the movement for global social justice' has been the World Social Forum in Porto Allegre, attended by 50,000 in 2002 (Wainwright, 2002).

65. Circular from Jubilee Plus (10 June 2001). A useful overview of global citizen action and the issues it raises can be found in Anheier *et al.* (2001); Edwards and Gaventa (2001). These issues include the need to distinguish between social movements and professional NGOs, underlined by Silliman (1999; see also Alvarez *et al.*, 1998). The latter have come under increasing criticism for their frequent lack of accountability and democracy, tendency to Northern domination and growing co-option by government (see also, Spivak, 1996; Weiss, 1999; Shaw Bond, 2000). Nor, as Halliday (2000) points out, is all non-governmental action 'civil', as it can also involve, for example, fundamentalist and anti-immigrant groups and violence (see also Stubbs, 1998). The journal *Red Pepper* is a good source of information on the globalisation of protest.

66. During the course of the 1995 Copenhagen Social Summit, for instance, provision was made for the lobbying of delegates through the medium of e-mail. The use made of the internet by global networks is discussed in Ribeiro (1998); UNDP (1999); Mayo (2000); Desai and Said (2001); Edwards and Gaventa (2001); Naughton (2001) who also emphasises how its full potential is undermined by the global digital divide.

67. The impact of women's networks on the UN conferences is discussed by Pettman (1996); Alvarez (1998); Desai (1999); Silliman (1999); Bunch *et al.* (2001). Despite the degree of unity achieved, tensions were identified between women in the North and the South and between NGOs and the wider women's movement. Mackie (2001) points to the long history of women's international networking.

68. Suarez Toro (1995) provides the example of Central America. Here cross-national networking among women's organisations played a crucial role in the lead up to the Beijing conference (see also Alvarez, 1998). Bunch *et al.* (2001) describe the work of DAWN, a network of women from the South concerned with, *inter alia*, economic justice and reproductive rights (see also Moghadam, 1999a, b). In the EU, some space has been provided for women's organisations to articulate their interests, especially through the non-governmental European Women's Lobby (www.womenlobby.org; Pillinger, 1992; Hoskyns, 1996, Hantrais, 2000). It has, though, been criticised for marginalising Black and migrant women, leading to a report by the EWL on Black and migrant women in the EU (European Women's Lobby, 1995).

69. See Düvell and Jordan (1999); Harris (2000); Hayter (2001). Sassen (1998, p. 14) underlines the tension between global capital's 'drives for border-free economic spaces' and immigration controls.

70. The principle of non-discrimination would include not only anti-sexism and anti-racism but also, for instance, discrimination against same-sex partnerships, disabled people and people with AIDS or other illnesses. An attempt to sketch out a framework for an anti-discriminatory immigration policy in the British context can be found in Cook *et al.* (1988) and Spencer (1994). Cohen (1995), however, argues that immigration controls are inherently racist. The demand for recognition of autonomous legal status was made by the Refugee and Migrant Women's Caucus in a statement to the Beijing Conference.

71. The term 'prefigurative political forms' comes from Rowbotham *et al.* and refers to 'the notion of organizations in which a transforming vision of what is possible develops out of the process of organizing' (1979, p. 146).

Chapter 3

1. The phrase 'false universalism' is taken from Williams (1989, p. 118). Williams (1996) also distinguishes between diversity, difference and division, making clear that they are not fixed categories. Diversity is used to refer to a shared collective experience which does not necessarily imply relations of subordination, for example based on age, nationality, sexual identity. Division occurs where diversity is translated into relations of subordination. Difference signifies a situation where diversity becomes the basis for resistance against such subordination.
2. In his history of divorce in England, Stone (1990, p. 13) writes that 'it is easy to forget that under the patriarchal system of values, as expressed in the enacted law as it endured until the nineteenth century, a married woman was the nearest approximation in a free society to a slave. Her person, her property, both real and personal, her earnings, and her children all passed on marriage into the absolute control of her husband'.
3. hooks (1982, p. 126); see also Spelman (1988). The impact of slavery on US citizenship is discussed by Shklar (1991) and Fraser and Gordon (1994b).
4. Peters and Wolper (1995); Sunstein (1995); UNDP (1995); Afary (1997); Balchin (2001). Castles and Davidson (2000, pp. 202–3) estimate nearly 10 per cent of the world's population are denied equal legal status. For more details of women's exclusion from civil rights in the US and UK, see Pateman (1988, 1989); Pahl (1989); Sapiro (1990); Fraser and Gordon (1994b).
5. Yuval-Davis and Werbner (1999, p. 14); Pourzand (1999). Marshall identified education (a social citizenship right in his schema) as 'a necessary prerequisite of civil freedom' (1950, p. 26). Education can also enable women to become 'agents of change' in traditional societies (Herzog, 1999, p. 351).
6. Walby (1994). The results of women's involvement in nationalist struggles are discussed by Rowbotham (1992); Coulter (1993); Basu (1995); Berkovitch and Moghadam (1999); Hammami and Johnson (1999); Herzog (1999).
7. Tilly (1997); see also Saraceno (1997); Siim (2000).
8. For feminist critiques of Marshall, see Stacey and Price (1981); Pascall (1986); Vogel (1991); Fraser and Gordon (1994b). Walby (1994) has provided a feminist analysis of Mann (1987) and Turner's (1990) critique of Marshall.
9. Fraser and Gordon (1994b, p. 88). My discussion of the exile of the female draws on a rich feminist literature including: Lloyd (1984, 1986); Coole (1988, 1993); Pateman (1988, 1989); Young (1989); Davidoff (1990); Gatens (1991a); Phillips (1991); Vogel (1991); Caverero (1992); Clark (1995). Ong (1999) provides an Islamic perspective, which in many ways mirrors Western gendered constructions.
10. For a discussion of the masculinist conceptualisation of the citizen-soldier see Hartsock (1985); Lloyd (1986) and of women's relationship to military citizenship today, Yuval-Davis (1991b, 1997a); Helman (1999).

11. In addition to Hartsock (1985, pp. 177–8), my discussion of the disembodied public citizen draws on the work of Elshtain (1981); Nicholson (1984); Jones (1990); Riley (1988); Collins (1991); Gatens (1991b, 1992); Young (1989, 1990a); Benhabib (1992); Finzi (1992); Pettman (1996). For an alternative perspective on embodied citizenship, see Bacchi and Beasley (2002).

12. Thus, it does not mean that women never entered the public sphere, the actual demarcation of which from the private has, in any case, varied in sharpness historically. Indeed, they carved out alternative public spheres (Fraser, 1997). However, the legitimacy of their presence was frequently disputed (Davidoff, 1990; Tronto, 1993). Economically, the maintenance of separate spheres was for some time a middle-class privilege (Clark, 1995). The historical significance of the public–private dichotomy is detailed by Elshtain (1981); Stacey and Price (1981); Pateman (1988, 1989); Gordon (1990); Pateman and Shanley (1991). The implications have though been different for Black women as will become clear in Chapter 5 where I return to the issue.

13. Davies (1994, p. 13); see also Pateman (1989), Jones (1990, 1993); Cockburn (1991). Fearon observers how 'sexualisation' was used by male members of the Northern Ireland Assembly 'as the preferred tool for undermining powerful women' (1999, p. 67). The exclusionary nature of male organisational culture is illustrated by Martin and Collinson (1999) and Bagilhole (2003).

14. This male bias is discussed by Jones and Jónasdóttir (1988); Okin (1989); Pateman and Shanley (1991); Caverero (1992); Jones (1993).

15. Young (1989, p. 255, 1990a, 1993); see also Collins (1991).

16. See, for instance, Bryan *et al.* (1985); Arber and Ginn (1991); Begum (1992); Carabine (1992, 1996); Nasir (1996); Meekosha (1998).

17. See Fraser and Nicholson (1990); Bryson (1992, 1999); Crowley and Himmelweit (1992); Stacey (1993); Afshar and Maynard (1994); Mirza (1997); Bhavnani (2001).

18. Jones (1993, p. 222). The distinction between 'weak' and 'strong' postmodernist claims, which have very different implications for feminism, is made by Benhabib (1992). The implications of postmodernism are discussed by Fraser and Nicholson (1990); Aziz (1992); Mouffe (1992b); Williams (1992a, 1996); Coole (1993); Featherstone and Fawcett (1994/5); Benhabib *et al.* (1995); Weedon (1997); Ahmed (1998); Fawcett (2000).

19. The Black feminist critique can be found in hooks, (1982, 1984); Amos and Parmar (1984); Carby (1984); Bhavnani and Coulson (1986); Spelman (1988); Collins (1991); Anthias and Yuval-Davis (1992); Aziz (1992); Bhavnani (1993, 2001); Afshar and Maynard (1994); Nasir (1996); Mirza (1997); Sudbury (1998). Examples of acknowledgement of White privilege are Adams (1989); Crowley and Himmelweit (1992); Dean (1997).

20. For feminist discussions of difference which do include class divisions, see hooks (1984); Phillips (1987); Collins (1991); Rowbotham (1992); Curthoys (1993); Larner (1993); Mayo and Weir (1993) and, in particular, Coole (1996); Phillips (1999).

21. The implications of religious and cultural differences are discussed by Anthias and Yuval-Davis (1992); Silverman (1992); Allen (1994); Modood (1994, 2000); Patel (1997); Yuval-Davis (1997a); Sudbury (1998); Parekh (2000).

22. Nussbaum, citing statistics of homophobic violence in the US, states that 'to live as a gay or lesbian in America is thus to live with fear' (1999, p. 190) In a 1996 British Stonewall survey, a quarter of lesbians had experienced homophobic violence at least once in the previous five years and Stonewall (2001) provides information on the denial of full citizenship rights in the UK. An international overview of the denial of lesbians' human rights is provided by Dorf and Careaga Pérez (1995) and *New Internationalist* (2000). A gradual extension of legal rights is taking place in some countries and in the EU a Directive requiring the outlawing of discrimination on grounds of sexual orientation has been passed. For a more theoretical account of citizenship's heterosexist trappings see Evans (1993); Herman (1993); Wilson (1995); Richardson (1996, 1998, 2000a, b); Waites (1996); Weeks (1996, 1998); Kaplan (1997); Hubbard (2001); Lister (2002b). The 'normal' heterosexual woman is discussed by Carabine (1992, 1996) and the term 'marginal citizens' come from Phelan (1995). Even more marginal is the citizenship of transgendered people (Evans, 1993; Foley, 1994).
23. Morris (1991); see also Begum (1992); Ellis (1995); Meekosha (1998) and for an attempt to incorporate disability perspectives into feminism, Fawcett (2000).
24. See also Ginn (1993); Bernard (2000); Older Women's Network Europe (http://own-europe.org/).
25. Citizenship is an increasingly prominent focus of the youth literature (see, for instance, Jones and Wallace 1992; Bynner *et al.*, 1997; France, 1998; Hall, Williamson and Coffey 1998, 1999; Hall and Wilkinson, 1999). Blackman and France (2001) provide a critical perspective on the notion of youth transitions to citizenship. The labour market context is discussed in Coles (1995); Furlong and Cartmel (1997); MacDonald (1997). The relationship of children to citizenship has been largely ignored by the general citizenship literature. There is, however, a discussion in Evans (1993) and Close (1995) and Turner (1986, 1993) alludes to the question.
26. A British survey of 'young carers' found that three-fifths were female (Dearden and Becker, 1995); see also Becker *et al.* (1998).
27. Hareven (1982, p. 6, cited by Jones and Wallace, 1992); see also Twine (1994) for the application of a life-course framework to citizenship theory.
28. Riley (1988, p. 112); see also Bacchi (1996); Nash (1998) and for a more general warning of the dangers to citizenship theory of total 'decentring' of the subject (Ellison, 1997). Black feminists who have argued for solidarity on the basis of shared interests include hooks (1984); Lorde (1984) and Collins (1991). The argument about women's agency has been put by Mouffe (1992a), McClure (1992) and Butler (1995). Young (1994, 2000), using similar arguments to those here, has advocated use of Sartre's concept of 'a serial collective' as a way of seeing 'women as a collective' without attributing a common identity or qualities to them.
29. Brewer (1993). See also Spelman (1988); Williams (1992a); Larner (1993); Ng (1993); Fraser (1996); Hirschmann and Di Stefano (1996, pp. 17–18); Sudbury (1998); Vernon (1998).
30. This argument has been put also by Gordon (1990); Yuval-Davis (1991a); Anthias (1992); Maynard (1994); Coole (1996); Hall (2000).
31. Phillips (1993); see also Nash (1998) and Squires (2000, 2001). These criticisms are exemplified by the attempt of a British local authority to set up three

community consultative committees around the issues of 'race', women and disability. What emerged was a women's committee which was all White and non-disabled; a minority ethnic committee which was all male and non-disabled; and a disability committee which was all male and all White. Only the women's committee was willing to accept co-options to achieve a more balanced group representation; the others refused on the grounds that it would dilute the representation of their particular groups. I am grateful to Barbara Bagilhole for this example.

32. Cain and Yuval-Davis (1990, p. 23) and Anthias and Yuval-Davis (1992). The dangers of fragmentation are also emphasised by Adams (1989); Phillips (1993) and Weeks (1993).

33. For some of these examples, see Basu (1995). Another is provided by Desai (1999) who describes how women, on opposite sides of a number of divides, achieved a 'negotiated solidarity' in order to develop the international women's human rights movement.

34. In addition to those specifically referenced in the text, I am drawing on Benhabib (1992); Mouffe (1992a, b); Frazer and Lacey (1993). See also Leonard (1997).

35. Yeatman (1994, p. 89). I deal here with the question of an inclusive politics of voice and will return to the issue of representation in Chapter 6. For a fuller discussion of the issues raised by such a commitment to diversity, see Kymlicka and Norman (1994, 2000); Kymlicka (1995, 2001); Young (2000).

36. Hobson and Lindholm (1997) propose a process-oriented model of 'identity formation' or 'cognitive framing' to analyse the creation of shared meanings and consciousness which provide the basis of collective citizen actions. See also Bhavnani and Phoenix (1994); Dean (1997); Hobson (1999).

37. Attention to sites of citizenship participation underlines the importance of locating citizenship in space and place (Jones, 1994; Hall *et al.*, 1999; Jones and Gaventa, 2002). The term 'dialogic democracy' is Giddens' (1994a); for a discussion of 'deliberative' or 'communicative' democracy, see Phillips (1995); Porter (2000); Young (2000) and, from a social policy perspective, Ellison (1999); Fitzpatrick (2002). For a review of practical examples, such as citizens' juries and consensus conferences, see Stewart J. (1995); Meehan (1996); Barnes (1999b); Smith and Wales (2000). Other examples are a British local needs audit (Percy Smith and Sanderson, 1992) and the participatory budget process pioneered in cities in Brazil and Uruguay (Baierle, 1998; Chavez, 1999).

38. The Northern Ireland Women's Coalition, established in 1996 to contest the election to seats at the Northern Ireland peace talks, has become an important force in Northern Ireland's politics. Its story is told in Fearon (1999); Fearon and McWilliams (2000). Cockburn (1998) provides a more in depth analysis of transversal politics in action and further examples can be found in *Soundings* (1999).

39. Williams (1993); Feldman *et al.*, 1998. Women's community activism is discussed in McCulloch (1997); Naples (1998a, b, c); Roulston and Davies (2000); anti-racist community activism by Gilroy (1987, reproduced in Bornat *et al.*, 1993) and Joseph (1994); and Black women's community activism by Sudbury (1998).

40. For a comprehensive feminist critique of communitarianism see Frazer and Lacey (1993).

41. Young (1990b, p. 301; 1990a); Yuval-Davis (1991a).
42. Frazer and Lacey (1993). Powerful challenges to the idea of a unified community have come from working-class women in British mining communities and minority ethnic women whose interests have been rendered invisible by male leaders who purport to speak on behalf of their communities. Southall Black Sisters, in particular, have been instrumental in challenging the power of male community leaders to speak on their behalf and to define and control the interests of their 'community', especially with regard to the issue of violence against women (Patel, 1990, 1999; see also Wilson, 1978; Trivedi, 1984; Patel, 1992; Ng, 1993). Gwinnett's case study of policing prostitution illustrates how community politics can reinforce gendered inequalities (1998).
43. Weeks (1993, p. 203; 1996); see also Benhabib (1992); Yeatman (1994); Hughes (1996).
44. Aziz (1992, p. 292, emphasis in original); Mani (1992, p. 320); see also Mirza (1997). There is a considerable literature that documents Black and 'Third World' women's historical and contemporary struggles: Carby (1982); hooks (1982, 1984); Trivedi (1984); Bryan *et al.* (1985); Mitter (1986); Foster-Carter (1987); Collins (1991); Rowbotham and Mitter (1994); Alexander and Mohanty (1997); Patel (1997); Sudbury (1998).
45. Silverman (1992). The denial of disabled women's agency as victims is discussed by Morris (1991, 1993b, 1996) and Meekosha (1998); and the stereotyping of older women by Arber and Ginn (1991); Bernard and Meade (1993); Bernard (2000). For a critical discussion of poverty research, see Beresford and Croft (1995); Beresford *et al.* (1999); Deacon and Mann (1999); Lister *et al.* (2000).
46. Bauböck (1994, p. 290). The point is made at greater length by Thompson and Hoggett who, from a social policy perspective, argue that 'any justifiable universalism or egalitarianism must take particularity and difference into account; and any legitimate particularism or politics of difference must employ some universal or egalitarian standard' (1996, p. 23).
47. The group-specific rights which I am discussing here are still exercised by individuals and as such can be distinguished from group-differentiated rights which are exercised by a group; the collective self-government rights exercised by indigenous American Indians are an example of the latter. The distinction is explained by Bauböck (1994), Kymlicka (1995, 2001), Isin and Wood (1999) and Parekh (2000) to whom I would refer the reader for a more in-depth discussion, from varying perspectives, of the case for a combination of universal and particularised rights and of the relationship between the two.
48. Castles (1994, 1996); Yeatman (1994) also discusses the Australian model, which has, more recently, been tarnished by the country's highly exclusionary stance towards asylum-seekers and growing xenophobia. The issue of language is important too for disabled people: recognition of sign language can be seen as both a reactive and proactive particular right. For a discussion of the rights of indigenous American Indians, see Young (1990a, p. 183, 1989, 1993) and Kymlicka (1995, 2001).
49. Silverman (1992); Favell (1998). The backlash against group rights is discussed in Eisenstein (1988); Young (1990a); Bader (1998); Castles and Miller (1998) and Castles and Davidson (2000). For a useful overview of the 'politics of affirmative action', see Bacchi (1996). Some of the dilemmas raised by policies

that attempt to promote both equality and cultural diversity are debated by
Modood and Parekh in Miliband (1994) and in the Report of the Commission
on the Future of Multi-Ethnic Britain (2000).

50. Taylor (1989, p. 27). See also, Taylor-Gooby (1991) who locates his defence of
welfare citizenship in a discussion of the relationship between needs and rights.
51. Doyal and Gough (1991, p. 74); see also Hewitt M. (1993, 1998); Leonard
(1997).
52. Young (1990a, p. 105); see also Benhabib (1992); Dean (1996).
53. Riley (1992, p. 187). Similar arguments can be found in Eisenstein (1991);
Phillips (1993); Yeatman (1993, 1994).
54. Mouffe (1993a, p. 13, 1993b); see also Gunew and Yeatman (1993); Ellison
(1999), who argues the need to move welfare theory beyond the universalis-
tic/particularist duality; and Parekh, who argues that human identity 'is a
product of the dialectical interplay between the universal and the particular'
(2000, p. 124).
55. Bunch (2001, pp. 228, 227); Thomas (1995; p. 357); see also Nussbaum and
Glover (1995); Desai (1999); Nussbaum (2000).
56. The relationship between the two is debated by Fraser (1995, 1996, 2000);
Young (1997, 2000); Phillips (1997, 1999) and in *Theory, Culture and Society*
(2001).
57. Weeks (1993, pp. 196). See also Leonard (1997), whose reconstruction of
welfare as an 'emancipatory' postmodern project represents another important
attempt to rethink social justice in the light of postmodernism.

Chapter 4

1. See, for instance, Scott (1988); Cornell (1991); Coole (1993); Frazer and Lacey
(1993); Lacey (1993); Squires (1993); Fawcett (2000).
2. Barrett and Phillips (1992, p. 8). The theme is developed by, among others,
Eisenstein (1988); Mohanty (1988); Bacchi (1990); Collins (1991); Young
(1990a, b, 1993); Benhabib (1992); Held, V. (1993); Squires (2001).
3. The range of feminist approaches to the 're-gendering' of citizenship (a notion
derived from discussion with Celia Davies) is discussed by Voet (1998);
Hutchings (1999); Siim (2000, ch.3); Squires (2000); Lister (2001).
4. Vogel (1994, p. 86); see also Jones (1990); Gatens (1991a).
5. These points are illustrated by Koven and Michel (1993) and Lewis and Åström
(1992).
6. Bryson, V. (1992, p. 88); see also Offen (1988); Bacchi (1990).
7. Koven and Michel (1993, p. 4); see also Bock and Thane (1991); Kornbluh
(1996); Sainsbury (2001).
8. Dietz (1991, p. 244). Among the key contemporary proponents of a maternalist
vision are: Ruddick (1980, 1989); Elshtain (1981); Held, V. (1993). Among the
most prominent critics are Dietz (1985, 1987, 1991) whose critique of the maternalist conception of citizenship will be discussed in Chapter 6 and Segal (1987).
9. Some of these conflicts are described by Eisenstein (1988); Bacchi (1990); Lewis
and Davies (1991); Rhode (1992). In Britain, the conflict was expressed partially

in class terms, as middle-class feminism tended to accentuate the case for equal rights and working-class that for better support for women as mothers (Dale and Foster, 1986; Phillips, 1987).

10. See Offen (1988); Bacchi (1990); Tronto (1993).

11. In addition to those specifically referenced, see MacKinnon (1989); Bacchi (1990); Bussemaker (1991); Gatens (1991a, b, 1992); Meehan and Sevenhuijsen (1991); Parvikko (1991); Mouffe (1992b); Pateman (1992); Coole (1993); Galeotti (1993); Fraser (1996); Holli (1997) upon whose arguments this section draws.

12. Parekh makes a similar point with regard to cultural difference and illustrates it with an example from the Netherlands of the withdrawal of unemployment benefit from a Turkish woman who refused to accept a job in which she would have been the only female. On appeal, the disqualification was ruled unjust on the grounds that the woman had been justified in refusing to accept the job 'under culturally and religiously unacceptable conditions'. Noting that a White woman's refusal on such grounds would have been rejected, Parekh observes that 'the two women are treated differently but equally, the equality consisting in the fact that they are judged impartially on the basis of the same criterion of what consists reasonable or acceptable working conditions for each' (1994, p. 105; 1998; 2000).

13. Bock (1992) analyses how certain forms of 'difference' were explicitly posited as inequality deriving from inferiority in the tenets of National Socialism under which equality and difference were racialised as well as gendered in that only the women of 'superior' ethnic groups were deemed different from men, fit to occupy 'separate spheres'. 'The "inferior" women and men, by contrast, whether Jews, blacks or gypsies' were subject to 'sexual levelling' (p. 92).

14. Isin and Wood (1999, p. 89) discuss the implications of 'transgendered identities' and Carver (1998) of multiple and 'marginalised sexualities' for 'sexual citizenship'.

15. Eisenstein (1988, pp. 2, 1). A similar position can be found within queer theory: Wilson argues that 'the equality which satisfies [lesbians and gays] must reflect not monolithic, repressive heterosexual values, but instead must respect the variety of values which result from our differences' (1993, p. 188).

16. See also Offen (1988) and Riley (1988) for a similar historical perspective and Cockburn (1991) and Rhode (1992) for an application of the argument to contemporary feminist strategy. Bader (1998) argues for just such a contextualised approach in relation to 'ethnic affirmative action'. The need to reconcile equality and difference is emphasised from a disability perspective by Silvers (1997).

17. Fraser's (1994) conception of gender equity comprises five main principles: anti-poverty; anti-exploitation; equality (sub-divided into income, leisure time and respect); anti-marginalisation and anti-androcentrism.

18. I am grateful to Jane Lewis for this point.

19. I am grateful to Fiona Williams for making the connection with Molyneux's argument.

20. See, for instance, Fraser and Nicholson (1990). For a general discussion see Meyers and Kittay (1987); Flanagan and Jackson (1987); Davis (1992); Bubeck (1995a).

21. Tronto (1987, 1993); see also Baier (1987); Sevenhuijsen (1991b). For a discussion of different understandings of the gendered nature of care, see Bubeck (1995a); Bowden (1997); Sevenhuijsen (1998).

22. Sevenhuijsen (1991a, 1992); the term 'compulsory altruism' was coined by Land and Rose (1985).

23. Young (1990a, p. 39). It is from her I take the distinction between the two justice paradigms. Gould, similarly, interprets justice as 'a principle of equal rights to the conditions of self-development' (1988, p. 60).

24. Flanagan and Jackson (1987, p. 628). In similar vein, Aafke E. Komter (1995) draws on Aristotle's moral theory to demonstrate how the universal and the particular are united within both the care and justice ethic. The two ethics inform notions of ecological citizenship also, as demonstrated in a special edition of *Social Policy and Administration* (2001) on environmental issues.

25. Held, V. (1993, pp. 228, 76); see also Bubeck (1995a) and Sevenhuijsen (1991a, b). The latter is, though, more ambivalent in her book. Here she warns that attempts to integrate the two ethics could 'serve to defuse the radical implications of the ethics of care', yet also concedes that questions concerning the distribution of care 'need to be reflected on in terms of justice' (1998, pp. 54, 86). Young (1990a) also argues for a synthesis from within the justice paradigm and Benhabib (1992) from the perspective of what is required in the development of the autonomous adult from the dependent child. Others who make the case include Bacchi (1990) and Phillips (1993). Williams (2001) suggests some 'points of commonality' between the arguments of care theorists and disability activists.

26. The historical link between independence and citizenship, in both its liberal and republican formulations, is discussed by Heater (1990); Mink (1990); Shklar (1991); Fraser and Gordon (1994a); Clark (1995); Yeatman (2001). Today, Hall and Held (1989), Taylor-Gooby (1991) and Dagger (1997) are among those who appeal to the ideal of autonomy. Saharso (2000) points out that it is a Western ideal and that 'the form and extent of autonomy' varies between cultures, reflecting different conceptions of the self.

27. Weale (1983) cited in Sapiro (1990, p. 51) who makes the link with women's dependence.

28. Wollstonecraft (1792/1985, p. 283). The importance historically of the issue of women's economic (in)dependence can be traced in Rathbone (1924/1986); Lewis (1980, 1994); Land (1990); Bock and Thane (1991); Koven and Michel (1993). An example from contemporary feminism is the Campaign for Legal and Financial Independence which pursued the 'fifth demand' of the British Women's Liberation Movement during the 1970s (see McIntosh, 1981; Lister, 1999). Its importance to feminist analysis is underlined by Acker (1988), although Daly (2000) points out that this is more the case in liberal Anglo-Saxon countries than in Continental European countries such as Germany. Nyberg (2002) offers a Scandinavian perspective.

29. See Blumberg (1991); Mosse (1993); Chen (1995); Sen (1999).

30. See Carby (1982); hooks (1982); Amos and Parmar (1984); Mirza (1997). The US welfare debate context is discussed by Fraser and Gordon (1994a).

31. Collins (1991, p. 110); see also Thorogood (1987); Brah and Shaw (1992); Graham (1993); Bhavnani (1994); Brah (1994, 1996); Reynolds (2001).

32. See Lister (1992); Hutton (1994); Joshi *et al.* (1995); Gornick (1999); Warren *et al.* (2001). Women are less likely to be economically dependent in the Nordic countries (Sørensen, 2001).

33. Morris (1991, 1993a, 1996). See also Marks (2001) and Keith (1992) who rightly criticises my earlier work for ignoring the needs of disabled people when discussing dependency and citizenship. The image of the dependent disabled woman is highlighted by Begum (1992) and Lloyd (1992).
34. Shakespeare warns that 'the disability community may have a major problem with those who wish to displace independence as a goal'. Instead, the aim is 'to break the link between physical and social dependency', although he concedes that 'there can be too much stress on independence and autonomy within disability rights discourse' (2000, pp. 62–3). Yeatman suggests an alternative formulation of 'individualized personhood' through which lack of independence would invite an ethic of 'moral respect and reciprocity' rather than one of 'paternalistic or maternalistic protection' (2001, pp. 146–7).
35. This argument is put by Waerness (1987, 1989); Pateman (1989); Young (1990a, 1995); Elshtain, 1992; Tronto (1993); Knijn (1994); Knijn and Kremer (1997); Sevenhuijsen (1998); Porter (2001). See also Hoggett (2000).
36. This viewpoint is expressed by Wilson (1983); Land (1989); Gordon (1990); Fraser and Gordon (1994a, b); Knijn (1994). For an analysis of how family relationships between kin typically represent an attempt to balance dependence and independence in line with a norm of reciprocity, see Finch (1989) and Finch and Mason (1993). Their study demonstrates how women and men of all ages try to avoid dependence on relatives and how where an imbalance occurs it involves issues of power and control, which can result in a position of subordination.
37. Pearce (1990); see also Graham (1983); Pateman (1989); Sapiro (1990); Williams (1999, 2000).
38. Fraser and Gordon (1994a, p. 23). I would suggest that 'reliance' is a less ideologically charged term than 'dependency' in the context of welfare, for it does not carry the same pejorative connotations and implications of individual inadequacy identified by Fraser and Gordon. These are also analysed, in the context of US welfare reform, by Naples (1997).
39. Relevant here also is the treatment of dependency in some of the traditional social policy literature, in particular the distinction made by Titmuss (1987) between 'natural' and 'man-made' dependencies. Included in the former are childhood, extreme old age and childbearing, whereas the latter refer to dependencies, such as unemployment, determined wholly or primarily by social and cultural factors. I have noted elsewhere (Lister, 1990b) that while women's economic dependency is very much man-made, it is widely perceived to be natural. See also the taxonomy of dependencies elaborated by Walker (1982).
40. Fraser (1994) drawing on Goodin (1988); see also Okin (1989).
41. See also O'Connor (1993) who points out that interdependence and involuntary economic dependence have very different implications for choice and the nature of relationships. When Sevenhuijsen (1998) argues against opposing autonomy to dependency she is, in effect, referring to 'socially necessary' dependence, without giving adequate consideration to the implications for autonomy of 'surplus' exploitative dependence.
42. Mayo and Weir (1993). An interesting historical perspective is provided on the relationship between men's independence and women's dependence by Lake (1993) who interprets the opposition to a motherhood endowment scheme in Australia in the early twentieth century as averting a threat to men's independent

citizenship, supported by their dependent wives for whom they provided, a relationship which would be upset if the latter were to be treated as economically independent citizen-mothers. A similar point is made by Lewis (1991, p. 81) in the British context where, quoting the Labour leader Ramsay MacDonald's opposition to mother's endowment, she suggests he saw it as 'a threat to the integrity of the family and to men's claim for a family wage, and as an attack on one of the basic underpinnings of late nineteenth- and early twentieth-century respectable working-class masculinity, viz. that a man should "keep" a wife and child'.

43. Einhorn (1993); Watson (1993); *Social Politics* (1995); Pascall and Manning (2000); Manning (2001).
44. See Hernes (1987); Borchorst and Siim (1987); Walby (1990, 1997).
45. Blumberg (1991). See also Okin (1989); Pahl (1989); Sen (1999, ch. 8). Research by Cragg and Dawson (1984); McLaughlin (1991); Callender (1992) confirms the importance to many women of an independent source of income. More recently, the British Social Attitudes Survey shows that, in 1999, 10 per cent of women gave 'to earn money of my own' as the main reason for working. Hinds and Jarvis suggest this indicates that some of the increase in women's labour market participation is driven 'by the desire for a greater sense of financial freedom' (2000, p. 105). Three-fifths of employed women in a 1998 Women's Unit survey mentioned financial independence as a reason for doing paid work (Bryson *et al.*, undated). Economic dependence – the reality and the ideology – is discussed further in Chapter 5.
46. Hobson (1990, pp. 237–8); see also Okin (1989) and Orloff (1993).
47. Pahl (1989, p. 118). See also Evason (1982); Homer *et al.* (1984, 1985). Hagemann-White (2000), however, warns that overall levels of male violence are not necessarily lower in societies where women have achieved greater economic independence.
48. Begum (1992); Meekosha (1998); Sale (2001).
49. James (1992, p. 50); see also Gatens (1991b); O'Connor (1993); Orloff (1993); Williams (1999).
50. Male violence and its threat are discussed in, for instance, Walby (1990); Kelly and Radford (1990/91); Fawcett *et al.* (1996); Maynard and Winn (1997); European Women's Lobby (1999); Hagemann-White (2000). With regard to racist violence, a British Home Office (1989) report has warned that 'if the fear of racial harassment deprives people from ethnic minorities of the freedom of choice over such fundamental matters as where they live or work, or if they are reluctant to leave home to take their children to school, to visit a doctor, to use public transport or libraries or parks, then they will be unable to play their full part in the life of this country or to feel that they have a stake in its future'. In the US, Boris (1995) emphasises how African-American men and women's citizenship is violated by attacks on their bodily integrity. Violence against lesbians is discussed by Kitzinger (1994) in the more general context of anti-lesbian harassment; a large-scale British Stonewall survey revealed that one in four lesbians and one in three gays had been the victim of a violent attack (*Independent*, 13 May 1996).
51. Pateman (1988); Frazer and Lacey (1993); Bagilhole (2003). For a more nuanced analysis of sexual harassment, which takes account of institutional,

geographical and historical context, see Brant and Lee Too (1994). Minson (1993) considers the issue of sexual harassment explicitly from the perspective of citizenship theory.

52. Lacey (1993, p. 105). The radical feminist position on pornography can be found in, for instance, Dworkin (1981); MacKinnon (1989). Segal (1987) and Eisenstein (1988) discuss the dangers. An overview of feminist positions is provided by Bryson (1999). Its racialised nature is discussed by Collins (1991) and Bhattacharyya (1994).

53. Benhabib (1992, p. 198). The issue of autonomy and its relationship to a care perspective is explored by a number of authors in Meyers and Kittay (1987).

54. Eisenstein (1987, p. 85). The distinction between autonomy on the one hand and egoism or selfish liberal individualism on the other is drawn by a number of contemporary political writers such as Giddens (1994a); Gray (1994); Miliband (1994).

Chapter 5

1. In addition to those specifically referenced, my discussion of the construction and rearticulation of the public–private split draws on the work of Nicholson (1984); O'Donovan (1985); Sassoon (1987); Young (1987, 1990a); Pateman (1988, 1989); Bacchi (1990); Fraser and Nicholson (1990); Okin (1991); Phillips (1991); Benhabib (1992); Frazer and Lacey (1993); Held, V. (1993); Lacey (1993); Tronto (1993); Pascall (1997). See also Prokhovnik (1998) and Landes' reader (1998).

2. Elshtain (1981); for a critique see Stacey (1986); Siim (1988) and Phillips (1991).

3. See Fraser who also uses an analysis of the Clarence Thomas/Anita Hill case to demonstrate 'women's greater vulnerability to unwanted, intrusive publicity and lesser ability to define and defend their privacy' (1997, p. 103).

4. For accounts of how feminism has helped to make public issues of sexuality and male violence see Hanmer and Maynard (1987); Lacey (1993); Richardson (1993); Hague and Malos (1994/5); Basu (1995); Gustafsson *et al.* (1997). More generally, the history of women's struggles demonstrates the ways in which they succeeded in placing a range of 'private' issues on the public agenda (see Brophy and Smart, 1985; Koven and Michel, 1993).

5. Black women, for instance, are sometimes wary of involving the law in cases of domestic violence because of racist treatment by the police (Mama, 1989a, b; 1992; Foley and Wright, 1994). The success of the anti-pornography campaign in making the private consumption of pornography a public issue affecting women's citizenship has nevertheless resulted in fierce divisions between feminists over the question of its legal censorship (Lovenduski and Randall, 1993; Bryson, 1999).

6. Brodie argues that 'different state forms rest on different negotiations of the public and the private', producing 'differently gendered citizens' (1997. p. 230). This is illustrated by Siim's comparison of perceptions of public/private in liberal, republican and social democratic states (2000). The culturally specific

nature of the divide is underlined by Joseph's analysis of the Lebanon in which she argues that it forms 'a boundary imagined by a state imagining its people' (1997, p. 88; 1999).

7. Einhorn (1993, pp. 6–7); see also Watson (1993); Matynia (1995); *Social Politics* (1995); Molyneux (2000) and Heinen (1997) who notes the continued resistance to the slogan 'the personal is the political' among those with experience of totalitarianism.
8. Scott (1994, p. 154); Lasch (1995); Eisenstein (1997).
9. Plummer (2001, pp. 243, 245). A more sceptical and radical perspective is provided by Hubbard (2001). For a discussion of the sexualised nature of the divide see Cooper (1993); Evans (1993); Sullivan (1995); Richardson (1996, 1998); Isin and Wood (1999); Lister (2002b). Fraser (1997) analyses multiple public spheres, which include 'counterpublics' created by subordinated social groups.
10. Hyatt (1993). She uses the example of a campaign against water-metering (which had caused soaring bills and damaging water-rationing) waged in this way by a group of working-class women on a Bradford housing estate in the North of England. Miethe (1999) writes of the power of kitchen table politics in the former GDR and how, following unification, the shift of the locus of political activity to the public sphere tilted the political gender balance in men's favour.
11. For a discussion of homeworking and the campaigns around it, see Rowbotham (1995, 1998); Tate (1994); Phizacklea and Wolkowitz (1995); Mohanty (1997). Cook (2000) underlines how homeworkers' location in the private sphere impedes access to public employment rights. The convergence of the public and private in childminding is discussed by Windebank (1996) and Gregory and Windebank (2000, p. 151).
12. Glenn (1991, 1992). See also Bhattacharjee, who argues that 'the condition of the domestic worker overturns a lot of conventional ideas regarding the private and the public' (1997, p. 316) and Graham (1991) who has developed the argument in the context of British feminist research into care.
13. Glenn (1991, p. 193); Collins (1991, p. 47). The point about White working-class women is made by Hyatt (1993), citing Ross (1983).
14. Turner (1990); see Walby (1994) for a more detailed critique. Pocock (1992); Okin (1992) provides a feminist response in the same volume.
15. The feminist case has been outlined by Eisenstein (1988, 1991). For an international human rights perspective, see Cook (1995). The Beijing Declaration included recognition of the right of women to control their health and in particular their fertility as basic to their empowerment.
16. UNDP (1995, p. 111); see also UNFPA (1995); CRLP (2000). An estimated 600,000 women die each year from pregnancy-related causes, including 78,000 from unsafe abortions (Browne, 2001). Van Eerdewijk (2001) warns against the appropriation of the notion of reproductive rights by a development discourse that discounts the agency of Southern women in comparison to that of Northern.
17. Alsop and Hockey (2001, p. 469); CRLP (2000). In some of the former Communist societies, there has been some re-liberalisation of abortion laws after an initially more restrictive stance. However, in Poland a more liberal law enacted in 1996, in part in response to women's campaigns, was overturned by the Constitutional Court in 1997 so that the legal abortion rate is near zero (Henshaw *et al.*, 1999; Watson, 1996). The US Bush Administration has

withdrawn funding from any charity worldwide that has anything to do with abortion, leading to the loss of many 'life-saving, poverty-reducing projects' (Browne, 2001).

18. Bryan *et al.* (1985) draw attention to the treatment of Black women. The position of women with learning difficulties and of women with mental health problems is discussed by Williams (1992b) and Sayce (2000) respectively; and that of disabled women more generally by Lonsdale (1990); Begum (1992); Meekosha (1998); Lloyd (2001).

19. McKiernan and McWilliams in Morris and Lyon (1996) a volume of 'new research perspectives' on the gendered interaction of public and private.

20. For a discussion see Morokvasic (1993); Bhabha and Shutter (1994); Goldberg (1995): Bhabha (1996, 1999); Jarvis and Stanley (1999); UNHCHR (2001); Oswin (2001) who, however, contends that too great an emphasis on private persecution deflects attention from public persecution and the interaction between the two.

21. Weeks (1998, p. 35); 2001. Richardson (2000a) suggests three kinds of sexual rights claims: 'practice-based' (the right to participate in sexual activity, to sexual pleasure and to sexual and reproductive autonomy); 'identity-based' (the recognition rights of self-definition, self-expression and self-realisation); and 'relationship-based' (rights of consent, of choice of sexual partners and to publicly recognised sexual relationships). See also Richardson (1998, 2000b) and Lister (2002b) on sexual citizenship.

22. Katz and Monk (1993, p. 266) conclude from their edited collection on women's geographies over the life-course that 'the theme of mobility has been pervasive' but that women's capacity for mobility 'is often severely constrained' by both ideological and material factors. Another edited collection on women's citizenship in Europe begins: 'mobility is one of the most pre-eminent experiences of the twentieth century and women have been actively involved in its processes and forms, crossing both material and symbolic frontiers' (Ferreira and Tavares, 1998).

23. Foley and Nelles write of Asian families in parts of Britain living 'under a self-imposed curfew within their own homes, afraid to walk the streets for fear of a racially motivated attack' (1993, pp. 8–9); see also Ginsburg (1989); Cook (1993). The British Crime Survey reveals women's fear of going out at night (Kershaw *et al.*, 2001); see also Hamilton and Jenkins (2000).

24. Hamilton and Jenkins (2000, p. 1794). The significance of transport is also discussed by Beuret (1991); Hamilton *et al.* (1991); Graham (1993); Jones (1996).

25. A study of the 2001 UK General Election found 69 per cent of polling stations surveyed were potentially inaccessible to some disabled voters (Scott and Morris, 2001). In contrast, Foley and Pratt (1994) cite the accessibility of 94 per cent of polling booths in New York in the 1993 mayoral elections, three years after the passage of the Americans with Disabilities Act. For a more general discussion of disabled people's autonomy see Oliver (1990, 1993, 1996); Morris (1991, 1993a); Keith (1992); Shakespeare (2000).

26. See Sassens (1998); Anthias (2000); Escrivá (2000); Kofman *et al.* (2000); Gibson *et al.*, (2001).

27. European Women's Lobby (1995, p. 88); see also Morokvasic (1984, 1991, 1993); Kofman and Sales (1992, 1998); Kofman *et al.* (2000); UNHCHR

(2001); and in the US context, Boris (1995); Bhattacharjee (1997); Narayan (1997b). In the UK, a concession was introduced in 1999 to protect from deportation women with proof of having been driven out of violent marriages during the 'probationary period'.

28. Bhavnani (1994). As against this, Brah (1994) found in her research that some young Asian women take paid work in order to be able to sponsor the entry of a prospective spouse from the Asian sub-continent so as to comply with the immigration law requirement that a sponsor must be able to provide support 'without recourse to public funds'.

29. See Brydon and Chant (1989); Doyal (1990, 1995); Mosse (1993); Sanchez (1993); UNDP (1995).

30. See Kiernan (1992); Central Statistical Office (1995); Kozak (1998). *Social Trends 2001* shows that, in 1999, in couples men spent 142 minutes to women's 235 minutes a day on household tasks (Office for National Statistics, 2001, p. 224). Where both partners work full time, the proportion of total domestic work time undertaken by the woman was 62 per cent in 1997 compared with 68 per cent in 1974/5 (Laurie and Gershuny, 2000).

31. Morris (1990, p. 190); see also Kremer and Montgomery (1993).

32. See Heinen (1990, 1997); Einhorn (1991; 1993); Broschart (1992); Corrin (1992); Bucur (1994); Makkai (1994).

33. Even in Denmark and Sweden, change has been slow (Carlsen and Larsen, 1993; Højgaard, 1993; Gould, 2001). Statistics from the Danish Equality Council (provided by Birte Siim) indicate that, in 1995, 62 per cent of women and 11 per cent of men did 51 per cent or more of the housework compared with 80 per cent and 4 per cent in 1976.

34. See Morris (1990); Blumberg (1991); Brannen and Moss (1991); Sullivan (2000); Kan (2001); Sullivan and Gershuny (2001).

35. Balbo (1987); see also Brannen and Moss (1991); Carlsen and Larsen (1993); Kremer and Montgomery (1993); Gregson and Lowe (1994a); Gregory and Windebank (2000); Tobío (2001).

36. Gardiner (1997) underlines the emotional and practical demands of childcare on women. The implications for health are discussed by Doyal (1990, 1995) and Graham (1993).

37. See Finch and Groves (1983); Ungerson (1987, 1990); Evandrou (1990); Janile-Bris (1993); Parker and Lawton (1994); Twigg and Atkin (1995); *Benefits* (2000).

38. Warde and Hetherington (1993); Gershuny (2000); Sullivan (2000) and Sullivan and Gershuny (2001) suggest convergence. However a study of 31 countries concluded that on average 'women put in 13 per cent more time than men do in market activities and unpaid work taken together' (UNDP, 1995, pp. 91–2; see also European Commission, 2000). UK evidence suggests women are especially less likely to have leisure time at weekends (cited in Hamilton and Jenkins, 2000). Luxton (1997) and Land (2002) argue that time use studies can underestimate the overall volume of domestic care work. Land (1991) underlines the fragmented nature of women's time, as does an EC study (2000). Drew (2000) points out that more of women's domestic work than men's is 'time-dependent', i.e. it has to fit in with externally imposed time frames such as those imposed by schools and shops.

39. For evidence, see Doyal (1990, 1995); Brannen and Moss (1991); Marsh (1991); Payne, S. (1991); Graham (1993); Fagan (1996); Siranni and Negrey (2000). Although Sullivan and Gershuny (2001, p. 344) suggest that time-use evidence does not support the view that 'time poverty' has increased, they point to how time is much more pressured for some groups, notably dual earner couples and lone parents. They also speculate that an increase in 'the number of activities engaged in simultaneously', which are not recorded in time-use studies, would produce a feeling of greater time pressure, especially among women combining child care and other domestic tasks. In the UK a *Good Housekeeping* survey (cited by Williams, 2001) found that three-quarters of working mothers reported stress because of lack of time from juggling paid work and care responsibilities.

40. Scheiwe (1994, p. 134) argues for an analytical framework for welfare state research which takes time seriously. She applies 'the concept of institutionalised "gendered times" to analyse how the time factor plays a role in access to social rights and insurance benefits through minimum working hours, contribution periods, continuity of employment or other time thresholds' (see also Daly, 2000, p. 114; Land, 2002). In relation to employment , Mutari and Figart (2001) offer a gendered analysis of European 'work time regimes' and Gornick *et al.* of school time schedules. Burns (2000) discusses 'time money schemes', such as time banks, which attempt to give recognition to the value of unpaid, invisible work (see also www.timebanks.co.uk).

41. The problematisation of the distribution of time and unpaid domestic work between the sexes is one of the distinguishing features of 'second-wave feminism' in contrast to earlier waves which took it for granted as a natural given (Okin, 1989, 1991; Gatens, 1996). In Denmark, time has become a public policy issue in the face of high, full-time labour market participation among women as well as men (Roll, 1992; Carlsen and Larsen, 1993). Pillinger (2000) describes a variety of time policies and initiatives including over 200 'time in the city' projects in Italy, initially pioneered in response to a grassroots women's legislative initiative: 'women change the time'. For a discussion of time as a resource, see also Lee and Piachaud (1992).

42. Chafetz (1991, p. 81); see also Cockburn (1991); Land (1991); Leira (1992); Glenn (1992).

43. Massey notes from research into high technology sectors how the design of demanding jobs requires that those employed in them, overwhelmingly men, 'do not do the work of reproduction and of caring for other people; indeed, it implies that, best of all, they have someone to look after *them*' (1994, p. 190, emphasis in original).

44. Moss (1988); Larsen and Sørenson (1993); Duncan and Edwards (1997); Gill and Davidson (2001). Others, though, have suggested that the absence of a father can mean less household work for women (Del Re, 1996; Oakley and Rigby, 1998).

45. Gregson and Lowe (1994a, p. 49) point to a 'resurgence in demand for waged domestic labour in Britain through the 1980s and its strong association with the care of pre-school children and general household cleaning'. They estimate that between 30 and 40 per cent of dual-career households employ some form of domestic labour. Their study also provides an historical and cross-national

overview of the evidence on the use of domestic labour. Evidence for Germany can be found in Friese (1995) and Rerrich (1996), for Italy in Andall (1995, 2000). In each case, the use of migrant female labour is emphasised. Gardiner (1997) and Bittman *et al.* (1999), in contrast, warn against exaggerating the extent to which women have substituted other women's labour for their own.

46. Bakan and Stasiulis (1995, p. 304), see also hooks (1982); Glenn (1991, 1992).
47. See Lewis (1993); Hantrais and Mangen (1994); OECD (1994); Scheiwe (1994); Rubery and Fagan (1995); Anttonen and Sipilä (1996); Gornick *et al.* (1997); Deven *et al.* (1998); Gornick (1999); Meyers *et al.* (1999) . It should though be stressed that the link between levels of public provision and of female participation in the public sphere is not an automatic one, as Maruani (1992), Hantrais and Letablier (1996) and O'Connor (1996) underline. Moreover, in a British–French study, Gregory and Windebank (2000) point out that the superior provision of state child care provision in France is not matched by greater male involvement in unpaid child care; if anything the gender division of domestic labour is more unequal than in Britain.
48. See Vaiou *et al.* (1991); Tobío (1996); Valentes (2000); Wall *et al.* (2001). Where mothers are nevertheless moving into paid work without such an infrastructure, they have to develop complex private strategies to cope (often involving their own mothers) (Del Re, 1996; Tobío, 2001).
49. The position with regard to the care of adults is rather more complex, as some in the disability movement would argue that adequate state provision in support of community care would obviate the need for the provision of informal care within the family (Morris, 1993a, 1996). For a general feminist analysis of adult care, which underlines the interaction between public and private, see Hooyman and Gonyea (1995).
50. See, for instance, Okin (1989); Pateman (1989); Cockburn (1991); Phillips (1991); Fraser (1994).
51. For a discussion of EU policy, see Hantrais and Letablier (1996); Hoskyns (1996); Hantrais (2000).
52. Cass (1994, p. 115). See also Taylor-Gooby (1991), who uses the concept of 'moral hazard' in relation to men's evasion of caring work.
53. Parker and Parker (1986) cited by Hooper (1996) and by Kraemer (1999). Flouri and Buchanan (2001) suggest research points to the positive impact on children of paternal involvement. Hester and Harne (1999) are among those who warn that encouraging greater male involvement can, in some circumstances, strengthen the power of abusive fathers. Pringle explores this tension, concluding that 'men's greater involvement in childcare activities does have a real and vital anti-oppressive potential, with possible benefits for children, women and men themselves' provided that it is grounded in 'a broad anti-oppressive framework which places issues of their power and violence centre-stage' (1998, p. 331).
54. Richardson (1993). This is a real and understandable fear; at the same time there are dangers in assuming women's automatic right to have custody of their children on marriage break-up, if the father has been genuinely actively involved in their care. Delphy (1994, p. 188), for instance, has criticised feminist arguments which lay a claim to mothers' 'exclusive ownership of children' as damaging to the interests of both women and children.

55. EC Childcare Network (1990, p. 5, emphasis in original). For a sceptical discussion of the benefits of shared parenting, however, see Segal (1987).
56. See Young (1995); Prokhovnik (1998); Sevenhuijsen (1998).
57. Chanan (1992); see also, in the British context, Campbell (1984); Coote and Pattullo (1990); Mackay (2001).
58. See Coote and Pattullo (1990, p. 43) and, with respect to British parliamentary politics, Norris and Lovenduski (1995) and Mackay (2001). In the Latin American context, Craske writes of the 'mobilisation fatigue' faced by women who 'already work long hours in the reproductive and productive arenas' so that engagement in grassroots political activity becomes a 'triple burden' (1998, p. 114). Pascall and Manning suggest that for women in Central/Eastern Europe, political action can represent a 'fourth burden' on top of domestic and paid work and the development and deployment of the network resources needed to cope (2000, p. 263).
59. Hernes (1987). Women's role in trade unions is discussed by Cockburn (1987, 1995); Walby (1997).
60. See Council of Europe (1984); Lovenduski (1986); Vianello and Siemienska (1990); Chapman (1991); Vaiou *et al.* (1991). Three-quarters of female Scottish councillors interviewed by Mackay cited the sexual division of labour and caring responsibilities as the 'major reason for women's relative absence from politics' (2001, p. 57).
61. Pateman (1989, p. 186); see also Shklar (1991), who emphasises the centrality of paid employment to US citizenship, and O'Connor (1996). However, O' Connor also points out that 'West German feminism has been reluctant to identify independence for women with employment' (p. 34). Military service still, none the less, has some significance for women's citizenship, even if in many societies it now represents a job rather than a special citizenship obligation (Yuval-Davis, 1991b, 1997a; Helman, 1999).
62. For British evidence of the importance of paid employment to many women see, for instance, Cragg and Dawson (1984); Brannen and Moss (1991); Callender (1992); Watson and Fothergill (1993); Thomson (1995); Brah (1996); Ford (1996); Hinds and Jarvis (2000); Bryson *et al.* (undated). Pascall and Manning cite research demonstrating the value placed on paid employment by women in eastern and central Europe (2000, p. 250; Watson, 1996). For a Third World perspective, see Chen (1995).
63. Randall (1987). Danish research has found that unemployment reduces women's access to politics more than it does men's (Siim, 1994). Barkman (1995) points to an association between high levels of female labour market participation and female political representation. However, Squires and Wickham-Jones (2001) are more sceptical, arguing that it is professional occupations, in which women are still under-represented, from which politicians are most likely to be recruited. In France it has been suggested that women's high labour market participation has been at the expense of political participation (Letablier, 1995).
64. Marshall (1950, p. 15) identified the right to work as 'the basic civil right' in the economic field. However, as Leisink and Coenen (1993) note, this referred to the easing of restrictions on employment during the seventeenth and eighteenth centuries and there is no substantive citizen right to work as such. O'Connor *et*

al. (1999) emphasise the significance of labour market location for the exercise of social rights.

65. Gershuny (1996). Gershuny *et al.* (1994) conclude that the continued gender bias in responsibility for domestic work means that the 'time, effort and attention' that women can devote to paid work is limited, with implications for their 'accumulation of human capital'. This, they suggest, must 'be an important factor in the explanation of the continuing differential between men's and women's levels of pay and occupational attainment' ensuring 'substantial advantages to the husband in terms of earnings and status' (see also Gershuny, 2000, p. 199).

66. A French study, cited by Le Feuvre (1996), has also shown how the sexual division of labour can be deployed as an alibi for promoting men over women in the workplace, despite the commitment of those women to continuous full-time career patterns. The result was to push some of the women back into a more traditional division of labour with their spouses. See also O'Connor (1996).

67. Walby, for instance, argues that 'the labour market is more important and the family less important as the determinant of women's labour force participation than is conventionally assumed' (1990, p. 56; 1997). Arber and Gilbert, in contrast, conclude that 'the nature and extent of women's participation in waged work is intimately connected with their unpaid domestic labour as mothers and housewives' (1992, p. 1). Evidence of this connection is also provided by Anderson *et al.* (1994); MacEwen Scott (1994); Employment Committee (1995); Crompton (1997); Gregory and Windebank (2000); Hantrais (2000).

68. See Hakim (1993); Jonung and Persson (1993); Land (1994); Forsberg *et al.* (2000). The account of women's employment which follows is inevitably broad-brush, glossing over some of the differences that exist between and within countries. Evidence of the national variations in women's employment position can be found in OECD (1994); Sainsbury (1994); Anker (1998); Kauppinen and Kandolin (1998); Duncan and Pfau-Effinger (2000); UNIFEM (2000); Grimshaw and Rubery (2001). The importance of intra-country variations is underlined by Duncan (1995).

69. See, for instance Sainsbury (1994); Sly (1994); O'Reilly and Fagan (1998); Walsh (1999).

70. See Brannen and Moss (1991); OECD (1994); Ferri and Smith (1996); Gregory and Windebank (2000); Siranni and Negrey (2000).

71. For evidence of the impact of adult care on labour market participation, see Jani-Le Bris (1993); Parker and Lawton (1994); Arber and Ginn (1995); Hooyman and Gonyea (1995); Phillips J. (1995, 1996); Caring Costs Alliance (1996); Deven *et al.* (1998); *Benefits* (2000); European Commission (2000, p. 83); Howard (2001).

72. See Watson and Fothergill (1993); Ginn and Arber (1994b); Kozak (1998).

73. Eurostat (2000) statistics show that in the EU female part-time employment is highest in the Netherlands (71 per cent), UK (44.5 per cent), Belgium (40 per cent), Germany (38 per cent) Denmark (35 per cent) and lowest (below 20 per cent) in the Southern countries plus Finland. The proportion working very short hours (10 or fewer) is highest in the UK and the Netherlands (Hantrais and Letablier, 1997; Lewis, 2001). In Sweden, where part-time work generally represents the exercise of a parent's right to opt for shorter hours, it has a different meaning from other countries (Hobson *et al.*, 1995; Daune-Richard, 1998). In

the former socialist countries of Central and Eastern Europe, part-time work was relatively uncommon. Outside Europe, rates of female part-time work are high in Australia and New Zealand and lower in the US, Canada and Japan (OECD, 1994). An international overview of women's part-time work can be found in O'Reilly and Fagan (1998).

74. Access to occupational welfare, and its accompanying fiscal advantages (in the UK at least), is also consequently skewed by gender (Sinfield, 1991; Ginn and Arber, 1993, 1998; Twine, 1994; Sainsbury, 1996; Rubery, 1998; Ginn *et al.*, 2001). In the Netherlands, however, the pay of female full time and part time workers is similar (Rubery, 1998).

75. McRae (1998); OECD (1999). The importance of training to women's advancement in the UK context is stressed by the Equal Opportunities Commission (1990); Payne, J. (1991); Metcalf (1997) and in the EU context by Whitting and Quinn (1989) and Pillinger (1992). The particular importance to Black and migrant women and the difficulties they face are highlighted by Bhavnani (1994) and the European Women's Lobby (1995). There is evidence that disabled women's rehabilitation and training needs receive low priority (John, 1988; Lonsdale, 1990; Boylan, 1991).

76. Despite the evidence of a female preference for part-time work in many countries, Walsh (1999) also demonstrates a significant minority of part-time female workers would prefer to work full time and a substantial number wanted to return to full-time work in the future (see also Fagan, 1996; Smith *et al.*, 1998). For a discussion of the meaning and implications of the 'preference' for part-time work see Hewitt, P. (1993); McRae (1998); O'Reilly and Fagan (1998). In the UK, Fagan suggests that the combination of very long hours in full time jobs and inadequate child care facilities 'encourages mothers to consider part-time work as the only viable form of employment'. Many women would prefer something in between long full-time and very short part-time hours (2001, p. 244). France is one country where mothers do not favour part-time work (Daune-Richard, 1998). The Netherlands is unusual in its attempt to 'normalise' part-time work, even if not totally successfully from a gender equality perspective (Kremer, 2001; Plantenga, 2002).

77. Walby (1997); Anker (1998); Kauppinen and Kandolin (1998); Smith *et al.* (1998); Grimshaw and Rubery (2001). Einhorn (1993), Heinen (1990), Makkai (1994) and Watson (1996) point to how Western patterns have been reflected in Eastern Europe. The degree of segregation in Scandinavian labour markets is highlighted by, for instance, Lewis and Åström (1992); Hobson *et al.* (1995); Forsberg *et al.* (2000); Gould (2001); Björnberg (2002). Hantrais and Letablier suggest that even for full-time workers, segregation may partly reflect the long working hours which may operate 'as an unwritten condition of employment' for some occupations (1997, p. 142; see also Fagan, 2001).

78. OECD (1994); European Commission (2001). The lower UK female unemployment rate is partly a reflection of the growth in part-time jobs available to women. The economic activity rate of UK disabled women is about 30 percentage points lower than that of non-disabled women (Equal Opportunities Commission, 2000). Women's employment rate has fallen sharply in the former socialist countries (UNIFEM, 2000), with damaging consequences (Watson, 1996).

79. For evidence of the gender wages gap in a range of countries see, for instance Gornick (1999); UNIFEM (2000); Clarke (2001). US data can be found in US Census Bureau (2001). Minority ethnic women's pay is discussed by Bruegel (1989); Bhavnani (1994); Street and Wilmoth (2001, p. 133); and disabled women's by Lonsdale (1990). The gap can be disaggregated into a 'gender' and a 'family' gap, the latter reflecting women's child care responsibilities (Harkness and Waldfogel, 1999).

80. See Brannen and Moss (1991); MacEwen Scott (1994); Vogler (1994); Kadalie (1995).

81. See, for instance, Siim (1993, 2000); Glover and Arber (1995); Harrop and Moss (1995); Macran *et al.* (1996); McRae (1996); Kozak (1998); Gregory and Windebank (2000) and Walby (1997, 2000) who also emphasises age or generational differences. Korpi (2000) argues that class inequalities have been more resistant to reduction than gender inequalities.

82. For UK evidence see, Bruegel (1989, 1994); Bhavnani (1994) and for the wider EU, European Women's Lobby (1995). However, according to Rake (2000) in the UK the average hourly pay of Black (though not Pakistani/Bangladeshi) women is higher than that of White women. The unemployment rate for Black African women was 3.5 times higher and for Pakistani/Bangladeshi women over 5 times higher than that for White women in 1999–2000 (Twomey, 2001).

83. See Brah and Shaw (1992); Bhavnani (1994); Phizacklea, (1994); Rowbotham and Mitter (1994); Phizacklea and Wolkowitz (1995); Mohanty (1997); Cook (2000); Felstead *et al.* (2001).

84. A study of north-western Europe suggests sexual harassment occurs in virtually all workplaces to varying degrees and that, on average, 30 to 50 per cent of women have experienced it in some form (Timmerman and Bajema, 1999). It has been shown to 'create an intimidating and unfriendly workplace atmosphere for hundreds of thousands of women around the EU' (Kauppinen and Kandolin, 1998). The connections with racial and homophobic harassment are made by Brant and Lee Too (1994).

85. For evidence regarding the discrimination which lesbians and disabled women might face see respectively, Foley (1994); Palmer (1995); Stonewall (2001) and Lonsdale (1990); Foley and Pratt (1994).

86. UNHCHR (2001) For the position in the EU and the UK see Glendinning and Millar (1992); Payne, S. (1991); Lister (1992, 1995b); Conroy and Flanagan (1993); Directorate General for Research (1994). Evidence of the 'feminisation of poverty' in Eastern Europe is provided by Einhorn (1993) and in the US is discussed by Nelson (1984); Fraser (1987); Polakow (1993) and Pearce (1990) who is credited with coining the term 'the feminisation of poverty'. The term is used also to describe the position of women in the South (Mosse, 1993), discussed also in IDS Bulletin (1997). Cross-national evidence is provided by Orloff (1996); Christopher (2001b).

87. See Amott (1990); Lonsdale (1990); Amin with Oppenheim (1992); Cook and Watt (1992); Roberts (1995); UNHCHR (2001).

88. See Ginn and Arber (1991, 1994a, 1996); Joshi (1992); Walker (1992); Groves (1992); Rake (2000); Ginn *et al.* (2001).

89. Lister (1992; 1995b). The work of Pahl and of Vogler has been particularly important in illuminating the extent to which household income is shared

unfairly to the disadvantage of women and the ways in which women bear the strain of managing a low income (Pahl, 1989; Vogler and Pahl, 1993, 1994; Vogler, 1994; Goode *et al.*, 1997; Molloy and Snape, 1999).

90. For a fuller account of the relationship between poverty and citizenship, see Lister (1990a); Dean (1995, 1999); Procacci (2001) and, from a historical perspective, Vincent (1991).

Chapter 6

1. Hoskyns (1996); European Women's Lobby (1995); European Database (2000).
2. Lovenduski (1986); Hernes (1987); Randall (1987); Cockburn (1995, 1996c); Phillips, A. (1995); Young (1996); Wirth (2001). In Scandinavia, though, women's representation on corporate bodies has increased, following government action (Siim, 2000; Skjeie and Siim, 2000). UNIFEM (2000) underlines the growing power of the corporate sector relative to parliament, just as women's parliamentary representation has grown.
3. Dölling (1991); Einhorn (1993); European Centre (1993); Watson (1993, 1996); Petrova, (1994); Herhoffer (1995); Pascall and Manning (2000); UNIFEM (2000). Female representation has, however, begun to rise again in some countries.
4. Examples can be found in *Social Politics* (1995); Miethe (1999); Franceschet (2001). Kadalie (1995); Seidman (1999); McEwan (2000) and Steady (2002) discuss South Africa.
5. See Vianello and Siemienska (1990); Norris (1991; 2001; 2002); Parry *et al.* (1992); Verba *et al.* (1995); Inglehart and Norris (2003).
6. Chanan (1992, p. 86, emphasis in original); see also McCulloch (1997); McCoy (2000). Research with young people, carried out with colleagues, found that qualitative interviewing can reveal examples of unstructured activism that a questionnaire failed to elicit (ESRC Project award no. L134 25 1039). A wide-ranging historical and cross-national account of women's radical political action is provided by Rowbotham (1992). See also Siim (1994, 2000) and Gustafsson *et al.* (1997) for a Scandinavian and Einhorn (1993) and Miethe (1999) for an East/Central European perspective. Contemporary studies of explicitly feminist politics can be found in Lovenduski and Randall (1993); Threlfall (1996) and Corrin (1999).
7. British studies include Campbell (1984); Coote and Pattullo (1990); Hyatt (1992a, b). Examples from the US can be found in Ferree and Martin (1995); Naples (1998a, c) and from the South in Basu (1995); *Social Politics* (1998); McEwan (2000).
8. See Carby (1982); Parmar (1982); Bryan *et al.* (1985); Brah (1987); Collins (1991); Cook and Watt (1992); Mirza (1997).
9. See Morris (1991, 1996); Lloyd (1992, 2001); Ginn (1993); Bristow and Wilson (1993); Wilson (1995); Corrin (1999).
10. See Donnison (1989); West and Blumberg (1990); Chanan (1992); Pardo (1995); McCulloch (1997).

11. The Opsahl Commission was established by Initiative '92 to seek a way forward for Northern Ireland; see Pollak (1993) and also Lister (1994a). Women's political action in Northern Ireland is discussed in NI Women and Citizenship Research Group (1995); Roulston and Davies (2000).
12. Pettman (1996, p. 124); see also Schirmer (1989); Jaquette (1994); Blacklock and Macdonald (1998) for discussion of mothers' protests, which reflect the weaving of motherhood 'through the history of women's citizenship in Latin America' (Molyneux, 2000, p. 134). Arat (1999) and Helman (1999) provide a Turkish and an Israeli perspective.
13. Riley (1988); see also Bacchi (1990); Koven (1993).
14. Pateman (1992, p. 19); Kornbluh (1996), however, argues that republican motherhood and maternalism are separate philosophies pertaining to different historical periods.
15. See Williams (1989, 1995a); Mink (1990); Boris (1993); Lake (1993, 1995); Roberts (1995); Brush (1996).
16. For a detailed critique, see Dietz (1985, 1987); Stacey (1986); Siim (1988).
17. Ruddick (1989, p. 24, 1980, p. 354, 1987, p. 251, 1989, p. 220, emphasis in original).
18. Dietz (1985, p. 20, 1987); see also Tronto (1993).
19. Segal (1987, p. 145). Ruddick (1989) herself is careful to acknowledge differences between women and that motherhood is itself historically constructed; nevertheless, as Delphy (1994) observes, this is not really reflected in her overall thesis.
20. See Schirmer (1989); Rowbotham (1992); Jaquette (1994); Franceschet (2001).
21. Mackay (2001, p.186); Sevenhuijsen (1998, p. 15). Bowden (1997) and McLaughlin (1997) also make the case for incorporating an ethic of care into the understanding and practice of political citizenship. Ruddick (1989, pp. 46–7) herself, whilst sympathetic to the argument, deliberately retains 'the maternal idiom' on the grounds that 'the maternal is not the whole of care and cannot be made to stand for it'.
22. Coote and Pattullo (1990), for instance, found that children's needs and domestic violence were the two main catalysts for women's political activity. The nature of this activity is summed up well by this extract from a statement from a women's community action conference: 'We are the women who organise summer playschemes, mother-and-toddler groups, and after-school care for our children. We do this work without pay so that our children will have opportunities to be together and have fun when all other schemes to serve their needs have been lost in endless budget cuts; We are the women who campaign for safe play areas and for better road safety, so that our children can be outdoors and can be protected from the dangers of traffic and death-riders; ... We are the women fighting against drugs, crime and violence, working to make the streets safer and to give our children hope for a better future, despite the unemployment statistics; We are the women who believe that by working together, both within our communities and by forming coalitions across the boundaries of different communities, we can create positive changes for our children, our partners and our neighbours; We are women living on council estates and in inner-city neighbourhoods. We are all races and colours. Many of us are lone parents; some of us are disabled' (Women's Stand for Community Action, 1994). Examples from the US can be found in Naples (1998c).

23. See Campbell (1984); Coote and Pattullo (1990); Rowbotham and Mitter (1994).
24. Lovenduski and Randall (1993, p. 124); see also Coote and Pattullo (1990); Hyatt (1992b). In the US, working class Appalachian women were similarly transformed by their involvement in support of a coal strike (Seitz, 1998). The transformative impact on women of collective action is also highlighted in Ferree and Martin's edited collection on feminist organisations in the US (1995) and by Mayo (1994), Suarez Toro (1995); Naples (1998a); Roulston and Whittock (2000).
25. Black supplementary schools, set up 'by and for the black community' offer education outside the formal school system. Mirza and Reay (2000b) found 60 in 15 London boroughs in a short space of time.
26. Women in Black (1993), cited in Hughes *et al.* (1995), emphasis in original. Helman likewise contrasts the mobilisation of motherhood for peace in Israel with the protests of Women in Black. Whereas the former failed to overcome ethnic and class divisions and to challenge 'the militaristic gender order', the latter claimed a voice in the public realm as female 'citizens of equal standing – not as the mother or wife of a soldier', thereby undermining 'the male monopoly on this realm' (1999, pp. 306–7).
27. Stacey and Price (1981, p. 189); see, more recently, Randall (1987) and Coote and Pattullo (1990).
28. For a discussion of the arguments see Hernes (1987); Phillips (1991, 1995, 2000); Squires (1999); Sawer (2000).
29. See Molyneux (1984); Phillips (1991, 1993, 1995); Pringle and Watson (1992); Squires (1999, 2001); Sawer (2000).
30. Childs (2001a, b). The failure of New Labour women MPs to vote against the legislation to abolish lone parent benefits was the subject of widespread criticism (see, for instance, Ward, 2000). Some, such as Fiona Mactaggart MP (2000), justify this failure on the grounds that behind the scenes pressure is more effective; Squires and Wickham-Jones (2001) and Russell *et al.* (2002) provide a more sympathetic overall assessment.
31. See Costain (1988); Meuller (1988); Burrell (1993); Bryson (1999). Inglehart and Norris (2000) suggest that a similar gender gap, in which women (especially younger women) favour more left-oriented parties, is beginning to emerge in other postindustrial societies. In the UK, the traditional gender gap, in which women have favoured the Conservatives, has narrowed overall and has reversed among younger women (Harman and Mattinson, 2000; Lovenduski, 2001; Russell *et al.*, 2002).
32. See Lewis and Åström (1992); Siim (1994, 2000); Hobson and Lindholm (1995); Gould (2001). In Ireland, an increase in female political representation has had a significant impact on the political agenda especially in the areas of social and family policy (Suibhne, 1995). In the UK, the jury is still out on the impact of women MPs at Westminster post-1997, but one verdict is that 'it appears that women have been more successful in challenging the male policy agenda bias' in Scotland and Wales, where they constitute a 'critical mass' (Squires and Wickham-Jones, 2001, p. 110). The position of women politicians in Scotland and Wales is discussed by Gill (1999) and Stephenson (2001) and at Westminster by Lovenduski (2001) and Childs (2001a, b).

33. See Hedlund (1988); Norris (1996); Mackay (2001). Nearly two-thirds of Labour women MPs, first elected in 1997, interviewed by Childs (2002) believed that women had a different political style. However, they saw this as an attribute of gender rather than sex, so that some 'new men' shared this style while some more established women did not.

34. Gould (1988, p. 294). Giddens (1994a, p. 16) makes a similar point when he argues that communication skills developed in the private sphere, 'a democracy of the emotions', provide a sound floor for the development of public democracy and citizenship.

35. For a discussion of quotas see Phillips (1991, 1995); Lovenduski and Norris (1993); Bryson (1999, pp. 119–121) and Squires and Wickham-Jones (2001) who point to their success in India in increasing women's participation in local politics. An example of the backlash a quota system can create and of the dangers of withdrawing quotas prematurely is provided by the decision of the British Labour Party, in 1993, to require all-women parliamentary shortlists in 50 per cent of its vacant and winnable seats. Following considerable opposition among some constituency parties, an industrial tribunal ruled that the policy breached the Sex Discrimination Act and the policy was abandoned. The proportion of women subsequently selected for winnable seats plummeted. However, following the 2001 General Election, when the number of Labour women MPs fell, the Government has legislated to permit positive discrimination in the selection of candidates (Russell *et al.*, 2002). Gill (1999) discusses the impact of other positive action mechanisms in Scotland and Wales and points out that the choice of mechanism needs to take account of the voting system used.

36. In the 2002 election, however, the largest parties, which could afford to forego the contribution to expenses, contingent on compliance, flouted the law (*Independent*, 31 May 2002).

37. Taken to its logical conclusion, this invokes the 'mirror principle', under which the composition of the population as a whole is mirrored in the make-up of the legislature. The difficulties with this are discussed by Phillips (1991, p. 152; 1995) and Kymlicka (1995) and the more general dilemma by Nash (1998) and Squires (1999, 2001).

38. Phillips (1994, 1995). She explores the debates in the US around a politics of presence, which has increased the representation of African Americans in city councils and state legislatures. One general problem she identifies is a tendency for a politics of presence to eclipse a politics of ideas, so that identity takes precedence over political ideas or programmes. She rejects the idea that the two are mutually exclusive: 'It is in the relationship between ideas and presence that we can best hope to find a fairer system of representation, not in a false opposition between one or the other' (1995, p. 25).

39. Norris (2000); Squires and Wickham-Jones (2001); also Barkman (1995) and Bryson who warns that PR does not, of itself, constitute 'a magic wand' (1999, p. 118).

40. Sawer (2000, p. 370); Gill (2000); Elgood *et al.* (2002).

41. Cockburn (1987, 1995, 1996c); Randall (1987); Coote and Pattullo (1990); Lovenduski and Randall (1993); Sawer (2000); Mackay (2001). Young's (2000) argument for more inclusive forms of political communication is also relevant in this context.

42. See Dahlerup (1986); Sainsbury (1993b); Skjeie (1993); Siim (2000) and, more generally, Randall (1998), Bryson (1999, p.122) and Sawer (2000).
43. See Chapter 3; also, Cain and Yuval-Davis (1990); Anthias and Yuval-Davis (1992); Rowbotham (1996).
44. These are discussed in Beresford and Croft (1993); Jacobs and Popple (1994); Chanan *et al.* (2000). The case for involving people in poverty is made by the Commission on Poverty, Participation and Power (2000) and Lister (2002a).
45. Pillinger (1992, p. 4); Hoskyns (1996); see also Meehan (1993a); Cockburn (1995); European Women's Lobby (1995, 2000). Cohen (1998, 2000) is more critical, emphasising the barriers faced by Black women and women in poverty from grassroots organisations.

Chapter 7

1. Koven and Michel (1993). See also Lewis (1980, 1994); Dale (1986); Dale and Foster (1986); Gordon (1990); Sarvasy (1992); Misra and Akins (1998); Siim (2000); Sainsbury (2001). A more negative assessment of their impact is provided by Pederson (1989, 1990).
2. Hobson *et al.* (1995); see also Dahlerup (1986); Randall (1987); Fox-Piven (1990); Lovenduski and Randall (1993); Doyal (1995); Mahon (1997); Hobson (1999); Siim (2000); Gould (2001); Peng (2001). Mink (1998), though, is critical of feminists' failure in the US to defend poor mothers' rights against punitive welfare reforms.
3. See David (1985); Balbo (1987). According to a British Government Minister, 91 per cent of women with school-age children say they normally take them to the doctor and 61 per cent to school (*House of Commons Hansard*, 2001). The point is not, however, necessarily true for all societies. Joseph, for instance, notes how in Lebanon 'patriarchy privileged the initiatives of males and seniors in such a way that women and juniors often had to have the involvement of males and seniors on their behalf in negotiations with public officials and agencies' (1994, p. 283).
4. See Hernes (1987); Fox-Piven (1990); Orloff (1993); O'Connor (1993, 1996); Naples (1998a, b); Hobson (1999); Pope (1999).
5. See Croft and Beresford (1989, 1992); Fraser (1989); Beresford and Croft (1993); Yeatman (1994); Barnes (1997, 1999a); Higgins (1999); Commission on Poverty, Participation and Power (2000).
6. Lewis (1994, p. 50); see also Dale and Foster (1986); Riley (1988).
7. See Lewis (1980, 1994); Mink (1990); Bellingham and Mathis (1994); Misra and Akins (1998).
8. Leira (1992, p. 126). Examples of alternative health projects are discussed by Doyal (1983, 1995); Lovenduski and Randall (1993); Cockburn (1998). Examples of women as alternative welfare providers can be found in Hyatt (1992a); Basu (1995); Behrend (1995). The dangers are also discussed by Silliman (1999) and Schild (2000).
9. Recent studies include Sainsbury (1996, 1999); O'Connor *et al.* (1999); Daly (2000).

10. See Hernes (1987); Sassoon (1987); Fox-Piven (1990); Kohlberg (1991); Lewis (1994); Meyer (1994).
11. See Bryan *et al.* (1985); Mama (1992); Foster (1996).
12. Pateman (1989, p. 195); see also Daly (1994); Kornbluh (1996); O'Connor (1996); Christopher (2001b).
13. Orloff (1997). Evidence of the domestic violence experienced by lone mothers can be found in, for instance, Bradshaw and Millar (1991); Marsh *et al.* (1997); Raphael (2000); Polakow *et al.* (2001).
14. Falkingham and Hills (1995); Daly (2000); Nyberg (2002).
15. See Nelson (1984, 1990); Fraser (1987); Fraser and Gordon (1994a).
16. Sainsbury (1996); Lewis (1997). This process has gone furthest in Australia, see Shaver (1993); O' Connor *et al.* (1999).
17. See Hoskyns and Luckhaus (1989); Millar (1989, 1996); Maier (1991); Lister (1992, 1994c); Sohrab (1994); O'Reilly and Fagan (1998); Daly (2000).
18. See Groves (1991, 1992); Davies and Ward (1992); Ginn and Arber (1991, 1992; 1994a); Twine (1994); Joshi *et al.* (1996); Gough (2001); Ginn *et al.*, 2001 and on fiscal welfare, Sainsbury (1999).
19. Lister (1992); Sainsbury (1996, 1999); Ginn *et al.* (2001).
20. Esping-Andersen (1990, p. 37). The gendered critique and development of his model includes, in addition to texts specifically referenced, Lewis (1993); Scheiwe (1994); Anttonen and Sipilä (1996); Gornick *et al.* (1997) and O' Connor *et al.*'s (1999) study of liberal regimes. Initial feminist analysis of welfare regimes and the 'male breadwinner' model has since been critiqued and refined in Sainsbury (1994, 1996, 1999); Lewis (plus Commentaries) (1997); Daly (2000) and Adams and Padamsee (2001).
21. McLaughlin and Glendinning (1994) have put forward the same concept of 'defamilialisation'. Subsequently Esping-Andersen (1999) has himself appropriated the term in his later work, which accords the family a key role (see also Mahon, 2001).
22. Orloff (1993, p. 320; 1997); O'Connor (1993, 1996); see also Hobson (1990); Bussemaker and van Kersbergen (1994); Lister (1995a) and Korpi (2000) who treats autonomy as an aspect of 'agency inequality'.
23. Lewis (2001, p. 163; 2000); Pascall and Lewis (2001). The Scandinavian version of the individualised model is discussed by Sainsbury (1996, 1999); Bergqvist and Jungar (2000); Siim (2000). Plantenga (2002) discusses the Netherlands. Pfau-Effinger (2001) identifies three 'modernisation paths of gender arrangements'.
24. See Einhorn (1993, 1999); Lykke *et al.* (1994); Matynia (1995); Pascall and Manning (2000).
25. Pringle and Watson (1992, pp. 70, 63); see also Dahlerup (1987); Eisenstein (1988); Cooper (1993); Curthoys (1993); Randall and Waylen (1998); Rai (1999); Squires (2000). Brown's more critical analysis of the state as a continued instrument of male dominance, producing disciplined gendered subjects, distinguishes between the state's juridical, capitalist, prerogative and bureaucratic facets (1995). A related issue is the role of the law, which like the state, is best understood as neither unitary nor homogeneous (Smart and Brophy, 1985). Feminist accounts of the law which are relevant to the issues pursued here include O'Donovan (1985); Dahl (1987); Holtmaat (1989); Smart (1989) and, in an EU context, Hoskyns (1996).

26. The implications of such transformations for gendered citizenship are discussed in Brodie (1997); Pettman (1999); Schild (2000); Crouch (2001). Lewis (1998) and Daly and Lewis (2000) analyse the implications of marketisation for care and Ginn *et al.* (2001) of privatisation for women's pensions.

27. The importance of the 'social services state' is underlined by Anttonen and Sipilä (1996); Sainsbury (1996); Anttonen (1998); Johansson and Jansson (1998).

28. Writing within the Finnish context, Silius (1995) cites as examples of the first point the tardy criminalisation of rape in marriage; the non-gender sensitive treatment of domestic violence; and the non-problematisation of pornography. Bacchi (1996) makes similar observations about Sweden where the political agenda has not reflected feminist concerns about such issues until only recently. Eduards (1997) and Gould (2001) describe how they are now taken more seriously in Sweden thanks to the feminist movement. The more general critique can be found in Leira (1992, 1993a, b); Sainsbury, (1999, pp. 94–5); Nyberg (2002).

29. See Williams (1989, 1995a); Shaver (1990, 1993); Anthias and Yuval-Davis (1992); Ginsburg (1992, 1994a); Boris (1995); Orloff (1996, 2002).

30. Mama (1992, p. 86); see also Bryan *et al.* (1985); Cook and Watt (1992); Nasir (1996); Douglas (1998).

31. See Shaver (1990); Carabine (1992, 1996); Cooper (1993); Alexander (1994); Richardson (1998). The promotion of heterosexual interests is not always to the disadvantage of lesbians and gays. Thus, for example, where homosexual partnerships are not recognised lesbian and gay couples escape the cohabitation rule applied to social security claims from heterosexuals deemed to be living as part of an unmarried couple.

32. See Lewis (1980); Bock and Thane (1991); Koven and Michel (1993); Frader (1996); Kornbluh (1996); Misra and Akins (1998). Lewis (1994) has, however, challenged the increasingly influential feminist interpretation of women's early welfare activism as being inspired solely by maternalism. Rather, she suggests, it represented primarily the expression of their perceived citizenship duties.

33. Pederson (1990, pp. 983, 1006); with regard to the US, see Gordon (1990) and Sarvasy (1992).

34. In contrast, Sainsbury contends that maternalists' 'influence on Norwegian social policy constitutes a major source of contemporary variations among Scandinavian welfare states', revealing 'a much sharper gender differentiation in social entitlements' (2001, pp. 137, 114).

35. Leira (1992, p. 171, 1989, p. 208). Arguments for such a concept are put also by, for instance, Knijn and Kremer (1997); Grace (1998); Sevenjuijsen (1998); McKie *et al.* (2001). Relevant here also are the growing demands worldwide, as expressed in the 1995 UN Platform for Action agreed at Beijing, for women's unpaid caring work to be treated as part of gross national product for economic accounting purposes in the same way that paid caring work is (Folbre, 1995). The limits of such a strategy are, however, pointed out by Gardiner (1997).

36. See Luckhaus and Dickens (1991); Lister (1992, 1994c); Commission on Social Justice (1994); Daly (1996).

37. For a discussion of the individualisation of social security benefits see Esam and Berthoud (1991); Roll (1991); Luckhaus (1994); Sainsbury (1996, 1999). Individualisation of contributory benefits would, though, have to be introduced

gradually so as not to hurt those, particularly older, women who had not built up their own contribution entitlement. I have argued elsewhere that individualisation is not appropriate in means-tested benefits on the grounds that 'short of measuring the actual flow of resources between partners (which would be unacceptably intrusive and could not, in any case, take account of the use of such resources for household or personal consumption), it is difficult to see how means-tested benefits can accurately target help on those in need, once concern shifts to the needs not of families but of the individuals that make up families' (Lister, 1992, p. 65, 1994c). This is, in my view, a strong argument against means-tested benefits *per se*, although Australia has shown that partial individualisation is possible (Millar, 1998).

38. Kremer (1994) and Knijn and Kremer (1997); see also Balbo and Nowotny (1986); Sassoon (1991); Knijn (1994).

39. Germany reformed its parental leave scheme in 2000, with the aim in part to raise fathers' take-up rate (Ostner, 2001).

40. Denmark introduced a two weeks father's quota in addition to two weeks existing paternity leave in 1999 (Rostgaard *et al.*, 1999). A proposal to extend the quota to three months fell with the change of government in 2001 (Siim, personal communication). A number of EC member states are taking steps to increase fathers' take-up (European Commission, 2001).

41. Deven *et al.* (1998); Moss and Deven (1999); Sainsbury (1999). The New Labour British Government, which introduced parental leave in the UK, has been widely criticised for its refusal to consider payment; as a result only a tiny percentage of fathers are making use of it.

42. Carlsen (1993, 1995); Deven *et al.* (1998); Moss and Deven (1999); Kröger (2001); Björnberg (2002).

43. See Brannen and Moss (1991); Cockburn (1991); Richardson (1993); Martin and Collinson (1999). The impact of attitudes on the sexual division of labour is stressed by Compton and Harris (1999).

44. Plantenga *et al.* (1999, p. 100); see also Knijn and van Wel (2001a, b); Kremer (2001); Plantenga (2002).

45. Marsh (1991, p. 80). See also Hernes (1987); Hewitt (1993); Folbre (1994); Employment Committee (1995); Pillinger (2000); and Sirianni and Negrey (2000) who point out that a feminist approach to working time would emphasise a shorter working day, work-time flexibility and limits on un-social hours rather than a shorter working week. A working time directive was agreed by the EU in 1993, but its limitations have reduced its impact (Hantrais and Letablier, 1997).

46. Critical feminists include Segal (1987) and Richardson (1993). In their study of Britain and France, Gregory and Windebank (2000), on the other hand, suggest that better state provisions might reinforce the sexual division of labour by relieving men of their responsibility in the domestic sphere. My emphasis on the balance between individual and state responsibility is not to discount the importance of informal and voluntary forms of collective provision that fall between the two. Examples in the field of childcare can be found, for instance, in Norway where mothers have developed a network of informal provisions (Leira, 1992) and the UK where there is a strong voluntary childcare movement (Lovenduski and Randall, 1993; Figes, 1994; Melzer, 1994).

47. Moss (1988); see too Cook and Watt (1992) with respect to the differential access to childcare facilities by 'race'.

48. Child care league tables suffer from problems of data comparison. These data are from the European Commission (2001) and include formal private as well as public provision. There is a growing trend in some countries to privately provided though publicly funded childcare (Lewis, 1998). For further information on childcare see O'Connor (1996); Sainsbury (1999); Deven *et al.* (1998); Randall (2000); Kröger (2001); Millar and Ridge (2001); Michel, Mahon (eds) (2002). Childcare is of importance not just to women but to children themselves (Daycare Trust, 2001; Polakow *et al.*, 2001), which underlines the importance of quality (La Valle *et al.*, 1999; Land, 2002).

49 The extension of parental leave in Eastern/Central Europe, for instance, is aimed at reducing spending on child care and depressing women's labour supply (Pascall and Manning, 2000).

50. For more detailed information about policies in Sweden and the other Nordic welfare states see Hobson *et al.* (1995); Kautto *et al.* (1999); Moss and Deven (1999); Sainsbury (1999); Bergqvist and Jungar (2000).

51. The dangers are discussed in Moss and Deven (1999). Bruning and Platenga (1999) suggest that a year is the optimal length. For evidence of the long-term impact of women's absence from the labour market, see Mertens *et al.* (1995); Joshi *et al.* (1996); McRae (1996); Rake (2000). The point still applies, albeit less so, even in those countries, such as Sweden, where those on parental leave are defined as in employment.

52. Information about child care allowances can be found in Leira (1998); Lewis (1998); Moss and Deven (1999). Their introduction in Sweden was shortlived (Bergqvist and Jungar, 2000). In an assessment of the debates in Finland and France around the relative merits of such allowances and formal child care, Heinen and Martiskainen Koenigswarter conclude that the outcome will 'dramatically affect ... the shape of women's citizenship' (2001, p. 176).

53. Ungerson (1995, 1997) makes the point that the growing incidence of paid volunteering and the diversification of modes of payment for care (in which she includes symbolic informal payments to kin, friends and neighbours) serves to undermine the dichotomy that she and others had previously drawn between formal and informal forms of care. More detailed information about payments for caring can be found in cross-national studies by Glendinning and McLaughlin (1993a, b); Evers *et al.* (1994), updated by Pijl (1995) and Lewis (1998). For a more general discussion of citizenship and the provision of care for frail elderly people, see Baldock and Evers (1991).

54. McLaughlin and Glendinning (1994). Until a ruling by the European Court of Justice, married/cohabiting women were excluded from entitlement on the grounds that 'they might be at home in any event'.

55. See Ungerson (1992, 1997); Glendinning and McLaughlin (1993b); Evers *et al.* (1994). Ungerson (2000) warns that, in the UK, the domiciliary care labour market is beginning to bifurcate into one part, offering very low wages and poor working conditions and the other, more skilled, not quite as low paid, work under better conditions. This mirrors growing inequalities between women in the labour market more generally.

56. The position of and policies for working carers are discussed by Jani-Le Bris (1993); Parker and Lawton (1994); Arber and Ginn, (1995); Evers *et al.* (1994, p. 38); Phillips J. (1995, 1996); Schunk (2000); Howard (2001).

57. Arber and Ginn (1995). The other two arguments can be found in McLaughlin and Glendinning (1994) and Ungerson (1993) respectively.
58. For a fuller discussion of the arguments for and against each of these positions see, for instance, Evers *et al.* (1994); Bransbury (1995); Ungerson (1995); Shakespeare (2000); Howard (2001); Daly (2002). A number of European countries are going down the road of payment to the care-user. Legislation to introduce direct payments was introduced in the UK in 1996. Ungerson suggests that 'these developments constitute the sharp end of commodified care and marketized intimacy' (1997, p. 170; 1999). The relationship that such payments set up between recipients and the state has been described as possibly heralding 'a new type of welfare citizenship' (Daly and Lewis, 1998, p. 4).
59. Ungerson (1993, pp. 144, 150, 1995, 1997). The importance of such a public framework is emphasised also in Hooyman and Gonyea's feminist model for family care, elaborated in the US context (1995).
60. Jordan (1989, p. 124). Among other writers who have advocated Citizen's or Basic Income (as it is also called) with reference to the principles of citizenship are Offe (1993), Vilrokx (1993); Twine (1994); Faulks (2000); McKay and VanEvery (2000). Roche (1992) also provides a critically sympathetic account. Williams (1992a) suggests that it could help to resolve the tension in social policy between universality and diversity but does not go into detail. The definition is taken from the *Citizen's Income Bulletin* (now Newsletter), published by the Citizen's Income Trust (*www.citizensincome.org*). The position of non-citizen residents under it is not clear.
61. Atkinson (1993); see also White (2000); Oppenheim (2001). As the Commission on Social Justice acknowledged, the definition of such a condition would need detailed consideration. Its own suggestion is that it would include all 'residents in employment or self-employment, those unable to work because of sickness, injury or disability, those unemployed but available for work, those in approved education or training, and those caring for young, elderly or disabled dependants' (1994, p. 264). Atkinson's formulation included, in addition, those engaged in voluntary work. Jordan *et al.*, however, doubt 'the ability of legislators to translate the notion of "participation" into a system which is both morally defensible and politically feasible' (2000, p. 68).
62. See Amott (1990); Meucci (1992); King (1995); Roberts (1995); Naples (1997); Mink (1998); Link and Bibus (2000); Clarke and Fox Piven (2001); Millar and Ridge (2001); Waldfogel *et al.* (2001); Wiseman (2001).
63. Gilder (1986, p. 39 cited in Roche, 1992). Elsewhere, Gilder (1987) explicitly condemns the position of Novak *et al.* (1987).
64. See Duncan and Edwards (1997); Lewis (1997); Kiernan *et al.* (1998); Millar and Rowlingson (2001).
65. Knijn and van Wel (2001a, b). Feminists have been divided in their responses to this policy shift. Some are in favour because they see it as opening up facilities and opportunities to lone mothers which would not be available so long as they are on social assistance; while others see it as an erosion of lone mothers' social rights.
66. For discussion of the UK see Millar and Rowlingson (2001); Gray (2001); Lister, (2002c). According to a study of OECD countries, the only other countries that do not require lone parents to seek work until their youngest child is

aged (at least) 16 are Ireland, Australia and New Zealand (Eardley *et al.*, 1996). See also Bradshaw *et al.* (1996). In Australia pressure to enter the labour market is growing and a requirement on lone parents to demonstrate some form of social or economic participation, broadly defined to include voluntary work, as a condition of receipt of social assistance is under consideration (Hancock, 2002; Saunders, 2002).

67. Kilkey and Bradshaw (1999, 2001); Pedersen *et al.* (2000); Chambaz (2001); Millar and Ridge (2001) provide information on lone mothers' poverty rates.

68. Waldfogel *et al.* (2001, p. 59). See also Duncan and Edwards (1997); Christopher (2001a); Polit *et al.* (2001); Verber (2001). In the context of the UK New Deal, the importance of sustainable employment and support from personal advisers for lone parents once in work is stressed by the National Council for One Parent Families (2001).

69. See, for instance, Duncan and Edwards (1997); Lewis (1997); Kiernan *et al.* (1998); Pedersen *et al.* (2000), Millar and Rowlingson (2001). Information about lone mothers own preferences and needs, in the UK context, can be found in Kemmer *et al.* (2001); Millar and Ridge (2001); National Council for One Parent Families (2001). Paid time off to care for sick children is of particular importance given the high incidence of ill health among children in lone parent families (Millar and Ridge, 2001).

70 The impact of education on lone mothers' economic situation is emphasised by Knijn and van Wel (2001a); Millar and Rowlingson (2001); Polakow *et al.* (2001).

71. See Knijn and van Wel (2001a, b) and also van Drenth *et al.* (1999). Black lone mothers in the UK are more likely to see the financial rewards from and example set by paid work as part of their moral responsibilities towards their children (Duncan and Edwards, 1999; Reynolds, 2001).

72. The stronger the expectation that lone mothers are in paid work, the more unreasonable is the competing expectation of their involvement in their children's schooling (Standing, 1999).

73. Hobson (1994, p. 171). See also Lewis (1997). However, a small qualitative study in Denmark warns that lone mothers 'readily fall through the ever-widening holes of a universalistic society which has failed to recognize the specific life-world obstacles of such families' and in which the failure of social citizenship rights 'to take account of the unique position of lone-mother families' leaves them 'diminished and impaired' (Polakow *et al.*) (2001, pp. 2–3).

Bibliography

Abbott, E. and Bompas, K. (1943) *The Woman Citizen and Social Security*, London: Mrs Bompas.

Acker, J. (1988) 'Class, gender and the relations of distribution', *Signs*, 13(3), pp. 473–97.

Ackers, L. (1996) 'Citizenship, gender, and dependence in the European Union: women and internal migration', *Social Politics*, 3(2/3), pp. 316–330.

Ackers, L. (1998), *Shifting Spaces. Women, Citizenship and Migration within the European Union*, Bristol: Policy Press.

Adams, J. and Padamsee, T. (2001) 'Signs and regimes: rereading feminist work on welfare states', *Social Politics*, 8(1), pp. 1–23.

Adams, M. L. (1989) 'There's no place like home: on the place of identity in feminist politics', *Feminist Review*, (31), pp. 22–33.

Adamson, W. (1987/1988) 'Gramsci and the politics of civil society', *Praxis International*, 7(3/4), p. 320.

Afary, J. (1997) 'The war against feminism in the name of the almighty: making sense of gender and Muslim fundamentalism', *New Left Review*, 224, pp. 89–110.

Afshar, H. and Maynard, M. (eds) (1994) *The Dynamics of 'Race' and Gender: Some Feminist Interpretations*, London: Taylor & Francis.

Aguiton, C. (2001) 'French connections', *Red Pepper*, July, pp. 28–9.

Ahmed, S. (1998) *Differences that Matter*, Cambridge: Cambridge University Press.

Albrow, M. (1996) *The Global Age*, Cambridge: Polity Press.

Aldridge, J. and Becker, S. (1995) 'The rights and wrongs of children who care', in B. Franklin (ed.) *The Handbook of Children's Rights*, London: Routledge.

Alexander, M. J. (1994) "Not just (any) body can be a citizen: the politics of law, sexuality and postcoloniality in Trinidad and Tobago and the Bahamas', *Feminist Review*, (48), pp. 5–23.

Alexander, M. J. and Mohanty, C. T. (1997) 'Introduction: genealogies, legacies, movements', in M. J. Alexander and C. T. Mohanty, *op. cit.*

Alexander, M. J. and Mohanty, C. T. (eds) (1997) *Feminist Genealogies, Colonial Legacies, Democratic Futures*, New York and London: Routledge.

Allen, S. (1994) 'Race, ethnicity and nationality. Some questions of identity', in H. Afshar and M. Maynard, *op. cit.*

Alsop, R. and Hockey, J. (2001) 'Women's reproductive lives as a symbolic resource in Central and Eastern Europe', *European Journal of Women's Studies*, 8(4), pp. 454–71.

249

Ålund, A. (1999a) 'Feminism, multi-culturalism, essentialism', in N. Yuval-Davis and P. Werbner, *op. cit.*

Ålund, A. (1999b) 'Ethnicity, multi-culturalism and the problem of culture', *European Societies*, 1(1), pp. 105–16.

Alvarez, S. E. (1998) 'Latin American feminisms "go global": trends of the 1990s and challenges for the new millennium', in S. E. Alvarez *et al.*, *op. cit.*

Alvarez, S.E., Dagnino, E. and Escobar, A. (eds) (1998) *Cultures of Politics, Politics of Cultures: Re-visioning Latin American Social Movements*, Boulder, CO and Oxford: Westview Press.

Amnesty International (1995) *Human Rights are Women's Rights*, London: Amnesty International.

Amos, V. and Parmar, P. (1984) 'Challenging imperial feminism', *Feminist Review*, (17), pp. 3–19.

Amott, T. L. (1990) 'Black women and AFDC: making entitlement out of necessity', in L. Gordon, *op. cit.*

Andall, J. (1995) 'Migrant women and gender role definition in the Italian context', *Journal of Area Studies*, 6, pp. 203–15.

Andall, J. (2000) *Gender, Migration and Domestic Service: The Politics of Black Women in Italy*, Aldershot: Ashgate.

Anderson, B. (1997) 'Servants and slaves: Europe's domestic workers', *Race & Class*, 39(1), pp. 37–49.

Anderson, B. (2000) *Doing the Dirty Work: The Global Politics of Domestic Labour*, London: Zed Books.

Anderson, M., Bechhofer, F. and Gershuny, J. (1994) *The Social and Political Economy of the Household*, Oxford: Oxford University Press.

Andrews, G. (1991) *Citizenship*, London: Lawrence & Wishart.

Anheier, H., Glasius, M. and Kaldor, M. (eds) (2001) *Global Civil Society 2001*, Oxford: Oxford University Press.

Anker, R. (1998) *Gender and Jobs: Sex Segregation of Occupations in the World*, Geneva: ILO.

Anthias, F. (1992) 'The problem of ethnic and race categories and the anti-racist struggle', in N. Manning and R. Page (eds) *Social Policy Review 4*, Canterbury: Social Policy Association.

Anthias, F. (2000) 'Metaphors of home: gendering new migrations to Southern Europe', in F. Anthias and C. Lazaridis (eds) *Gender and Migration in Southern Europe: Women on the Move*, Oxford and New York: Berg.

Anthias, F. and Yuval-Davis, N. (1992) *Racialized Boundaries*, London: Routledge.

Anttonen, A. and Sipilä, J. (1996) 'European social care services: is it possible to identify models?, *Journal of European Social Policy*, 6(2), pp. 87–100.

Arat, Y. (1999) 'Democracy and women in Turkey: in defense of liberalism', *Social Politics*, 6(3), pp. 370–387.

Arber, S. and Gilbert, N. (eds) (1992) *Women and Working Lives*, Basingstoke: Macmillan.

Arber, S. and Ginn, J. (1991) *Gender and Later Life*, London: Sage.

Arber, S. and Ginn, J. (1995) 'Gender differences in the relationship between paid employment and informal care', *Work, Employment and Society*, 9(3), pp. 445–71.

Arber, S. and Ginn, J. (1995), *Connecting Gender and Ageing: A Sociological Approach*, Buckingham: Open University Press.

Arendt, H. (1958) *The Human Condition*, Chicago: University of Chicago Press.

Arnot, M. and Dillabough, J. (eds) (2000) *Challenging Democracy. International Perspectives on Gender, Education and Citizenship*, London and New York: Routledge.

Ashworth, G. (1992) *When will Democracy Include Women?*, London: Change.

Atkinson, A. B. (1991) *Poverty, Statistics and Progress in Europe*, London: STICERD/LSE.

Atkinson, A. B. (1993) *Beveridge, the National Minimum, and its Future in a European Context*, London: STICERD/LSE.

Aziz, R. (1992) 'Feminism and the challenge of racism: deviance or difference?', in H. Crowley and S. Himmelweit, *op. cit.*

Bacchi, C. (1990) *Same Difference*, Sydney: Allen & Unwin.

Bacchi, C. (1991) 'Pregnancy, the law and the meaning of equality', in E. Meehan and S. Sevenhuijsen, *op. cit.*

Bacchi, C. (1996) *The Politics of Affirmative Action*, London: Sage.

Bacchi, C. L. and Beasley, C. (2002) 'Citizen bodies: is embodied citizenship a contradiction in terms?', *Critical Social Policy* 22(2), pp. 324–352.

Bader, V. M. (1998) 'Dilemmas of ethnic affirmative action. Benign state-neutrality or relational ethnic neutrality?', *Citizenship Studies*, 2(3), pp. 435–473.

Bagilhole, B. (2003) *Women in Non Traditional Occupations*, Basingstoke: Palgrave Macmillan.

Baier, A. C. (1987) 'Hume, the women's moral theorist?', in D.T. Meyers and E. F. Kittay, *op. cit.*

Baierle, S. G. (1998) 'The explosion of experience: the emergence of a new ethical-political principle in popular movements in Porto Alegre, Brazil', in Alvarez *et al.*, *op. cit.*

Bakan, A. B. and Stasiulus, D. K. (1995) 'Making the match: domestic placement agencies and the racialization of women's household work', *Signs*, 20(2), pp. 303–35.

Balbo, L. (1987) 'Crazy quilts', in A. S. Sassoon, *op. cit.*

Balbo, L. and Nowotny, H. (eds) (1986) *Time to Care in Tomorrow's Welfare Systems*, Vienna: European Centre for Social Welfare Training and Research.

Balchin, C. (2001) 'Feminist front', *Red Pepper*, December, pp. 24–5.

Baldock, J. and Evers, A. (1991) 'Citizenship and frail old people: changing patterns of provision in Europe', in N. Manning (ed.) *Social Policy Review 1990–91*, Harlow: Longman.

Baldock, J. and May, M. (eds) (1995) *Social Policy Review 7*, Canterbury: Social Policy Association.

Baldock, J. and Ungerson, C. (1991) 'What d'ya want if you don't want money?: a feminist critique of "paid volunteering"', in M. Maclean and D. Groves (eds) *Women's Issues in Social Policy*, London: Routledge.

Baldwin-Edwards, M. (1991a) 'Immigration after 1992', *Policy and Politics*, 19(3), pp. 199–211.

Baldwin-Edwards, M. (1991b) 'The socio-political rights of migrants in the European Community', in G. Room, *op. cit.*

Barbalet, J. M. (1988) *Citizenship*, Milton Keynes: Open University Press.

Barkman, K. (1995) 'Politics and gender: the need for electoral reform', *Politics*, 15(3), pp. 141–6.

Barnes, M. (1997) *Care, Communities and Citizens*, London and New York: Longman.

Barnes, M. (1999a) 'Users as citizens: collective action and the local governance of welfare', *Social Policy & Administration*, 33(1), pp. 73–90.

Barnes, M. (1999b) *Building a Deliberative Democracy: An Evaluation of Two Citizens' Juries*, London: Institute for Public Policy Research.

Barnett, A., Ellis, C. and Hirst, P. (eds) (1993) *Debating the Constitution*, Cambridge: Polity Press.

Barrett, M. and Macintosh, M. (1982/1991) *The Anti-Social Family*, London: Verso.

Barrett, M. and Phillips, A. (eds) (1992) *Destabilising Theory*, Cambridge: Polity Press.

Barton, L. (1993) 'The struggle for citizenship: the case of disabled people', *Disability, Handicap & Society*, 8(3), pp. 235–48.

Barton, L. (1996) 'Citizenship and disabled people: a cause for concern' in J. Demaine and H. Entwistle, *op. cit.*

Basu, A. (ed.) (1995) *The Challenge of Local Feminisms*, Boulder, CO and Oxford: Westview Press.

Bauböck, R. (1991) 'Migration and citizenship', *New Community*, 18(1), pp. 27–48.

Bauböck, R. (1994) *Transnational Citizenship: Membership and Rights in International Migration*, Aldershot: Edward Elgar.

Becker, S. (ed.) (1995) *Young Carers in Europe*, Loughborough: Young Carers Research Group.

Becker, S., Aldridge, J. and Dearden, C. (1998) *Young Carers and Their Families*, Oxford: Blackwell.

Begum, N. (1992) 'Disabled women and the feminist agenda', *Feminist Review*, 40, pp. 70–84.

Behnke, A. (1997) 'Citizenship, nationhood and the production of political space', *Citizenship Studies*, 1(2), pp. 243–65.

Behrend, H. (1995) 'East German women and the Wende', *European Journal of Women's Studies*, 2(2), pp. 237–55.

Bellah, R., Madsen, R., Sullivan, W., Swidler, A. and Tipton, S. (1985) *Habits of the Heart: Individualism and Commitment in American Life*, Berkeley and Los Angeles: University of California Press.

Bellingham, B. and Mathis, M. P. (1994) ' Race, citizenship and the bio-politics of the maternalist welfare state: "traditional" midwifery in the American South under the Sheppard-Towner Act, 1921–29', *Social Politics*, 1(2), pp. 157–89.

Benefits (2000) 'Carers', *Benefits*, 28.

Benhabib, S. (1992) *Situating the Self*, Cambridge: Polity Press.

Benhabib, S., Butler, J., Cornell, D., Fraser, N. (1995) *Feminist Contentions. A Philosophical Exchange*, New York and London: Routledge.

Beresford, P, Green, D., Lister, R. and Woodard, K. (1999) *Poverty First Hand*, London: CPAG.

Beresford, P. (1999) 'Making participation possible: movements of disabled people and psychiatric survivors', in T. Jordan and A. Lent (eds) *Storming the Millennium: The New Politics of Change*, London: Lawrence & Wishart.

Beresford, P. and Croft, S. (1993) *Citizen Involvement*, Basingstoke: Macmillan.

Beresford, P. and Croft, S. (1995) 'It's our problem too! Challenging the exclusion of poor people from poverty discourse', *Critical Social Policy*, 44/45, pp. 75–97.

Bergqvist, C. and Jungar, A. (2000) 'Adaptation or diffusion of the Swedish gender model?' in L. Hantrais, *op. cit.*

Berkovitch, N. and Moghadam, V. (1999) 'Middle East politics and women's collective action: challenging the status quo', *Social Politics*, 6(3), pp. 273–91.

Bernard, M. (2000) *Promoting Health in Old Age: Critical Issues in Self Health Care*, Buckingham: Open University Press.

Bernard, M. and Meade, K. (1993) *Women Come of Age*, London: Edward Elgar.

Beuret, K. (1991) 'Women and transport', in M. Maclean and D. Groves (eds) *Women's Issues in Social Policy*, London: Routledge.

Bhabha, J. (1996) 'Embodied rights: gender persecution, state sovereignty, and refugees', *Public Culture*, 9, pp. 3–32.

Bhabha, J. (1999) 'Embodied rights: gender persecution, state sovereignty and refugees', in N. Yuval-Davis and P. Werbner, *op. cit.*

Bhabha, J. and Shutter, S. (1994) *Women's Movement: Women under Immigration, Nationality and Refugee Law*, Stoke-on-Trent: Trentham Books.

Bhattacharjee, A. (1997) 'The public/private mirage: mapping homes and un-domesticating violence work in the South Asian immigrant community', in M. J. Alexander and C. T. Mohanty, *op. cit.*

Bhattacharyya, G. (1994) 'Offence is the best defence? Pornography and racial violence', in C. Brant and Y. Lee Too, *op. cit.*

Bhavnani, K. (1993) 'Towards a multi-cultural Europe? "Race", nation and identity in 1992 and beyond', *Feminist Review*, (45), pp. 30–45.

Bhavnani, K. (ed.) (2001) *Feminism and 'Race'*, Oxford: Oxford University Press.

Bhavnani, K. and Coulson, M. (1986) 'Transforming socialist-feminism: the challenge of racism', *Feminist Review*, (23), pp. 81–92.

Bhavnani, K. and Phoenix, A. (1994) 'Shifting identities shifting racisms', *Feminism and Psychology*, 4(1), pp. 5–18.

Bhavnani, R. (1994) *Black Women in the Labour Market: A Research Review*, Manchester: Equal Opportunities Commission.

Bickford, S. (1997) 'Anti-anti-identity politics: feminism, democracy and the complexities of citizenship', *Hypatia*, 12(4), pp. 111–31.

Bittman, M., Matheson, G. and Meagher, G. (1999) 'The changing boundary between home and market: Australian trends in outsourcing domestic labour', *Work, Employment and Society*, 13(2), pp. 249–73.

Björnberg, U. (2002) 'Ideology and choice between work and care: Swedish family policy for working parents', *Critical Social Policy*, 22(1), pp. 33–52.

Björnsdóttir, I. D. and Kristmundsdóttir, S. D. (1995) 'Purity and defilement: essentialism and punishment in the Icelandic women's movement', *European Journal of Women's Studies*, 2(2), pp. 171–83.

Blacklock, C. and Jenson, J. (1998) 'Citizenship: Latin American perspectives', *Social Politics*, 5(2), pp. 127–31.

Blacklock, C. and Macdonald, L. (1998) 'Human rights and citizenship in Guatemala and Mexico: from "strategic" to "new" universalism?', *Social Politics*, 5(2), pp. 132–57.

Blackman, S. and France, A. (2001) 'Youth marginality under "postmodernism"', in N. Stevenson, *op. cit.*

Blumberg, R. L. (ed.) (1991) *Gender, Family and Economy: The Triple Overlap*, Newbury Park, London, New Delhi: Sage.

Bock, G. (1992) 'Equality and difference in National Socialist racism', in G. Bock and S. James, *op. cit.*

Bock, G. and James, S. (eds) (1992) *Beyond Equality and Difference*, London: Routledge.

Bock, G. and Thane, P. (eds) (1991) *Maternity and Gender Policies*, London: Routledge.

Bolderson, H. and Roberts, S. (1995) 'New restrictions on benefits for migrants: xenophobia or trivial pursuits?', *Benefits*, 12, pp. 11–15.

Borchorst, A. (1999) 'Feminist thinking about the welfare state', in M. M. Ferree, J. Lorber and B. B. Hess (eds) *Revisioning Gender*, Thousand Oaks, CA: Sage.

Borchorst, A. and Siim, B. (1987) 'Women and the advanced welfare state: a new kind of patriarchal power?', in A. S. Sassoon, *op. cit.*

Boris, E. (1993) 'The power of motherhood: black and white activist women redefine the "political"', in S. Koven and S. Michel, *op. cit.*

Boris, E. (1995) 'The racialized gendered state: constructions of citizenship in the United States', *Social Politics*, 2(2), pp. 160–80.

Bornat, J., Pereira, C., Pilgrim, D. and Williams, F. (eds) (1993) *Community Care: A Reader*, Basingstoke: Macmillan/Open University.

Bovenkerk, F., Miles, R. and Verbunt, G. (1990) 'Racism, migration and the state in Western Europe: a case for comparative analysis', *International Sociology*, 5(4), pp. 475–90.

Bovenkerk, F., Miles, R. and Verbunt, G. (1991) 'Comparative studies of migration and exclusion on the grounds of "race" and ethnic background in Western Europe: A critical appraisal', *International Migration Review* (25), pp. 375–91.

Bowden, P. (1997) *Caring: Gender-Sensitive Ethics*, London and New York: Routledge.

Boylan, E. (1991) *Women and Disability*, London and New York: Zed Books.

Bradshaw, J. and Millar, J. (1991) *Lone Parent Families in the UK*, London: HMSO.

Bradshaw, J., Kennedy, S., Kilkey, M., Hutton, S., Corden, A., Eardley, T., Holmes, H. and Neale, J. (1996) *The Employment of Lone Parents: A Comparison of Policy in 20 Countries*, London: Family Policy Studies Centre.

Brah, A (1996) *Cartographies of Diaspora*, London and New York: Routledge.

Brah, A. (1993) 'Re-framing Europe: en-gendered racisms, ethnicities and nationalisms in contemporary Western Europe', *Feminist Review*, 45, pp. 9–45.

Brah, A. (1994) '"Race" and "culture" in the gendering of labour markets', in H. Afshar and M. Maynard, *op. cit.*

Brah, A. and Shaw, S. (1992) *Working Choices: South Asian Young Muslim Women and the Labour Market*, London: Department of Employment, Research Paper no. 91.

Brannen, J. and Moss, P. (1991) *Managing Mothers*, London: Unwin Hyman.

Bransbury, L. (1995) 'Shouting the odds', *Community Care*, 28 September–4 October, p. 18.

Brant, C. and Lee Too, Y. (eds) (1994), *Rethinking Sexual Harassment*, London: Pluto Press.

Breckenridge, C. A. and Voglar, C. (2001) 'The critical limits of embodiment: disability's criticism', *Public Culture*, 13(3), pp. 349–57.

Breitenbach, E., Mackay, F., Brown, A. (1999) 'A Voice and a Place: Women and the Politics of the Scottish Parliament', Women and Political Action conference, Middlesex University, 18–19 June.

Brewer, R. (1993) 'Theorizing race, class and gender: the new scholarship of Black feminist intellectuals and Black women's labor', in S. James and A. Busia (eds) *Theorizing Black Feminisms: The Visionary Pragmatism of Black Women*, London: Routledge.

Bristow, J. and Wilson, A. R. (eds) (1993) *Activating Theory: Lesbian, Gay, Bisexual Politics*, London: Lawrence & Wishart.

Brocas, A., Cailloux, A. and Oget, V. (1990) *Women and Social Security: Progress Towards Equality of Treatment*, Geneva: International Labour Office.

Brodie, J. (1997) 'Meso-discourses, state forms and the gendering of liberal-democratic citizenship', *Citizenship Studies*, 1(2), pp. 223–42.

Brophy, J. and Smart, C. (eds) (1985) *Women in Law: Explorations in Law, Family and Sexuality*, London: Routledge & Kegan Paul.

Broschart, K. R. (1992) 'An analysis of "women's place" in contemporary Soviet society', in S. Arber and N. Gilbert, *op. cit.*

Brown, W. (1995) *States of Injury: Power and Freedom in Late Modernity*, Princeton: Princeton University Press.

Browne, A. (2001) 'The Bush edict that kills women', *New Statesman*, 23 July.

Brubaker, W. R. (1990) 'Immigration, citizenship and the nation-state in France and Germany: a comparative historical analysis', *International Sociology*, 5(4), pp. 379–407.

Brubaker, W. R. (1992) *Citizenship and Nationhood in France and Germany*, Cambridge, MA: Harvard University Press.

Brubaker, W. R. (ed.) (1989) *Immigration and the Politics of Citizenship in Europe and North America*, Lanham and London: University Press of America.

Bruegel, I. (1989) 'Sex and race in the labour market', *Feminist Review*, 32, pp. 49–68.

Bruegel, I. (1994) 'Labour market prospects for women from ethnic minorities', in R. Lindley (ed.) *Labour Market Structures and Prospects for Women*, Manchester: Equal Opportunities Commission.

Bruning, G. and Plantenga, J. (1999) 'Parental leave and equal opportunities: experiences in eight European countries', *Journal of European Social Policy*, 9(3), pp. 195–209.

Brush, L. D. (1996) 'Love, toil and trouble: motherhood and feminist politics', *Signs*, 21(2), pp. 429–54.

Bryan, B., Dadzie, S. and Scafe, S. (1985) *The Heart of the Race*, London: Virago.

Brydon, L. and Chant, S. (1989) *Women in the Third World*, Aldershot: Edward Elgar.

Bryson, C., Budd, T., Lewis, J. and Elam, G. (undated) *Women's Attitudes to Combining Paid Work and Family Life*, London: Cabinet Office.

Bryson, L. (2000) 'Citizenship, caring and commodification', in B. Hobson (ed.) *Gender and Citizenship in Transition*, Basingstoke: Macmillan.

Bryson, L., Bittman, M. and Donath, S. (1994) 'Men's welfare state, women's welfare state: tendencies to converge in practice and theory?', in D. Sainsbury, *op. cit.*

Bryson, V. (1992) *Feminist Political Theory*, Basingstoke: Macmillan.

Bryson, V. (1999) *Feminist Debates, Issues of Theory and Political Practice*, Basingstoke: Macmillan.

Bubeck, D. (1995a) *Care, Gender and Justice*, Oxford: Clarendon Press.

Bubeck, D. (1995b) *A Feminist Approach to Citizenship*, Florence: European University Institute.

Bucur, M. (1994) 'An American feminist in Romania', *Social Politics*, 1(2), pp. 223–30.

Buijs, G. (ed.) (1993) *Migrant Women: Crossing Boundaries and Changing Identities*, Providence, RI: Berg.

Bulmer, M. and Rees, A. M. (eds) (1996) *Citizenship Today*, London: UCL Press.

Bunch, C. with Antrobus, P., Frost, S. and Reilly, N. (2001) 'International networking for women's human rights', in M. Edwards and J. Gaventa, *op. cit.*

Bunyan, T. (1993) *Statewatching the New Europe*, London: Statewatch.

Burns, S. (2000) 'New economy, new equality? The need to recognise the value of unpaid work', *New Economy*, pp. 111–13.

Burrell, B. C. (1993) 'Party decline, party transformation and gender politics: the USA', in J. Lovenduski and P. Norris, (eds) *Gender and Party Politics*, London: Sage.

Bussemaker, J. (1991) 'Equality, autonomy and feminist politics', in E. Meehan and S. Sevenhuijsen, *op. cit.*

Bussemaker, J. (1998) 'Vocabularies of citizenship and gender: the Netherlands, *Critical Social Policy* 18(3), pp. 333–54.

Bussemaker, J. and van Kersbergen, K. (1994) Gender and welfare states: some theoretical reflections', in D. Sainsbury, *op. cit.*

Bussemaker, J. and Voet, R. (1998) 'Citizenship and gender: theoretical approaches and historical legacies', *Critical Social Policy*, 18(3), pp. 277–307.

Butler, J. (1995) 'For a careful reading', in S. Benhabib *et al.*, *op. cit.*

Bynner, J., Chisholm, L., and Furlong, A. (eds) (1997), *Youth, Citizenship and Social Change in a European Context*, Aldershot: Ashgate.

Bynoe, I. (1991) 'The case for anti-discrimination legislation', in I. Bynoe, M. Oliver and C. Barnes, *op. cit.*

Bynoe, I., Oliver, M. and Barnes, C. (1991) *Equal Rights for Disabled People*, London: Institute for Public Policy Research.

Cain, H. and Yuval-Davis, N. (1990) '"The equal opportunities community" and the anti-racist struggle', *Critical Social Policy*, 29, pp. 5–26.

Callender, C. (1992) 'Redundancy, unemployment and poverty', in C. Glendinning, and J. Millar, *op. cit.*

Campbell, B. (1984) *Wigan Pier Revisited*, London: Virago.

Campbell, B. (1993) *Goliath*, London: Methuen.

Campbell, B. (1995) 'Old fogeys and angry young men: a critique of communitarianism', *Soundings*, 1, pp. 47–64.

Camus-Jacques, G. (1989) 'Refugee women: the forgotten majority', in G. Loescher and L. Monahan, *op. cit.*

Canefe, N. (1998) 'Citizens versus permanent guests: cultural memory and citizenship laws in a reunified Germany', *Citizenship Studies*, 2(3), pp. 519–44.

Carabine, J. (1992) 'Constructing women: women's sexuality and social policy', *Critical Social Policy*, 34, pp. 23–37.

Carabine, J. (1996) 'Heterosexuality and social policy', in D. Richardson, *op. cit.*

Carby, H. (1982) 'White women listen: black feminism and the boundaries of sisterhood', in Centre for Contemporary Cultural Studies, *The Empire Strikes Back*, London: Hutchinson.

Carens, J. (1989) 'Membership and morality: admission to citizenship in liberal democratic states', in W. R. Brubaker, *op. cit.*

Carens, J. H. (2000) *Culture, Citizenship and Community*, Oxford: Oxford University Press.

Caring Costs Alliance (1996) *The True Cost of Caring. A Survey of Carers' Lost Income*, London: Caring Costs.

Carlsen, S. (1993) 'Men's utilization of parental leave and paternity leave schemes', in S. Carlsen and J. E. Larsen, *op. cit.*

Carlsen, S. (1995) 'When working men become fathers', in P. Moss (ed.) *Father Figures: Fathers in the Families of the 1990s*, Edinburgh: Children in Scotland/HMSO.

Carlsen, S. and Larsen, J. E. (eds) (1993) *The Equality Dilemma*, Copenhagen: Danish Equal Status Council.

Carroll, L. (1871) *Alice Through the Looking Glass*, London: Macmillan.

Carver, T. (1996) '"Public man" and the critique of masculinities', *Political Theory*, 24(4), pp. 673–86.

Carver, T. (1998) 'Sexual citizenship. Gendered and de-gendered narratives' in T. Carver and V. Mottier (eds) *Politics of Sexuality: Ideology, Gender, Citizenship*, London and New York: Routledge.

Cass, B. (1994) 'Citizenship, work and welfare: the dilemma for Australian women', *Social Politics*, 1(1), pp. 106–24.

Castles, S. (1994) 'Democracy and multi-cultural citizenship. Australian debates and their relevance for Western Europe', in R. Bauböck (ed.) *From Aliens to Citizens: Redefining the Status of Immigrants in Europe*, Aldershot: Avebury.

Castles, S. and Davidson, A. (2000) *Citizenship and Migration*, Basingstoke: Macmillan.

Castles, S. and Miller, M. J. (1998) *The Age of Migration* (2nd edn), Basingstoke: Macmillan.

Caverero, A. (1992) 'Equality and sexual difference: amnesia in political thought', in G. Bock and S. James, *op. cit.*

Central Statistical Office (1995) *Social Focus on Women*, London: HMSO.

Cesarini, D. and Fulbrook, M. (eds) (1996) *Citizenship, Nationality and Migration in Europe*, London: Routledge.

Chafetz, J. S. (1991) 'The gender division of labor and the reproduction of female disadvantage: toward an integrated theory', in R. L. Blumberg, *op. cit.*

Chambaz, C. (2001) 'Lone-parent families in Europe: a variety of economic and social circumstances', *Social Policy & Administration*, 35(6), pp. 658–71.

Chanan, G. (1992) *Out of the Shadows: Local Community Action and the European Community*, Dublin: European Foundation for the Improvement of Living and Working Conditions.

Chanan, G., Garratt, C. and West, A. (2000) *The New Community Strategies. How to Involve Local People*, London: Community Development Foundation.

Chang, J. (1991) *Wild Swans*, London: HarperCollins.

Chapman, J. (1991) *The Political versus the Personal: Participatory Democracy and Feminism*, Strathclyde: Strathclyde Papers on Government and Politics, no. 81.

Chappell, A. L. (1994/95) 'Disability, discrimination and the criminal justice system', *Critical Social Policy*, (42), pp. 19–33.

Charter 88 (2000) *Unlocking Democracy*, London: Charter 88.

Chavez, D. (1999) 'Cities for people', *Red Pepper*, June, pp. 19–21.

Chen, M. (1995) 'A matter of survival: women's right to employment in India and Bangladesh', in M. Nussbaum and J. Glover, *op. cit.*

Childs, S. (2001a) '"Attitudinally feminist': the New Labour women MPs and the substantive representation of women', *Politics*, 21(3), pp. 178–85.

Childs, S. (2001b) 'In their own words: New Labour women and the substantive representation of women', *British Journal of Politics and International Relations*, 3(2), pp. 173–90.

Childs, S. (2002) 'Women MPs in the House of Commons: A women's style of politics?' Mimeo: PSA Women and Politics Group conference, London, 23 February.

Christopher, K. (2001a) 'Single motherhood, employment or social assistance: why are US women poorer than women in other affluent nations?' *Luxembourg Income Study Paper No. 285*: Luxembourg: Luxembourg Income Study.

Christopher, K. (2001b) 'Caregiving, welfare states and mothers' poverty', *Luxembourg Income Study Paper No. 287*, Luxembourg: Luxembourg Income Study.

Citizenship Studies (1999) 'Special Issue: Gender and Citizenship in Muslim Communities', *Citizenship Studies* 3(3).

Citizenship Studies (2001) 'Special Issue: Citizenship and Democracy in Hong Kong', *Citizenship Studies*, 5(2).

Clark, A. (1995) *The Struggle for the Breeches: Gender and the Making of the British Working Class*, London: Rivers Oram Press.

Clarke, J. (2001) 'Globalization and welfare states: some unsettling thoughts', in R. Sykes *et al.*, *op. cit.*

Clarke, J. and Fox Piven, F. (2001) 'United States: an American welfare state?' in P. Alcock and G. Craig (eds) *International Social Policy*, Basingstoke: Palgrave.

Clarke, J., Dam, E. van and Gooster, L. (1998) 'New Europeans: naturalisation and citizenship in Europe', *Citizenship Studies*, 2(1), pp. 43–67.

Clarke, S. (2001) 'Earnings of men and women in the EU: the gap narrowing but only slowly', *Statistics in Focus*, Theme 3 – 5/2001.

Close, P. (1995) *Citizenship, Europe and Change*, Basingstoke: Macmillan.

Cockburn, C. (1987) *Women, Trade Unions and Political Parties*, London: Fabian Society.

Cockburn, C. (1991) *In the Way of Women*, Basingstoke: Macmillan.

Cockburn, C. (1995) 'Strategies for gender democracy', *Social Europe*, Supplement 4, Luxembourg: European Commission (DGV).

Cockburn, C. (1996a) 'Different together: women in Belfast', *Soundings*, 2, pp. 32–47.

Cockburn, C. (1996b) 'Mixing it', *Red Pepper*, September, pp. 22–4.

Cockburn, C. (1996c) 'Strategies for gender democracy: strengthening the representation of trade union women in the European social dialogue', *European Journal of Women's Studies*, 3(1), pp. 7–26.

Cockburn, C. (1998) *The Space Between Us: Negotiating Gender and National Identities in Conflict*, London and New York: Zed Books.

Coenen, H. and Leisink, P. (eds) (1993) *Work and Citizenship in the New Europe*, Aldershot: Edward Elgar.

Cohen, B. (1999) 'Parental leave in Europe: policy implications', in P. Moss and F. Deven, *op. cit.*

Cohen, J. L. (1999) 'Changing paradigms of citizenship and the exclusiveness of the demos', *International Sociology*, 14(3), pp. 245–68.

Cohen, P. (1997) 'Beyond the community romance', *Soundings*, 5, pp. 29–51.

Cohen, S. (1985) 'Anti-semitism, immigration controls and the welfare state', *Critical Social Policy*, (13), pp. 73–92.

Cohen, S. (1995) 'The mighty state of immigration controls', in J. Baldock and M. May, *op. cit.*

Cohen, S. (1998) 'Body, space and presence: women's social exclusion in the politics of the European Union', *European Journal of Women's Studies*, 5(3–4), pp. 367–380.

Cohen, S. (2000) 'Social solidarity in the Delors period', in C. and M. Newman (eds) *Democratizing the European Union: Issues for the Twenty-first Century*, Manchester/New York: Manchester University Press.

Coles, B. (1995) *Youth and Social Policy: Youth Citizenship and Young Careers*, London: UCL Press.

Collins, P. H. (1991) *Black Feminist Thought*, London: Routledge.

Commission of the European Communities (2001) *Assessment of the Implementation of the 2001 Employment Guidelines*, SEC (2001) 1398, Brussels: Commission of the European Communities.

Commission on Poverty, Participation and Power (2000) *Listen Hear: The Right to be Heard*, Bristol: Policy Press.

Commission on Social Justice (1994) *Social Justice: Strategies for National Renewal*, London: Vintage.

Commission on the Future of Multi-Ethnic Britain (2000), *The Future of Multi-Ethnic Britain*, London: Runnymede Trust.

Comor, E. A. (1998) 'Governance and the "commoditization" of information', *Global Governance*, 4, pp. 217–33.

Connelly, M. P. (1996) 'Gender matters: global restructuring and adjustment', *Social Politics*, 3(1), pp. 12–31.

Conover, P. J., Crewe, I. M., Searing, D. D. (1991) 'The nature of citizenship in the United States and Great Britain: empirical comments on theoretical themes', *Journal of Politics*, 53(3), pp. 800–32.

Conroy, P. and Flanagan, N. (1993) *Women and Poverty in the European Community*, Brussels: European Commission (DGV).

Cook, D. (1993) 'Racism, citizenship and exclusion', in D. Cook and B. Hudson (eds) *Racism and Criminology*, London: Sage.

Cook, D., Mactaggart, F., Misrahi, B. and Rahman, H. (1988) 'A race to exclusion', *Marxism Today*, January, pp. 20–3.

Cook, J. (2000) 'Flexible employment – implications for a gendered political economy of citizenship', in J. Cook, J. Roberts and G. Waylen (eds) *Towards a Gendered Political Economy*, Basingstoke: Macmillan.

Cook, J. and Watt, S. (1992) 'Racism, women and poverty', in C. Glendinning and J. Millar, *op. cit.*

Cook, R. J. (1995) 'International human rights and women's reproductive health', in J. Peters and A. Wolper, *op. cit.*

Coole, D. (1988) *Women in Political Theory: From Ancient Misogyny to Contemporary Feminism*, Brighton: Wheatsheaf Books.

Coole, D. (1993) *Women in Political Theory* (2nd edn), Hemel Hempstead: Harvester Wheatsheaf.

Coole, D. (1996) 'Is class a difference that makes a difference?', *Radical Philosophy*, 77, pp. 17–25.

Coomaraswamy, R. (1999) 'Reinventing international law. Women's rights as human rights in the international community', in P. van Ness, *op. cit.*

Cooper, D. (1992/3) 'Off the banner and into the agenda: the emergence of a new municipal lesbian and gay politics, 1979–86', *Critical Social Policy*, 36, pp. 20–39.

Cooper, D. (1993) 'An engaged state: sexuality, governance, and the potential for change', in J. Bristow and A. R. Wilson, *op. cit.*

Coote, A. and Pattullo, P. (1990) *Power and Prejudice*, London: Weidenfeld & Nicolson.

Cornell, D. (1991) *Beyond Accommodation*, New York: Routledge.

Cornell, D. (1992) 'Gender, sex and equivalent rights', in J. Butler and J. W. Scott (eds) *Feminists Theorize the Political*, New York: Routledge.

Cornwall, A. and Gaventa, J. (2000) 'From users and choosers to makers and shapers: repositioning participation in social policy', *IDS Bulletin*, 31(4), pp. 50–62.

Correa, S. and Petchesky, R. (1994) 'Reproductive and social rights: a feminist perspective', in G. Sen, A. Germain and L. C. Cohen (eds) *Population Policies Considered*, Cambridge, MA: Harvard University Press.

Corrin, C. (1999) *Feminist Perspectives on Politics*, Harlow: Longman.

Corrin, C. (ed.) (1992) *Superwomen and the Double Burden*, London: Scarlet Press.

Costain, A. N. (1988) 'Representing women: the transition from social movement to interest group', in E. Boneparth and E. Stoper (eds) *Women, Power and Policy: Toward the Year 2000*, New York: Pergamon Press.

Coulter, C. (1993) *The Hidden Tradition, Feminism, Women and Nationalism in Ireland*, Cork: Cork University Press.

Council of Europe (1984) *The Situation of Women in the Political Process* in Europe, Strasbourg: Directorate of Human Rights.

Council of Ministers (1992) *Council Recommendation on Child Care*, 92/241/EEC1992.

Cowan, J. K., Dembour, M. and Wilson, R. (eds) (2001) *Culture and Rights: Anthropological Perspectives*, Cambridge: Cambridge University Press.

Cox, R. H. (1998) 'The consequences of welfare reform: how conceptions of social rights are changing', *Journal of Social Policy*, 21(1), pp. 1–16.

Cragg, A. and Dawson, T. (1984) *Unemployed Women: A Case Study of Attitudes and Experiences*, London: Department of Employment.

Craske, N. (1998) 'Remasculinisation and the neoliberal state in Latin America' in V. Randall and G. Waylen (eds) *Gender, Politics and the State*, London and New York: Routledge.

Crawley, H. (2000) 'Gender, persecution and the concept of politics in the asylum determination process', *Forced Migration Review*, 9, pp. 17–20.

Crick, B. (1998) *Education for Citizenship and the Teaching of Democracy in Schools* (Final Report of the Advisory Group on Citizenship), London: Qualifications and Curriculum Authority.

Critical Social Policy (1998) 'Special Issue: Vocabularies of Citizenship and Gender in Northern Europe', *Critical Social Policy*, 18(3).

CRLP (2000) *Women of the World: Laws and Policies Affecting Their Reproductive Lives: East Central Europe*, New York: Centre for Reproductive Law and Policy.

Croft S. (1986) 'Women, caring and the recasting of need – a feminist reappraisal', *Critical Social Policy*, 16, pp. 23–39.

Croft, S. and Beresford, P. (1989) 'User-involvement, citizenship and social policy', *Critical Social Policy*, 26, pp. 5–18.

Croft, S. and Beresford, P. (1992) 'The politics of participation', *Critical Social Policy*, 35, pp. 20–44.

Crompton, R. (1997) *Women and Work in Modern Britain*, Oxford: Oxford University Press.

Crompton, R. and Harris, F. (1999) 'Attitudes, women's employment and the changing domestic division of labour: a cross-national analysis', in R. Crompton (ed.) *Restructuring Gender Relations and Employment: The Decline of the Male Breadwinner*, Oxford: Oxford University Press.

Crompton, R. and Sanderson, K. (1990) *Gendered Jobs and Social Change*, London: Unwin Hyman.

Cross, M. (1993) 'Generating the "new poverty": a European comparison', in R. Simpson and R. Walker, *op. cit.*

Crossley, N. (2001) 'Citizenship, intersubjectivity and the lifeworld' in N. Stevenson, *op. cit.*

Crouch, C., Eder, K., Tambini, D. (eds) (2001) *Citizenship, Markets and the State*, Oxford: Oxford University Press.

Crowley, H. and Himmelweit, S. (eds) (1992) *Knowing Women*, Cambridge: Polity/Open University Press.

Curthoys, A. (1993) 'Feminism, citizenship and national identity', *Feminist Review*, 44, pp. 19–38.

Dagger, R. (1997) *Civic Virtues. Rights, Citizenship and Republican Liberalism*, New York and Oxford: Oxford University Press.

Dagnino, E. (1998) 'Culture, citizenship and democracy', in Alvarez *et al.*, *op. cit.*

Dahl, T. S. (1987) *Women's Law: An Introduction to Feminist Jurisprudence*, Oslo: Norwegian University Press.

Dahlerup, D. (1986) *The New Women's Movement*, London: Sage.

Dahlerup, D. (1987) 'Confusing concepts – confusing reality: a theoretical discussion of the patriarchal state', in A. S. Sassoon, *op. cit.*

Dahlerup, D. (1988) 'From a small to a large minority: women in Scandinavian politics', *Scandinavian Political Studies*, 11(4) pp. 275–98.

Dahlerup, D. (1994) 'Learning to live with the state – state, market, and civil society: women's need for state intervention in East and West', *Women's Studies International Forum*, 17(2/3) pp. 117–27.

Dahrendorf, R. (1988) 'Citizenship and the modern social conflict', in R. Holme and M. Elliott (eds) *The British Constitution: 1688–1988*, Basingstoke: Macmillan.

Dahrendorf, R. (1989) Untitled Mimeo: paper presented to the Commission on Citizenship Seminar, April.

Dahrendorf, R. (1994) 'The changing quality of citizenship', in B. van Steenbergen, *op. cit.*

Dahrendorf, R. (1996) 'Citizenship and social class', in M. Bulmer and A. M. Rees, *op. cit.*

Dale, J. (1986) 'Feminists and the development of the welfare state – some lessons from our history', *Critical Social Policy*, (16), pp. 57–65.

Dale, J. and Foster, P. (1986) *Feminists and State Welfare*, London: Routledge & Kegan Paul.

Daly, M. (1994) 'A matter of dependency? The gender dimension of British income maintenance provision', *Sociology*, 28(3), pp. 779–97.

Daly, M. (1997) 'Welfare states under pressure: cash benefits in European welfare states over the last ten years', *Journal of European Social Policy*, 7(2), pp. 129–46.

Daly, M. (2000) *The Gender Division of Welfare: The Impact of the British and German Welfare States*, Cambridge: Cambridge University Press.

Daly, M. (2002) 'Care as a good for social policy' *Journal of Social Policy*, 31(2), pp. 251–70.

Daly, M. and Lewis, J. (1998) 'Introduction: Conceptualising social care in the context of welfare state restructuring', in J. Lewis, *op. cit.*

Daly, M. and Lewis, J. (2000) 'The concept of social care and the analysis of contemporary welfare states', *British Journal of Sociology*, 51(2), pp. 281–98.

Daune-Richard, A. (1998) 'Part-time work in France, the UK and Sweden', in J. O' Reillly and C. Fagan, *op. cit.*

David, M. (1985) 'Motherhood and social policy – a matter of education?', *Critical Social Policy*, 12, pp. 28–43.

Davidoff, L. (1990) '"Adam spoke first and named the orders of the world": masculine and feminine domains in history and sociology', in H. Corr and L. Jamieson (eds) *Politics of Everyday Life: Continuity and Change in Work and Family*, Basingstoke: Macmillan.

Davies, B. and Ward, S. (1992) *Women and Personal Pensions*, London: Equal Opportunities Commission/HMSO.

Davies, C. (1994) 'The masculinity of organisational life', Mimeo: 'Women and Public Policy' Conference, Rotterdam, December.

Davis, K. (1991) 'Critical sociology and gender relations', in K. Davis *et al.*, *op. cit.*

Davis, K. (1992) 'Toward a feminist rhetoric: the Gilligan debate revisited', *Women's Studies International Forum*, 15(2), pp. 219–31.

Davis, K., Leijenao, M. and Oldersma, J. (eds) (1991) *The Gender of Power*, London: Sage.

Deacon, A. (1997) 'The case for compulsion', *Poverty*, 98, pp. 8–10.

Deacon, A. and Mann, K. (1999) 'Agency, modernity and social policy', *Journal of Social Policy*, 28(3), pp. 413–35.

Deacon, B. (2000) 'Globalisation: a threat to equitable social provision?' in H. Dean, R. Sykes and R. Woods (eds) *Social Policy Review 12*, Newcastle: Social Policy Association.

Deacon, B. (2001) 'International organizations, the EU and global social policy', in R. Sykes *et al.*, *op. cit.*

Deacon, B. (with Hulse, M. and Stubbs, P.)(1997) *Global Social Policy*, London: Sage.

Dean, H. (1995) *Welfare, Law and Citizenship*, Hemel Hempstead: Prentice Hall/Harvester Wheatsheaf.

Dean, H. (2001) 'Green citizenship', *Social Policy & Administration*, 35(5), pp. 490–05.

Dean, H. with Melrose, M. (1999) *Poverty, Riches and Social Citizenship*, Basingstoke: Macmillan.

Dean, J. (1996) *Solidarity of Strangers: Feminism after Identity Politics*, Berkeley: University of California Press.

Dean, J. (1997) 'The reflective solidarity of democratic feminism', in J. Dean, *op. cit.*

Dean, J. (ed.) (1997) *Feminism and the New Democracy: Resiting the Political*, London: Sage.

Dearden, C. and Becker, S. (1995) *Young Carers: The Facts*, Sutton: Reed Business Publishing/Young Carers Research Group.

Deem, R. (1996) 'No time for a rest? An exploration of women's work, engendered leisure and holidays', *Time & Society*, 5(1), pp. 5–25.

DEG/DSS, (1994) *Jobseeker's Allowance* (White Paper) London: HMSO.

Del Re, A. (1996) 'The relationship between women's paid and unpaid work', in L. Hantrais and M. Letablier (eds) *Comparing Families and Family Policies in Europe*, Loughborough: Cross-national Research Group.

Delanty, G. (1997a) 'Models of citizenship: defining European identity and citizenship', *Citizenship Studies*, 1(3), pp. 285–303.

Delanty, G. (1997b) 'Habermas and occidental rationalism', *Sociological Theory* 15(1), pp. 30–59.

Delanty, G. (1998) 'Dilemmas of citizenship: recent literature on citizenship and Europe', *Citizenship Studies*, 2(2), pp. 353–8.

Delanty, G. (2000) *Citizenship in a Global Age*, Buckingham: Open University Press.

Delphy, C. (1994) 'Changing women in a changing Europe: is "difference" the future for feminism', *Women's Studies International Forum*, 17(2/3), pp. 187–201.

Demaine, J. and Entwistle, H. (eds) (1996) *Beyond Communitarianism. Citizenship, Politics and Education*, Basingstoke: Macmillan.

Deprez, L. S. and Butler, S. S. (2001) 'In defense of women's economic security: securing access to higher education under welfare reform', *Social Politics*, 8(2), pp. 210–27.

Desai, M. (1999) 'From Vienna to Beijing: Women's human rights activism and the human rights community', in P. van Ness, *op. cit.*

Desai, M. and Said, Y. (2001) 'The new anti-capitalist movement: money and global civil society', in H. Anheier *et al.*, *op. cit.*

Deven, F., Inglis, S., Moss, P. and Petrie, P. (1998) *State of the Art Review on the Reconciliation of Work and Family Life for Men and Women and the Quality of Care Services*, London: Department for Education and Employment.

Dietz, M. (1985) 'Citizenship with a feminist face: the problem with maternal thinking', *Political Theory*, 13(1), pp. 19–37.

Dietz, M. (1987) 'Context is all: feminism and theories of citizenship', *Daedalus*, 116(4), pp. 1–24.

Dietz, M. (1991) 'Hannah Arendt and feminist politics', in M. L. Shanley and C. Pateman, *op. cit.*

Directorate General for Research (1994) *Women and Poverty in Europe*, Luxembourg: European Parliament.

Dirks, G. E. (1998) 'Factors underlying migration and refugee issues: responses and co-operation among OECD member states', *Citizenship Studies*, 2(3), pp. 377–95.

Dodds, S. (1998) 'Citizenship, justice and indigenous group-specific rights – citizenship and indigenous Australia', *Citizenship Studies*, 2(1), pp. 105–19.

Dölling, I. (1991) 'Between hope and helplessness: women in the GDR after the "turning point"', *Feminist Review*, (39), pp. 3–15.

Donnison, D. (1989) 'Social policy: the community-based approach', in M. Bulmer, J. Lewis and D. Piachaud (eds) *The Goals of Social Policy*, London: Unwin Hyman.

Dorf, J. and Careaga Pérez, G. (1995) 'Discrimination and the tolerance of difference: international lesbian human rights', in J. Peters and A. Wolper, *op. cit.*

Douglas, J. (1998) 'Meeting the health needs of women from black and minority ethnic communities', in L. Doyal (ed.) *Women and Health Services*, Buckingham: Open University Press.

Doyal, L. (1983) 'Women, health and the sexual division of labour: a case study of the women's health movement in Britain', *Critical Social Policy*, 7, pp. 21–33.

Doyal, L. (1990) 'Waged work and women's well being', *Women's Studies International Forum*, 13(6), pp. 587–604.

Doyal, L. (1995) *What Makes Women Sick*, Basingstoke: Macmillan.

Doyal, L. and Gough, I. (1991) *A Theory of Human Need*, Basingstoke: Macmillan.

Drew, E. P. (2000) 'Reconciling divisions of labour', in S. Duncan and B. Pfau-Effinger (eds) *Gender, Economy and Culture in the European Union*, London: Routledge.

Drover, G. and Kerans, P. (eds) (1993) *New Approaches to Welfare Theory*, Aldershot: Edward Elgar.

Dummett, A. (1991) 'Racial equality and "1992"', *Feminist Review*, 39, pp. 85–90.

Duncan, S. (1995) 'Theorizing European gender systems', *Journal of European Social Policy*, 5(4), pp. 263–84.

Duncan, S. and Edwards, R. (eds) (1997) *Single Mothers in an International Context*, London: UCL Press.

Duncan, S. and Edwards, R. (1999) *Lone Mothers, Paid Work and Gendered Moral Rationalities*, Basingstoke: Macmillan.

Düvell, F. and Jordan, B. (1999) 'Immigration, asylum and citizenship', *Imprints*, 4(1), pp. 15–36.

Dworkin, A. (1981) *Pornography: Men Possessing Women*, London: The Women's Press.

Dwyer, P. (2000) *Welfare Rights and Responsibilities. Contesting Social Citizenship*, Bristol: Policy Press.

EAPN (1995/6) *Network News*, no. 35, Newsletter of the European Anti-Poverty Network.

Eardley, T., Bradshaw, J., Ditch, J., Gough, I. and Whiteford, P. (1996) *Social Assistance in OECD Countries: Synthesis Report*, London: HMSO.

EC Childcare Network (1990) *Men as Carers for Children*, Brussels: Commission of the European Communities.

EC Childcare Network (1993) *Men as Carers*, Brussels: Commission of the European Communities.

Eduards, M. (1994) 'Women's agency and collective action', *Women's Studies International Forum*, 17(2/3), pp. 181–6.

Eduards, M. (1997) 'The women's shelter movement', in G. Gustafsson *et al.*, *op. cit.*

Edwards, M. and Gaventa, J. (2001) *Global Citizen Action*, Boulder: Lynne Rienner.

Einhorn, B. (1991) 'Where have all the women gone? Women and the women's movement in East Central Europe', *Feminist Review*, 39, pp. 16–36.

Einhorn, B. (1993) *Cinderella Goes to Market*, London: Verso.

Einhorn, B. (1999) 'Gender and citizenship in the context of democratisation and economic transformation in East Central Europe', Mimeo: Equality, Democracy, and the Welfare State conference: Stanford University, 10–11 May.

Eisenstein, Z. (1987) 'Elizabeth Cady Stanton: radical-feminist analysis and liberal-feminist strategy', in A. Phillips, *op. cit.*

Eisenstein, Z. (1988) *The Female Body and the Law*, Berkeley and Los Angeles: University of California Press.

Eisenstein, Z. (1991) 'Privatising the state: reproductive rights, affirmative action and the problem of democracy', *Frontiers*, xii(1), pp. 98–125.

Eisenstein, Z. (1997) 'Women's publics and the search for new democracies', *Feminist Review*, 57, pp. 140–67.

Elgood, J., Vinter, L. and Williams, R. (2002) *Man Enough for the Job? A Study of Parliamentary Candidates*, Manchester: Equal Opportunities Commission.

Ellis, B. (1995) 'The experiences of disabled women', *Social Policy Research Findings* 81, York: Joseph Rowntree Foundation.

Ellison, N. (1997) 'Towards a new social politics: citizenship and reflexivity in late modernity', *Sociology*, 31(4), pp. 697–717.

Elshtain, J. B. (1981) *Public Man, Private Woman*, Oxford: Martin Robertson.

Elshtain, J. B. (1987) 'Against androgyny', in A. Phillips, *op. cit.*

Elshtain, J. B. (1992) 'The power and powerlessness of women', in G. Bock and S. James, *op. cit.*

Employment Committee (1995) *Mothers in Employment: First Report Session 1994–95*, HC 227–1, London: HMSO.

Entrèves, M. P. d, (1992) 'Hannah Arendt and the idea of citizenship', in C. Mouffe, *op. cit.*

Equal Opportunities Commission (1990) *Women and Training: An EOC Review of Recent Research and Policy*, Manchester: Equal Opportunities Commission.

Esam, P and Berthoud, R. (1991) *Independent Benefits for Men and Women*, London: Policy Studies Institute.

Escrivá, A. (2000) 'The position and status of migrant women in Spain', in F. Anthias and C. Lazaridis (eds) *Gender and Migration in Southern Europe: Women on the Move*, Oxford and New York: Berg.

Espada, J. C. (1996) *Social Citizenship Rights. A Critique of F. A. Hayek and Raymond Plant*, Basingstoke: Macmillan.

Esping-Andersen, G. (1990) *The Three Worlds of Welfare Capitalism*, Cambridge: Polity Press.

Esping-Andersen, G. (1999) *Social Foundations of Postindustrial Economies*, Oxford: Oxford University Press.

Etzioni, A. (1993) *The Spirit of Community*, New York: Simon & Schuster.

Etzioni, A. (2000) *The Third Way to a Good Society*, London: Demos.

European Commission (1994) *European Social Policy: A Way Forward for the Union* (White Paper), Luxembourg: Office for Official Publications of the European Communities.

European Commission (1998) *Education and Active Citizenship in the European Union*, Luxembourg: Office for Official Publications of the European Communities.

European Commission (2000) *The Social Situation in the European Union 2000*, Luxembourg: Office for Official Publications of the European Communities.

European Commission (2001) *Assessment of the Implementation of the 2001 Employment Guidelines.* Supporting Document to the Joint Employment Report 2001 {COM(2001)438 final}, Commission Staff Working Paper, Brussels: Commission of the European Communities.

European Commission Network on Childcare and Other Measures to Reconcile Employment and Family Responsibilities (1996) *European Childcare Network: A Decade of Achievements 1986–1996*, Brussels: Commission on European Communities.

European Database (2000) *Women in Political Decision-Making Positions: Facts and Figures, 2000*, Berlin: European Database – Women in Decision-Making.

European Ministerial Conference (1986) *Declaration on Equality between Women and Men in Political and Public Life*, 4 March, Strasbourg, MEG 86(8).

European Network of Experts (1994) *Women in Decision-making*, Brussels: Network of the European Commission: 'Women in Decision-making'.

European Women's Lobby (1995) *Confronting the Fortress – Black and Migrant Women in the European Union*, Luxembourg: European Parliament.

European Women's Lobby (1999) *Unveiling the Hidden Data on Domestic Violence in the European Union.* Report to European Commission Conference on Domestic Violence, Brussels: European Women's Lobby.

European Women's Lobby (2000) *Annual Report 2000*, Brussels, European Women's Lobby.

European Women's Lobby (2001) *Young Women's Guide to Equality between Women and Men in Europe*, Brussels: European Women's Lobby.

Eurostat (1995) *Women and Men in the European Union: A Statistical Portrait*, Luxembourg: Office for Official Publications of the European Communities.

Evandrou, M. (1990) *Challenging the Invisibility of Carers: Mapping Informal Carers Nationally*, London: STICERD, London School of Economics.

Evans, D. T. (1993) *Sexual Citizenship*, London: Routledge.

Evans, J., Hills, J., Hunt, K., Meehan, E., Tusscher, T., Vogel, U. and Waylen, G. (1986) *Feminism and Political Theory*, London: Sage.

Evason, E. (1982) *Hidden Violence: A Study of Battered Women in Northern Ireland*, Belfast: Farset Press.

Evers, A., Pijl, M. and Ungerson, C. (eds) (1994) *Payments for Care: A Comparative Overview*, Aldershot: Avebury.

Expert Group on Fundamental Rights (1999) *Affirming Fundamental Rights in the European Union*, Luxembourg: Office for Official Publications of the European Communities.

Fagan, C. (1996) 'Gendered time schedules: paid work in Great Britain', *Social Politics*, 3(1), pp. 72–106.

Fagan, C. (2001) 'Time, money and the gender order: work orientations and working time preferences', *Gender, Work and Organization*, 8(3), pp. 239–66.

Fagnani, J. (1999) 'Parental leave in France', in P. Moss and F. Deven, *op. cit.*

Faist, T. (1997) 'Immigration, citizenship and nationalism. Internal internationalization in Germany and Europe', in M. Roche, R. van Berkel, *op. cit.*

Falk, R. (1994) 'The making of global citizenship', in B. van Steenbergen, *op. cit.*

Falk, R. (1996) 'An inquiry into the political economy of the world order', *New Political Economy*, 1(1), pp. 13–26.

Falkingham, J. and Hills, J. (1995) *The Dynamic of Welfare*, Hemel Hempstead: Prentice Hall/Harvester Wheatsheaf.

Falks, K. (1998) *Citizenship in Modern Britain*, Edinburgh: Edinburgh University Press.

Faulks, K. (2000) *Citizenship*, London: Routledge.

Favell, A. (1998) *Philosophies of Integration*, Basingstoke: Macmillan.

Fawcett, B. (2000) *Feminist Perspectives on Disability*, Harlow: Prentice Hall.

Fawcett, B., Featherstone, B., Hearn, J. and Toft, C. (eds) (1996) *Violence and Gender Relations*, London: Sage.

Fearon, K. (1999) *Women's Work. The Story of the Northern Ireland Women's Coalition*, Belfast: Blackstaff Press.

Fearon, K. and McWilliams, M. (2000) 'Swimming against the mainstream: the Northern Ireland Women's Coalition', in C. Roulston and C. Davies, *op. cit.*

Featherstone, B. and Fawcett, B. (1994/5) 'Feminism and child abuse: opening up some possibilities?', *Critical Social Policy*, 42, pp. 61–80.

Fekete, L. (ed.) (1997) *Europe: The Wages of Racism*, London: Institute for Race Relations (*Race & Class*, 39(1)).

Feldman, R. M., Stall, S. and Wright, P. A. (1998) '"The community needs to be built by us"', in N. Naples, *op. cit.*

Felstead, A., Jewson, N., Phizacklea, A. and Walters, S. (2001) 'Working at home: statistical evidence for seven key hypotheses', *Work, Employment and Society*, 15(2), pp. 215–31.

Ferguson, C. (1999) *Global Social Policy Principles: Human Rights and Social Justice*, London: Department for International Development.

Ferree, M. M. and Martin, P. Y. (eds) (1995) *Feminist Organisations: Harvest of the New Women's Movement*, Philadelphia: Temple University Press.

Ferreira, V. and Tavares, T. (1998) 'Introduction. Women and mobility: shifting bonds and bounds in Europe', in V. Ferreira, T. Tavares and S. Portugal, *op. cit.*

Ferreira, V., Tavares, T. and Portugal, S. (eds) (1998) *Shifting Bonds, Shifting Bounds. Women, Mobility and Citizenship in Europe*, Oeiras, Portugal: Celta.

Ferri, E. and Smith, K. (1996) *Parenting in the 1990s*, London: Family Policy Studies Centre.

Figes, K. (1994) *Because of Her Sex*, Basingstoke: Macmillan.

Finch, J. (1989) *Family Obligations and Social Change*, Cambridge: Polity Press.

Finch, J. (1990) 'The politics of community care in Britain', in C. Ungerson, *op. cit.*

Finch, J. and Groves, D. (eds) (1983) *A Labour of Love: Women, Work and Caring*, London: Routledge & Kegan Paul.

Finch, J. and Mason, J. (1993) *Negotiating Family Responsibilities*, London: Routledge.

Fink, J., Lewis, G. and Clarke, J. (eds) (2001) *Rethinking European Welfare*, London: Sage.

Finzi, S. V. (1992) 'Female identity between sexuality and maternity', in G. Bock and S. James, *op. cit.*

Fitzpatrick, T. (2001) *Welfare Theory: An Introduction*, Basingstoke: Palgrave.

Fitzpatrick, T. (2002) 'In search of a welfare democracy', *Social Policy and Society*, 1(1), pp. 11–20.

Flanagan, O. and Jackson, K. (1987) 'Justice, care and gender: the Kohlberg–Gilligan debate revisited', *Ethics*, 97, pp. 622–37.

Flax, J. (1992) 'Beyond equality: gender, justice and difference', in G. Bock and S. James, *op. cit.*

Florini, A. M. (2001) 'Transnational civil society', in M. Edwards and J. Gaventa, *op. cit.*

Flouri, E. and Buchanan, A. (2001) 'Fathertime', *Community Care*, 4–10 October 2001, p. 42.

Folbre, N. (1994) *Who Pays for the Kids?*, London and New York: Routledge.

Folbre, N. (1995) '"Holding hands at midnight": the paradox of caring labor', *Feminist Economics*, 1(1), pp. 73–92.

Foley, C. (1994) *Sexuality and the State*, London: Liberty/Outrage!/Stonewall.

Foley, C. and Nelles, S. (1993) *Racism: the Destruction of Civil and Political Liberties*, London: Liberty/Anti-Racist Alliance.

Foley, C. and Pratt, S. (1994) *Access Denied: Human Rights & Disabled People*, London: Liberty/British Council of Organisations of Disabled People.

Foley, C. and Wright, C. (1994) *Women's Rights, Human Rights*, London: Liberty/Southall Black Sisters/Change.

Fonseca, M. (1998) 'The transformation of the Guatemalan public sphere', *Social Politics*, 5(2), pp. 188 213.

Forsberg, G., Gonäs, L. and Perrons, D. (2000) 'Paid work participation, inclusion and liberation', in S. Duncan and B. Pfau-Effinger (eds) *Gender, Economy and Culture in the European Union*, London: Routledge.

Foster, P. (1996) 'Women and health care', in C. Hallett, *op. cit.*

Foster-Carter, O. (1987) 'Ethnicity: the fourth burden of Black women – political action', *Critical Social Policy*, 20, pp. 46–56.

Fox-Piven, F. (1990) 'Ideology and the state: women, power and the welfare state', in L. Gordon, *op. cit.*

Frader, L. L. (1996) 'Social citizens without citizenship: working class women and social policy in interwar France', *Social Politics*, 3(2/3), pp. 111–35.

France, A. (1998) '"Why should we care?" Young people, citizenship and questions of social responsibility', *Journal of Youth Studies*, 1(1), pp. 97–111.

Franceschet, S. (2001) 'Women in politics in post-transitional democracies' *International Feminist Journal of Politics*, 3(2), pp. 207–36.

Fraser, N. (1987) 'Women, welfare and the politics of need interpretation', *Hypatia*, 2(1), pp. 103–19.

Fraser, N. (1989) *Unruly Practices*, Cambridge: Polity Press.

Fraser, N. (1994) 'After the family wage: gender equity and the welfare state', *Political Theory*, 22(4), pp. 591–618.

Fraser, N. (1995) 'From redistribution to recognition? Dilemmas of justice in a "post-socialist" age', *New Left Review*, 212, pp. 68–93.

Fraser, N. (1996) 'Equality, difference and radical democracy: the United States feminist debates revisited', in D. Trend, *op. cit.*

Fraser, N. (1997) *Justice Interruptus*, New York and London: Routledge.

Fraser, N. (2000) 'Rethinking recognition', *New Left Review*, 3, pp. 107–20.

Fraser, N. and Gordon, L. (1994a) '"Dependency" demystified: inscriptions of power in a keyword of the welfare state', *Social Politics*, 1(1), pp. 4–31.

Fraser, N. and Gordon, L. (1994b) 'Civil citizenship against social citizenship?', in B. van Steenbergen, *op. cit.*

Fraser, N. and Nicholson, L. J. (1990) 'Social criticism without philosophy; an encounter between feminism and postmodernism', in L. J. Nicholson (ed.) *Feminism/Postmodernism*, London: Routledge.

Frazer, E. and Lacey, N. (1993) *The Politics of Community*, Hemel Hempstead: Harvester Wheatsheaf.

Freedland, M. (2001) 'The marketization of public services', in C. Crouch *et al., op. cit.*

Freeman, M. A. (1995) 'The human rights of women in the family: issues and recommendations for implementation of the Women's Convention', in J. Peters and A. Wolper, *op. cit.*

Friedan, B. (1963/1986) *The Feminist Mystique*, London: Gollancz/ Harmondsworth: Penguin.

Friese, M. (1995) 'East European women as domestics in Western Europe: the new social inequality and division of labour among women', *Journal of Area Studies*, 6, pp. 194–202.

Fulbrook, M. and Cesarini, D. (1996) 'Conclusion', in D. Cesarini and M. Fulbrook, *op. cit.*

Furlong, A. and Cartmel, F. (1997) *Young People and Social Change*, Buckingham: Open University Press.

Galbraith, J. K. (1996) *The Good Society*, London: Sinclair-Stevenson.

Galeotti, A. E. (1993) 'Citizenship and equality: the place for toleration', *Political Theory*, 21(4), pp. 585–605.

Gallagher, J. (1995) 'Fortress Europe?', *New Times*, 28 October, pp. 2–3.

Gallie, W. B. (1956) 'Essentially contested concepts', *Proceedings of the Aristotelian Society*, 56.

Gardiner, J. (1997) *Gender, Care and Economics*, Basingstoke: Macmillan.

Gardner, J. P. (1990) 'What lawyers mean by citizenship', appendix to Commission on Citizenship, *Encouraging Citizenship*, London: HMSO.

Gaspard, F. (1998) 'Invisible, demonised and instrumentalised: female migrants and their daughters in Europe', in V. Ferreira *et al., op. cit.*

Gatens, M. (1991a) *Feminism and Philosophy: Perspectives on Difference and Equality*, Cambridge: Polity Press.

Gatens, M. (1991b) '"The oppressed state of my sex": Wollstonecraft on reason, feeling and equality', in M. L. Shanley and C. Pateman, *op. cit.*

Gatens, M. (1992) 'Power, bodies and difference', in M. Barrett and A. Phillips (eds) *Destabilising Theory*, Cambridge: Polity Press.

Gaventa, J. (2001) 'Global citizen action: lessons and challenges' in M. Edwards and J. Gaventa, *op. cit.*

Geddes, A. (2002) 'The borders of absurdity and fear', *The Times Higher Education Supplement*, 24 May, p. 17.

Gerhard, U. (1997) 'Feminism and the law: towards a feminist and contextualized concept', *Gender and Citizenship: Equality Revisited*, 3, Report of 'Gender and Citizenship' seminar, Stockholm, 3–4 October.

Gershuny, J. (1996) 'From gemstone to millstone', *The Times Higher Education Supplement*, 2 September.

Gershuny, J. (2000) *Changing Times: Work and Leisure in Postindustrial Society*, Oxford: Oxford University Press.

Gershuny, J., Godwin, M. and Jones, S. (1994) 'The domestic labour revolution: a process of lagged adaptation', in M. Anderson *et al., op. cit.*

Gewirth, A. (1982) *Human Rights: Essays on Justification and Applications*, Chicago: University of Chicago Press.

Gibson, K., Law, L. and McKay, D. (2001) 'Beyond heroes and victims: Filipina contract migrants, economic activism and class transformations', *International Feminist Journal of Politics*, 3(3), pp. 367–86.

Giddens, A. (1991) *Modernity and Self-Identity*, Cambridge: Polity Press.

Giddens, A. (1994a) *Beyond Left and Right*, Cambridge: Polity Press.

Giddens, A. (1994b) 'Brave new world: the new context of politics', in D. Miliband, *op. cit.*

Giddens, A. (1998) *The Third Way: The Renewal of Social Democracy*, Cambridge: Polity Press.

Giddens, A. (2000) *The Third Way and its Critics*, Cambridge: Polity Press.

Giddens, A. and Hutton, W. (2000) 'Fighting back' in W. Hutton and A. Giddens, *op. cit.*

Gilder, G. (1986) *Men and Marriage*, Louisiana: Pelican.

Gilder, G. (1987) 'The collapse of the American family', *The Public Interest*, 89, pp. 20–5, reproduced in B. Turner and P Hamilton (eds) (1994) *Citizenship: Critical Concepts*, Vol. 2, London and New York: Routledge.

Gill, B. (1999) *Winning Women: Lessons from Scotland and Wales*, London: Fawcett.

Gill, B. (2000) *Losing Out Locally. Women and Local Government*, London: Fawcett.

Gill, S. and Davidson, M. J. (2001) 'Problems and pressures facing lone mothers in management and professional occupations – a pilot study', *Women in Management Review*, 16(8), pp. 383–99.

Gilleard, C. and Higgs, P. (2000) *Cultures of Ageing: Self, Citizen and the Body*, London: Pearson Education.

Gilligan, C. (1982) *In a Different Voice*, Cambridge, MA: Harvard University Press.

Gilroy, P. (1987) *There Ain't No Black in the Union Jack*, London: Hutchinson.

Ginn, J. (1993) 'Grey power: age-based organisations' response to structured inequalities', *Critical Social Policy*, 38, pp. 23–47.

Ginn, J. and Arber, S. (1994b) 'Midlife women's employment and pension entitlement in relation to coresident adult children', *Journal of Marriage and the Family*, November, pp. 813–19.

Ginn, J. and Arber, S. (1991) 'Gender, class and income inequalities in later life', *British Journal of Sociology*, 42(3), pp. 369–96.

Ginn, J. and Arber, S. (1992) 'Towards women's independence: pension systems in three contrasting European welfare states', *Journal of European Social Policy*, 4(2), pp. 255–77.

Ginn, J. and Arber, S. (1993) 'Pension penalties: the gendered division of occupational welfare', *Work, Employment & Society*, 7(1), pp. 47–70.

Ginn, J. and Arber, S. (1994a) 'Gender and pensions in Europe: current trends in women's pension acquisition', in P. Brown and R. Crompton (eds) *A New Europe: Economic Restructuring and Social Exclusion*, London: UCL Press.

Ginn, J. and Arber, S. (1996) 'Patterns of employment, gender and pensions: the effects of work history on older women's non-state pensions', *Work, Employment & Society*, 10(3), pp. 469–90.

Ginn, J. and Arber, S. (1998) 'How does part-time work lead to low pension income?' in J. O' Reillly and C. Fagan, *op. cit.*

Ginn, J., Street, D. and Arber, S. (eds) (2001) *Women, Work and Pensions. International Issues and Prospects*, Buckingham: Open University Press.

Ginsburg, N. (1989) 'Racial harassment policy and practice: the denial of citizenship', *Critical Social Policy*, 26, pp. 66–81.

Ginsburg, N. (1992) *Divisions of Welfare*, London: Sage.

Ginsburg, N. (1994a) '"Race", racism and social policy in western Europe', in J. Ferris and R. Page (eds) *Social Policy in Transition: Anglo-German Perspectives in the New European Community*, Aldershot: Avebury.

Ginsburg, N. (1994b) 'Agendas and prognoses for social policy – a selective review', in R. Page and J. Baldock (eds) *Social Policy Review 6*, Canterbury: Social Policy Association.

Glendinning, C. and McLaughlin, E. (1993a) *Paying for Care: Lessons from Europe*, London: Social Security Advisory Committee/HMSO.

Glendinning, C. and McLaughlin, E. (1993b) 'Paying for informal care: lessons from Finland', *Journal of European Social Policy*, 3(4), pp. 239–53.

Glendinning, C. and Millar, J. (1987) *Women and Poverty*, Brighton: Wheatsheaf.

Glendinning, C. and Millar, J. (1992) *Women and Poverty in Britain: The 1990s*, Hemel Hempstead: Harvester Wheatsheaf.

Glenn, E. N. (1991) 'Racial ethnic women's labor: the intersection of race, gender, and class oppression', in R. L. Blumberg, *op. cit.*

Glenn, E. N. (1992) 'From servitude to service work: historical continuities in the racial division of paid reproductive labor', *Signs*, 18(1), pp. 1–43.

Glover, J. and Arber, S. (1995) 'Polarization in mothers' employment', *Gender, Work and Organization*, 2(4), pp. 165–79.

Glucksman, M. A. (1998) '"What a difference a day makes": A theoretical and historical explanation of temporality and gender', *Sociology* 32(2), pp. 239–58.

Goldberg, P. (1995) 'Where in the world is there safety for me?: women fleeing gender-based persecution', in J. Peters and A. Wolper, *op. cit.*

Golding, P. (1990) 'Political communication and citizenship: democracy in an inegalitarian social order', in M. Ferguson (ed.) *Public Communications: The New Imperatives*, London: Sage.

Golding, P. (1994) 'Telling stories: sociology, journalism and the informed citizen', *European Journal of Communication*, 9, pp. 461–84.

Golding, P. (1996) 'World wide wedge: division and contradiction in the global information infrastructure', *Monthly Review*, 48(3), pp. 72–85.

Golding, P. and Murdock, G. (2001) 'Digital divides. Communications policy and its contradictions', *New Economy*, 8(2), pp. 110–15.

Golding, P. and Murdock, G. (2002) 'Digital possibilities, market realities: the contradictions of communications convergence', in L. Panitch and C. Leys (eds) *Socialist Register 2002 – A World of Contradictions*, Rendlesham: Merlin Press.

Goode, J., Callender, C. and Lister, R. (1998) *Purse or Wallet? Gender Inequalities within Families on Benefits*, London: Policy Studies Institute.

Goodin, R. E. (1988) *Reasons for Welfare: The Political Theory of the Welfare State*, Princeton, NJ: Princeton University Press.

Gordon, L. (ed.) (1990) *Women, the State and Welfare*, Madison: University of Wisconsin Press.

Gordon, P. (1989) *Citizenship for Some? Race and Government Policy 1979–1989*, London: Runnymede Trust.

Gordon, P. (1991) 'Forms of exclusion: citizenship, race and poverty', in S. Becker (ed.) *Windows of Opportunity*, London: CPAG.

Gornick, J. C. (1999) 'Gender equality in the labour market', in D. Sainsbury, *op. cit.*

Gornick, J. C., Meyers, M. K. and Ross, K. E. (1997) 'Supporting the employment of mothers: policy variation across fourteen welfare states', *Journal of European Social Policy*, 7(1), pp. 45–70.

Gough, I. (1992) 'What are human needs?', in J. Percy-Smith and I. Sanderson, *op. cit.*

Gough, O. (2001) 'The impact of the gender pay gap on post-retirement earnings', *Critical Social Policy*, 21(3), pp. 311–34.

Gould, A. (2001) *Developments in Swedish Social Policy: Resisting Dionysus*, Basingstoke: Palgrave.

Gould, C. (1988) *Rethinking Democracy*, Cambridge: Cambridge University Press.

Gould, C. (ed.) (1984) *Beyond Domination*, Totowa, NJ: Rowman & Allanheld.

Grace, M. (1998) 'The work of caring for young children: priceless or worthless?' *Women's Studies International Forum*, 21(4), pp. 401–13.

Graham, H. (1983) 'Caring: a labour of love', in J. Finch and D. Groves, *op. cit.*

Graham, H. (1991) 'The concept of caring in feminist research: the case of domestic service', *Sociology*, 25(1), pp. 61–78.

Graham, H. (1993) *Hardship and Health in Women's Lives*, Hemel Hempstead: Harvester Wheatsheaf.

Gray, A. (2001) '"Making work pay": Devising the best strategy for lone parents in Britain', *Journal of Social Policy*, 30(2), pp. 189–207.

Gray, J. (1994) *The Undoing of Conservatism*, London: Social Market Foundation.

Gray, L. (1996) 'The road to the referendum', *New Times*, 20 July, pp. 10–11.

Gregory, A. and Windebank, J. (2000) *Women's Work in Britain and France*, Basingstoke: Macmillan.

Gregson, N. and Lowe, M. (1994a) *Servicing the Middle Classes: Class, Gender and Waged Domestic Labour in Contemporary Britain*, London and New York: Routledge.

Gregson, N. and Lowe, M. (1994b) 'Waged domestic labour and the renegotiation of the domestic division of labour within dual career households', *Sociology*, 28(1), pp. 55–78.

Grewal, I. (1999) '"Women's rights as human rights": feminist practices, global feminism, and human rights regimes in transnationality', *Citizenship Studies*, 3(3), pp. 337–54.

Grieve Smith, J. (2000) *Closing the Casino: Reform of the Global Financial System*, London: Fabian Society.

Grimshaw, D. and Rubery, J. (2001) *The Gender Pay Gap: A Research Review*, Manchester: Equal Opportunities Commission.

Grimshaw, J. (1988) 'Autonomy and identity in feminist thinking', in M. Griffiths and M. Whitford (eds) *Feminist Perspectives in Philosophy*, Basingstoke: Macmillan.

Groves, D. (1991) 'Women and financial provision for old age', in M. Maclean and D. Groves, (eds) *Women's Issues in Social Policy*, London: Routledge.

Groves, D. (1992) 'Occupational pension provision and women's poverty in old age', in C. Glendinning and J. Millar, *op. cit.*

Groves, D. (1994) 'The older woman as citizen: some issues', Mimeo: Gender and Welfare ESRC Seminar, Bath, December.

>`::>

Gunew, S. and Yeatman, A. (eds) (1993) *Feminism and the Politics of Difference*, Australia: Allen & Unwin.

Gustafsson, G., Eduards, M. and Rönnblom, M. (1997) *Towards a New Democratic Order? Women's Organizing in Sweden in the 1990s*, Stockholm: Publica.

Gustafsson, S. (1994) 'Childcare and types of welfare state', in D. Sainsbury, *op. cit.*

Gwinnett, B. (1998) 'Policing prostitution', in V. Randall and G. Waylen (eds) *Gender, Politics and the State*, London and New York: Routledge.

Hagemann-White, C. (2000) 'Male violence and control: constructing a comparative European perspective', in S. Duncan and B. Pfau-Effinger (eds) *Gender, Economy and Culture in the European Union*, London: Routledge.

Hague, G. and Malos, E. (1994/5) 'Domestic violence, social policy and housing', *Critical Social Policy*, 42, pp. 112–25.

Hakim, C. (1993) 'The myth of rising female employment', *Work, Employment and Society*, 7(1), pp. 97–120.

Halisi, C. R. D., Kaiser, P. J. and Ndegwa, S. N. (1998) 'Introduction: the multiple meanings of citizenship – rights, identity and social justice in Africa', *Africa Today*, 45(3–4), pp. 337–50.

Hall, S. (2000) 'Multicultural citizens, monocultural citizenship?' in N. Pearce and J. Hallgarten, *op. cit.*

Hall, S. and Held, D. (1989) 'Left and rights', *Marxism Today*, June, pp. 16–23.

Hall, T. and Williamson, H. (1999) *Citizenship and Community*, Leicester: Youth Work Press.

Hall, T. Coffey, A. and Williamson, H. (1999) 'Self, space and place: youth identities and citizenship', *British Journal of Sociology of Education*, 20 (4), pp. 501–13.

Hall, T., Williamson, H. and Coffey, A. (1998) 'Conceptualizing citizenship: young people and the transition to adulthood', *Journal of Education Policy*, 13 (3), pp. 301–15.

Hallett, C. (1996) *Women and Social Policy: An Introduction*, Hemel Hempstead: Harvester Wheatsheaf.

Halliday, F. (2000) 'Global governance: prospects and problems', *Citizenship Studies*, 4(1), pp. 19–33.

Hamilton, K. and Jenkins, L. (2000) 'A gender audit for public transport: a new policy tool in the tackling of social exclusion', *Urban Studies*, 37(10), pp. 1793–1800.

Hamilton, K., Jenkins, L. and Gregory, A. (1991) *Women and Transport*, Bradford: University of Bradford.

Hammami, R. and Johnson, P. (1999) 'Equality with a difference: gender and citizenship in transition Palestine', *Social Politics*, 6(3), pp. 314–43.

Hammar, T. (1990) *Democracy and the Nation State*, Aldershot: Avebury.

Hancock, L. (2002) 'The care crunch: changing work, families and welfare in Australia', *Critical Social Policy*, 22(1), pp. 119–40.

Hanmer, J. (1978) 'Violence and the social control of women', in G. Littlejohn, B. Smart, J. Wakeford and N. Yuval-Davis (eds) *Power and the State*, London: Croom Helm.

Hanmer, J. and Maynard, M. (eds) (1987) *Women, Violence and Social Control*, Basingstoke: Macmillan.

Hansen, P. (2000) '"European citizenship" or where neoliberalism meets ethno-culturalism', *European Societies*, 2(2), pp. 139–65.

Hantrais, L. (1993) 'Women, work and welfare in France', in J. Lewis, *op. cit.*

Hantrais, L. (2000) *Social Policy in the European Union*, (2nd edn) Basingstoke: Macmillan.

Hantrais, L. (ed.) (2000) *Gendered Policies in Europe*, Basingstoke: Macmillan.

Hantrais, L. and Letablier, M. (1996) *Families and Family Policies in Europe*, London and New York: Longman.

Hantrais, L. and Letablier, M. (1997) 'The gender of paid and unpaid work time: a European problem', *Time & Society*, 6(2/3), pp. 131–49.

Hantrais, L. and Mangen, S. (1994) *Family Policy and the Welfare of Women*, Loughborough: Cross-National Research Group.

Haq, J. (1994) 'Urban women fighting back!', in Women's Stand for Community Action, *op. cit.*

Harding, S. (1987) 'The curious coincidence of feminine and African moralities', in D. T. Meyers and E. F. Kittay, *op. cit.*

Hardt, M. and Negri, A. (2000) *Empire*, Cambridge MA and London: Harvard University Press.

Harkness, S. and Waldfogel, J. (1999) *The Family Gap in Pay: Evidence from Seven Industrialised Countries*, London: Centre for Analysis of Social Exclusion.

Harman, H. and Mattinson, D. (2000) *Winning for Women*, London: Fabian Society.

Harris, D. (1987) *Justifying State Welfare: The New Right versus the Old Left*, Oxford: Basil Blackwell.

Harris, N. (2000) 'Playing the numbers game', *Red Pepper*, May, pp. 22–3.

Harris, P. (1999) 'Public welfare and liberal governance', in A. Petersen, I Barns, J. Dudley and P. Harris, *Poststructuralism, Citizenship and Social Policy*, London: Routledge.

Harrop, A. and Moss, P. (1995) 'Trends in parental employment', *Work, Employment and Society*, 9(3), pp. 421–44.

Hartsock, N. (1985) *Women, Sex and Power*, Boston: Northeastern University Press.

Harvey, D. (1993) 'Class relations, social justice and the politics of difference', in J. Squires, *op. cit.*

Hayter, T. (2001) 'Going nowhere', *Red Pepper*, January, p. 25.

Hearn, J. (2001) 'Men, fathers and the state: national and global relations', in B. Hobson (ed.) *Making Men into Fathers*, Cambridge: Cambridge University Press.

Heater, D. (1999) *Citizenship*, London: Longman.

Hedlund, G. (1988) 'Women's interests in local politics', in K. B. Jones and A. G. Jónasdóttir, *op. cit.*

Heinen, J. (1990) 'The impact of social policy on the behaviour of women workers in Poland and East Germany', *Critical Social Policy*, 29, pp. 79–91.

Heinen, J. (1997) 'Public/private: gender – social and political citizenship in Eastern Europe', *Theory and Society*, 26, pp. 577–97.

Held, D. (1987) *Models of Democracy*, Cambridge: Polity Press.

Held, D. (1989) *Political Theory and the Modern State*, Cambridge: Polity Press.

Held, D. (1991a) 'Between state and civil society: citizenship', in G. Andrews, *op. cit.*

Held, D. (1991b) 'Democracy, the nation state and the global system', in D. Held (ed.) *Political Theory Today*, Cambridge: Polity Press.

Held, D. (1994) 'Inequalities of power, problems of democracy', in D. Miliband, *op. cit.*

Held, D. (1995) *Democracy and the Global Order*, Cambridge: Polity Press.

Held, V. (1993) *Feminist Morality: Transforming Culture, Society and Politics*, Chicago and London: University of Chicago Press.

Helman, S. (1999) 'From soldiering and motherhood to citizenship: a study of four Israeli peace protest movements', *Social Politics*, 6(3), pp. 292–313.

Henig, R. and Henig, S. (2001) *Women and Political Power: Europe since 1945*, London: Routledge.

Henshaw, K., Singh, A. and Haas, T. (1999) 'Recent trends in abortion rates world-wide', *International Family Planning Perspectives*, 25(1), pp. 44–8.

Herhoffer, A. (1995) 'Autonomy versus integration – East German women and political participation', *Journal of Area Studies*, 6, pp. 179–93.

Herman, D. (1993) 'The politics of law reform: lesbian and gay struggles into the 1990s', in J. Bristow and A. R. Wilson, *op. cit.*

Hernes, H. (1987) *Welfare State and Woman Power*, Oslo: Norwegian University Press.

Hernes, H. (1988) 'The welfare state citizenship of Scandinavian women', in K. B. Jones and A. G. Jónasdóttir, *op. cit.*

Hervey, T. and Shaw, J. (1998) 'Women, work and care: women's dual role and double burden in EC sex equality law', *Journal of European Social Policy*, 8(1), pp. 43–63.

Herzog, H. (1999) 'A space of their own: social-civil discourses among Palestinian–Israeli women in peace organizations', *Social Politics*, 6(3), pp. 344–69.

Hester, M. and Harne, L. (1999) 'Fatherhood, children and violence: placing the UK in an international context', in S. Watson and L. Doyal (eds) *Engendering Social Policy*, Buckingham: Open University Press.

Hewitt, M. (1993) 'Social movements and social need: problems with postmodern political theory', *Critical Social Policy*, (37), pp. 52–74.

Hewitt, M. (1998) 'Social policy and human need', in N. Ellison and C. Pierson (eds) *Developments in British Social Policy*, Basingstoke: Macmillan.

Hewitt, P. (1993) *About Time: The Revolution in Work and Family Life*, London: Rivers Oram Press.

Hills, J. (2001) 'Poverty and social security: what rights? whose responsibilities?', in A. Park, J. Curtice, K. Thomson, L. Jarvis and C. Bromley (eds) *British Social Attitudes. The 18th Report*, London: Sage.

Hindess, B. (1993) 'Citizenship in the modern West', in B. Turner, *op. cit.*

Hindess, B. (1998) 'Divide and rule: the international character of modern citizenship', *European Journal of Social Theory*, 1(1), pp. 57–70.

Hinds, K. and Jarvis, L. (2000) 'The gender gap', in R. Jowell, J. Curtice, A. Park, K. Thomson, L. Jarvis, C. Bromley, N. Stratford (eds) *British Social Attitudes Survey: the 17th Report*, Thousand Oaks/London: Sage.

Hirsch, D. (1999) *Welfare Beyond Work. Active Participation in a New Welfare State*, York: Joseph Rowntree Foundation.

Hirschmann, N. J. (1996) 'Rethinking obligation for feminism', in N. J. Hirschmann and C. Di Stefano (eds) *Revisioning the Political*, Boulder, CO: Westview Press.

Hirschmann, N. J. and Di Stefano, C. (1996) 'Introduction' in N. J. Hirschmann and C. Di Stefano (eds) *Revisioning the Political*, Boulder, CO: Westview Press.

Hirst, P. and Thompson, G. (1999) *Globalization in Question* (2nd edn) Cambridge: Polity Press.

Hobsbawm, E. (1994) *Age of Extremes*, London: Michael Joseph.

Hobson, B. (1990) 'No exit, no voice: women's economic dependency and the welfare state', *Acta Sociologica*, 33(3), pp. 235–50.

Hobson, B. (1994) 'Solo mothers, social policy regimes, and the logics of gender', in D. Sainsbury, *op. cit.*

Hobson, B. (1999) 'Women's collective agency, power resources, and the framing of citizenship rights', in M. Hanagan and C. Tilly (eds) *Extending Citizenship, Reconfiguring States*, Lanham, Boulder, New York and Oxford: Rowman & Littlefield.

Hobson, B. (with Takahashi, M.) (2001) 'The framing of gender equality in the Swedish welfare state and the power of actors within families', Mimeo: Academy Colloquium, Solidarity between the sexes and generations: transformations in Europe, Amsterdam, 28–29 June.

Hobson, B. and Lindholm, M. (1997) 'Collective identities, women's power resources, and the making of welfare states', *Theory and Society*, 26, pp. 475–508.

Hobson, B. and Lister, R. (2002) 'Keyword: citizenship', in J. Lewis, B. Hobson and B. Siim (eds) *Contested Concepts in Gender and Social Politics*, Cheltenham: Edward Elgar.

Hobson, B., Johansson, S., Olah, L. and Sutton, C. (1995) 'Swedish welfare: policy and provision', in E. Brunsdon and M. May (eds) *Swedish Welfare: Policy and Provision*, London: Social Policy Association.

Hochschild, A. R. (2000) 'Global care chains and emotional surplus value', in W. Hutton and A. Giddens, *op. cit.*

Hocking, B. J. and Hocking, B. A. (1998) 'A comparative view of indigenous citizenship issues', *Citizenship Studies*, 2(1), pp. 121–31.

Hoggett, P. (2000) *Emotional Life and the Politics of Welfare*, Basingstoke: Macmillan.

Hoggett, P. (2001) 'Agency, rationality and social policy', *Journal of Social Policy*, 30(1), pp. 37–56.

Højgaard, L. (1993) 'Work and family life – life's inseparable pair', in S. Carlsen and J. E. Larsen, *op. cit.*

Holli, A. M. (1997) 'On equality and Trojan horses: the challenges of the Finnish experience to feminist theory', *European Journal of Women's Studies*, 4(2), pp. 133–64.

Holmes, H. (1984) 'A feminist analysis of the Universal Declaration of Human Rights', in C. Gould, *op. cit.*

Holtmaat, R. (1989) 'The power of legal concepts: the development of a feminist theory of law', *International Journal of the Sociology of Law*, 17, pp. 481–502.

Home Office (1989) *The Response to Racial Attack and Harassment*, London: HMSO.

Homer, M., Leonard, A. E. and Taylor, M. P. (1984) *Private Violence: Public Shame*, Cleveland: Cleveland Refuge Aid for Women and Children.

Homer, M., Leonard, A. E. and Taylor, M. P. (1985) 'The burden of dependency', in N. Johnson (ed.) *Marital Violence*, London: Routledge & Kegan Paul.

hooks, b. (1982) *Ain't I a Woman?*, London: Pluto.

hooks, b. (1984) *Feminist Theory from Margin to Center*, Boston: South End Press.

Hooper, C. (1996) 'Men's violence and relationship breakdown: can violence be dealt with as an exception to the rule?', in C. Hallett, *op. cit.*

Hooyman, N. R. and Gonyea, J. (1995) *Feminist Perspectives on Family Care,* Thousand Oaks and London: Sage.

Horsman, M. and Marshall, A. (1994) *After the Nation State,* London: HarperCollins.

Hoskyns, C. (1996) *Integrating Gender: Women, Law and Politics in the European Union,* London: Verso.

Hoskyns, C. and Luckhaus, L. (1989) 'The European Community Directive on Equal Treatment in Social Security', *Policy and Politics,* 17(4), pp. 321–5.

Hoskyns, C. and Rai, S. M. (1998) 'Gender, class and representation: India and the European Union', *European Journal of Women's Studies,* 5(3–4), pp. 345–65.

Howard, M. (2001) *Paying the Price. Carers, Poverty and Social Exclusion,* London: Child Poverty Action Group.

Hrafnsdóttir, S. (2002) 'Fire, ice and paternity', *Community Care,* 14–20 March, p. 43.

Hubbard, P. (2001) 'Sex zones: intimacy, citizenship and public space' *Sexualities,* 4(1), pp. 51–71.

Hughes, D. M., Mladjenovic, L. and Mrsevic, Z. (1995) 'Feminist resistance in Serbia', *European Journal of Women's Studies,* 2(4), pp. 509–32.

Hughes, G. (1996) 'Communitarianism and law and order', *Critical Social Policy,* 16(4), pp. 17–41.

Huq, S. P. (2000) 'Gender and citizenship: What does a rights framework offer women?', *IDS Bulletin,* 31(4), pp. 74–82.

Hutchings, K. and Dannreuther, R. (eds) (1999) *Cosmopolitan Citizenship,* Basingstoke: Macmillan.

Hutton, S. (1994) 'Men and women's incomes: evidence from survey data', *Journal of Social Policy,* 23(1), pp. 21–40.

Hutton, W. (1995) *The State We're In,* London: Jonathan Cape.

Hutton, W. and Giddens, A. (eds) (2000) *On the Edge,* London: Jonathan Cape.

Hyatt, S. (1992a) *'Putting Bread on the Table'. The Women's Work of Community Activism,* Bradford: Work & Gender Research Unit.

Hyatt, S. (1992b) 'Accidental activists: women and politics on a council estate', *Crosscurrents,* 5, pp. 93–102.

Hyatt, S. (1993) 'Across the great divide? Women's politics and the genealogy of public/private space', Mimeo: Christian Urban Resources Unit seminar, University of Bradford.

IDS Bulletin (1997) 'Tactics and trade-offs: revising the links between gender and poverty', *IDS Bulletin,* 28(3).

Ignatieff, M. (1989) 'Citizenship and moral narcissism', *Political Quarterly,* 60(1), pp. 63–74.

Inglehart, R. and Norris, P. (2000) 'The developmental theory of the gender gap: women's and men's voting behaviour in global perspective', *International Political Science Review,* 21(4), pp. 441–63.

Inter-Parliamentary Union (2001) *Women in National Parliaments,* http://www.ipu.org/wmn-e/world.htm, as at 5 December.

Isin, E. F. and Wood, P. K. (1999) *Citizenship and Identity,* London: Sage.

Jacobs, S. (1985) 'Race, empire and the welfare state: council housing and racism', *Critical Social Policy,* 13, pp. 6–28.

Jacobs, S. and Popple, K. (eds) (1994) *Community Work in the 1990s*, Nottingham: Spokesman.

Jacquette, J. S. (1994) 'Women's movements and the challenge of democratic politics in Latin America', *Social Politics*, 1(3), pp. 335–40.

James, S. (1992) 'The good-enough citizen: citizenship and independence', in G. Bock, and S. James, *op. cit.*

Jani-le-Bris, H. (1993) *Family Care of Dependent Older People in the European Community*, Dublin: European Foundation for the Improvement of Living and Working Conditions.

Janoski, T. (1998) *Citizenship and Civil Society: A Framework of Rights and Obligations in Liberal, Traditional and Social Democratic Regimes*, Cambridge: Cambridge University Press.

Jarvis, C. and Stanley, A. (1999) 'Recent developments in immigration law', *Legal Action*, July, pp. 10–14.

Jayasuriya, K. (2001) 'Autonomy, liberalism and the new contractualism', *Law in Context*, 18(2), pp. 57–78.

Jelin, E. (2000) 'Towards a global environmental citizenship', *Citizenship Studies*, 4(1), pp. 47–63.

Jenkins, S. (1991) 'Poverty measurement and the within-household distribution: agenda for action', *Journal of Social Policy*, 20(4), pp. 457–83.

Jenson, J. (1997) 'Who cares? Gender and welfare regimes', *Social Politics*, 4(2), pp. 182–87.

Jenson, J. and Phillips, S. D. (2001) 'Redesigning the Canadian citizenship regime: remaking the institutions of representation', in C. Crouch *et al.*, *op. cit.*

Jenson, J. and Sineau, M. (1995) 'Family policy and women's citizenship in Mitterrand's France', *Social Politics*, 2(3), pp. 244–69.

Joaquim, T. (1998) 'Social citizenship and motherhood', in V. Ferreira *et al.*, *op. cit.*

Jónasdóttir, A. (1988) 'On the concept of interests, women's interests and the limitations of interest theory', in K. B. Jones and A. Jónasdóttir, *op. cit.*

Jones, C. (1999) *Global Justice. Defending Cosmopolitanism*, Oxford: Oxford University Press.

Jones, E. and Gaventa, J. (2002) *Concepts of Citizenship: A Review*, Brighton: Institute for Development Studies.

Jones, G. and Wallace, C. (1992) *Youth, Family and Citizenship*, Buckingham: Open University Press.

Jones, K. B. (1988) 'Towards the revision of politics', in K. B. Jones and A. G. Jónasdóttir, *op. cit.*

Jones, K. B. (1990) 'Citizenship in a woman-friendly polity', *Signs*, 15(4), pp. 781–812,

Jones, K. B. (1993) *Compassionate Authority: Democracy and the Representation of Women*, New York: Routledge.

Jones, K. B. (1994) 'Identity, action and locale: thinking about citizenship, civic action and feminism', *Social Politics*, 1(3), pp. 256–70.

Jones, K. B. and Jónasdóttir, A. G. (1988) *The Political Interests of Gender*, London: Sage.

Jones, L. (1996) 'Putting transport on the social policy agenda', in M. May, E. Brunsdon and G. Craig (eds) *Social Policy Review 8*, London: Social Policy Association.

Jonung, C. and Persson, I. (1993) 'Women and market work: the misleading tale of participation rates in international comparisons', *Work, Employment and Society*, 7(2), pp. 259–74.

Jordan, B. (1989) *The Common Good: Citizenship, Morality and Self-Interest*, Oxford: Basil Blackwell.

Jordan, B. (1997) 'Citizenship, association and immigration: theoretical issues', in M. Roche, R. van Berkel, *op. cit.*

Jordan, B. (1998) *The New Politics of Welfare*, London: Sage.

Jordan, B., Agulnik, P., Burbidge, D. and Duffin, S. (2000) *Stumbling Towards Basic Income*, London: Citizen's Income Study Centre.

Joseph, S. (1994) 'Problematizing gender and relational rights: experiences from Lebanon', *Social Politics*, 1(3), pp. 271–85.

Joseph, S. (1997) 'The public/private – the imagined boundary in the imagined nation/state/community: the Lebanese case', *Feminist Review*, 57, pp. 73–92.

Joseph, S. (1999) 'Descent of the nation: kinship and citizenship in Lebanon', *Citizenship Studies* 3(3), pp. 295–318.

Joshi, H. (1992) 'The cost of caring', in C. Glendinning and J. Millar, *op. cit.*

Joshi, H., Dale, A., Ward, C. and Davies, H. (1995) *Dependence and Independence in the Finances of Women aged 33*, London: Family Policy Studies Centre.

Joshi, H., Davies, H. and Land, H. (1996) *The Tale of Mrs Typical*, London: Family Policy Studies Centre.

Kadalie, R. (1995) 'Constitutional equality: the implications for women in South Africa, *Social Politics*, 2(2), pp. 208–24.

Kamerman, S. B. and Kahn, A. J. (eds) (1991) *Child Care, Parental Leave, and the Under 3s. Policy Innovation in Europe*, New York: Auburn House.

Kan, M. Y. (2001) 'Gender asymmetry in the division of domestic labour', mimeo: British Household Panel Survey conference, University of Essex, July.

Kaplan, M. B. (1997) *Sexual Justice: Democratic Citizenship and the Politics of Desire*, New York and London: Routledge.

Katz, C. and Monk, J. (eds) (1993) *Full Circles: Geographies of Women Over the Life Course*, London: Routledge.

Katz, I. (ed.) (2001) *Welcome to Britain*, London: Guardian Newspapers.

Kauppinen, K. and Kandolin, I. (1998) *Gender and Working Conditions in the European Union*, Luxembourg: Office for Official Publications of the European Communities.

Kautto, M., Heikkila, M., Hvinden, B., Marklund, S. and Ploug, N. (1999) *Nordic Social Policy: Changing Welfare States*, London and New York: Routledge.

Kay, D. and Miles, R. (1992) *Refugees or Migrant Workers? European Volunteer Workers in Britain 1946–1951*, London: Routledge.

Keane, J. (1994) 'Public spheres', *Centre for the Study of Democracy Bulletin*, II(1), pp. 10–11.

Keith, L. (1992) 'Who cares wins? Women, caring and disability', *Disability, Handicap & Society*, 7(2), pp. 167–75.

Keith, L. and Morris, J. (1996) 'Easy targets: a disability rights perspective on the "children as carers" debate', in J. Morris, *op. cit.*

Kelly, L. and Radford, J. (1990/91) '"Nothing really happened": the invalidation of women's experience of sexual violence', *Critical Social Policy*, 30, pp. 39–53.

Kemmer, D., Cunningham-Burley, S. and Backett-Milburn, K. (2001) 'How does working work for lone mothers on low incomes?' *Benefits*, 32, pp. 10–14.

Kemp, A., Madlala, N., Moodley, A. and Salo, E. (1995) 'The dawn of a new day: redefining South African feminism', in A. Basu, *op. cit.*

Kershaw, C., Chivite-Matthews, N., Thomas, C. and Aust, R. (2001) *The 2001 British Crime Survey*, London: Home Office Statistical Bulletin.

Kiernan, A. K. (1997) 'Citizenship – the real democratic deficit of the European Union?', *Citizenship Studies*, 1(3), pp. 323–34.

Kiernan, K. (1992) 'Men and women at work and at home', in R. Jowell, L. Brook, G. Prior and B. Taylor (eds) *British Social Attitudes: The 9th Report*, Aldershot: Dartmouth.

Kiernan, K., Land, H. and Lewis, J. (1998) *Lone Motherhood in Twentieth-Century Britain*, Oxford: Clarendon Press.

Kildal, N. (1999) 'Justification of workfare: the Norwegian case', *Critical Social Policy*, 19(3), pp.353–70.

Kildal, N. (1999b) 'Social rights and individual responsibilities', mimeo: European Sociological Association Conference, Amsterdam, August.

Kilkey, M. and Bradshaw, J. (1999) 'Lone mothers, economic well-being and policies', in D. Sainsbury, *op. cit.*

Kilkey, M. and Bradshaw, J. (2001) 'Making work pay policies for lone parents', in J. Millar and K. Rowlingson, *op. cit.*

Kilmurray, A. (1991) 'Rural women and socio-economic development policies: the case of South Armagh', in C. Davies and E. McLaughlin (eds) *Women, Employment and Social Policy in Northern Ireland: A Problem Postponed?*, Belfast: Northern Ireland Policy Research Institute.

King, D. S. (1987) *The New Right: Politics, Markets and Citizenship*, Basingstoke: Macmillan.

King, D. S. (1995) *Actively Seeking Work? The Politics of Unemployment and Welfare Policy in the United States and Great Britain*, Chicago and London: University of Chicago Press.

Kingdom, E. (1991) *What's Wrong with Rights? Problems for Feminist Politics of Law*, Edinburgh: Edinburgh University Press.

Kingdom, E. (1996) 'Gender and citizenship rights', in J. Demaine and H. Entwistle, *op. cit.*

Kitzinger, C. (1994) 'Anti-lesbian harassment', in C. Brant and Y. Lee Too, *op. cit.*

Knijn, T. (1994) 'Fish without bikes: revision of the Dutch welfare state and its consequences for the (in)dependence of single mothers', *Social Politics*, 1(1), pp. 83–105.

Knijn, T. and Kremer, M. (1997) 'Gender and the caring dimension of welfare states: towards inclusive citizenship', *Social Politics*, 4(3), pp. 328–61.

Knijn, T. and van Wel, F. (2001a) 'Careful or lenient: welfare reform for lone mothers in the Netherlands', *Journal of European Social Policy*, 11(3), pp. 235–51.

Knijn, T. and van Wel, F. (2001b) 'Does it work? Employment policies for lone parents in the Netherlands', in J. Millar and K. Rowlingson, *op. cit.*

Knocke, W. (1995) 'Migrant and ethnic minority women: the effects of gender-neutral legislation in the European Community', *Social Politics*, 2(2), pp. 225–38.

Knocke, W. (1998) 'Problematizing multiculturalism: respect, tolerance and the limits to tolerance', in V. Ferreira *et al.*, *op. cit.*

Kofman, E. (1995) 'Citizenship for some but not for others: spaces of citizenship in contemporary Europe', *Political Geography*, 14(2), pp. 121–37.

Kofman, E. and Sales, R. (1992) 'Towards Fortress Europe?', *Women's Studies International Forum*, 15(1), pp. 29–39.

Kofman, E. and Sales, R. (1998) 'Migrant women and exclusion in Europe', *European Journal of Women's Studies*, 5(3–4), pp. 381–98.

Kofman, E., Phizacklea, A., Raghuran, P. and Sales, R. (2000) *Gender and International Migration in Europe*, London and New York: Routledge.

Kohlberg, J. E. (1991) 'The gender dimension of the welfare state', *International Journal of Sociology*, 21(2), pp. 119–48.

Komter, A. E. (1995) 'Justice, friendship and care. Aristotle and Gilligan – two of a kind?', *European Journal of Women's Studies*, 2(2), pp.151–69.

Kornbluh, F. A. (1996) 'The new literature on gender and the welfare state: the U.S. case', *Feminist Studies*, 22(1), pp. 171–97.

Korpi, W. (2000) 'Faces of inequality: gender, class, and patterns of inequalities in different types of welfare states', *Social Politics*, 7(2), pp.127–91.

Kosambi, M. (1995) 'An uneasy intersection: gender, ethnicity and crosscutting identities in India', *Social Politics*, 2(2), pp. 181–94.

Kosko, B. (1993) *Fuzzy Thinking: The New Science of Fuzzy Logic*, London: Harper-Collins.

Koven, S. (1993) 'Borderlands: women, voluntary action, and child welfare in Britain, 1840 to 1914', in S. Koven and S. Michel, *op. cit.*

Koven, S. and Michel, S. (1993) *Mothers of a New World*, London: Routledge.

Kraemer, S. (1995) 'Fathers roles: research findings and policy implications', Mimeo, London: Tavistock Clinic.

Krauss, C. (1998) 'Challenging power. Toxic waste and the politicization of white, working-class women', in N. Naples, *op. cit.*

Kremer, J. and Montgomery, P. (1993) *Women's Working Lives*, Belfast: Equal Opportunities Commission for Northern Ireland/HMSO.

Kremer, M. (1994) 'Interpretations of Citizenship', Mimeo: MA thesis, University of Utrecht.

Kremer, M. (2001) 'A Dutch miracle for women?', *Social Politics*, 8(2), pp. 182–5.

Kröger, T. (2001) *Comparative Research on Social Care: The State of the Art*, Brussels: European Commission.

Kveinen, E. (2002) 'Citizenship in a post-Westphalian community: beyond external exclusion?', *Citizenship Studies* 6(1), pp. 21–35.

Kymlicka, W. (1995) *Multicultural Citizenship: A Liberal Theory of Minority Rights*, Oxford: Clarendon Press.

Kymlicka, W. (2001) *Politics in the Vernacular. Nationalism, Multiculturalism and Citizenship*, Oxford: Oxford University Press.

Kymlicka, W. and Norman, W. (1994) 'Return of the citizen', *Ethics* (104), January, pp. 352–81.

Kymlicka, W. and Norman, W. (2000) 'Citizenship in culturally diverse societies: issues, contexts, concepts', in W. Kymlicka and W. Norman (eds), *Citizenship in Diverse Societies*, Oxford: Oxford University Press.

La Valle, I., Finch, S., Nove, A. Lewis, C. (1999) *Parents' Demand for Childcare*, London: Department for Education and Employment.

Lacey, N. (1993) 'Theory into practice? Pornography and the public/private dichotomy', *Journal of Law and Society*, 20, pp. 93–113.

Laclau, E. (1996) *Emancipation(s)*, London, New York: Verso.

Lagergren, M. (1986) 'Time to care in the advanced welfare state – some observations from a Swedish futures study "Care in society"', in L. Balbo and H. Nowotny, *op. cit.*

Lake, M. (1993) 'A revolution in the family: the challenge and contradictions of maternal citizenship in Australia', in S. Koven and S. Michel, *op. cit.*

Lake, M. (1995) 'Introduction', *Social Politics*, 2(2), pp. 123–6.

Land, H. (1989) 'The construction of dependency', in M. Bulmer, J. Lewis and D. Piachaud (eds) *The Goals of Social Policy*, London: Unwin Hyman.

Land, H. (1990) 'Eleanor Rathbone and the economy of the family', in H. L. Smith (ed.) *British Feminism in the Twentieth Century*, Aldershot: Edward Elgar.

Land, H. (1991) 'Time to care', in M. Maclean and D. Groves (eds) *Women's Issues in Social Policy*, London: Routledge.

Land, H. (1994) 'The demise of the male breadwinner – in practice but not in theory: a challenge for social security systems', in S. Baldwin and J. Falkingham (eds) *Social Security and Social Change: New Challenges to the Beveridge Model*, Hemel Hempstead: Harvester Wheatsheaf.

Land, H. (2002) 'Spheres of care in the UK: separate and unequal', *Critical Social Policy*, 22(1), pp. 13–32.

Land, H. and Rose, H. (1985) 'Compulsory altruism for some or an altruistic society for all?', in P. Bean, J. Ferris and D. Whynes (eds) *In Defence of Welfare*, London: Tavistock.

Landes, J. B. (ed.) (1998) *Feminism, the Public and the Private*, Oxford: Oxford University Press.

Langan, M. and Ostner, I. (1991) 'Gender and welfare', in G. Room, *op. cit.*

Larner, W. (1993) 'Changing contexts: globalization, migration and feminism in New Zealand', in S. Gunew and A. Yeatman, *op. cit.*

Larsen, J. E. and Sørenson, A. M. (1993) 'Lone parents', in S. Carlsen and J. E. Larsen, *op. cit.*

Lasch, C. (1995) *The Revolt of the Elites and the Betrayal of Democracy*, New York: W. W. Norton.

Laurie, J. and Gershuny, J. (2000) 'Couples, work and money', in R. Berthoud and J. Gershuny (eds) *Seven Years in the Lives of British Families*, Bristol: Policy Press.

Layton-Henry, Z. (1991) 'Citizenship and migrant workers in Western Europe', in U. Vogel and M. Moran, *op. cit.*

Le Feuvre, N. (1996) 'Sociological perspectives on the family-employment relationship in France', in L. Hantrais and M. Letablier (eds) *Comparing Families and Family Policies in Europe*, Loughborough: Cross-National Research Group.

Leca, J. (1992) 'Questions on Citizenship', in C. Mouffe, *op. cit.*

Lee, T. and Piachaud, D. (1992) 'The time-consequences of social services', *Time and Society*, 1(1), pp. 65–80.

Lehning, P. B. and Weale, A. (eds) (1997) *Citizenship, Democracy and Justice in the New Europe*, London and New York: Routledge.

Leira, A. (1989) *Models of Motherhood*, Oslo: Institutt for Samfunns Forskning.

Leira, A. (1992) *Welfare States and Working Mothers*, Cambridge: Cambridge University Press.

Leira, A. (1993a) 'Mothers, markets and the state: a Scandinavian "model"?', *Journal of Social Policy*, 22(3), pp. 329–47.

Leira, A. (1993b) 'The "woman-friendly" welfare state?: the case of Norway and Sweden', in J. Lewis, *op. cit.*

Leira, A. (1998) 'Caring as a social right: cash for child care and daddy leave', *Social Politics*, 5(3), pp. 362–78.

Leira, A. (1999) 'Cash-for-child care and daddy leave', in P. Moss and F. Deven, *op. cit.*

Leisink, P. (1997) 'Work and citizenship in Europe', in M. Roche, R. van Berkel, *op. cit.*

Leisink, P. and Coenen, H. (1993) 'Work and citizenship in the New Europe', in H. Coenen and P. Leisink, *op. cit.*

Leitner, S. (2001) 'Sex and gender discrimination within EU pension systems', *Journal of European Social Policy*, 11(2), pp. 99–115.

Leonard, P. (1997) *Postmodern Welfare: Reconstructing an Emancipatory Project*, London: Sage.

Letablier, M. (1995) 'Women's labour market participation in France: the paradox of the nineties', *Journal of Area Studies*, 6, pp. 108–16.

Lewis, G. (1998) 'Citizenship', in G. Hughes (ed.) *Imagining Welfare Futures*, London and New York: Routledge.

Lewis, J. (1980) *The Politics of Motherhood: Child and Maternal Welfare Policies in England 1900–1939*, London: Croom Helm.

Lewis, J. (1991) 'Models of equality for women: the case of state support for children in twentieth-century Britain', in G. Bock and P. Thane, *op. cit.*

Lewis, J. (1992a) 'Gender and the development of welfare regimes', *Journal of European Social Policy*, 2(3), pp. 159–73.

Lewis, J. (1992b) *Women in Britain since 1945*, Oxford: Basil Blackwell.

Lewis, J. (1993) *Women and Social Policies in Europe*, Aldershot: Edward Elgar.

Lewis, J. (1994) 'Gender, the family and women's agency in the building of "welfare states": the British case', *Social History*, 19(1), pp. 37–55.

Lewis, J. (1997) 'Gender and welfare regimes: further thoughts', *Social Politics*, 4(2), pp. 160–77.

Lewis, J. (2000) 'Work and care', in H. Dean, R. Sykes and R. Woods (eds) *Social Policy Review 12*, Newcastle: Social Policy Association.

Lewis, J. (2001) 'The decline of the male breadwinner model: implications for work and care', *Social Politics*, 8(2), pp. 152–69.

Lewis, J. (ed.) (1997) *Lone Mothers in European Welfare Regimes*, London and Philadelphia: Jessica Kingsley.

Lewis, J. (ed.) (1998) *Gender, Social Care and Welfare State Restructuring in Europe*, Aldershot: Ashgate.

Lewis, J. and Åström, G. (1992) 'Equality, difference and state welfare: labour market and family policies in Sweden', *Feminist Studies*, 18(1), pp. 59–87.

Lewis, J. and Davies, C. (1991) 'Protective legislation in Britain, 1870–1990: equality, difference and their implications for women', *Policy and Politics*, 19(1), pp. 13–25.

Lewis, J. and Piachaud, D. (1992) 'Women and poverty in the twentieth century', in C. Glendinning and J. Millar, *op. cit.*

Lingsom, S. (1993) 'Norway', in A. Evers, M. Pijl and C. Ungerson, *op. cit.*

Link, R. J. and Bibus, A. A. (with Lyons, K.) (2000) *When Children Pay: US Welfare Reform and its Implications for UK Policy*, London: CPAG.

Linklater, A. (1998) 'Cosmopolitan citizenship', *Citizenship Studies*, 2(1), pp. 23–41.

Lister, R. (1990a) *The Exclusive Society: Citizenship and the Poor*, London: Child Poverty Action Group.

Lister, R. (1990b) 'Women, economic dependency and citizenship', *Journal of Social Policy*, 19(4), pp. 445–67.

Lister, R. (1992) *Women's Economic Dependency and Social Security*, Manchester: Equal Opportunities Commission.

Lister, R. (1993) 'Welfare rights and the constitution', in A. Barnett *et al.*, *op. cit.*

Lister, R. (1994a) 'Social policy in a divided community: reflections on the Opsahl Report on the future of Northern Ireland', *Irish Journal of Sociology*, 4, pp. 27–50.

Lister, R. (1994b) ' "She has other duties" – women, citizenship and social security', in S. Baldwin and J. Falkingham (eds) *Social Security and Social Change: New Challenges to the Beveridge Model*, Hemel Hempstead: Harvester Wheatsheaf.

Lister, R. (1995a) 'Dilemmas in engendering citizenship', *Economy and Society*, 24(1), pp. 1–40.

Lister, R. (1995b) 'Women in poverty', in K. Funken and P. Cooper (eds) *Old and New Poverty: The Challenge for Reform*, London: Rivers Oram Press.

Lister, R. (1999) ' "Reforming welfare around the work ethic": new gendered and ethical perspectives on work and care', *Policy and Politics*, 27(2), pp. 233–46.

Lister, R. (2000) 'Citizenship and gender', in K. Nash and A. Scott (eds) *The Blackwell Companion to Political Sociology*, Oxford: Blackwell.

Lister, R. (2001) 'Doing good by stealth: The politics of poverty and inequality under New Labour', *New Economy*, 8(2), pp. 65–70.

Lister, R. (2002a) 'A politics of recognition and respect: involving people with experience of poverty in decision making that affects their lives', *Social Policy and Society*, 1(1), pp. 37–46.

Lister, R. (2002b) 'Sexual citizenship', in E. F. Isin and B. S. Turner (eds) *Handbook of Citizenship Studies*, London: Sage.

Lister, R. (2002c) 'The responsible citizen: creating a new British welfare contract', in Kingfisher, C. (ed.) *Western Welfare in Decline: Women's Poverty in the Age of Gobalization*, Philadelphia: University of Pennsylvania Press.

Lister, R., Middleton, S. and Smith, N. (2001) *Young People's Voices: Citizenship Education*, Leicester: Youth Work Press.

Little, A. and Hughes, G. (1999) 'Theorising community and solidarity: the politics of differentiated universalism', mimeo: Rethinking Citizenship conference, Leeds, 29–30 June.

Lloyd, G. (1984) *The Man of Reason: 'Male' and 'Female', in Western Philosophy*, London: Methuen.

Lloyd, G. (1986) 'Selfhood, war and masculinity', in C. Pateman and E. Gross, *op. cit.*

Lloyd, J. (1998) 'The dream of global justice', *New Statesman*, 25 September, pp. 28–9.

Lloyd, M. (1992) 'Does she boil eggs? Towards a feminist model of disability', *Disability, Handicap and Society*, 7(3), pp. 207–21.

Lloyd, M. (2001) 'The politics of disability and feminism: discord or synthesis?', *Sociology*, 35(3), pp. 715–28.

Lødemel, I. and Trickey, H. (eds) (2001) *'An offer you can't refuse'. Workfare in International Perspective*, Bristol: Policy Press.

Loescher, G. and Monahan, L. (eds) (1989) *Refugees and International Relations*, Oxford: Oxford University Press.

Lonsdale, S. (1990) *Women and Disability*, Basingstoke: Macmillan.

Lorde, A. (1984) 'Age, race, class and sex: women redefining difference', reproduced in H. Crowley and S. Himmelweit (1992), *op. cit.*

Lovenduski, J. (1986) *Women and European Politics, Contemporary Feminism and Public Policy*, Brighton: Harvester Press.

Lovenduski, J. (2001) 'Women and politics: minority representation or critical mass?', *Parliamentary Affairs*, 54(4), pp. 743–58.

Lovenduski, J. and Norris, P. (1993) *Gender and Party Politics*, London: Sage.

Lovenduski, J. and Randall, V. (1993) *Contemporary Feminist Politics*, Oxford: Oxford University Press.

Lovett, T., Gillespie, N. and Gunn, D. (1995) *Community Development, Education and Community Relations*, Belfast: Community Research and Development Centre, University of Ulster.

Lowndes, V. (1995) 'Citizenship and urban politics', in D. Judge, G. Stoker and H. Wolman (eds) *Theories of Urban Politics*, London: Sage.

Lowndes, V. (2000) 'Women and social capital: a comment on Hall's "Social capital in Britain"', *British Journal of Political Science*, 30, pp. 533–40.

Luckhaus, L. (1994) 'Individualisation of social security benefits', in C. McCrudden (ed.) *Equality of Treatment between Women and Men in Social Security*, London, Dublin, Edinburgh: Butterworths.

Luckhaus, L. and Dickens, L. (1991) *Social Protection of Atypical Workers in the United Kingdom*, Brussels: Report for the European Commission.

Lustiger-Thaler, H. and Shragge, E. (1993) 'Social movements and social welfare: the political problem of needs', in G. Drover and P. Kerans (eds) *New Approaches to Welfare Theory*, Aldershot: Edward Elgar.

Lutz, H. (1997) 'The limits of European-ness: Immigrant women in Fortress Europe', *Feminist Review*, 57, pp. 93–111.

Lykke, N., Ravn, A. and Siim, B. (1994) 'Images from women in a changing Europe', *Women's Studies International Forum*, 17(2/3), pp. 111–16.

Macaulay, F. (1995) 'Gender relations and the democratization of local politics in the transition to democracy in Brazil and Chile', Mimeo: Political Studies Association Conference, York, April.

MacDonald, R. (ed.) (1997) *Youth, the 'Underclass' and Social Exclusion*, London and New York: Routledge.

MacEwen Scott, A. (ed.) (1994) *Gender Segregation and Social Change*, Oxford: Oxford University Press.

Macey, M. (1995) 'Towards racial justice? A re-evaluation of anti-racism', *Critical Social Policy*, 44/45, pp. 126–46.

Mackay, F. (2001) *Love and Politics: Women Politicians and the Ethics of Care*, London and New York: Continuum.

MacKian, S. (1998) 'The citizen's new clothes: care in a Welsh community', *Critical Social Policy*, 18(1), pp. 27–50.

Mackie, V. (2001) 'The language of globalization, transnationality and feminism', *International Feminist Journal of Politics*, 3(2), pp. 180–206.

MacKinnon, C. (1989) *Towards a Feminist Theory of the State*, Cambridge, MA: Harvard University Press.

Macran, S., Joshi, H. and Dex, S. (1996) 'Employment after childbearing: a survival analysis', *Work, Employment and Society*, 10(2), pp. 273–96.

Mactaggart, F. (2000) *Women in Parliament: Their Contribution to Labour's First 1000 Days*, London: Fabian Society.

Mahon, R. (1997) 'Child care in Canada and Sweden: policy and politics', *Social Politics*, 4(3), pp. 382–418.

Mahon, R. (2001) 'Theorizing welfare regimes: toward a dialogue?', *Social Politics*, 8(1), pp 24–35.

Maier, F. (1991) 'Part-time work, social security protection and labour law: an international comparison', *Policy and Politics*, 19(1), pp. 1–11.

Makkai, T. (1994) 'Social policy and gender in Eastern Europe', in S. Sainsbury, *op. cit.*

Mama, A. (1989a) 'Violence against black women: gender, race and state responses', *Feminist Review*, 32, pp. 30–48.

Mama, A. (1989b) *The Hidden Struggle – Statutory and Voluntary Sector Responses to Violence against Black Women in the Home*, London: Race and Housing Research Unit/Runnymede Trust.

Mama, A. (1992) 'Black women and the British state', in P. Braham, A. Rattansi and R. Skellington (eds) *Racism and Anti-racism*, London: Sage.

Mani, L. (1992) 'Multiple mediations: feminist scholarship in the age of multinational reception', in H. Crowley and S. Himmelweit, *op. cit.*

Mann, M. (1987) 'Ruling class strategies and citizenship', *Sociology*, 21(3), pp. 339–54.

Mann, P. S. (1997) 'Musing as a feminist in a postfeminist era', in J. Dean, *op. cit.*

Manning, N. (2001) 'Copenhagen + 5: what should be done about the transition in Eastern Europe?', in R. Sykes, C. Bochel and N. Ellison (eds) *Social Policy Review 13*, Bristol: Policy Press.

Marcos, S. (1999) 'Twenty-five years of Mexican feminisms', *Women's Studies International Forum*, 22(4), pp. 431–33.

Marfleet, P. (2001) 'Europe's civilising mission', in J. Fink *et al.*, *op. cit.*

Marks, D. (2001) 'Disability and cultural citizenship: exclusion, "integration" and resistance', in Stevenson, *op. cit.*

Marquand, D. (1991) 'Civic republicans and liberal individualists: the case of Britain', *Archive Européenne de Sociologie*, XXXII, pp. 329–44.

Marques-Pereira, B. (1995) 'Citoyenneté sociale et liberté reproductive: l'approche de T.H. Marshall est-elle pertinente?' Mimeo: European Sociological Association Conference, Budapest, August/September.

Marsh, A., Ford, R. and Finlayson, L. (1997) *Lone Parents, Work and Benefits*, London: The Stationery Office.

Marsh, C. (1991) *Hours of Work of Women and Men in Britain*, London: Equal Opportunities Commission/HMSO.

Marshall, T. H. (1950) *Citizenship and Social Class*, Cambridge: Cambridge University Press.

Martin, J. and Roberts, C. (1984) *Women and Employment: A Lifetime Perspective*, London: Department of Employment/OPCS/HMSO.

Martin, P. Y. and Collinson, D. L. (1999) 'Gender and sexuality in organizations', in M. M. Ferree, J. Lorber, and B. B. Hess (eds) *Revisioning Gender*, Thousand Oaks: Sage.

Maruani, M. (1992) 'The position of women in the labour market', *Women of Europe*, no. 36, Brussels: Commission of the European Communities.

Massey, D. (1994) *Space, Place and Gender*, Cambridge: Polity Press.

Massey, D. (1995) 'Making spaces: or geography is political too', *Soundings*, 1, pp. 193–208.

Matynia, E. (1995) 'Finding a voice: women in postcommunist Central Europe', in A. Basu, *op. cit.*

Maynard, M. (1993) 'Violence towards women', in D. Richardson and V. Robinson (eds) *Introducing Women's Studies*, Basingstoke: Macmillan.

Maynard, M. (1994) '"Race", gender and the concept of "difference" in feminist thought', in H. Afshar and M. Maynard, *op. cit.*

Mayo, M. (1994) *Communities and Caring*, New York: St Martin's Press.

Mayo, M. (2000) *Cultures, Communities, Identities: Cultural Strategies for Participation and Empowerment*, Basingstoke: Palgrave.

Mayo, M. and Weir, A. (1993) 'The future for feminist social policy', in R. Page and J. Baldock (eds) *Social Policy Review 5*, Canterbury: Social Policy Association.

McClure, K. (1992) 'On the subject of rights: pluralism, plurality and political identity', in C. Mouffe, *op. cit.*

McCoy, G. (2000) 'Women, community and politics in Northern Ireland', in C. Roulston and C. Davies, *op. cit.*

McCulloch, A. (1997) '"You've fucked up the estate and now you're carrying a briefcase!"', in P. Hoggett (ed.) *Contested Communities*, Bristol: Policy Press.

McEwan, C. (2000) 'Engendering citizenship: gendered spaces of democracy in South Africa', *Political Geography*, 19, pp. 627–51.

McGlone, F. (1995) 'State support boosts motherhood in Hungary', *Family Policy Bulletin*, July, p. 15.

McGrew, A. G. (1992) 'A global society?', in S. Hall, D. Held and A. McGrew (eds) *Modernity and its Futures*, Cambridge: Polity Press.

McIntosh, M. (1981) 'Feminism and social policy', *Critical Social Policy*, 1(1), pp. 32–42.

McKay, A. and VanEvery, J. (2000) 'Gender, family, and income maintenance: a feminist case for citizens basic income', *Social Politics*, 7(2), pp. 266–84.

McKie, L, Bowlby, S. and Gregory, S. (2001) 'Gender, caring and employment in Britain', *Journal of Social Policy*, 30(2), pp. 233–58.

McKinnon, C. (2000) 'Civil citizens', in C. McKinnon and I. Hampsher-Monk, *op. cit.*

McKinnon, C. and Hampsher-Monk, I. (eds) (2000) *The Demands of Citizenship*, London and New York: Continuum.

McLaughlin, E. (1991) *Social Security and Community Care: The Case of the Invalid Care Allowance*, London: Department of Social Security/HMSO.

McLaughlin, E. and Glendinning, C. (1994) 'Paying for Care in Europe: is there a feminist approach?', in L. Hantrais and S. Mangen, *op. cit.*

McLaughlin, J. (1997) 'An ethic of care: a valuable political tool?' *Politics*, 17(1), pp. 17–23.

McMillan, J. (2001) 'Will Scottish devolution make a difference?', in B. Crick (ed.) *Citizens: Towards a Citizenship Culture*, Oxford: Blackwell.

McRae, S. (1996) *Women's Employment during Family Formation*, London: Policy Studies Institute.

McRae, S. (1998) 'Part-time employment in a European perspective', in E. Drew, R. Emerek and E. Mahon (eds) *Women, Work and the Family in Europe*, London: Routledge.

Mead, L. (1986) *Beyond Entitlement: the Social Obligations of Citizenship*, New York: The Free Press.

Meehan, E. (1993a) *Citizenship and the European Community*, London: Sage.

Meehan, E. (1993b) 'Women's rights in citizens' Europe', in A. Barnett *et al., op. cit.*

Meehan, E. (1993c) 'Women's rights in the European Community', in J. Lewis, *op. cit.*

Meehan, E. (1996) 'Democracy unbound', in R. Wilson (ed.) *Reconstituting Politics*, Belfast: Democratic Dialogue.

Meehan, E. and Sevenhuijsen, S. (1991) *Equality, Politics and Gender*, London: Sage.

Meekosha, H. (1998) 'Body battles: bodies, gender and disability', in T. Shakespeare (ed.) *The Disability Reader*, London and New York: Continuum.

Meekosha, H. and Dowse, L. (1997) 'Enabling citizenship: gender, disability and citizenship in Australia', *Feminist Review*, 57, pp. 49–72.

Melzer, H. (1994) *Day Care Services for Children*, London: OPCS/HMSO.

Merry, S. E. (2001) 'Changing rights, changing culture', in J. K. Cowan *et al., op. cit.*

Mertens, N., Schippers, J. and Siegers, J. (1995) 'Career interruptions and women's life-time earnings', *European Journal of Women's Studies*, 2(4), pp. 469–91.

Metcalf, H. (ed.) (1997) *Half Our Future: Women, Skill Development and Training*, London: Policy Studies Institute.

Meucci, S. (1992) 'The moral context of welfare mothers: a study of US welfare reform in the 1980s', *Critical Social Policy*, 34, pp. 52–74.

Meuller, C. M. (ed.) (1988) *The Politics of the Gender Gap*, California, London and New Delhi: Sage.

Meyer, T. (1994) 'The German and British welfare states as employers: patriarchal or emancipatory?', in D. Sainsbury, *op. cit.*

Meyers, D. T. and Kittay, E. F. (eds) (1987) *Women and Moral Theory*, New Jersey: Rowman & Littlefield.

Meyers, M. K., Gornick, J. C. and Ross, K. E. (1999) 'Public childcare, parental leave, and employment', in D. Sainsbury, *op. cit.*

Michel, S., Mahon R. (eds) (2002) *Child Care Policy at the Crossroads: Gender and Welfare State Restructuring*, New York: Routledge.

Miethe, I. (1999) 'From "mother of the revolution" to "fathers of unification": concepts of politics among women activists following German unification', *Social Politics*, 6(1), pp. 1–22.

Miliband, D. (ed.) (1994) *Reinventing the Left*, Cambridge: Polity Press.

Millar, J. (1989) 'Social security, equality and women in the UK', *Policy and Politics*, 17(4), pp. 311–19.

Millar, J. (1996) 'Women, poverty and social security', in C. Hallett, *op. cit.*

Millar, J. (1998) 'Making work pay: integration of family payments in Australia', in J. Millar, D. Hole, *Integrated Family Benefits in Australia and Options for the UK Tax Return System*, York: Joseph Rowntree Foundation.

Millar, J. and Ridge, T. (2001) *Families, Poverty, Work and Care*, Leeds: Department for Work and Pensions/Corporate Document Services.

Millar, J. and Rowlingson, K. (eds) (2001) *Lone Parents, Employment and Social Policy*, Bristol: Policy Press.

Miller, A. G. (1988) 'Basic incomes and women', in A. G. Miller (ed.) *Proceedings of the First International Conference on Basic Income*, Antwerp: Basic Income European Network.

Miller, D. (1987) 'Foreword' to D. Harris, *op. cit.*

Miller, D. (1999) 'Bounded citizenship', in K. Hutchings and R. Dannreuther, *op. cit.*

Miller, D. (2000) *Citizenship and National Identity*, Cambridge: Polity Press.

Miller, M. (1989) 'Political participation and representation of non-citizens', in W. G. Brubaker, *op. cit.*

Miller, S. and Peroni, F. (1992) 'Social politics and the Citizen's Charter', in N. Manning and R. Page (eds) *Social Policy Review 4*, Canterbury: Social Policy Association.

Mills, C. Wright (1959/1970) *The Sociological Imagination*, Harmondsworth: Penguin.

Mink, G. (1990) 'The lady and the tramp: gender, race and the origins of the American welfare state', in L. Gordon, *op. cit.*

Mink, G. (1998) 'Feminists, welfare reform, and welfare justice', *Social Justice*, 25(1), pp. 146–57.

Minson, J. (1993) *Questions of Conduct: Sexual Harassment, Citizenship, Government*, Basingstoke: Macmillan.

Mirza, H. S. (ed.) (1997) *Black British Feminism: A Reader*, London and New York: Routledge.

Mirza, H. S. and Reay, D. (2000a) 'Redefining citizenship: Black women educators and "the third space"', in M. Arnot and J. Dillabough, *op. cit.*

Mirza, H. S. and Reay, D. (2000b) 'Spaces and places of black educational desire: rethinking black supplementary schools as a new social movement', *Sociology*, 34(3), pp. 521–44.

Mishra, R. (1999) *Globalization and the Welfare State*, Cheltenham and Northampton, MA: Edward Elgar.

Misra, J. and Akins, F. (1998) 'The welfare state and women: structure, agency and diversity', *Social Politics*, 5(3), pp. 259–85.

Mitchell, H. (1977) *The Hard Way Up*, London: Virago.

Mitchell, M. and Russell, D. (1994) 'Race, citizenship and "Fortress Europe"', in P. Brown and R. Crompton (eds) *A New Europe? Economic Restructuring and Social Exclusion*, London: UCL Press.

Mitter, S. (1986) *Common Fate, Common Bond: Women in the Global Economy*, London: Pluto Press.

Modood, T. (1994) 'Ethnic difference and racial equality: new challenges for the Left', in D. Miliband, *op. cit.*

Modood, T. (2000) 'Anti-essentialism, multiculturalism, and the "recognition" of religious groups', in W. Kymlicka and W. Norman (eds), *Citizenship in Diverse Societies*, Oxford: Oxford University Press.

Moghadam, V. M. (1999a) 'Gender and the global economy', in M. M. Ferree, J. Lorber and B. B. Hess (eds) *Revisioning Gender*, Thousand Oaks: Sage.

Moghadam, V. M. (1999b) 'Gender and globalization: female labor and women's mobilization', *Journal of World-Systems Research* 5(2), pp. 301–14.

Mohanty, C. (1988) 'Under western eyes: feminist scholarship and colonial discourses,' *Feminist Review*, 30, pp. 61–88.

Mohanty, C. (1992) 'Feminist encounters: locating the politics of experience', in M. Barrett and A. Phillips, *op. cit.*

Mohanty, C. T. (1997) 'Women workers and capitalist scripts: ideologies of domination, common interests, and the politics of solidarity', in M. J. Alexander and C. T. Mohanty, *op. cit.*

Molloy, D. and Snape, D. (1999) *Financial Arrangements of Couples on Benefit: A Review of the Literature*, Leeds: Corporate Document Services

Molyneux, M. (1984) 'Mobilisation without emancipation?', *Critical Social Policy*, 10, pp. 59–75.

Molyneux, M. (2000) 'Comparative perspectives on gender and citizenship: Latin America and the former socialist states', in J. Cook, J. Roberts and G. Waylen (eds) *Towards a Gendered Political Economy*, Basingstoke: Macmillan.

Monk, J. and Katz, C. (1993) 'When in the world are women?', in C. Katz and J. Monk (eds), *op. cit.*

Monks, J. (1999) '"It works both ways": belonging and social participation among women with disabilities', in N. Yuval-Davis and P. Werbner, *op. cit.*

Moore, R. (1993) 'Citizenship and the underclass', in H. Coenen and P. Leinsink, *op. cit.*

Morokvasic, M. (1984) 'Birds of passage are also women', *International Migration Review*, xviii(4), pp. 886–907.

Morokvasic, M. (1991) 'Fortress Europe and migrant women', *Feminist Review*, 39, pp. 69–84.

Morokvasic, M. (1993) 'In and out of the labour market: immigration and minority women in Europe', *New Community*, 19(3), pp. 459–83.

Morris, J. (1991) *Pride against Prejudice*, London: Women's Press.

Morris, J. (1993a) *Independent Lives*, Basingstoke: Macmillan.

Morris, J. (1993b) 'Feminism and disability', *Feminist Review*, 43, pp. 57–70.

Morris, J. (ed.) (1996) *Encounters with Strangers: Feminism and Disability*, London: Women's Press.

Morris, L. (1990) *The Workings of the Household*, Cambridge: Polity Press.

Morris, L. (1994) *Dangerous Classes*, London: Routledge.

Morris, L. (1997) 'A cluster of contradictions: the politics of migration in the European Union, *Sociology*, 31(2), pp. 241–59.

Morris, L. (1998) 'Governing at a distance: the elaboration of controls in British immigration', *International Migration Review*, 32, pp. 949–73.

Morris, L. (2000) 'Rights and controls in the management of migration: the case of Germany', *Sociological Review*, 48(2), pp. 224–40.

Morris, L. and Lyon, E. S. (eds) (1996) *Gender Relations in Public and Private: New Research Perspectives*, Basingstoke: Macmillan.

Moss, P. (1988) *Childcare and Equality of Opportunity*, London: European Commission.

Moss, P. (1996) 'Child care', in B. Arve-Parès (ed.) *Reconciling Work and Family Life – A Challenge for Europe?*, Stockholm: Ministry of Health and Social Affairs.

Moss, P. and Deven, F. (eds) (1999) *Parental Leave: Progress or Pitfall?*, Brussels: NIDI/CBGS Publications.

Mosse, J. C. (1993) *Half the World, Half a Chance: An Introduction to Gender and Development*, Oxford: Oxfam.

Mouffe, C. (ed.) (1992a) *Dimensions of Radical Democracy*, London: Verso.

Mouffe, C. (1992b) 'Feminism, citizenship and radical democratic politics', in J. Butler and J. W. Scott (eds) *Feminists Theorize the Political*, New York and London: Routledge.

Mouffe, C. (1993a) *The Return of the Political*, London: Verso.

Mouffe, C. (1993b) 'Liberal socialism and pluralism: which citizenship?', in J. Squires, *op. cit.*

Muetzelfeldt, M. and Smith, G. (2002) 'Civil society and global governance: the possibilities for global citizenship', *Citizenship Studies* 6(1), pp. 55–75.

Munn-Giddings, C. (1998) 'Self-help/mutual aid, gender and citizenship', in V. Ferreira *et al.*, *op. cit.*

Murdock, G. and Golding, P. (1989) 'Information poverty and political inequality: citizenship in the age of privatised communications', *Journal of Communication*, 39(3), pp. 180–95.

Murrell, A. J. (1996) 'Sexual harassment and women of color', in M. S. Stockdale (ed.) *Sexual Harassment in the Workplace: Perspectives, Frontiers and Responsive Strategies*, Thousand Oaks: Sage.

Mutari, E. and Figart, D. M. (2001) 'Europe at a crossroads: harmonization, liberalization, and the gender of work time', *Social Politics*, 8(1), pp. 36–64.

Naples, N. A. (1997) 'The "new consensus" on the gendered "social contract": the 1987–1988 US Congressional hearings', *Signs*, 22(4), pp. 907–45.

Naples, N. A. (1998a) *Grassroots Warriors. Activist Mothering, Community Work, and the War on Poverty*, New York and London: Routledge.

Naples, N. A. (1998b) 'Toward a multiracial feminist social-democratic praxis: lessons from grassroots warriors in the U.S. War on Poverty', *Social Politics*, 5(3), pp. 286–313.

Naples, N. A. (ed.) (1998c) *Community Activism and Feminist Politics. Organizing Across Race, Class and Gender*, New York and London: Routledge.

Narayan, U. (1997a) 'Towards a feminist vision of citizenship: rethinking the implications of dignity, political participation, and nationality', in M. L. Shanley and U. Narayan (eds) *Reconstructing Political Theory. Feminist Perspectives*, Cambridge: Polity Press.

Narayan, U. (1997b) '"Male-order" brides: immigrant women, domestic violence and immigration law', in P.DiQuinzio and I. M. Young (eds) *Feminist Ethics and Social Policy*, Bloomington and Indianapolis: Indiana University Press.

Nash, K. (1998) 'Beyond liberalism? Feminist theories of democracy', in V. Randall and G. Waylen (eds) *Gender, Politics and the State*, London and New York: Routledge.

Nasir, S. (1996) ' "Race", gender and social policy', in C. Hallett, *op. cit.*

National Council for One Parent Families (2001) *Lone Parents and Employment. The Facts*, London: NCOPF.

Naughton, J. (2001) 'Contested space: the internet and global civil society', in H. Anheier *et al.*, *op. cit.*

Neff, S. C. (1999) 'International law and the critique of cosmopolitan citizenship', in K. Hutchings and R. Dannreuther, *op. cit.*

Nelson, B. J. (1984) 'Women's poverty and women's citizenship: some political consequences of economic marginality', *Signs*, 10(2), pp. 209–31.

Nelson, B. J. (1990) 'The origins of the two-channel welfare state: workmen's compensation and mothers' aid', in L. Gordon, *op. cit.*

Newby, H. (1996) 'Citizenship in a green world: global commons and human stewardship', in M. Bulmer and A. M. Rees, *op. cit.*

Ng, R. (1993) 'Sexism, racism and Canadian nationalism', in S. Gunew and A. Yeatman, *op. cit.*

Nicholson, L. J. (1984) 'Feminist theory: the private and the public', in C. Gould, *op. cit.*

Nielson, K. (1995) 'Reconceptualizing civil society for now: some Gramscian turnings', in M. Waltzer (ed.) *Toward a Global Civil Society*, Providence: Berghahn Books.

NIWC (undated) *Common Cause: The Story of the Northern Ireland Women's Coalition*, Belfast: *Northern Ireland Women's Coalition.*

Nkiwane, T. C. (2000) 'Gender, citizenship and constitutionalism in Zimbabwe: the fight against Amendment 14', *Citizenship Studies*, 4(3), pp. 325–38.

Noddings, N. (1984) *Caring: A Feminist Approach to Ethics and Moral Education*, Berkeley and Los Angeles: University of California Press.

Norris, P. (1987) *Politics and Sexual Equality: The Comparative Position of Women in Western Democracies*, London: Wheatsheaf Books.

Norris, P. (1991) 'Gender difference in political participation in Britain: traditional, radical and revisionist models', *Government and Opposition*, 26(1), pp. 56–74.

Norris, P. (1996) 'Women politicians: transforming Westminster?', in J. Lovenduski and P. Norris (eds) *Women in Politics*, Oxford: Oxford University Press.

Norris, P. (2000) 'Women's representation and electoral systems', in R. Rose (ed.) *The International Encyclopaedia of Elections*, Washington, DC: CQ Press.

Norris, P. (2001) 'Women's Power at the Ballot Box', in *Voter Turnout from 1945 to 2000: A Global Report on Political Participation*, Stockholm: International IDEA.

Norris, P. (2002) 'The gender gap: theoretical frameworks and new approaches', in S. Carroll (ed.) *Women and American Politics: New Questions, New Directions*, New York: Oxford University Press.

Norris, P. and Lovenduski, J. (1995) *Political Recruitment: Gender, Race and Class in the British Parliament*, Cambridge: Cambridge University Press.

Northern Ireland Women and Citizenship Research Group (1995) *Women and Citizenship: Power, Participation and Choice*, Belfast: WCRG.

Novak, M., Cogan, J., Bernstein, B. *et al.* (1987) *A Community of Self-Reliance: the New Consensus on Family and Welfare*, Milwaukee: American Enterprise Institute for Public Policy Research.

Nussbaum, M. C. (1999) *Sex and Social Justice*, New York and Oxford: Oxford University Press.

Nussbaum, M. C. (2000) *Women and Human Development: The Capabilities Approach*, Cambridge: Cambridge University Press.

Nussbaum, M. C. and Glover, J. (eds) (1995) *Women, Culture and Development: A Study of Human Capabilities*, Oxford: Oxford University Press.

Nyberg, A. (2002) 'Gender, (de)commodification, economic (in)dependence and autonomous households: the case of Sweden', *Critical Social Policy*, 22(1), pp. 72–95.

O'Connor, J. S., Orloff, A. S. and Shaver, S. (1999) *States, Markets, Families. Gender, Liberalism and Social Policy in Australia, Canada, Great Britain and the United States*, Cambridge: Cambridge University Press.

O'Connor, J. S. (1993) 'Gender, class and citizenship in the comparative analysis of welfare state regimes: theoretical and methodological issues', *British Journal of Sociology*, 44(3), pp. 501–18.

O'Connor, J. S. (1996) 'From women in the welfare state to gendering welfare state regimes,' *Current Sociology* (Trend report), 44(2), pp. 1–130.

O'Donovan, K. (1985) *Sexual Divisions in Law*, London: Weidenfeld & Nicolson.

O'Leary, S. (1996) *European Union Citizenship*, London: Institute for Public Policy Research.

O'Reilly, J. and Fagan, C. (eds) (1998) *Part-time Prospects: An International Comparison of Part-time Work in Europe, North America and the Pacific Rim*, London: Routledge.

Oakley, A. and Rigby, A. S. (1998) 'Are men good for the welfare of women and children?', in J. Popay, J. Hearn and J. Edwards (eds) *Men, Gender Divisions and Welfare*, London and New York: Routledge.

OECD (1994) *Women and Structural Change*, Paris: OECD.

OECD (1999) *Employment Outlook. How Do Part-time Jobs Compare with Full-Time Jobs?*, Paris: OECD.

Offe, C. (1993) 'A non-productivist design for social policies', in H. Coenen and P. Leisink, *op. cit.*

Offen, K. (1988) 'Defining feminism: a comparative historical approach', *Signs*, 14(1), pp. 119–57.

Office for National Statistics (2001) *Social Trends*, 31, London: Stationery Office.

Okin, S. M. (1989) *Justice, Gender and the Family*, New York: Basic Books.

Okin, S. M. (1991) 'Gender, the public and the private', in D. Held (ed.) *Political Theory Today*, Cambridge: Polity Press.

Okin, S. M. (1992) 'Women, equality and citizenship', *Queen's Quarterly*, 99(1), pp. 56–71.

Okin, S. M. (1994) 'Political liberalism, justice and gender, *Ethics*, 105, pp. 23–43.

Okin, S. M. (1998) 'Gender, the public, and the private', in A. Phillips (ed.) *Feminism and Politics*, Oxford: Oxford University Press.

Oláh, L. S. '"Sweden, the middle way": a feminist approach', *European Journal of Women's Studies*, 5(1), pp. 47–67.

Oldfield, A. (1990) *Citizenship and Community, Civic Republicanism and the Modern World*, London: Routledge.

Oliver, D. and Heater, D. (1994) *The Foundations of Citizenship*, Hemel Hempstead: Harvester Wheatsheaf.

Oliver, M. (1990) *The Politics of Disablement*, Basingstoke: Macmillan.

Oliver, M. (1993) *Disability, Citizenship and Empowerment*, Milton Keynes: The Open University.

Oliver, M. (1996) *Understanding Disability: From Theory to Practice*, Basingstoke: Macmillan.

Oliver, M. and Barnes, C. (1991) 'Discrimination, disability and welfare: from needs to rights', in I. Bynoe *et al.*, *op. cit.*

Ong, A. (1996) 'Cultural citizenship as subject-making: immigrants negotiate racial and cultural boundaries in the United States', *Current Anthropology*, 37(5), pp. 737–62.

Ong, A. (1999) 'Muslim feminism: citizenship in the shelter of corporate Islam', *Citizenship Studies*, 3(3), pp. 355–71.

Oppenheim, C. (2001) 'Enabling participation? New Labour's welfare-to-work policies', in S. White (ed.) *New Labour. The Progressive Future?*, Basingstoke: Palgrave.

Orloff, A. S. (1993) 'Gender and the social rights of citizenship: the comparative analysis of gender relations and welfare states', *American Sociological Review*, 58 (June), pp. 303–28.

Orloff, A. S. (1996) 'Gender and the welfare state', Discussion Paper no. 1082–96, Wisconsin: Institute for Research on Poverty.

Orloff, A. S. (1997) 'Comment on Jane Lewis's "Gender and welfare regimes: further thoughts"', *Social Politics*, 4(2), pp. 188–202.

Orloff, A. S. (2002) 'Explaining US welfare reform: power, gender, race and the US policy legacy', *Critical Social Policy*, 22(1), pp. 96–118.

Osler, A. (2000) 'The Crick Report: difference, equality and racial justice', *The Curriculum Journal* 11(1), pp. 25–37.

Osler, A. and Starkey, H. (2001) 'Citizenship education and national identities in France and England: inclusive or exclusive?', *Oxford Review of Education*, 27(2), pp. 287–305.

Ostner, I. (1993) 'Slow motion: women, work and the family in Germany', in J. Lewis, *op. cit.*

Ostner, I. (2001) 'What are children for, why care, and who should care?', Mimeo: Academy Colloquium, Solidarity between the sexes and generations: transformations in Europe, Amsterdam, 28–29 June.

Oswin, N. (2001) 'Rights spaces: an exploration of feminist approaches to refugee law', *International Feminist Journal of Politics*, 3(3), pp. 347–64.

Pahl, J. (1989) *Money and Marriage*, London: Macmillan.

Pahl, R. (1990) 'Prophets, ethnographers and social glue: civil society and social order', Mimeo: ESRC/CNRS Workshop on Citizenship, Social Order and Civilising Processes, Cumberland Lodge, September.

Pakulski, J. (1997) 'Cultural citizenship', *Citizenship Studies*, 1(1), pp.73–86.

Palmer, A. (1995) 'Lesbian and gay rights campaigning: a report from the coalface', in A. R. Wilson, *op. cit.*

Pardo, M. (1995) 'Doing it for the kids: Mexican American community activists, border feminists?', in M. M. Ferree and P. Y. Martin, *op. cit.*

Parekh, B. (1991) 'British citizenship and cultural difference', in G. Andrews, *op. cit.*

Parekh, B. (1994) 'Minority rights, majority values', in D. Miliband, *op. cit.*

Parekh, B. (1998) 'Equality in a multicultural society', *Citizenship Studies*, 2(3), pp. 397–411.

Parekh, B. (2000) *Rethinking Multiculturalism*, Basingstoke: Macmillan.

Parker, G. and Lawton, D. (1994) *Different Types of Care, Different Types of Carer*, London: Social Policy Research Unit/HMSO.

Parker, H. (1991) *Basic Income and the Labour Market*, London: Basic Income Research Group.

Parker, H. (1993) *Citizen's Income and Women*, London: Citizen's Income.

Parker, H. and Parker, S. (1986) 'Father–daughter sexual abuse: an emerging perspective', *American Journal of Orthopsychiatry*, 56(4), pp. 531–49.

Parker, J. (1998) *Citizenship, Work and Welfare*: Basingstoke: Macmillan.

Parmar, P. (1982) 'Gender, race and class: Asian women in resistance', in Centre for Contemporary Cultural Studies, *The Empire Strikes Back*, London: Hutchinson.

Parmar, P. (1989) 'Other Kinds of Dreams', *Feminist Review*, 31, pp. 55–65.

Parry, G. (1991) 'Conclusion: paths to citizenship', in U. Vogel and M. Moran, *op. cit.*

Parry, G., Moyser, G. and Day, N. (1992) *Political Participation and Democracy in Britain*, Cambridge: Cambridge University Press.

Parvikko, T. (1991) 'Conceptions of gender equality: similarity and difference', in E. Meehan and S. Sevenhuijsen, *op. cit.*

Pascall, G. (1993) 'Citizenship – a feminist analysis', in G. Drover and P. Kerans (eds) *New Approaches to Welfare Theory*, Aldershot: Edward Elgar.

Pascall, G. (1997) *Social Policy: A New Feminist Analysis*, London: Routledge.

Pascall, G. and Lewis, J. (2001) 'Care work beyond Beveridge', *Benefits*, 32, pp. 1–6.

Pascall, G. and Manning, N. (2000) 'Gender and social policy in Central and Eastern Europe and the former Soviet Union', *Journal of European Social Policy*, 10(3), pp. 240–66.

Patel, P. (1990) 'Southall boys', in *Southall Black Sisters 1979–1989*, London: Southall Black Sisters.

Patel, P. (1992) 'Citizenship: whose rights', in A. Ward *et al.*, *op. cit.*

Patel, P. (1997) 'Third wave feminism and black women's activism', in H. S. Mirza, *op. cit.*

Patel, P. (1999) 'Difficult alliances: treading the minefield of identity and solidarity politics', *Soundings*, 12, pp. 115–26.

Pateman, C. (1988) *The Sexual Contract*, Cambridge: Polity Press.

Pateman, C. (1989) *The Disorder of Women*, Cambridge: Polity Press.

Pateman, C. (1992) 'Equality, difference, subordination: the politics of motherhood and women's citizenship', in G. Bock and S. James, *op. cit.*

Pateman, C. and Gross, E. (eds) (1986) *Feminist Challenges: Social and Political Theory*, Sydney, London and Boston: Allen & Unwin.

Pateman, C. and Shanley, M. L. (1991) 'Introduction', in M. L. Shanley and C. Pateman, *op. cit.*

Patten, A. (2000) 'Equality of recognition and the liberal theory of citizenship', in C. McKinnon and I. Hampsher-Monk, *op. cit.*

Paul, R. (1991) 'Black and Third World peoples' citizenship', *Critical Social Policy*, 32, pp. 52–64.

Payne, J. (1991) *Women, Training and the Skills Shortage: The Case for Public Investment*, London: Policy Studies Institute.

Payne, S. (1991) *Women, Health and Poverty: An Introduction*, Hemel Hempstead: Harvester Wheatsheaf.

Pearce, D. (1990) 'Welfare is not for women: why the war on poverty cannot conquer the feminization of poverty', in L. Gordon, *op. cit.*

Pearce, N. and Hallgarten, J. (eds) (2000) *Tomorrow's Citizens: Critical Debates in Citizenship and Education*, London: Institute for Public Policy Research.

Peck, J. (1998a) 'Workfare in the sun: politics, representation, and method in US welfare-to-work strategies', *Political Geography*, 17(5), pp. 535–66.

Peck, J. (1998b) 'Workfare: a political etymology', *Environment and Planning D: Society and Space*, 16, pp. 133–61.

Pederson, L., Weise, H., Jacobs, S. and White, M. (2000) 'Lone mothers' poverty and employment', in D. Gallie and S. Paugam (eds) *Welfare Regimes and the Experience of Unemployment in Europe*, Oxford: Oxford University Press.

Pederson, S. (1989) 'The failure of feminism in the making of the British welfare state,' *Radical History Review*, 43, pp. 86–110.

Pederson, S. (1990) 'Gender, welfare and citizenship in Britain during the Great War', *American Historical Review*, 95(4), pp. 983–1006.

Peng, I. (2001) 'Women in the middle: welfare state expansion and devolution in Japan', *Social Politics*, 8(2), pp. 191–6.

Percy-Smith, J. and Sanderson, I. (1992) *Understanding Local Needs*, London: Institute of Public Policy Research.

Perez-Bustillo, C. (2000) 'The indigenous question in Latin America: from social policy to social revolution', in H. Dean, R. Sykes and R. Woods (eds) *Social Policy Review 12*, Newcastle: Social Policy Association.

Peruzzotti, E. (2002) 'Towards a new politics: citizenship and rights in contemporary Argentina', *Citizenship Studies* 6(1), pp. 77–93.

Peters, J. and Wolper, A. (eds) (1995) *Women's Rights, Human Rights*, London: Routledge.

Peterson, V. S. (1996) 'The politics of identification in the context of globalization', *Women's Studies International Forum*, 19(1/2), pp. 5–15.

Petersson, O. (1989) *Medborgerskab och makt* (Citizenship and power), Stockholm: Carlssons.

Petrova, D. (1994) 'What can women do to change the totalitarian cultural context', *Women's Studies International Forum*, 17(2/3), pp. 267–71.

Pettman, J. J. (1996) *Worlding Women: A Feminist International Politics*, London and New York : Routledge.

Pettman, J. J. (1999) 'Globalisation and the gendered politics of citizenship', in N. Yuval-Davis and P. Werbner, *op. cit.*

Pfau-Effinger, B. (1998) 'Gender cultures and the gender arrangement: a theoretical framework for cross-national gender research', *Innovation*, 11(2), pp. 147–66.

Pfau-Effinger, B. (2002) 'Changing welfare states and labour markets in the context of European gender arrangements', in J. G. Andersen and P. H. Jensen (eds) *Changing Labour Markets, Welfare Policies and Citizenship*, Bristol: Policy Press.

Phelan, S. (1995) 'The space of justice: lesbians and democratic politics', in A. R. Wilson, *op. cit.*

Phillips, A. (1991) *Engendering Democracy*, Cambridge: Polity Press.

Phillips, A. (1993) *Democracy and Difference*, Cambridge: Polity Press.

Phillips, A. (1994) 'Dealing with difference: a politics of ideas or a politics of presence?', *Constellations*, 1(1), pp. 74–91.

Phillips, A. (1995) *The Politics of Presence*, Oxford: Clarendon Press.

Phillips, A. (1997) 'From inequality to difference: a severe case of displacement?', *New Left Review*, 224, pp. 143–53.

Phillips, A. (1999) *Which Equalities Matter?*, Cambridge: Polity Press.

Phillips, A. (2000) 'Second class citizenship', in N. Pearce and J. Hallgarten, *op. cit.*

Phillips, A. (ed.) (1987) *Feminism and Equality*, Oxford: Basil Blackwell.

Phillips, A. (ed.) (1998) *Feminism and Politics*, Oxford: Oxford University Press.

Phillips, J. (1996) *Working and Caring: Developments at the Workplace for Family Carers of Disabled and Older People*, Dublin: European Foundation for the Improvement of Living and Working Conditions.

Phillips, J. (ed.) (1995) *Working Carers*, Aldershot: Avebury.

Phizacklea, A. (1994) 'A single or segregated market? Gendered and racialized divisions', in H. Afshar and M. Maynard, *op. cit.*

Phizacklea, A. and Wolkowitz, C. (1995) *Homeworking Women: Gender, Ethnicity and Class at Work*, London: Sage.

Pianta, M. (2001) 'Parallel summits of global civil society', in H. Anheier *et al.*, *op. cit.*

Pierson, C. (1998) *Beyond the Welfare State?* (2nd edn), Cambridge: Polity Press.

Pierson, P. (ed.) (2001) *The New Politics of the Welfare State*, Oxford: Oxford University Press.

Pijl, M. (1995) 'Ageing, care policies and social services', *Eurosocial* (65/66), Vienna: European Centre, pp. 35–7.

Pillinger, J. (1992) *Feminising the Market: Women's Pay and Employment in the European Community*, Basingstoke: Macmillan.

Pillinger, J. (2000) 'Redefining work and welfare in Europe: new perspectives on work, welfare and time', in G. Lewis, S. Gewirtz and J. Clarke (eds) *Rethinking Social Policy*, London: Sage.

Plant, R. (1988) *Citizenship, Rights and Socialism*, London: Fabian Society.

Plant, R. (1989) 'Citizenship. Dilemmas of Definition', Mimeo: background paper, London: Speaker's Commission on Citizenship.

Plant, R. (1990) 'Citizenship and rights', in R. Plant and N. Barry, *Citizenship and Rights in Thatcher's Britain: Two Views*, London: IEA Health and Welfare Unit.

Plant, R. (1991) 'Citizenship and civilising processes: a political science perspective', in B. Turner, *op. cit.*

Plant, R. (1992) 'Citizenship, rights and welfare', in A. Coote (ed.), *The Welfare of Citizens*, London: Institute of Public Policy Research/Rivers Oram Press.

Plantenga, J. (2002) 'Combining work and care in the polder model: an assessment of the Dutch part-time strategy', *Critical Social Policy*, 22(1), pp. 53–71.

Plantenga, J., Schippers, J. and Siegers, J. (1999) 'Towards an equal division of paid and unpaid work: the case of the Netherlands', *Journal of European Social Policy*, 9(2), pp. 99–110.

Plummer, K. (1995) *Telling Sexual Stories: Power, Change and Social Worlds*, London: Routledge.

Plummer, K. (2001) 'The square of intimate citizenship: some preliminary proposals', *Citizenship Studies*, 5(3), pp. 237–53.

Pocock, J. G. A. (1992) 'The ideal of citizenship since classical times', *Queen's Quarterly*, 99(1), pp. 33–55.

Polakow, V. (1993), *Chicago & Lives on the Edge: Single Mothers and their Children in the Other America* London: University of Chicago Press.

Polakow, V., Halskov, T. and Jørgensen, P. S. (2001), *Diminished Rights. Danish Lone Mother Families in International Context*, Bristol: Policy Press.

Polit, D. F., Widom, R., Edin, K., Bowie, S., London, A. S., Scott, E.K., Valenzuela, A. (2001) *Is Work Enough? The Experiences of Current and Former Welfare Mothers Who Work*, New York: Manpower Demonstration Research Corporation.

Pollak, A. (ed.) (1993) *A Citizen's Enquiry: The Opsahl Report on Northern Ireland*, Dublin: Lilliput Press/Initiative '92.

Pope J. (1999) 'Women in the welfare rights struggle', in L. Kushnick and J. Jennings (eds) *A New Introduction to Poverty: The Role of Race, Power and Politics*, New York and London: New York University Press.

Porter, E. (1997) 'Diversity and commonality: women, politics and Northern Ireland', *European Journal of Women's Studies*, 4(1), pp. 83–100.

Porter, E. (2000) 'Participatory democracy and the challenge of dialogue across difference', in C. Roulston and C. Davies, *op. cit.*

Porter, E. (2001) 'Interdependence, parenting and responsible citizenship', *Journal
of Gender Studies*, 10(1), pp. 5–15.

Pourzand, N. (1999) 'Female education and citizenship in Afghanistan: a turbulent
relationship', in N. Yuval-Davis and P. Werbner, *op. cit.*

Pratt, G. and Hanson, S. (1993) 'Women and work across the life course', in C. Katz
and J. Monk, *op. cit.*

Pringle, K. (1998) 'Men and childcare: policy and practice', in J. Popay, J. Hearn and
J. Edwards (eds) *Men, Gender Divisions and Welfare*, London and New York:
Routledge.

Pringle, R. and Watson, S. (1992) '"Women's interests" and the post-structuralist state',
in M. Barret and A. Phillips (eds) *Destabilising Theory*, London: Polity Press.

Procacci, G. (2001) 'Poor citizens: social citizenship versus individualization of
welfare', in C. Crouch *et al.*, *op. cit.*

Pugh, R. and Thompson, N. (1999) 'Social work, citizenship and constitutional
change in the UK', in W. Lorenz, (ed.) *International Perspectives in Social Work –
Social Work and the State*. Brighton: Pavilion Publishing.

Purdy, D. (1994) 'Citizenship, basic income and the state', *New Left Review*, (208),
pp. 30–48.

Putnam, R. D. (1993) 'The prosperous community: social capital and public life', *The
American Prospect*, (13), pp. 35–42.

Rai, S. M. (1999) 'Fractioned states and negotiated boundaries: gender and law in
India', in H. Afshar and S. Barrientos (eds) *Women, Globalization and
Fragmentation in the Developing World*, Basingstoke: Macmillan.

Rake, K. (2000) *Women's Incomes over the Lifetime*, London: Cabinet Office.

Randall, V. (1987) *Women and Politics*, Basingstoke: Macmillan.

Randall, V. (1998) 'Gender and power', in V. Randall and G. Waylen (eds) *Gender,
Politics and the State*, London and New York: Routledge.

Randall, V. (2000) *The Politics of Child Care in Britain*, Oxford: Oxford University
Press.

Raphael, J. (2000) *Saving Bernice: Battered Women, Welfare, and Poverty*, Boston:
Northeastern University Press.

Rathbone, E. (1924/1986) *The Disinherited Family*, Bristol: Falling Wall Press.

Raz, J. (1994) 'Multiculturalism: a liberal perspective', *Dissent*, Winter.

Rees, A. M. (1995a) 'The other T. H. Marshall', *Journal of Social Policy*, 24(3),
pp. 341–62.

Rees, A. M. (1995b) 'The promise of social citizenship', *Policy and Politics*, 23(4),
pp. 313–25.

Rees, A. M. (1996) 'T. H. Marshall and the progress of citizenship', in M. Bulmer
and A. M. Rees, *op. cit.*

Reiger, K. (2000) 'Reconceiving citizenship: the challenge of mothers as political
activists', *Feminist Theory*, 1(3), pp. 309–27.

Rerrich, M. S. (1996) 'Modernizing the patriarchal family in West Germany: some
findings on the redistribution of family work between women', *European Journal
of Women's Studies*, 3(1), pp. 27–37.

Reynolds, T. (2001) 'Black mothering, paid work and identity', *Ethnic and Racial
Studies*, 24(6), pp. 1046–64.

Rhode, D. L. (1992) 'The politics of paradigms: gender difference and gender disadvantage', in G. Bock, and S. James, *op. cit.*

Richards, P. (2000) 'Reviving social rights in Latin America: the potential role of international human rights documents', *Citizenship Studies*, 4(2), pp. 189–206.

Richardson, D. (1993) *Women, Motherhood and Childrearing*, Basingstoke: Macmillan.

Richardson, D. (1998) 'Sexuality and citizenship', *Sociology*, 32(1), pp. 83–1000.

Richardson, D. (2000) 'Constructing sexual citizenship', *Critical Social Policy*, 20(1), pp. 105–35.

Richardson, D. (2001) 'Extending citizenship: cultural citizenship and sexuality', in N. Stevenson, *op. cit.*

Richardson, D. (ed.) (1996) *Theorising Heterosexuality*, Buckingham: Open University Press.

Riley, D. (1988) *Am I that Name?*, Basingstoke: Macmillan.

Riley, D. (1992) 'Citizenship and the welfare state', in J. Allen, P. Braham and P. Lewis (eds) *Political and Economic Forms of Modernity*, Cambridge: Polity Press.

Roberts, A. (2002) 'Just the beginning', *The Guardian*, 8 April.

Roberts, D. E. (1995) 'Race, gender, and the value of mothers' work', *Social Politics*, 2(2), pp. 195–207.

Robertson, R. (1990) 'Mapping the global condition: globalization as the central concept', *Theory, Culture and Society*, 7(2–3), pp. 15–30.

Roche, M. (1992) *Rethinking Citizenship*, Cambridge: Polity Press.

Roche, M. and van Berkel R. (eds) (1997) *European Citizenship and Social Exclusion*, Aldershot: Ashgate.

Roll, J. (1991) *What is a Family? Benefit Models and Social Realities*, London: Family Policy Studies Centre.

Roll, J. (1992) *Lone Parent Families in the European Community*, London and Birmingham: European Family and Social Policy Unit.

Rooney, F. and Woods, M. (1992) *Women, Community and Politics in Northern Ireland*, Coleraine: University of Ulster.

Rosanvallon, P. (2000) *The New Social Question. Rethinking the Welfare State*, Princeton, NJ: Princeton University Press.

Ross, E. (1983) 'Survival networks: women's neighbourhood sharing in London before World War I', *History Workshop Journal*, (15), pp. 4–27.

Rostgaard, T., Christoffersen, M. N. and Weise, H. (1999) 'Parental leave in Denmark', in P. Moss and F. Deven, *op. cit.*

Roulston, C. and Davies, C. (eds) (2000) *Gender, Democracy and Inclusion in Northern Ireland*, Basingstoke: Palgrave.

Roulston, C. and Whittock, M. (2000) '"We are these women....": self-conscious structures for a women's centre', in C. Roulston and C. Davies, *op. cit.*

Rowbotham, S. (1974) *Hidden from History*, London: Pluto.

Rowbotham, S. (1989) *The Past is Before Us*, London: Pandora Press.

Rowbotham, S. (1992) *Women in Movement*, London: Routledge.

Rowbotham, S. (1995) *Women and the Global Economy*, London: War on Want.

Rowbotham, S. (1996) 'Introduction: Mapping the women's movement', in M. Threlfall, *op. cit.*

Rowbotham, S. and Mitter, S. (1994) *Dignity and Daily Bread*, London: Routledge.

Rowbotham, S., Segal, L. and Wainwright, H. (1979) *Beyond the Fragments*, London: Merlin Press.

Rubery, J. (1998) 'Part-time work: a threat to labour standards', in J. O' Reillly and C. Fagan, *op. cit.*

Rubery, J. and Fagan, C. (1995) 'Gender segregation in societal context', *Work, Employment and Society*, 9(2), pp. 213–40.

Rubery, J., Smith, M., Fagan, C. and Grimshaw, D. (1998) *Women and European Employment*, London and New York: Routledge.

Ruddick, S. (1980) 'Maternal thinking', *Feminist Studies*, 6(2), pp. 342–67.

Ruddick, S. (1987) 'Remarks on the sexual politics of reason', in E. F. Kittay and D. T. Meyers, *op. cit.*

Ruddick, S. (1989) *Maternal Thinking, Towards a Politics of Peace*, London: Women's Press.

Russell, M., Lovenduski, J. and Stephenson, M. (2002) *Women's Political Participation in the UK*, Manchester: The British Council.

Saharso, S. (2000) 'Female autonomy and cultural imperative: two hearts beating together', in W. Kymlicka and W. Norman (eds), *Citizenship in Diverse Societies*, Oxford: Oxford University Press.

Sainsbury, D. (1993a) 'Dual welfare and sex segregation of access to social benefits: income maintenance policies in the UK, the US, the Netherlands and Sweden', *Journal of Social Policy*, 22(1), pp. 69–98.

Sainsbury, D. (1993b) 'The politics of women's increased representation: the Swedish case', in J. Lovenduski and P. Norris (eds) *Gender and Party Politics*, London: Sage.

Sainsbury, D. (ed.) (1994) *Gendering Welfare States*, London: Sage.

Sainsbury, D. (1996) *Gender, Equality and Welfare States*, Cambridge: Cambridge University Press.

Sainsbury, D. (2001) 'Gender and the making of welfare states: Norway and Sweden', *Social Politics*, 8(1), pp.113–43.

Sainsbury, D. (ed.) (1999) *Gender and Welfare State Regimes*, Oxford: Oxford University Press.

Sale, A. U. (2001) 'Nowhere to go', *Community Care*, 19–25 July.

Sales, R. and Gregory, J. (1996) 'Employment, citizenship, and European integration: the implications for migrant and refugee women', *Social Politics*, 3(2/3), pp. 331–50.

Samers, M. (1998) 'Immigration, "ethnic minorities", and "social exclusion" in the European Union: a critical perspective', *Geoforum*, 29(2), pp. 123–44.

Sanchez, L. (1993) 'Women's power and the gendered division of domestic labor in the Third World', *Gender and Society*, 7(3), pp. 434–59.

Santos, B. de S. (1998) 'Participatory budgeting in Porto Alegre: toward a redistributive democracy', *Politics and Society*, 26(4), pp. 461–510.

Santos, B. de S. (1999) 'Towards a multicultural conception of human rights', in M. Featherstone and S. Lash (eds) *Spaces of Culture*, London: Sage.

Santos, B. de S. (2001) 'Nuestra America: reinventing a subaltern paradigm of recognition and redistribution', *Theory, Culture & Society*, 18(2–3), pp. 185–217.

Sapiro, V. (1981) 'When are interests interesting? The problem of political representation of women', *American Political Science Review*, 75(2), pp. 701–16.

Sapiro, V. (1990) 'The gender basis of American social policy', in L. Gordon, *op. cit.*

Saraceno, C. (1997) 'Reply: citizenship is context-specific', *International Labor and Working-Class History*, 52, pp. 27–34.

Sarvasy, W. (1992) 'Beyond the difference versus equality policy debate: postsuffrage feminism, citizenship and the quest for a feminist welfare state', *Signs*, 17(2), pp. 329–62.

Sarvasy, W. (1994) 'From man and philanthropic service to feminist social citizenship, *Social Politics*, 1(3), pp. 306–25.

Sarvasy, W. (1997) 'Social citizenship from a feminist perspective', *Hypatia*, 12(4), pp. 54–73.

Sarvasy, W. and Siim, B. (1994) 'Gender, transitions to democracy, and citizenship', *Social Politics*, 1(3), pp. 249–55.

Sassen, S. (1998) *Globalization and its Discontents*, New York: New Press.

Sassoon, A. S. (1991) 'Equality and difference: the emergence of a new concept of citizenship', in D. McLellan and S. Sayers (eds) *Democracy and Socialism*, Basingstoke: Macmillan.

Sassoon, A. S. (ed.) (1987) *Women and the State*, London: Hutchinson.

Saunders, P. (2002) 'Mutual obligation, participation and popularity: social security reform in Australia', *Journal of Social Policy*, 31(1), pp. 21–38.

Sawer, M. (2000) 'Parliamentary representation of women: from discourses of justice to strategies of accountability', *International Political Science Review*, 21(4), pp. 361–80.

Sawicki, J. (1991) *Disciplining Foucault: Feminism, Power and the Body*, London: Routledge.

Sayce, L. (2000) *From Psychiatric Patient to Citizen*, Basingstoke: Macmillan.

Scheiwe, K. (1994) 'German pension insurance, gendered times and stratification', in D. Sainsbury, *op. cit.*

Schild, V. (2000) 'Neo-liberalism's new gendered market citizens: the "civilizing" dimension of social programmes in Chile', *Citizenship Studies*, 4(3), pp. 275–305.

Schirmer, J. G. (1989) '"Those who die for life cannot be called dead"', *Feminist Review*, 32, pp. 3–29.

Schunk, M. (2000) 'A place for support: new policies for informal carers in long-term care programmes', *Benefits*, 28, pp. 22–5.

Schuster, L. and Solomos, J. (2002) 'Rights and wrongs across European borders: migrants, minorities and citizenship', *Citizenship Studies* 6(1), pp. 37–54.

Scobey, D. (2001) 'The specter of citizenship' *Citizenship Studies*, 5(1), pp. 11–26.

Scott, J. (1992) *Citizenship and Privilege*, Leicester: University of Leicester.

Scott, J. (1993) 'Wealth and privilege', in A. Sinfield (ed.) *Poverty, Inequality and Justice*, Edinburgh: New Waverly Papers, University of Edinburgh.

Scott, J. (1994) *Poverty and Wealth: Citizenship, Deprivation and Privilege*, Harlow: Longman.

Scott, J. W. (1988) 'Deconstructing equality versus difference: or, the uses of post-structuralist theory for feminism', *Feminist Studies*, 14(1), pp. 33–50.

Scott, R. and Morris, G. (2001) *Polls Apart, 3: Campaigning for Accessible Democracy*, London: Scope.

Segal, L. (1987) *Is the Future Female? Troubled Thoughts on Contemporary Feminism*, London: Virago.

Seidman, G. W. (1999) 'Gendered citizenship: South Africa's democratic transition and the construction of a gendered state', *Gender & Society*, 13(3), pp. 287–307.

Seitz, V. R. (1998) 'Class, gender and resistance in the Appalachian coalfields', in N. Naples, *op. cit.*

Selbourne, D. (1994) *The Principle of Duty*, London: Sinclair-Stevenson.

Selwyn, N. (2002) '"E-stablishing" an inclusive society? Technology, social exclusion and UK government policy making', *Journal of Social Policy*, 31(1), pp. 1–20.

Sen, A. (1999) *Development as Freedom*, Oxford: Oxford University Press.

Sevenhuijsen, S. (1991a) 'Justice, moral reasoning and the politics of child custody', in E. Meehan and S. Sevenhuijsen, *op. cit.*

Sevenhuijsen, S. (1991b) 'The morality of feminism, *Hypatia*, 6(2), pp. 173–91.

Sevenhuijsen, S. (1992) 'Paradoxes of gender: ethical and epistemological perspectives on care in feminist political theory', Mimeo: BSA/PSA Conference 'The politics of care', London, February.

Sevenhuijsen, S. (1998) *Citizenship and the Ethics of Care*, London and New York: Routledge.

Sevenhuijsen, S. (2000) 'Caring in the third way. The relation between obligation, responsibility and care in third way discourse', *Critical Social Policy*, 20(1), pp. 5–37.

Shachar, A. (2000) 'Should church and state be joined at the altar? Women's rights and the multicultural dilemma', in W. Kymlicka and W. Norman (eds), *Citizenship in Diverse Societies*, Oxford: Oxford University Press.

Shakespeare, T. (1993) 'Disabled people's self-organisation: a new social movement?', *Disability, Handicap and Society*, 8(3) pp. 249–64.

Shakespeare, T. (2000) 'The social relations of care', in G. Lewis, S. Gewirtz and J. Clarke (eds) *Rethinking Social Policy*, London: Sage.

Shakespeare, T. (ed.) (1998) *The Disability Reader: Social Science Perspectives*, London and New York: Continuum.

Shanley, M. L. and Pateman, C. (eds) (1991) *Feminist Interpretations and Political Theory*, Cambridge: Polity Press.

Shaver, S. (1990) *Gender, Social Policy Regimes and the Welfare State*, New South Wales: Social Policy Research Centre.

Shaver, S. (1993) *Women and the Australian Social Security System: From Difference towards Equality*, New South Wales: Social Policy Research Centre.

Shaver, S. (1993/4) 'Body rights, social rights and the liberal welfare state', *Critical Social Policy*, 39, pp. 66–93.

Shaw Bond, M. (2000) 'The backlash against NGOs', *Prospect*, April, pp. 52–5.

Sheffield Group (1989) *The Social Economy and the Democratic State*, London: Lawrence & Wishart.

Shiva, V. (2000) 'The world on the edge', in W. Hutton and A. Giddens, *op. cit.*

Shklar, J. (1991) *American Citizenship: The Quest for Inclusion*, Cambridge, MA: Harvard University Press.

Siim, B. (1988) 'Towards a feminist rethinking of the welfare state', in K. B. Jones and A. G. Jónasdóttir, *op. cit.*

Siim, B. (1991) 'Welfare state, gender politics and equality policies: women's citizenship in the Scandinavian welfare states', in E. Meehan and S. Sevenhuijsen, *op. cit.*

Siim, B. (1993) 'The gendered Scandinavian welfare states: the interplay between women's roles as mothers, workers and citizens in Denmark', in J. Lewis, *op. cit.*

Siim, B. (1994) 'Engendering democracy: social citizenship and political participation for women in Scandinavia', *Social Politics*, 1(3), pp. 286–305.

Siim, B. (1998) 'Vocabularies of citizenship and gender: Denmark', *Critical Social Policy*, 18(3), pp. 375–96.

Siim, B. (1999) 'Gender, citizenship and empowerment', in I. Gough and G. Olofsson (eds) *Capitalism and Social Cohesion*, Basingstoke: Macmillan.

Siim, B. (2000) *Gender and Citizenship*, Cambridge: Cambridge University Press.

Silius, H. (1995) 'Gendering citizenship: changing gender relations in the Finnish welfare state', Mimeo: European Sociological Association Conference, Budapest, August/September.

Silliman, J. (1999) 'Expanding civil society: shrinking political spaces – the case of women's nongovernmental organizations', *Social Politics*, 6(1), pp. 23–53.

Silverman, M. (1992) *Deconstructing the Nation*, London: Routledge.

Silvers, A. (1997) 'Reconciling equality to difference: caring (f)or justice for people with disabilities', in P. DiQuinzio and I. M. Young (eds) *Feminist Ethics and Social Policy*, Bloomington and Indianapolis: Indiana University Press.

Simonen, L. (1991) 'The Finnish caring state in transition – reversing the emancipatory mothering?', Mimeo: European Feminist Research Conference, Aalborg, August.

Simpson, R. (1993) 'Fortress Europe?', in R. Simpson and R. Walker, *op. cit.*

Simpson, R. and Walker, R. (eds) (1993) *Europe: For Richer or Poorer?*, London: Child Poverty Action Group.

Sinfield, A. (1991) 'Why some are more secure than others', *Benefits*, 2, pp. 2–5.

Sipilä, J. (1995) 'The right to choose: day care for children or money for parents?', in J. Baldock and M. May, *op. cit.*

Sirianni, C. and Negrey, C. (2000) 'Working time as gendered time', *Feminist Economics*, 6(1), pp. 59–76.

Sivanandan, A. (1993) 'Beyond state-watching', in T. Bunyan, *op. cit.*

Skinner, Q. (1984) 'The idea of negative liberty: philosophical and historical perspective', in R. Rorty, J. B. Schneewind and Q. Skinner (eds) *Philosophy in History*, Cambridge: Cambridge University Press.

Skinner, Q. (1992) 'On justice, the common good and the priority of liberty', in C. Mouffe, *op. cit.*

Skjeie, H. (1993) 'Ending the male political hegemony: the Norwegian experience', in J. Lovenduski and P. Norris, (eds) *Gender and Party Politics*, London: Sage.

Skjeie, H. and Siim, B. (2000) 'Scandinavian feminist debates on citizenship', *International Political Science Review*, 21(4), pp. 345–60.

Sly, F. (1994) 'Mothers in the labour market', *Employment Gazette*, November, pp. 403–13.

Smart, C. (1989) *Feminism and the Power of the Law*, London: Routledge.

Smart, C. and Brophy, J. (1985) 'Locating law: a discussion of the place of law in feminist politics', in J. Brophy and C. Smart, *op. cit.*

Smith, G. and Wales, C. (2000) 'Citizens juries and deliberative democracy', *Political Studies*, 48, pp. 51–65.

Soares, V., Costa, A., Buarque, C., Dora, D. and Sant'anna, W. (1995) 'Brazilian feminism and women's movements', in A. Basu, *op. cit.*

Social Politics (1995) 'Special issue: between East and West', *Social Politics*, 2(1).

Social Politics (1998) 'Special issue: Citizenship in Latin America', *Social Politics*, 5(2).

Sohrab, J. A. (1994) 'An overview of the equality directive on social security and its implementation in four social security systems', *Journal of European Social Policy*, 4(4), pp. 263–76.

Sørensen, A. (2001) 'Gender Equality in Earnings at Work and at Home', *Luxembourg Income Study Working Paper No 251*, Luxembourg: Luxembourg Income Study.

Sørensen, A. and McLanahan, S. (1987) 'Married women's economic dependency 1940–1980', *American Journal of Sociology*, 93(3), pp. 659–87.

Soundings (1999), 'Transversal politics', *Soundings*, 12.

Soysal, Y. N. (1994) *Limits of Citizenship: Migrants and Post-national Membership in Europe*, Chicago and London: University of Chicago.

Sparks, H. (1997) 'Dissident citizenship: democratic theory, political courage, and activist women', *Hypatia*, 12(4), pp. 54–110.

Sparr, P. (ed.) (1996) *Mortgaging Women's Lives: Feminist Critiques of Structural Adjustment*, London: Zed Books.

Spelman, E. V. (1988) *Inessential Woman: Problems of Exclusion in Feminist Thought*, Boston: Beacon Press.

Spencer, S. (1994) *Strangers and Citizens*, London: Institute for Public Policy Research.

Spivak, G. C. (1996) 'A dialogue on democracy', in D. Trend, *op. cit.*

Squires, J. (1998) 'Citoyennes?', *Imprints*, 2(3), pp. 263–75.

Squires, J. (1999) 'Rethinking the boundaries of political representation', in S. Walby (ed.) *New Agendas for Women*, Basingstoke: Macmillan.

Squires, J. (2000) 'The state in (and of) feminist visions of political citizenship', in C. McKinnon and I. Hampsher-Monk, *op. cit.*

Squires, J. (2001) 'Representing groups, deconstructing identities', *Feminist Theory*, 2(1), pp. 7–27.

Squires, J. (ed.) (1993) *Principled Positions*, London: Lawrence & Wishart.

Squires, J. and Wickham-Jones, M. (2001) *Women in Parliament: A Comparative Analysis*, Manchester: Equal Opportunities Commission.

Stacey, J. (1986) 'Are feminists afraid to leave home? The challenge of conservative pro-family feminism', in J. Mitchell and A. Oakley (eds) *What is Feminism?*, Oxford: Basil Blackwell.

Stacey, J. (1993) 'Untangling feminist theory', in D. Richardson and V. Robinson (eds) *Introducing Women's Studies*, Basingstoke: Macmillan.

Stacey, M. and Price, M. (1981) *Women, Power and Politics*, London: Tavistock.

Standing, K. (1999) 'Lone mothers and "parental" employment: A contradiction in policy?' *Journal of Social Policy*, 28(3), pp. 479–95.

Starr, A. (2000) *Naming the Enemy: Anti-Corporate Movements Confront Globalization*, London and New York: Zed Books.

Stasiulis, D. and Bakan, A. B. (1997) 'Negotiating citizenship: the case of foreign domestic workers in Canada', *Feminist Review*, 57, pp. 112–39.

Steady, F. C. (2002) 'Engendering change through egalitarian movements: the African experience', in C. N. Murphy (ed.) *Egalitarian Politics in the Age of Globalization*, Basingstoke and New York: Palgrave.

Stephen, A. (2001) 'Bush dumps American values', *New Statesman*, 26 November, p. 11.

Stephen, L. (2001) 'Gender, citizenship and the politics of identity', *Latin American Perspectives*, 121(28), pp. 54–69.

Stephenson, M. (2001) 'Feminising politics: lessons from Scotland and Wales', *Soundings*, 18, pp. 198–207.

Stevenson, N. (ed.) (2001) *Culture and Citizenship*, London: Sage.

Steward, F. (1991) 'Citizens of planet earth', in G. Andrews, *op. cit.*

Stewart, A. (1995) 'Two conceptions of citizenship', *British Journal of Sociology*, 46(1), pp. 63–78.

Stockman, N., Bonney, N. and Xuewen, S. (1995) *Women's Work in East and West*, London: UCL Press.

Stokes, W. (1995) 'Women and political representation', Mimeo: Political Studies Association Conference, York, April.

Stone, D. (1986) 'Stormy weather: A round table discussion on women and poverty', *Poverty*, 63, pp. 9–12.

Stone, L. (1990) *Road to Divorce, England 1530–1987*, Oxford: Oxford University Press.

Stonewall (2001) *Equal as Citizens. Action for a New Century.* London: Stonewall.

Street, D. and Wilmoth, J. (2001) 'Social insecurity? Women and pensions in the US', in J. Ginn *et al.*, *op. cit.*

Stubbs, P. (1998) 'Non-governmental organizations and global social policy: towards a socio-cultural framework', in B. Deacon, M. Koivusalo and P. Stubbs. *Aspects of Global Social Policy Analysis*, Helsinki: National Research and Development Centre for Welfare and Health.

Stychin, C. F. (2001) 'Sexual citizenship in the European Union', *Citizenship Studies*, 5(3), pp. 285–301.

Suarez Toro, M. (1995) 'Popularizing women's human rights at the local level', in J. Peters and A. Wolper, *op. cit.*

Sudbury, J. (1998) *'Other Kinds of Dreams': Black Women's Organisations and the Politics of Transformation*, London and New York: Routledge.

Suibhne, M. N. (1995) 'All the president's women', *Guardian*, 23 October.

Sullivan, A. (1995) *Virtually Normal*, London: Picador.

Sullivan, O. (2000) 'The division of domestic labour: twenty years of change?' *Sociology*, 34(3), pp. 437–56.

Sullivan, O. and Gershuny, J. (2001) 'Cross-national changes in time-use: some sociological (hi)stories re-examined', *British Journal of Sociology*, 52(2), pp. 331–47.

Sunstein, C. R. (1995) 'Gender, caste and law', in M. Nussbaum and G. Glover, *op. cit.*

Swedish Ministry of Labour (1988) *Equality between Men and Women in Sweden*, Stockholm.

Sykes, R., Palier, B. and Prior, P. M. (eds) *Globalization and European Welfare States: Challenges and Change*, Basingstoke: Palgrave.

Tam, H. (1998) *Communitarianism: A New Agenda for Politics and Citizenship*, Basingstoke: Macmillan.

Tambini, D. (2001) 'Post-national citizenship', *Ethnic and Racial Studies*, 24(2), pp. 195–217.

Tambini, D. (2001) 'The civic networking movement: the internet as a new democratic public space?', in C. Crouch *et al.*, *op. cit.*

Tassin, E. (1992) 'Europe: A political community?', in C. Mouffe, *op. cit.*

Tate, J. (1994) 'Homework in West Yorkshire', in S. Rowbotham and S. Mitter, *op. cit.*

Taylor, D. (1989) 'Citizenship and social policy', *Critical Social Policy*, 26, pp. 19–31.

Taylor, D. (1991/2) 'The Big Idea for the nineties? The rise of the citizen's charters', *Critical Social Policy*, 33, pp. 87–94.

Taylor, K. (1994) 'Towards a Europe of regions?' *Centre for the Study of Democracy Bulletin*, 2(1), p. 1.

Taylor-Gooby, P. (1991) *Social Change, Social Welfare and Social Science*, Hemel Hempstead: Harvester Wheatsheaf.

Teague, P. (1998) 'Monetary union and social Europe', *Journal of European Social Policy*, 8(2), pp. 117–37.

Theodore, N. and Peck, J. (1999) 'Welfare-to-work: national problems, local solutions?' *Critical Social Policy*, 19(4), pp. 485–510.

Theory, Culture and Society (2001), 'Special issue on Recognition and Difference', *Theory, Culture and Society*, 18(2–3).

Thomas, D. Q. (1995) 'Conclusion', in J. Peters and A. Wolper, *op. cit.*

Thomas, M. (2001) 'One rule for the Americans, one rule for the rest', *New Statesman*, 15 October, p. 9.

Thomas, N. (1996) 'Tongues tied', *Times Higher Education Supplement*, 21 June.

Thompson, S. and Hoggett, P. (1996) 'Universalism, selectivism and particularism: towards a post-modern social policy', *Critical Social Policy*, 16(1), pp. 21–43.

Thomson, K. (1995) 'Working mothers: choice or circumstance', in R. Jowell, J. Curtice, A. Park, L. Brook and D. Ahrendt with K. Thomson (eds) *British Social Attitudes, 12th Report*, London: Dartmouth.

Thorogood, N. (1987) 'Race, class and gender: the politics of housework', in J. Brannen and G. Wilson (eds), *Give and Take in Families*, London: Allen & Unwin.

Threlfall, M. (ed.) (1996) *Mapping the Women's Movement*, London and New York: Verso.

Tilly, L. T. (1997) 'Women, work and citizenship', *International Labor and Working-Class History*, 52, pp. 1–26.

Timmerman, G. and Bajema, C. (1999) 'Sexual harassment in north-west Europe: A cross-cultural comparison', *European Journal of Women's Studies*, 6(4), pp. 419–39.

Titmuss, R. (1987) 'The social division of labour', reproduced in B. Abel-Smith and K. Titmuss (eds) *The Philosophy of Welfare*, London: Allen & Unwin.

Titterton, M. (1992) 'Managing threats to welfare: the search for a new paradigm of welfare', *Journal of Social Policy*, 21(1), pp. 1–23.

Tobío, C. (1996) 'Changing gender roles and family-employment strategies in Spain', in L. Hantrais and M. Letablier (eds) *Comparing Families and Family Policies in Europe*, Loughborough: Cross-National Research Group.

Tobío, C. (2001) 'Working and mothering. Women's strategies in Spain', *European Societies*, 3(3), pp. 339–71.

Townsend, P. (1993) *The International Analysis of Poverty*, Hemel Hempstead: Harvester Wheatsheaf.

Townsend, P. (1995) *The Rise of International Social Policy*, Bristol: The Policy Press.

Trend, D. (ed.) (1996) *Radical Democracy*, New York: Routledge.

Trivedi, P. (1984) 'To deny our fullness: Asian women in the making of history', *Feminist Review*, 17, pp. 37–50.

Tronto, J. (1987) 'Beyond gender difference to a theory of care', *Signs*, 12(4), pp. 644–63.

Tronto, J. (1993) *Moral Boundaries*, New York: Routledge.

Tully, J. (2000) 'The challenge of reimagining citizenship and belonging in multicultural and multinational societies', in C. McKinnon and I. Hampsher-Monk, *op. cit.*

Turner, B. (1986) *Citizenship and Capitalism: The Debate over Reformism*, London: Allen & Unwin.

Turner, B. (1990) 'Outline of a theory of citizenship', *Sociology*, 24(2), pp. 189–217.

Turner, B. (1991) 'Reply to comments and civilicisms relating to "Prolegoma to a general theory of social order"', in B. Turner (ed.) *Citizenship, Civil Society and Social Cohesion*, Colchester: University of Essex.

Turner, B. (1994) 'Post-modern culture/modern citizens', in B. van Steenbergen, *op. cit.*

Turner, B. (1997) 'Citizenship studies: a general theory', *Citizenship Studies*, 1(1), pp. 5–18.

Turner, B. (ed.) (1993) *Citizenship and Social Theory*, London: Sage.

Turner, B. S. (2001) 'The erosion of citizenship', *British Journal of Sociology*, 52(2): 189–209.

Turner, J. and Grieco, M. (2000) 'Gender and time poverty: the neglected social policy implications of gendered time, transport and travel', *Time and Society* 9(1), pp. 129–36.

Twigg, J. and Atkin, K. (1995) 'Carers and services: factors mediating service provision', *Journal of Social Policy*, 24(1), pp. 5–30.

Twine, F. (1994) *Citizenship and Social Rights*, London: Sage.

Twomey, B. (2001) 'Labour market participation of ethnic groups', *Labour Market Trends*, 109(1), p. 29.

UN (1995a) *The World's Women 1995*, New York: United Nations.

UN (1995b) *The United Nations and the Advancement of Women 1945–1995*, New York: United Nations.

UN (2000) *The World's Women*, New York: United Nations.

UNDP (1995) *Human Development Report 1995*, New York and Oxford: Oxford University Press.

UNDP (1996) *Human Development Report 1996*, New York and Oxford: Oxford University Press.

UNDP (1999) *Human Development Report 1999*, New York and Oxford: Oxford University Press.

UNDP (2000) *Human Development Report 2000*, New York and Oxford: Oxford University Press.

UNFPA (1995) *The State of World Population*, New York: United Nations.

Ungerson, C. (1987) *Policy is Personal: Sex, Gender and Informal Care*, London: Tavistock.

Ungerson, C. (1992) 'Payment for caring – mapping a territory?', Mimeo: Social Policy Association Annual Conference, Nottingham, July.

Ungerson, C. (1993) 'Caring and citizenship: a complex relationship', in J. Bornat *et al.*, *op. cit.*

Ungerson, C. (1994) 'Morals and politics in "payments for care": an introductory note', in A. Evers *et al.*, *op. cit.*

Ungerson, C. (1995) 'Gender, cash and informal care: European perspectives and dilemmas', *Journal of Social Policy*, 24(1), pp. 31–52.

Ungerson, C. (1996) 'The "commodification of care" and the new generational contracts', Mimeo: 'Family, generations and social policies', EU conference, Rome, May.

Ungerson, C. (1997) 'Social politics and the commodification of care', *Social Politics*, 4(3), pp. 362–81.

Ungerson, C. (1999) 'Personal assistants and disabled people: an examination of a hybrid form of work and care', *Work, Employment and Society*, 13(4), pp. 583–600.

Ungerson, C. (2000) 'Thinking about the production and consumption of long-term care in Britain: does gender still matter?', *Journal of Social Policy*, 29(4), pp. 623–43.

Ungerson, C. (ed.) (1990) *Gender and Caring*, Hemel Hempstead: Harvester Wheatsheaf.

UNHCHR (2001) *Gender Dimensions of Racial Discrimination*, Geneva: Office of the High Commission for Human Rights.

UNHCR (2001) *Women, Children and Older Refugees*, Geneva: Population and Geographic Data Section UNHCR.

UNIFEM (2000) *Progress of the World's Women*, New York: UNIFEM.

Urry, J. (1999) 'Globalisation and citizenship', *Journal of World-Systems Research* 5(2), pp. 263–73.

US Census Bureau (2001) *Current Population Survey*, Washington: US Government Printing Office.

Vaiou, D., Georgiou, Z. and Stratigaki, M. (1991) *Women of the South in European Integration: Problems and Prospects*, Brussels: Commission of the European Communities (DGV).

Valiente, C. (2000) 'Reconciliation policies in Spain', in L. Hantrais, *op. cit.*

van Drenth, A., Knijn, T. and Lewis, J. (1999) 'Sources of income for lone mother families: policy changes in Britain and The Netherlands and the experiences of divorced women', *Journal of Social Policy*, 28(4), pp. 619–41.

van Eerdewijk, A. (2001) 'How sexual and reproductive rights can divide and unite', *European Journal of Women's Studies*, 8(4), pp. 421–39.

van Gunsteren, H. (1994) 'Four conceptions of citizenship', in B. van Steenbergen, *op. cit.*

Van Ness, P. (ed.) (1999) *Debating Human Rights*, London: Routledge.

van Steenbergen, B. (1994) (ed.) *The Condition of Citizenship*, London: Sage.

Vandenberg, A. (2000) 'Contesting citizenship and democracy in a global era', in A. Vandenberg (ed.) *Citizenship and Democracy in a Global Era*, Basingstoke: Macmillan.

Vargas, V. and Olea, C. (1999) 'An agenda of one's own: the tribulations of the Peruvian feminist movement', in N. Yuval-Davis and P. Werbner, *op. cit.*

Verba, S., Schlozman, K. L. and Brady, H. E. (1995) *Voice and Equality*, Cambridge, MA and London: Harvard University Press.

Verber, J. (2001) 'Mothers who fall through the safety net: poor women and welfare reform in an American city', *Social Politics*, 8(2), pp. 197–202.

Vernon, A. (1998) 'Multiple oppression and the disabled people's movement', in T. Shakespeare (ed.) *The Disability Reader*, London and New York: Continuum.

Vianello, M. and Siemienska, R. (1990) *Gender Inequality: A Comparative Study of Discrimination and Participation*, London: Sage.

Vilrokx, J. (1993) 'Basic income, citizenship and solidarity: towards a dynamic for social renewal', in H. Coenen and P. Leisink, *op. cit.*

Vincent, D. (1991) *Poor Citizens*, Harlow; Longman.

Voet, R. (1998) *Feminism and Citizenship*, London: Sage.

Vogel, U. (1988) 'Under permanent guardianship; women's condition under modern civil law', in K. B. Jones and A. G. Jónasdóttir, *op. cit.*

Vogel, U. (1991) 'Is citizenship gender-specific?', in U. Vogel and M. Moran, *op. cit.*

Vogel, U. (1994) 'Marriage and the boundaries of citizenship', in van Steenbergen, *op. cit.*

Vogel, U. and Moran, M. (eds) (1991) *The Frontiers of Citizenship*, Basingstoke: Macmillan.

Vogler, C. (1994) 'Money in the household', in M. Anderson *et al.*, *op. cit.*

Vogler, C. and Pahl, J. (1993) 'Social and economic change and the organisation of money within marriage', *Work, Employment and Society*, 7(1), pp. 71–95.

Vogler, C. and Pahl, J. (1994) 'Money, power and inequality within marriage', *Sociological Review*, 42(2), pp. 263–88.

von Bredow, W. (1998) 'The changing character of national borders', *Citizenship Studies*, 2(3), pp. 365–76.

Waerness, K. (1987) 'On the rationality of caring', in A. S. Sassoon, *op. cit.*

Waerness, K. (1989) 'Dependency in the welfare state', in M. Bulmer, J. Lewis and D. Piachaud (eds) *The Goals of Social Policy*, London: Unwin Hyman.

Wainwright, H. (1991) 'New forms of democracy for socialist renewal', in D. McLelland and S. Sayers, *Democracy and Socialism*, Basingstoke: Macmillan.

Wainwright, H. (2002) 'Ante upped', *Guardian Society*, 13 February.

Waites, M. (1996) 'Lesbian and gay theory, sexuality and citizenship', *Contemporary Politics*, 2(3), pp. 139–49.

Walby, S. (1990) *Theorising Patriarchy*, Oxford: Basil Blackwell.

Walby, S. (1992) 'Women and nation', *International Journal of Comparative Sociology*, 33(1–2), pp. 81–100.

Walby, S. (1994) 'Is citizenship gendered?' *Sociology*, 28(2), pp. 379–95.

Walby, S. (1997) *Gender Transformations*, London and New York: Routledge.

Walby, S. (1999) 'The European Union and equal opportunities policies', *European Societies*, 1(1), pp. 59–80.

Walby, S. (2000) 'The restructuring of the gendered political economy: transformations in women's employment', in J. Cook, J. Roberts and G. Waylen (eds) *Towards a Gendered Political Economy*, Basingstoke: Macmillan.

Waldfogel, J., Danziger, S. K., Danziger, S. and Seefeldt, K. S. (2001) 'Welfare reform and lone mothers' employment in the US', in J. Millar and K. Rowlingson, *op. cit.*

Walker, A. (1982) 'Dependency and old age', *Social Policy and Administration*, 16(2), pp. 115–35.

Walker, A. (1992) 'The poor relation: poverty among older women', in C. Glendinning and J. Millar, *op. cit.*

Wall, K., Aboim, S., Cunha, V. and Vasconcelos, P. (2001) 'Families and informal support networks in Portugal: the reproduction of inequality', *Journal of European Social Policy*, 11(3), pp. 213–33.

Walsh, J. (1999) 'Myths and counter-myths: an analysis of part-time female employees and their orientations to work and working hours', *Work, Employment and Society*, 13(2), pp. 179–203.

Waltzer, M. (1970) *Obligations: Essays on Disobedience, War and Citizenship*, Cambridge, MA: Harvard University Press.

Waltzer, M. (1992) 'The civil society argument', in C. Mouffe, *op. cit.*

Ward, A., Gregory, J. and Yuval-Davies, N. (eds) (1992) *Women and Citizenship in Europe*, Stoke: Trentham Books/European Forum of Socialist Feminists.

Ward, C., Dale, A. and Joshi, H. (1996) 'Combining employment with childcare; an escape from dependence?', *Journal of Social Policy*, 25(2), pp. 223–47.

Ward, L. (2000) 'Learning from the 'Babe' experience: how the finest hour became a fiasco', in A. Coote (ed.) *New Gender Agenda*, London: Institute for Public Policy Research.

Ward, S. (1986) 'Power, politics and poverty', in P. Golding (ed.) *Excluding the Poor*, London: Child Poverty Action Group.

Warde, A. and Hetherington, K. (1993) 'A changing domestic division of labour? Issues of measurement and interpretation', *Work, Employment and Society*, 7(1), pp. 23–45.

Warren, T. (2000) 'Diverse breadwinner models: a couple-based analysis of gendered working time in Britain and Denmark', *Journal of European Social Policy*, 10(4), pp. 349–71.

Warren, T., Rowlingson, K. and Whyley, C. (2001) 'Female finances: gender wage gaps and gender assets gaps', *Work, Employment and Society*, 15(3), pp. 465–88.

Watson, G. and Fothergill, B. (1993) 'Part-time employment and attitudes to part-time work', *Employment Gazette*, May, pp. 213–20.

Watson, P. (1993) 'Eastern Europe's silent revolution: gender', *Sociology*, 27(3), pp. 471–87.

Watson, P. (1996) 'The rise of masculinism in Eastern Europe', in M. Threlfall, *op. cit.*

Weale, A. (1983) *Political Theory and Social Policy*, London: Macmillan.

Weale, A. (1991) 'Citizenship beyond borders', in U. Vogel and M. Moran, *op. cit.*

Weedon, C. (1997) *Feminist Practice and Poststructuralist Theory*, 2nd edn, Oxford: Blackwell.

Weeks, J. (1993) 'Rediscovering values', in J. Squires, *op. cit.*

Weeks, J. (1996) 'The idea of a sexual community', *Soundings*, 2, pp. 71–84.

Weeks, J. (1998) 'The sexual citizen', *Theory, Culture & Society*, 15(3–4), pp. 35–52.

Weeks, J. (2001) 'Live and let love? Reflections on the unfinished sexual revolution of our times', in R. Edwards and J. Glover (eds) *Risk and Citizenship*, London and New York: Routledge.

Weiss, T. G. (1999) *International NGOs, Global Governance, and Social Policy in the UN System*, Helsinki: National Research and Development Centre for Welfare and Health.

Welsch, W. (1999) 'Transculturality: the puzzling form of cultures today', in M. Featherstone and S. Lash (eds) *Spaces of Culture*, London: Sage.

Werbner, P. (1996) 'Reversing the moral terms of citizenship: transnational belonging and political activism of Pakistani diasporic women', Mimeo, Women, Citizenship and Difference Conference, University of Greenwich, July.

Werbner, P. (1999) 'Political motherhood and the feminisation of citizenship: women's activisms and the transformation of the public sphere', in N. Yuval-Davis and P. Werbner, *op. cit.*

Werbner, P. and Yuval-Davis, N. (1999) 'Introduction: women and the new discourse of citizenship', in N. Yuval-Davis and P. Werbner, *op. cit.*

West, G. and Blumberg, R. L. (eds) (1990) *Women and Social Protest*, New York and Oxford: Oxford University Press.

Whitaker, R. (1998) 'Refugees: the security dimension', *Citizenship Studies*, 2(3), pp. 413–34.

White, S. (1995) 'Liberal equality, exploitation and the case for an unconditional basic income', in J. Lovenduski and J. Stanyer, (eds) *Contemporary Political Studies 1995*, Exeter: Political Studies Association.

White, S. (2000) 'Review article: social rights and the new social contract – political theory and the new welfare politics', *British Journal of Political Science*, 30, pp. 507–32.

White, S. and Gardner, D. (2000) 'Juggling with reciprocity: towards a better balance', in A. Coote (ed.) *New Gender Agenda*, London: Institute for Public Policy Research.

Whitting, G. and Quinn, J. (1989) 'Women and work: preparing for an independent future', *Policy and Politics*, 17(4), pp. 337–45.

Wiener, A. (1999) 'From *special* to *specialized* rights: the politics of citizenship and identity in the European Union', in M. Hanagan and C. Tilly (eds) *Extending Citizenship, Reconfiguring States*, Lanham, Boulder, New York and Oxford: Rowan & Littlefield.

Wilkinson, S. and Kitzinger, C. (eds) (1996) *Representing the Other*, London: Sage.

Williams, C. C. and Windebank, J. (1997) 'The informal sector in the European Union. Mitigating or reinforcing economic exclusion?', in M. Roche, R. van Berkel, *op. cit.*

Williams, F. (1989) *Social Policy: A Critical Introduction*, Cambridge: Polity Press.

Williams, F. (1992a) 'Somewhere over the rainbow: universality and diversity in social policy', in N. Manning and R. Page (eds) *Social Policy Review 4*, Canterbury: Social Policy Association.

Williams, F. (1992b) 'Women with learning difficulties are women too', in M. Langan and L. Day (eds) *Women, Oppression and Social Work*, London: Routledge.

Williams, F. (1993) 'Women and community', in J. Bornat *et al.*, *op. cit.*

Williams, F. (1995a) 'Race/ethnicity, gender and class in welfare states: a framework for comparative analysis', *Social Politics*, 2(2), pp. 127–59.

Williams, F. (1995b) 'Barrett', in V. George and R. Page (eds) *Modern Thinkers on Welfare*, Hemel Hempstead: Prentice Hall/Harvester Wheatsheaf.

Williams, F. (1996) 'Postmodernism, feminism and the question of difference', in N. Parton (ed.) *Sociological Theory, Social Change and Social Work*, London: Routledge.

Williams, F. (2001) 'In and beyond New Labour: Towards a new political ethics of care', *Critical Social Policy*, 21(4), pp. 425–47.

Williams, F., Popay, J. and Oakley A. (eds) (1999) *Welfare Research: A Critical Review*, London: UCL Press.

Wilson, A. (1978) *Finding A Voice*, London: Virago.

Wilson, A. R. (1993) 'Which equality? Toleration, difference or respect', in J. Bristow *et al.*, *op. cit.*

Wilson, A. R. (ed.) (1995) *A Simple Matter of Justice? Theorizing Lesbian and Gay Politics*, London and New York: Cassell.

Wilson, E. (1983) 'Feminism and social policy', in M. Loney, D. Boswell, and J. Clarke (eds) *Social Policy and Social Welfare*, Milton Keynes: Open University Press.

Windebank, J. (1996) ' To what extent can social policy challenge the dominant ideology of mothering? A cross-national comparison of Sweden, France and Britain',
Journal of European Social Policy, 6(2), pp. 147–61.

Wirth, L. (2001) *Breaking Through the Glass Ceiling: Women in Management*,
Geneva: ILO.

Wolf, N. (1993) *Fire with Fire*, London: Chatto & Windus.

Wolffensperger, J. (1991) 'Engendered structure: Giddens and the conceptualization
of gender', in K. Davis *et al.*, *op. cit.*

Wolin, S. (1992) 'What revolutionary action means today', in C. Mouffe, *op. cit.*

Wollstonecraft, M. (1792/1985) *Vindication of the Rights of Woman*, London:
Penguin.

Women in Black (ed.) (1993) *Women for Peace Anthology*, Belgrade: Women in
Black.

Women into Politics website, http://www.canto.org.uk.

Women's Stand for Community Action (1994) *Report of the 1994 Women's Stand for
Community Action Conference*, Bradford: Women's Stand for Community Action.

Women's Studies International Forum (1999) 'Special issue: Feminism and
Globalization', *Women's Studies International Forum*, 22(4).

Wood, R. (1991) 'Care of disabled people', in G. Dalley (ed.) *Disability and Social
Policy*, London: Policy Studies Institute.

World Bank (1999) *World Development Report 1999*, Washington: World Bank.

Yeandle, S. (1996) 'Work and care in the life course; understanding the context for
family arrangements', *Journal of Social Policy*, 25(4), pp. 507–27.

Yeatman, A. (1993) 'Voice and representation in the politics of difference', in S.
Gunew and A. Yeatman, *op. cit.*

Yeatman, A. (1994) *Post-modern Revisionings of the Political*, London: Routledge.

Yeatman, A. (1997) 'Feminism and power', in M. L. Shanley and U. Narayan (eds)
Reconstructing Political Theory: Feminist Perspectives, Cambridge: Polity Press.

Yeatman, A. (2001) 'Feminism and citizenship', in N. Stevenson, *op. cit.*

Young, B. (1996) 'The German state and feminist politics: a double gender marginal-
ization', *Social Politics*, 3(2/3), pp. 159–84.

Young, I. M. (1987) 'Impartiality and the civic public: some implications of feminist
critiques of moral and political theory', in S. Benhabib and D. Cornell (eds)
Feminism as Critique, Oxford: Polity Press.

Young, I. M. (1989) 'Polity and group difference: a critique of the ideal of universal
citizenship', *Ethics*, 99, pp. 250–74.

Young, I. M. (1990a) *Justice and the Politics of Difference*, Oxford: Princeton
University Press.

Young, I. M. (1990b) 'The ideal of community and the politics of difference', in
L. J. Nicholson, *Feminism/Postmodernism*, New York: Routledge.

Young, I. M. (1993) 'Together in difference: transforming the logic of group political conflict', in J. Squires, *op. cit.*

Young, I. M. (1994) 'Gender as seriality: thinking about women as a social collective', *Signs*, 19(3), pp. 713–38.

Young, I. M. (1995) 'Mothers, citizenship and independence: a critique of pure
family values' *Ethics*, 105, pp. 535–56.

Young, I. M. (1997) 'Unruly categories: a critique of Nancy Fraser's dual systems
theory', *New Left Review*, 222, pp. 147–60.

Young, I. M. (2000) *Inclusion and Democracy*, Oxford: Oxford University Press.

Yuval-Davis, N. (1991a) 'The citizenship debate: women, ethnic processes and the state', *Feminist Review*, 39, pp. 58–68.

Yuval Davis, N. (1991b) 'The gendered Gulf War: women's citizenship and modern warfare', in H. Bresheeth and N. Yuval-Davis (eds) *The Gulf War and the New World Order*, London: Zed Books.

Yuval-Davis, N. (1992) 'Women and citizens', in A. Ward *et al.*, *op. cit.*

Yuval-Davis, N. (1993) 'Gender and nation', *Ethnic and Racial Studies*, 16(4), pp. 621–32.

Yuval-Davis, N. (1994) 'Women, ethnicity and empowerment', *Feminism and Psychology*, 4(1), pp. 179–97.

Yuval-Davis, N. (1996) 'Women, citizenship and difference', Mimeo: background paper, 'Women, Citizenship and Difference', Conference, University of Greenwich.

Yuval-Davis, N. (1997a) *Gender and Nation*, London: Sage.

Yuval-Davis, N. (1997b) 'Ethnicity, gender relations and multiculturalism', in P. Werbner and T. Modood (eds) *Debating Cultural Hybridity*, London and New York: Zed Books.

Yuval-Davis, N. (1999) 'What is "transversal politics"?', *Soundings*, 12, pp. 94–8.

Yuval-Davis, N. and Anthias, F. (1989) *Woman-Nation-State*, Basingstoke: Macmillan.

Yuval-Davis, N. and Werbner, P. (eds) (1999) *Women, Citizenship and Difference*, London and New York: Zed Press.

Author Index

Subject Index

abortion, 126–7
  see also reproductive rights
accidental activism, 146–7
  see also political activism
active citizenship, 2, 23–4, 40
activist mothering, 147
  see also motherhood
affirmative action, 87–8, 160–1
age, 76–7
agency, *see* human agency
Amsterdam Treaty, 54
anti-globalisation movement, 28
Argentina, motherhood, 148
asylum-seekers, 2
  and citizenship, 4
  and human rights, 61, 67
  and immigration control, 47–8,
    65, 67
  see also immigration; refugees
Australia
  division of labour, 134–5
  and feminist citizenship, 6
  multi-culturalism, 87
  political participation, 156
  public–private divide, 123
  reproductive rights, 126
Austria
  childcare provision, 183
  parental leave, 180
autonomy, 7, 17, 39, 106–7
  and economic dependence,
    113, 172
  and economic independence,
    111, 113
  and ethic of care, 114
  and feminism, 107
  and immigration migration, 65,
    129
  and interdependence, 106,
    114–15
  and nation-states, 56
  political, 53
  and public–private divide, 121,
    125–30, 166
  relational, 114–15

Beijing World Conference on
  Women, 59, 60, 64, 202
Belgium, childcare provision, 183
Beveridge Plan, 171
binarism, 9, 94, 115–16
  equality/difference, 101,
    115–16, 197–8
  ethic of care/justice, 197
  public–private divide, 71–2, 73
  see also dichotomies
Black peoples, exclusion of, 74
Black women
  and the body, 72

and community, 85
and definitions of 'woman',
  75–6
and economic independence,
  108
and employment, 108, 170
and marginalisation, 81
and political activism, 5, 146,
  152–3
and public–private divide, 124
and welfare states, 174
bodily integrity, 200–1
  and married women, 69
  and public–private divide, 121,
    125–8, 142
  as a right, 113
body, and citizenship, 72–3, 95,
  98, 113
Brazil, political participation,
  164–5
Britain, *see* UK
British General Household Survey,
  132

Cairo Conference on Population
  and Development, 64
Canada
  migrant workers, 134
  political participation, 155
  refugees, 127
  reproductive rights, 126
care
  of adults, 132, 185–9
  children for parents, 77
  and citizenship, 9, 22–3, 104,
    177–9, 188–9
  and dependence, 103
  and division of labour, 132,
    134, 179–80, 187, 189,
    194
  and economic dependence, 110
  and employment, 139, 190–4
  and equality, 103, 176–7
  and gender, 169
  male participation in, 131–2,
    135–6
  payment for, 177–8, 185–8,
    189
  public–private balance of, 142,
    182–90
  receivers of, 187–8
  recognition of, 176–8
  and social security schemes, 186
  state provision, 182
  time to, 180–1, 182, 183, 184,
    185, 201
  see also childcare; ethic of care
careful citizenship, 179
Charter for Global Democracy, 62

childcare, 133–5, 170, 183–5
  and division of labour, 131,
    184–5
  and employment, 193–4, 200
  and European Commission,
    179–80, 183
  and income, 185
  see also care; lone parents;
    parental leave
children
  citizenship of, 77
  importance to political partici-
    pation, 147, 149, 150
  UN Convention on the Rights
    of, 77
China, public–private divide, 122
'citizen', conceptions of, 26–30,
  33–4
citizen-mothers, 100 *see also*
  motherhood
citizen, the carer, 10, 167, 176–8,
  199–200
  see also care; ethic of care
citizen, the earner or worker, 10,
  167, 172–3, 176–8,
  199–200
  see also employment; incomes
citizen, the worker-carer, 167
Citizen's Constitution, 35
Citizen's Income, 189–90
Citizens of the Union, 54
citizenship, 2, 3–5, 7, 35–6
  concepts of, 68
  contradictory nature of, 4–5
  definitions, 8, 13, 14, 15, 41–2,
    44, 60, 104, 175–6
  discourse of, 2
  male nature of, 4, 31, 34, 68,
    70, 71–2, 73, 98, 197,
    199
  negative connotations, 4, 5, 8
  as practice, 2, 8, 33–4, 41–2,
    69, 196, 199
  as status, 8, 14–15, 41–2, 69,
    92, 195–6
  see also active, careful, cultural,
    dissident, dual, ecological,
    European, everyday–life,
    feminist, formal, gender-
    differentiated/gender-
    neutral, gender-inclusive,
    global, intimate, liberal,
    lived, multi-layered,
    performative, political,
    post national, sexual,
    social, substantive,
    woman-friendly citizenship
citizenship education, 2, 4
citizenship regime, 3

316